William Henry Bishop

Old Mexico And Her Lost Provinces

William Henry Bishop

Old Mexico And Her Lost Provinces

ISBN/EAN: 9783741118043

Manufactured in Europe, USA, Canada, Australia, Japa

Cover: Foto ©Andreas Hilbeck / pixelio.de

Manufactured and distributed by brebook publishing software (www.brebook.com)

William Henry Bishop

Old Mexico And Her Lost Provinces

LAS CASAS PROTECTING THE AZTECS.
By Felix Parra.

OLD MEXICO

AND HER LOST PROVINCES

A JOURNEY IN

MEXICO, SOUTHERN CALIFORNIA, AND ARIZONA
BY WAY OF CUBA

By WILLIAM HENRY BISHOP

AUTHOR OF "DETMOLD" "THE HOUSE OF A MERCHANT PRINCE" ETC.

WITH ILLUSTRATIONS

NEW YORK
HARPER & BROTHERS, FRANKLIN SQUARE
1883

Entered according to Act of Congress, in the year 1883, by

HARPER & BROTHERS,

In the Office of the Librarian of Congress, at Washington.

All rights reserved.

CONTENTS.

Part I.—OLD MEXICO.

		PAGE
I.	By Way of Cuba and the Spanish Main	1
II.	Vera Cruz	16
III.	Up the Long Mountain Slope	24
IV.	The Capital	37
V.	The Projectors	54
VI.	The Ferro-carriles	70
VII.	The Railways at Work	80
VIII.	The Question of Money, and Shopping	96
IX.	Social Life, and some Notable Institutions	107
X.	The Fine Arts and Literature	120
XI.	Some Traits of Peculiar History, and the Mexican "Warwick"	134
XII.	Cuatitlan, and Around Lakes Xochimilco and Chalco	149
XIII.	To Old Tezcoco	162
XIV.	Popocatepetl Ascended	175
XV.	A Banquet, and a Tragedy, at Cuautla-Morelos	185
XVI.	San Juan, Orizaba, and Cordoba Revisited	192
XVII.	Puebla, Cholula, Tlaxcala	210
XVIII.	Mines and Mining Traits, at Pachuco and Regla	227
XIX.	A Week at a Mexican Country-house	245
XX.	On Horseback and Muleback to Acapulco	263
XXI.	Conversations by the Way with a Colonel	275

vi   CONTENTS.

Part II.—THE LOST PROVINCES.

		PAGE
XXII.	San Francisco	295
XXIII.	San Francisco (Continued)	324
XXIV.	The Villas of the Bonanza Kings	343
XXV.	The Vintage Season, and Monterey	359
XXVI.	A Wondrous Valley, and a Desert that Blossoms like the Rose	380
XXVII.	Visalia, Bakersfield, and Life on a Spacious Ranch	399
XXVIII.	Los Angeles	421
XXIX.	To San Diego, and the Mexican Frontier	448
XXX.	Across Arizona	469
XXXI.	Tombstone	482
XXXII.	Camp Lowell, Tucson, and San Xavier del Bac	496

ILLUSTRATIONS.

	PAGE
LAS CASAS PROTECTING THE AZTECS. By Felix Parra	*Frontispiece*
MEXICO, SHOWING PRESENT AND OLD FRONTIER	5
CATHEDRAL OF MEXICO	9
DOMES OF VERA CRUZ	17
MAP OF ENGLISH RAILROAD FROM VERA CRUZ TO MEXICO	25
TRANSCONTINENTAL PROFILE OF MEXICO	31
A RAILWAY JUDAS	33
A FLOWER-SHOW IN THE ZOCALO	43
COMPARATIVE LEVELS OF LAKES	46
THE HOMES OF THE POOR	49
ENTRANCE TO A TENEMENT-HOUSE	51
OLD SPANISH PALACE IN THE CALLE DE JESUS	56
SEMI-VILLA ON THE PASEO OF BUCARELLI	57
THE MODERN STYLE	58
PORCELAIN HOUSE IN SAN FRANCISCO STREET	59
THE DRIVE TO CHAPULTEPEC	63
GENERAL RAILWAY SYSTEM OF MEXICO	75
THE GREAT SPANISH DRAINAGE CUT	85
PAY CARAVAN ON THE MEXICAN NATIONAL ROAD	91
"NOT HERE FOR THEIR HEALTH"	93
MODERN SHOP-FRONTS AT MEXICO	99
THE "PORTALES" AT MEXICO	102
A "MERCERIA" AT PUEBLA	106
INTERIOR COURT-YARD OF MEXICAN RESIDENCE	111
MEXICAN COURTSHIP	113
THE DEATH OF ATALA. By Luis Monroy	123

ILLUSTRATIONS.

	PAGE
GENERAL PORFIRIO DIAZ, EX-PRESIDENT OF MEXICO	139
GENERAL MANUEL GONZALES, PRESIDENT OF MEXICO	143
ENVIRONS OF MEXICO	150
SUNDAY DIVERSIONS AT SANTA ANITA	153
CREW OF "LA NINFA ENCANTADORA"	165
THE "FIND"	169
IN TIERRA CALIENTE	186
THE HILL OF EL BORREGO, AT ORIZABA	196
PRISONERS WEAVING SASHES AT CHOLULA	217
OLD FONT AT TLAXCALA	222
THE FIRST CHRISTIAN PULPIT IN AMERICA. TLAXCALA	223
PART OF CONVENT OF SAN FRANCISCO. TLAXCALA	224
SUPERINTENDENT'S HOUSE AT REGLA	241
PLOUGHMAN IN GRASS CLOAK	243
THE HACIENDA OF TEPENACASCO	246
THE THRESHING-FLOOR	249
THE TLACHIQUERO	251
NURSE AND CHILDREN AT THE HACIENDA	261
THE "DILIGENCIA"	267
OUR CAVALCADE AT IGUALA	281
THE BELLS OF SAN BLAS	290
ALCATRAZ ISLAND	297
"NOB" HILL, FROM THE BAY	299
CALIFORNIA STREET, SAN FRANCISCO	305
LONE MOUNTAIN	309
"HIGH JINKS" OF THE BOHEMIAN CLUB AMONG THE BIG TREES	313
GOLDEN GATE, FROM GOAT ISLAND	317
HIGH-GRADE RESIDENCES	327
CHINESE FISHING-BOATS IN THE BAY	331
CHINESE QUARTER, SAN FRANCISCO	335
A BALCONY IN THE CHINESE QUARTER	337
IN A CHINESE THEATRE	339
RAILWAY ROUTE: SOUTHERN CALIFORNIA AND ARIZONA	345
PALO ALTO	354
RALSTON'S COUNTRY HOUSE	357
BOTTLING CHAMPAGNE AT SAN FRANCISCO	361
A BRANDY CELLAR, SAN JOSE	363

ILLUSTRATIONS. ix

	PAGE
A BIT OF OLD MONTEREY	365
LOOKOUT STATION	367
CUTTING UP THE WHALE	369
THE HOTEL DEL MONTE, MONTEREY	371
CLIFFS AND FOREST AT MONTEREY	373
CHINESE FISHING VILLAGE	375
SAN CARLOS'S-DAY AT THE OLD MISSION	376
DRYING FISH AT CHINESE VILLAGE	377
COURT-HOUSE AT FRESNO	387
PRIVATE RESIDENCE AT FRESNO	393
FIRST BUILDING IN VISALIA	400
AN OLD-TIMER	401
LOGGING, BACK OF VISALIA	403
CHINATOWN, BAKERSFIELD	409
GYPSY CAMP AT BAKERSFIELD	411
A TYPICAL RANCH-HOUSE	414
SAN LUIS OBISPO	416
A RODEO	418
THE KERN RIVER CAÑON	419
TEHACHAPI PASS	422
MAIN STREET, LOS ANGELES	425
DON PIO PICO	428
MONGOLIAN AND MEXICAN	430
PARADISE	437
A MEXICAN WEDDING AT SAN GABRIEL	441
THE VINTAGE, SAN GABRIEL	443
IRRIGATING AN ORANGE-ORCHARD	445
A SYLVAN GLIMPSE AT RIVERSIDE	449
ADOBE RESIDENCE AT RIVERSIDE	451
ADOBE RESIDENCE AT RIVERSIDE	452
OLD MISSION AT SANTA BARBARA	455
PLAZA OF SAN DIEGO, OLD TOWN	457
OLD MISSION AT SAN DIEGO	460
DON JUAN FORSTER	461
SEÑORA FORSTER	462
FORSTER'S RANCH	463
SAN LUIS REY	465

1*

x   ILLUSTRATIONS.

	PAGE
A TICHBORNE CLAIMANT	466
THE COLORADO RIVER AT YUMA	473
PASQUAL, CHIEF OF THE YUMAS	476
YUMA INDIANS AT HOME	477
DISTANT VIEW OF TOMBSTONE	484
"ED" SCHIEFFELIN	487
A TOMBSTONE SHERIFF AND CONSTITUENTS	494
APACHE PRISONERS AT CAMP LOWELL	497
AN ARIZONA WATERING-PLACE	499
CACTUS GROWTHS OF THE DESERT	501
STREET VIEW IN TUCSON	503
EXTERIOR OF MISSION CHURCH OF SAN XAVIER DEL BAC	505
INTERIOR OF CHURCH OF SAN XAVIER DEL BAC	507

PART I.
OLD MEXICO.

OLD MEXICO.

I.

BY WAY OF CUBA AND THE SPANISH MAIN.

I.

Boom! Two ruddy old castles domineering a narrow harbor entrance; on the other side a city, gray, warm-colored, and time-stained, and the bells of the Church of the Angels chiming for very early morning service! It was Havana!

I began this journey to Old Mexico and her Lost Provinces by sailing away from the foot of Wall Street, East River, on the 31st day of March, 1881. Some would have begun it, no doubt, by taking the railroad to our Southern confines, and sailing by the steamers, of medium size, which ply from New Orleans, Galveston, and Morgan City—all places feeling very much the new stimulus lately given to Mexican trade. Others—and very likely they could not do better—would have taken direct the excellent Alexandre Line, which carries the mail from New York, calling at Havana, Progreso, Campeachy, Frontera, and Vera Cruz.

Others, perchance, more adventurous, and fond of mixing as much hardship as possible in their pleasure, might have crossed the frontier at Texas, and, the new railroads being yet unfinished, been bumped and thumped a thousand miles to the capital in the wretched *diligencias* (stage-coaches) of the country.

I did none of these. I shall not be guilty of the egotism of insisting that I did any better; but I had formed a little plan of infusing variety into the trip without making it too onerous. I stood boldly upon the deck of the luxurious steamer *Newport*, bound for Cuba only. From there I was to take the French packet making regular trips from the ports of St. Nazaire and Santander to Vera Cruz, and bringing much of the French and Spanish migration; or a British steamer from Southampton, or a Spanish one from Cadiz, might be taken in the same way. The fare by any and all of the direct sea routes is about the same, and may be set down roughly at $85.00. The time consumed, where all connections are expeditiously made, should be about eleven days.

II.

There was no uncontrollable excitement on that raw 31st of March when we took our departure. People in the great financial mart, hurrying about their stocks and bonds, even blockaded us in an unthinking way as we came down to the steamer. It might have been simply a case of going to Europe, or anything else quite usual and of little import. It was, instead, a case of going to a land remote far beyond its distance in miles; shrouded in an atmosphere of mystery and danger; little travelled or sought for; the very antipodes of our own, though adjoining it; venerable with age, though a part of a new world; and said to have been suddenly awakened from slumber by the first touches of a phenomenal new development.

There are those of us whose conception of Mexico has been composed principally of the cuts in our early school geography, and the brief telegrams in the morning papers announcing new revolutions. We rest satisfied with this kind of concept about many another part of the globe as well till the necessity arrives for going there or otherwise clearing it up. I saw, I think, a snow volcano, and a string of donkeys, conducted by a broad-brim hatted peasant across a cactus-covered plain. I heard dimly isolated pistol-shots fired by brigands, and high-sounding *pronunciamentos* and cruel fusillades accompanying the overthrow from the Presidency of General this by General that, who would be served in the same way by General somebody else to-morrow. To this should be added some reminiscence of actions in the Mexican War, and notably the portraits of General Scott and bluff old Zachary Taylor.

To this, again, I would add fancies of buried cities in Central America, and of Aztec antiquity, and the valor and astuteness of Hernando Cortez and his cavaliers, remaining from Prescott's history of the Conquest. One of the most captivating of volumes, this had seemed almost mythical in its remoteness; and as to the idea of actually verifying its scenes in person, it was beyond the wildest imagination.

But now all at once this uncertain territory had become real. The railroad had penetrated it, and made it accessible to the average private citizen. Not that it could yet be reached by railway, for the first international line is still incomplete, though its termination is near at hand; but a multitude of lines, undertaken by American capital and enterprise, and aided by a Government of liberal ideas, were traced over every part of the land,

and some of them in progress. The locomotive screamed along-side the troops of laden donkeys and in sight of the snow volcanoes. Even the brigands were said to have been dislodged from their fastnesses, the revolutions had ceased, and a reign of peace and security begun.

Momentous rumors from these new enterprises were frequent in the newspapers, and predictions indulged in of the great increase of trade and population to result to Mexico by them. General Grant, to whose personal influence much of the turning of public attention in this unwonted direction, after his first visit, should certainly be ascribed, had taken the presidency of one of them. Their stocks and bonds were being prepared in bank-parlors, but as yet there was no "boom," little that was overt.

III.

I did not quite know, when standing on the deck of the departing steamer, that I was to return to this dense New York, with its tall towers and mansards and fairy-like bridge, from the other side of the world. This journey lengthened out into a long, desultory ramble, beginning with Cuba, and, after Mexico, concluding with the most remote, novel, and characteristic of our own possessions on the Pacific slope. There is unity of subject, and even a certain pathos, in the recollection that this latter was once Mexican territory also. Its most obvious basis of life is still Spanish, and it may be sentimentally considered a kind of Alsace-Lorraine—a part of the sister republic when it was well-nigh as large and powerful as ourselves.

It was naturally cold on the 31st day of March, and blustering weather followed us down the coast as far as it dared. Then I awoke one morning early, at the warm gleam of summer in the yellow lattices of my cabin window, and, looking out, saw that we were voyaging, on an even keel, on the placid blue sea of the tropics. Fra-

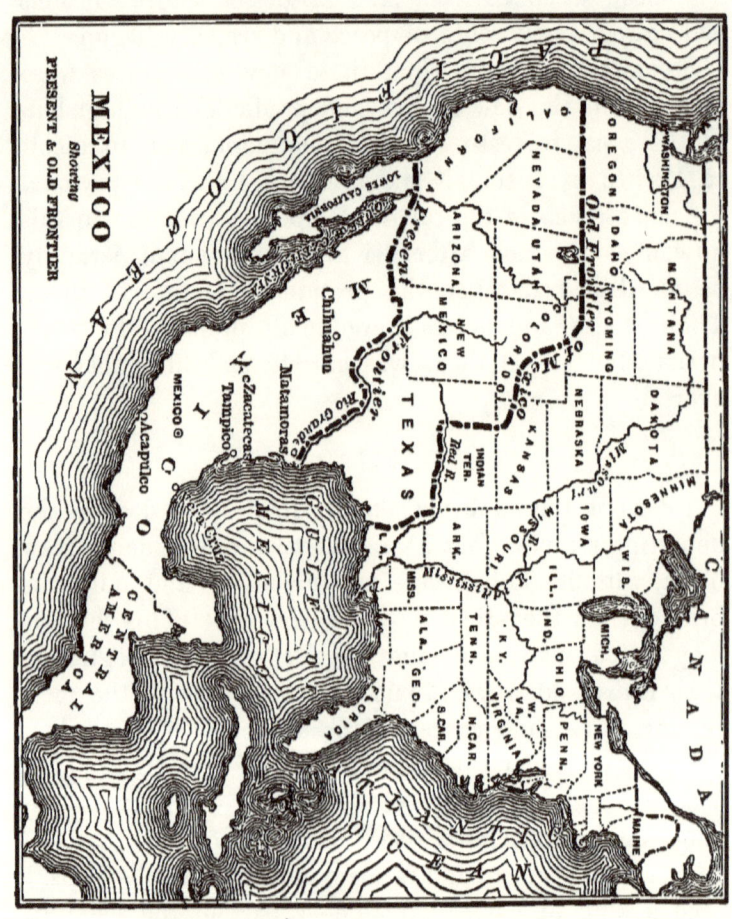

grant odors were wafted over to us from Florida, though we did not see the land. The Pan of Matanzas came in sight, and we studied the long, bold outline of the island of Cuba. It was the Spanish Main. It was the perfection of weather for piracy. If the "long, low, suspicious-looking craft, with raking masts," which used to steal out from sheltered covers to plunder rich galleons, had many such days for their occupation, it was, so far at least, an enviable one.

We had on board a Cuban who had married a Connecticut wife, and lived so long in a Connecticut village that he had a kind of Connecticut accent himself, and he was taking his wife to see his family, where, no doubt, much astonishment awaited her.

The captain, a merry and entertaining soul, had promised us, for our last day's dinner, a baked ice-cream. He endeavored to get up bets on the improbability of his being able to accomplish it; but there, sure enough, it was, and doubters were put to scorn. There was a form of ice-cream, frozen hard and firm, and a crust over it, brown and smoking—a dish, as it were, typical of our situation, as a hardy Northern element in the embrace of the tropics. Not to continue the mystery of it, and as an earnest that there shall be no "tales of a traveller" in this record which are not strictly true, let it be explained that the ice had been covered with a light froth of white of egg, which was rapidly browned and scorched at the cook's galley before the interior had time to be dissolved.

IV.

And so, as I say, two ruddy stone castles, full of green old bronze guns (we found that out afterward), looking down upon a narrow harbor-entrance; and it was Havana!

It was the morning of the 5th of April on which we entered it. We steamed up the strait to where it widens out into a basin, made fast to a buoy, and had our first glimpse of cocoa-palms, growing, unfortunately, around a cluster of coaling-sheds. Some harbor boats took us ashore. We landed at broad stone steps pervaded by smells, passed into the Custom-house (which had been an old convent), and out of it into paved lanes full of donkeys, negroes, soldiers, sellers of fruits and lottery-tickets, engaged in transactions in a debased fractional currency. The money of the debt-ridden island is that of our "shin-plaster" war period, of unhappy memory. A couple of boiled eggs in a common restaurant cost forty cents; a ride in a horse-car, thirty-five. The wages of a minor clerk at the same time were but $30 or $40 a month. How does he make ends meet and provide for his future? He buys regularly a certain amount of hope in the Government lottery. "A demoralizing system indeed!" I said, as I frowned over the wares of a dealer who had lost a leg in the insurrection. I think it was No. 11,014 I bought, however, in a grand extra drawing, the first prize of which was to be a million, in paper. I trust the gentle reader will feel that I repented when I heard the result, some months after, in Mexico, and that I should have tried just as hard to repent had I won.

The Havanese were exercised just then over the discovery of great frauds in their Marine Department. Forty million dollars had been stolen, by collusion between contractors and the commissariat, since the outbreak of the rebellion in 1868. The Morro Castle was full of prisoners of distinction—officers, marquises, and counts, of the sugar aristocracy of the island, and Old Spain—awaiting their trial by court-martial. The principal operator, one Antonio Gassol, had already been sentenced to two years' confinement and the restitution of a million of his ill-gotten gains.

The talk of not a few intelligent persons was, that the

ten years' insurrection had been purposely kept alive by rings of contractors for purposes of spoliation, and by ambition for military advancement. Dulce, they said—going through the list of Captains-General—had married a Cuban wife, and was secretly a traitor; De Rodas, when asked for re-enforcements at a certain place, withdrew a portion of the troops already there; Pieltan was occupied in intriguing for the republican cause in Spain, and the easy-going Concha for the cause of King Alfonso. Finally, Martinez Campos and Jovellar were sent out, and, yielding to the demand of the universal weariness, by a little display of vigor, the one in the cabinet, the other in the field, made an end of the languishing struggle.

This may have been, however, merely the story of the discontented, which should be taken with a grain of salt. It is true, on the one hand, that the area of the island is not great, and the despatch of forces from Spain easy; the insurgents never held a town, and received no aid worth mentioning from without. But, on the other hand, there were no railroads of consequence, the ordinary roads were wretched, and there was the wild *manigua*, as it is called, half forest, half swamp, with which a good part of the island has abounded from the date of Christopher Columbus down. It was in the *manigua* that the insurgents found refuge from pursuit.

V.

It so happened that the *Ville de Brest* was delayed in her coming, and I had six or seven days of leisure in the island. I employed part of it in a run down to Matanzas, the second city. I saw on the way the *manigua*, which is sentimentally pretty, from a distance, with

CATHEDRAL OF MEXICO.

masses of laurel, cypress, and graceful palms; but within it is a thicket of intertwisted cactus, thorns, and creepers, through which a way must be opened with the *machete*, a formidable half knife, half cleaver, carried by the peasants for general uses on the plantations, and which served also as their weapon in the strife.

There was an International Exhibition in progress at Matanzas, easily rivalled by almost any American county fair. The railway ride of three hours and a half by a ram-shackle train, run by a Chinese engineer, was hot and dusty, but how well repaid by the first deep draughts of satisfaction in understanding at last the heart of a tropical country! There was the thatched cabin, shaded by the broad-leafed banana. It was like "Paul and Virginia." Where was the faithful negro Domingo? The hedges were of cactus and dwarf pine-apple. There were groves of cocoa-nuts like apple-orchards with us, and unknown fruits too numerous to mention. It was as if each peasant proprietor had cultivated a gigantic conservatory, and were indulging himself in the luxuries of life in consideration of foregoing its necessities.

Matanzas was dull, even with its Exposition, a pretty plaza, and the memory of a locally immortal poet, Milanes, of whom a tablet in a wall testified that he was born and died in a certain house. I looked into his works at a book-stall. He wrote on "Tears," "The Sea," "Spring and Love," "The Fall of the Leaves," "To Lola," and "A Coquette." "Your mother little thought, when she held you an infant in her arms," he says, in substance, to the coquette, "of what wiles and perfidies you would be capable. Your beauteous aspect will in time fade away, and what remorseful memories will you not then have to look back upon!"

With this dip into the poetic inspiration of the heart

of the island of Cuba let me take the train back to town, having made a beginning of the discovery that a glib rhyming talent—and facility in speech-making as well—is common among the Spanish-Americans.

I visited a sugar plantation, where the negro slaves, swarming out of a great stone barracks—the men in ragged coffee-sacks, the women in bright calicoes—were as wild and uncouth as if just from the Congo. Next I went to the bathing suburb of Chorrera, where there is a battered old fort that has done service against the pirates, and where the American game of base-ball has been acclimated.

VI.

Havana was gay with parks, opera-houses, clubs, and military music. Awnings were stretched completely across the two narrow streets of principal shops. Bright tinting of the modern walls contrasted with a gray old rococo architecture. An interior court of my hotel was colored of so pure an azure that it was puzzling at the first glance to say where the sky began and the wall ended. The more important mansions were of a size and stateliness within which is probably nowhere surpassed, but neither in them nor the shabby little attempt at a gallery were there any pictures worthy of the name.

"You will find all that—the treasures of art—in Mexico," the Havanese say. "Yes indeed! that is the place for them."

They speak with great respect of Mexico, with which, perhaps, they have no very intimate personal acquaintance. Up to the independence of the latter, in 1821, it was the richest and greatest of all the Spanish possessions; and Cuba, made more important in its turn by this independence, was but a stopping-place on the way to it.

It is worth while to have seen Havana and Cuba as a preliminary to Mexico. The Spanish tradition pervading both is the same, with local modifications. It was here, too, that Hernando Cortez prepared his immortal expedition of discovery and conquest. Since I am preparing my own, to follow over exactly the same course, why should I repine that the *Ville de Brest* is a day or two longer in coming?

He was a wild young fellow in the island in early days, this Cortez, his chroniclers say, and gave little promise of the great qualities he developed in the enterprise which steadied him. The shilly-shally Velasquez would have stopped the sailing of his expedition and thrown him into prison, but he dropped down the harbor before his preparations were half completed and finished them elsewhere. He put to sea at last, with five hundred and fifty men, in nine small vessels, to undertake the conquest of an empire teeming with millions. The largest of his vessels was of a hundred tons, and some were mere open boats. In these he conveyed, too, sixteen horses, which cost him, it is said of them, "inexpressibly dear."

We make a boast of our hardihood sometimes, yet grumble at sea-sickness, delays, the ordinary mischances of the traveller. But think of it! To set out in such a fashion, without steam, without charts, subject to every bodily ill for which modern science has found a remedy, and carrying your horses, worth well-nigh their weight in gold, to proceed against an unknown empire! Why, we do not know the first principles of boldness!

VII.

At last, on the 11th of April, the *Ville de Brest* came in, and went out again on the same day. She was a steady-going, *bourgeois*-looking craft, as compared with the elegant American steamer, and showed traces of hard knocks in her long, plodding journey of twenty days to this point. She treated us well enough, however, and presented the novelty of surroundings for which I had come aboard. There was a little, gold-laced captain, and the crew wore white canvas hats and suits of two shades of blue cotton, as if equipped for some charming nautical opera. I believe I was the only English-speaking passenger; and as it has never been known to occur to a foreigner to practise his English, it was an excellent opportunity for practising the languages likely to be needed in the new country.

There was a young Frenchman who had been back to his own country to marry a wife, and brought her with him. There was a French engineer coming to report for principals in Paris on Mexican mines; an agent of a scheme for the establishment of a national bank. A young Italian of Novara, who had "Student" printed on his visiting-card, had secured an engagement as clerk in the capital for three years. An elderly Spaniard was coming over to look into the subject of forgotten heritages; another had obtained a position in the mines at Guanajuato. There were commercial men, and a well-to-do Mexican family, returning from their travels, with a son who had studied law at a Spanish university.

It has been proposed to call this body of water—made up of the Caribbean Sea and the Gulf of Mexico—the Columbian Sea, in compliment to sadly-neglected Columbus; and it seems a good idea, but it will hardly now be carried out. My predecessors have seen many an interesting sight on this tropical old Spanish Main, the source, too, of that greatest of natural mysteries, the Gulf Stream. But these must have been in times long gone by. In the day of steam, with the swift prow always in motion, the ocean is vacant. There is no catching of sharks and dolphins, hardly even a covey of flying-fish. Those things were for the long, lazy periods of calm, when the denizens of the deep gathered curiously around the craft half quiescent among them.

One of my predecessors in 1839—Madame Calderon de la Barca, whose book on Mexico remains full of interest still—was twenty-five days making the voyage from Havana to Vera Cruz. She saw, too, as she approached, the snow-clad peaks of Orizaba and the Cofre of Perote, thirty leagues inland. We saw nothing of these. The sky was of an opaque gray above low sand-hills, on which a white surf was tumbling. We made our transit in three days, including some stoppage by a "norther." The norther is of peculiar moment to the Mexican harbors of the eastern coast; they are little more than open roadsteads, and when it blows they cannot be entered.

II.

VERA CRUZ.

I.

The sea of the subsiding "norther" was still running heavily toward Vera Cruz, as if it would overwhelm it. It was a little Venice that we saw when we came to it. A half-mile or so of buildings, compact and solid, with blackened old rococo domes and steeples; yellow for the most part, scarlet, pink, green, and blue, in patches; a stone landing-quay, and a long, light iron pier projecting from it. At the end of the pier from a crane hung an iron hook, and to this the imagination instantly hooked on. It was the termination of the English railway to the capital. By that road, with all possible expedition, we should be borne up out of the miasmatic lands of the coast — the over-luxuriant *Tierra Caliente* — to the wonders of the interior.

To the left a reddish castellated fort. No suburbs—not a sign of them—only long, dreary stretches of sand. Very far down on the sand, with the sea breaking white over her, was the English steamer *Chrysolite*, dragged from her moorings by the gale and wrecked. We came in at evening, and joined ourselves to a little cluster of steamers and sailing-vessels made fast to buoys under the lee of a coral reef, on which stands the disreputable old castle of San Juan d'Ulloa. It is whitewashed in part, and partly as blackened by time and powder as the reef itself.

VERA CRUZ.

DOMES OF VERA CRUZ.

A revolving lantern moved round on its summit. It was told to the confiding that the Government kept prisoners there to turn it; and they were instructed to look for their dark, flitting forms and hear their lugubrious cries. We heard all night, at any rate, the creaking of the pumps of an American bark along-side, which had come disabled into port, with a freight of logs from Alvarado, and could barely keep afloat.

It so happened that it was the anniversary of the arrival of Cortez, in the year 1519. He had arrived on the evening of Thursday of Holy Week, and so had I. It was on the morning of Good Friday that I went ashore. We were taken off in small boats, and our ship unloaded by lighters, for there is not one of these Mexican harbors where a ship can lie up to a wharf in safety.

More than the usual embarrassments await the ordinary traveller on the quay at Vera Cruz, by so much as he is apt to know less of Spanish than of French—in which most of the dearly-bought early foreign experience is acquired—and nobody will tell him the truth. Let it be fixed in mind that but one train a day starts for the capital, and this at eleven at night. The designing by-standers make you take your baggage to a hotel, pretending that no other course is possible. Take it, instead, to the depot at once and get rid of it, and then see the town.

For the town is by all means to be seen. One had not expected much of a place the reputed home of pestilence, and I shall not advise a lengthened stay; but, from the point of view of the picturesque, it has some pleasant surprises.

Founded by the Count de Monterey in the early part of the seventeenth century—for it is not quite the site of the original Vera Cruz of Cortez, which was above—it has now attained a population of about seventeen thousand. The principal shops had a large, well-furnished aspect, especially those in groceries and heavy hardware. The Custom-house square was piled to repletion with bales of cotton, railroad iron, and miscellaneous goods awaiting transit.

I walked, the very first thing, into a large, cool public library, which had once been a convent. It was not much of a public library, the books being few, and to a certain extent bound in vellum, as if they too had belonged to the convent; but it was public, and what one did not expect.

The churches were of a well-proportioned, solid, grandiose, rococo architecture, and had charming bells. The principal one, in a little shaded plaza, had its dome encrusted with colored china tiles, which shone in the sun —a feature waiting in plenty farther on. They were draped in black, and crowded with worshippers to-day, and abounded in strange figures of bleeding Christs, with other evidences of a florid form of devotion.

Grass grew in joints of the pavement in the minor streets, as I had seen it, for instance, in some such place as Mantua. Long water-spouts project from the tops of the flat-roofed white and yellow houses, and upon these sit the solemn zopilotes. All the world knows that the street-cleaning of Vera Cruz is conducted by the ravens, or buzzards; but all the world does not know with what a dignity these large zopilotes, of a glossy blackness, often pose themselves immovably on the eaves against the deep blue sky. They might be carved there for ornament. Many a street-cleaning department is at least less sculpturesque, and perhaps less efficient.

The principal thoroughfare, called of the Independence, leads to a short, concrete-covered promenade, bordered with benches and a double row of cocoanut-palms, and this to the open country. It is an early discovery that the Mexican is patriotic. He is fond of naming his streets and squares after his military achievements, and particularly the Cinco de Mayo (the Fifth of May). We shall hear plenty more of it, this Cinco de Mayo. It was won at Puebla over the French, in 1862. He attaches also to cities the names of his heroes. Thus Vera Cruz itself is Vera Cruz of Llave, a general and governor; Oaxaca, Oaxaca of Juarez, the sagacious President; and Puebla, Puebla of Zaragoza, its commandant on the 5th of May above-named.

There were notices of a bull-fight posted on the dead walls. Nearly all typical notes are struck at once—plaza, Renaissance churches, patriotism, bull-fight, and tropical vegetation. I took a tram-car of a peculiar, wide, open pattern (made, however, in New York) out to the open fields, and saw a dancing-place, a ball-ground, and the dark, heavily walled-in cemetery.

The road to this latter should not be grass-grown, if half the tales of dread told abroad be true. And yet there are apologists even for the yellow-fever, or rather those who say that its ravages are greatly magnified.

I fell in with the Yankee captain of the disabled bark which had lain by us during the night. He was sitting on a low stone post at a street corner, and was half disconsolate, half desperate, by turns. He could find no dry-dock in which to lie up for repairs; and he could get no steam-pump, by the aid of which he might have kept on his way. He was condemned to see his venture sold for a song, for want of means to save it.

If little, as I say, was expected from the land at this place, a good deal, on the other hand, was expected from the water, at an ancient port, the New York of Mexico, receiving nine-tenths of the commerce of a nation of ten million people. But not a year passes without a number of disasters, which has led the underwriters to make their risks to Vera Cruz about five times higher than to most other ports. The aggregate of these losses for a brief time would pay the cost of works needed to make the inhospitable roadstead a harbor.

A few rudimentary preparations are absolutely necessary before Mexico can enter upon the expected period of prosperity, and the creation of harbors in some degree commensurate with the new transportation facilities is one of them. A breakwater plan will, no doubt, have to be adopted like that so much in use on our great lakes and the Channel ports of Europe. It was of interest to hear, during my stay in the country, that this need had impressed itself upon the authorities at Vera Cruz and Tampico, and that they had taken the step of counselling on what was best to be done with the American engineer, Captain Eads, who was engaged in his unique scheme of a ship railway across the Isthmus of Tehuantepec.

II.

I had the pleasure of spending the evening, pending the departure of the train, in a large, cool, roomy house, with the American consul. He had been a resident for twelve years, and had brought up a family of daughters here. It did not seem, at first sight, an attractive place in which to bring up a family; but they saw a good deal of company from the ships in port, took an occasional run to the capital, or a vacation at Jalapa or Cordova, above the danger-line, and seemed well content.

The consul was himself a physician, and had much to say on the subject of the yellow-fever. He insisted that it was epidemic, but not contagious. The local authorities put afflicted patients in their hospitals along-side others suffering from ordinary sickness, and these latter do not take it.

"Great damage," he said, "is done to the commercial interests of both countries by the annoying restrictions of quarantine arising from this cause. There is no more need of quarantine against yellow-fever than against common fever and ague, since it cannot be transmitted."

He quoted eminent medical authority at New Orleans as sharing his views. From which it would seem that the subject is worth careful looking into from official sources, in order that, if there be a mere popular delusion, it may be dispelled. As I write the Mexican Government has just granted authority to the steamer line which carries the mail into New Orleans to reduce the number of its trips to one each month during the quarantine, increase its freight and passenger rates fifty per cent., and, if the traffic does not pay even under the increase, to abandon it entirely.

The consul, in conclusion, had known but one countryman of ours to die of it during his stay, and only a few to be attacked. I may say, however, that the consul succeeding this one—who has since gone away—arrived fresh from Minnesota, and died at his post within a week.

Another interesting subject of talk with the consul was the tariff laws and the usages of the port of entry, naturally of leading importance here. The tariff system, based on an original law of 1872, has been greatly tampered with since, and is in a confused state; so that, with the best intentions, importers are apt to be visited with double duties, fines, detentions of goods, and law-suits. There are some three hundred and seventy-eight articles in the specified list. New articles are charged for after the manner of those which they resemble. Thus, when the article of celluloid was first introduced there was doubt whether it ought to be taxed twenty-nine cents a kilogram as bone, or $2.20 a kilogram as ivory, and the decision was finally in favor of the latter.

The merchant must use the names employed in the country. Thus, our "muslin" should be merely "shirting" or "calico;" while what is understood here by muslin is really lawn, taxed twice as much. The least variation in a label or form of package is visited with penalties. Storage in the warehouses, too, is estimated, not by the space occupied, but by the package, which is a hardship. A case is told of where ordinary *argenté* hooks-and-eyes, which should pay nineteen cents a kilogram, were charged for as "plated silver," which pays $1.15, and then a double duty imposed for "false declaration," making the total $2.30 a kilogram. As a rule, a "venture" is not a success. The laws, framed with excessive severity against contrabandists, whom they often fail to reach, afflict well-meaning persons. They make the consignee of goods subject to all the penalties; and many of these latter are afraid to touch, without the most ample guarantees, consignments of goods which they have not specifically ordered. The Germans succeed best in this traffic, through their painstaking attention to the local requirements.

"I will tell you a story," said the consul, "of an unlucky fellow who came here from England with a small venture of fancy goods, part free of duty. The whole cost him originally $1200; and he had consulted the Mexican consul at Liverpool, and thought he knew what he was about. When he got through the Custom-house his total charges and fines had amounted to $2850. He sold his stock for $2000, and borrowed money to pay the difference and get out of the country."

III.

UP THE LONG MOUNTAIN SLOPE.

I.

There is but one train a day, each way, on the English railway, and the journey occupies twenty hours. The road is a great piece of engineering, and has been described more than anything else in Mexico. Photographs —almost the only good ones to be had in the country— are plentiful, displaying its notable points. It climbs seven thousand six hundred feet to the table-land in a distance of about two hundred miles, the whole way to the capital being about two hundred and sixty. It has the transporting of the greater amount of construction material brought into the country for the new roads, and has lately been quite profitable. A first-class fare is $16; a second-class, $12.50; and baggage is charged for, as on the Continent of Europe.

Behold us at last at the station, at eleven o'clock at night, ready to climb to the capital—but how unlike our great predecessor, Cortez—by railway. No, indeed; poor hero! he had to linger at the coast for months before beginning his long and painful march, with a battle at every step. Nor was it by the same route. He went in by Tlaxcala, Cholula, Puebla, and so over between the great snow-peaks of Popocatepetl and Ixtacihuatl (the White Woman), down to the gleaming lakes and palaces

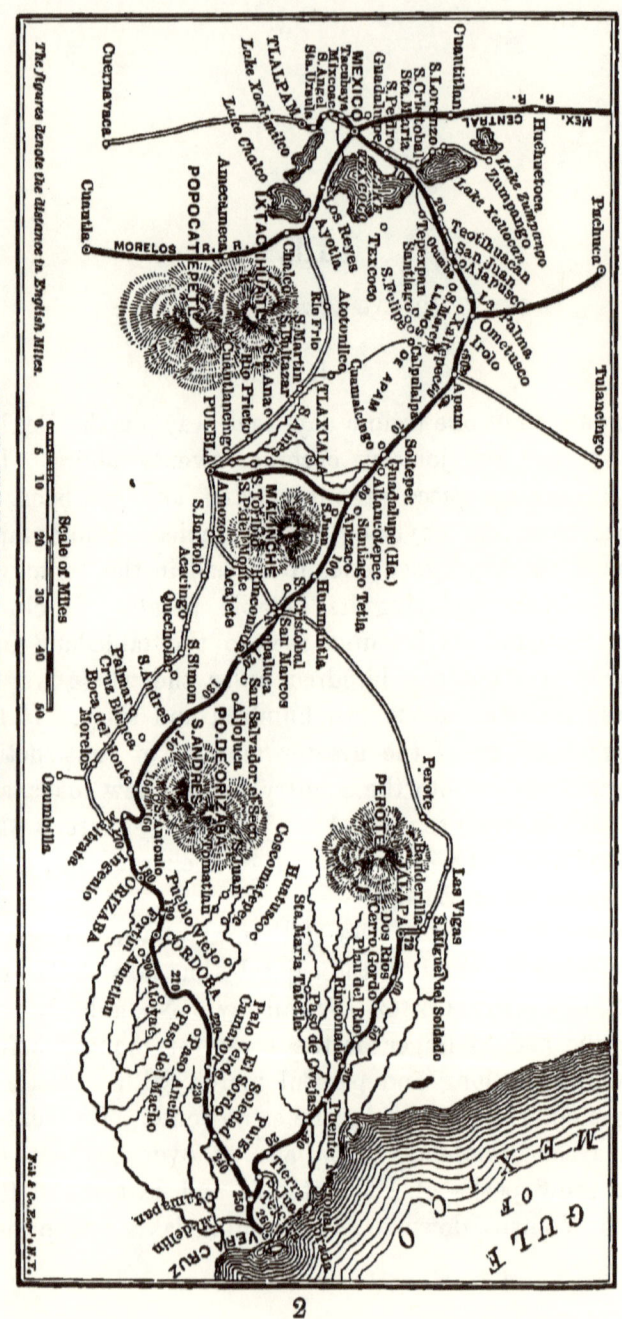

MAP OF ENGLISH RAILROAD FROM VERA CRUZ TO MEXICO.

of ancient Tenochtitlan. In this course he was followed by General Scott in his turn. The old diligence road—of their adventures on which my predecessors have written so much—continued practically the same route, going first by National Bridge and beautiful Jalapa.

I say beautiful Jalapa—although I have not been there myself—because all testimonies point with such a unanimity to the charms of soil and climate, and the beauty of the feminine type, in what is considered a peculiarly favored spot, that I think there can be no doubt about it.

There were no sleeping-cars; but the carriages, divided into compartments for eight, and comfortably padded (on the European plan), filled their place very well. The passengers in the third-class cars had already begun the night with a boisterous singing and playing of harmonicas. To-morrow was the *Sabado de Gloria* (or Holy Saturday), an occasion of merry-making, and they were taking an earnest of it. A car containing half a company of dusky Indian soldiers, who act as an escort, was coupled on to the train.

The associates in the compartment in which I established myself were the French engineer sent out to report for principals in Paris on Mexican mines, and the young Frenchman bringing back a bride from his own country. All at once there entered it so lawless and bizarre-looking a figure that the French engineer sent out to report on mines to his principals in Paris thought it prudent to descend hastily and seek quarters elsewhere. The rest of us, though remaining, were, perhaps, in no small trepidation. It was the first view at close quarters of a dashing type of Mexican costume and aspect which is peculiarly national.

Our new friend was dressed in a short black jacket,

under which showed a navy revolver, in a sash; tight pantaloons, adorned up and down with rows of silver coins; a great felt sombrero, bordered and encircled with silver braid; and a red handkerchief knotted around his neck. A person in such a hat seemed capable of anything. And I had forgotten to mention silver spurs, weighing a pound or two each, upon boots with exaggerated high and narrow heels. This last, by-the-way, is a peculiarity of all boots and shoes in the market, which aim thus, it would seem, to continue the old Castilian tradition of a high instep.

Would it be his plan to overawe us with his huge revolver, alone?

Or would he, at a preconcerted signal, be joined by confederates from the third-class car or a way-station, who would assist him to slaughter us?

The traveller is rare who arrives in Mexico for the first time without a head full of stories of violence. The numerous revolutions, the confused intelligence which reaches us from the country, give a color to anything of the kind; and the stories retain their hold for a time even in the most frequented precincts.

We got under way. The new arrival, instead of devouring us, proved the most amiable of persons, and we were soon upon excellent terms with him. He was a wealthy young hacendado, or planter, returning to estates of his, on which he said six hundred hands were employed. He offered cigars, gave us details in answer to our eager curiosity about his novel dress; and we had shortly even tried on—bride and all—the formidable sombrero, and learned that the price of such an one in the market is from $20 to $30. The silver-bound sombrero, and ornaments of coins, are a favorite kind of Mexican extravagance even among the lower classes, which is perhaps accounted for by the lack of proper places of deposit for savings in other forms.

II.

It was moonlight. Sleep on such a night was out of the question. Not a foot of the scenery ought to be lost. But the padded coach was comfortable; the fatigues of the day had been severe. The lively conversation became fitful, then lapsed into long silences. The events of that first night, half dozing, half waking, sometimes even alighting at the little stations, seem wholly like a dream —the waking part, if possible, stranger than the other.

Palms and bananas and dense coffee shrubbery, with hamlets of thatched cottages sleeping peacefully among them; a glimpse of a cataract; an Indian mother singing to her baby; perfumes coming in at the window; statuesque, silent men in blankets, and Moorish-looking women, offering fruits; stations from the outer doors of which, when reached, no town was visible, but only an immense darkness; persons taking coffee in lighted interiors; the dusky soldiers laughing loud in their compartment; a few startling words of English, sometimes with a Southern or even Hibernian accent, spoken by imported employés of the line meeting to exchange a comment, generally unfavorable, on their situation— these are the impressions that stamp themselves upon the memory.

As soon as the first gray of daylight appears it seems incumbent on us to begin to admire the country. We are not far past Cordoba, the centre of its most important coffee-growing interest.

"*Pouf!*" says our friend, the hacendado, with an air of disdain.

He will not take the trouble to look out of the window. He expects things very much better. We have, in fact, passed remarkable scenes in the night, but the best is still before us, and presently begins.

At a little station called Fortin we commence to wind along the side of one of the vast sudden gorges which impede travel in the country, the *barranca* of Metlac. There are horseshoe curves which almost permit the traditional feat in which the brakeman of the rear car is said to light his pipe at the locomotive. We pass tunnels and trestle bridges, see our route above and below us on the hills in such varied ways that it is hardly possible to understand that these are not so many different roads instead of the same. There is a point above Maltrata, distant but two and a half miles in a direct line, which must be reached by twenty miles of zigzag.

The history of this road, from the political point of view, presents hardly fewer obstacles and vicissitudes than those opposed by nature to its engineers. It has passed, in its time, under the rule of forty different presidencies, and lost and recovered its charter in the revolutions. Though of so moderate length it required over thirty years and $30,000,000 to build it.

The passengers ran out at the small stations for flowers, with which we adorned ourselves. So, too, wreaths were hung about the neck of Cortez's horse in his progress, and a chaplet of roses upon his helmet. We gave the new bride heliotrope, roses, jasmine, and the splendid large scarlet flower — the tulipan — which may pass for the type of tropical beauty.

The sun came up and lighted Orizaba, rising 17,375 feet beside us to the right, making it first rosy-red, then golden. The peak is a perfect sugar-loaf in form, with nothing splintered and savage about it, as in Switzerland. It seems almost too tame at first—a sort of drawing-master's mountain—and, above the tropical landscape, is like snow in sherbet. The city of Orizaba is an important small place, the scene of a dashing surprise of the Mexicans by the French, at the hill of El Borrego. It has charming torrents, which furnish water-power for cotton and paper mills. One of these torrents, conveyed in an arched aqueduct, turns the machinery of the *ingenio*, or sugar plantation, of Jalapilla, once a country residence of Maximilian.

A delegation of relatives had come down the night before to await our young couple here. What embracing and chattering! A Mexican embrace has a character of its own. The parties fall upon each other's necks, as we are accustomed to see done on the stage. It is given, too, between mere acquaintances, almost as commonly as shaking hands.

A vivacious sister-in-law aimed to give the new-comer an idea of what was before her in her future home. "Such flowers as I have in the court-yard!" she said, raising her eyes, with an expressive gesture; "such oranges, camellias, azaleas! Ah yes, indeed, I believe it well."

"And Jack?" inquired the husband, addressed as Prosper; "how always goes poor Jack?"

"Ah! he is dead," replied the vivacious sister-in-law. "I regret to tell you, but so it is."

It appeared that Jack was a favorite monkey, and for a moment his untimely fate cast a certain gloom over the company.

III.

From the heights where we were little villages, with squares of cultivated fields around them, were seen at vast distances below, with the effect of those miniature topographical preparations in relief displayed at international exhibitions.

It greatly simplifies Mexico to remember that, in profile, it is a long, continuous mountain-slope, rising from the Atlantic to a central table-land, and falling, though more gradually, on the other side to the Pacific. Along the ascents, as well as at the top, are some benches, or level breathing-places. These table-lands are the chief seats of population, and they are utilized as much as possible for the lines of the north and south railways.

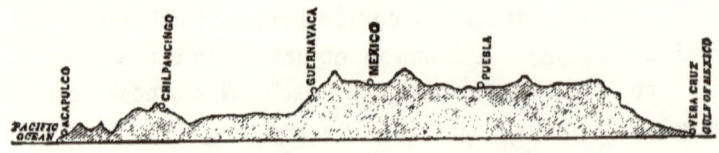

TRANSCONTINENTAL PROFILE OF MEXICO.

This steep formation accounts for absence of navigable streams and for the existence of climates verging from tropical to temperate, nearly side by side. The sharpness of contrasts in climate is scarcely to be appreciated by the hasty voyager. The really tropical vegetation is succeeded by a kind which to the eye of the American of the North is quite as exotic. Banana and cocoa-nut are followed by a hardy kind of fan-palm; by nopal, or prickly-pear, as large as the apple-tree with us; by the tall, straight organ-cactus, in use for hedges; and the remarkable maguey, or century-plant.

What would not some of our American conservatories or a certain well-known New York club give for some of these splendid specimens! The spiky maguey, like a sheaf of sword-blades, grows eight and ten feet high. It is the typical production of the central table-land. Its sap furnishes in extraordinary quantities the beverage called *pulque*—the wine of the country. From it, in addition, are made thatch, fuel, rope, paper, and even stuffs for wearing apparel.

'Our third-class passengers celebrated their *Sabado de Gloria* with great spirit, by shouting, and firing pistols and Chinese crackers from the car windows. Teams of mules, with their load, whatever it might be, gayly adorned, showed that it was being equally observed in the country. It is a day devoted by custom to the particular abasement of Judas, who is treated as a kind of Guy Fawkes and dishonored in effigy. Venders parade the streets with grotesque images of him, and children at this time estimate their fortune in the number of Judases they possess, just as at the season of All-Souls it is in cakes, gingerbread, and even more substantial viands, fashioned into death's-heads, cross-bones, and coffins.

At Apizaco, the junction of a branch-road to Puebla, we met a merry excursion, decorated with rosettes and streamers. It had two mammoth Judases, stuffed with fire-works, one on the locomotive, the other on a baggage-car. The former was blown up, as a kind of compliment to us by way of exchange of ceremonies with our own train, amid hilarious uproar.

We had now entered upon the central table-land of Mexico. Long, dotted, perspective lines of maize and maguey stretched to distant volcanic-looking hills. A few laborers in white cotton were ploughing with wooden ploughs, after the pattern of the ancient Egyptians. At the stations squads of a mounted rural police, in buff leather uniforms and crimson sashes, which give them a certain resemblance to Cromwell's troopers, salute the train.

The sparse towns consist of a nucleus of excellently built old churches amid an environment of mud-colored habitations. They are in crying need of whitewash. Will they ever get it?

The face of the country was not the verdant paradise that may have been expected, but parched and brown.

A RAILWAY JUDAS.

We had come at the end of the rainy season. Small columns of dust, whirling like water-spouts, were a constant feature of the landscape. A stage-coach going along a distant road was marked by its own dust, as a locomotive by its smoke.

Isolated houses there were none, with the exception of (at long intervals) some gloomy, square, fort-like hacienda, with straw-stacks and flocks and herds near it.

Indian peasants offered for sale, all along the way, cakes spiced with green and red peppers. The village of Apam is the centre of the Bordelais of the *pulque* industry. The new-comer here usually makes his first trial of that beverage, milk-like in aspect, but somewhat viscid and sour to the taste, with heady properties. It does not commend itself to favor on a first acquaintance. Wry and contemptuous grimaces are made over it, but in time, as occurred in my own case, it may become very palatable, as it is said to be healthful. It is poured into little earthen pitchers from bags of whole sheep-skins, with the wool-side in, like the wine-skins of the East and "Don Quixote." These bags, resembling dressed pigs, lie about on the ground or the freight-car, with their legs dumbly kicking up in the air, in many a grotesque attitude.

But one glimpse of real Aztec antiquity along the way, and that at San Juan Teotihuacan, thirty miles from the capital. The deceptive shapes of the hills, which assume symmetrical forms, had frequently produced a throb of half self-delusion, but here are two genuine pagan teocallis, pyramids dedicated to the sun and moon, and a great area covered with broken fragments and vestiges of tombs. It is thought to have been old and ruined even in the time of the Aztecs. Children offer at the train *caritas*, as they call them ("little faces"), and other fragments of earthen-ware, together with occasional pots and idols of large size, which they represent as having been dug up out of the soil. They have certainly been buried in the soil; but later, finding that the manufacture of spurious antiquities is a thriving industry, one takes leave to question for what length of time.

And yet, what can it matter? These ancient-seeming jars, with their symbols and images of the war-god and what not upon them, are at least unique and historically correct. One does well to bring home what he can get, for default of better, and not ask too many questions.

San Juan is a place that one mentally makes a note of as to be returned to; and I spent some pleasant days there later, poking among the potsherds of the past, and picking up ordinary *caritas* and bits of flint weapons, for myself.

IV.

But no dallying now. The shades of evening draw on. We are weary and travel-stained with the twenty hours' journey and the many excitements of the day; but the great moment is at hand. Gleams of distant water, thickets of maguey and cacti, with a peasant stealing mysteriously among them, behind a troop of donkeys! The geography picture is realized to the life. The water comes nearer; we skirt its borders. Can it be that these lonesome, shallow expanses, without vestige of sail or even skiff, their muddy shores white with a deposit of salt and alkali—can it be that these are the great lakes of Tenochtitlan, on which Cortez launched his brigantines? And the famous floating gardens, where are they? All in good time! We shall see. The sacred hill of the Virgin of Guadalupe, with a cluster of interesting-looking churches upon it, is passed. Remains of ruined haciendas and fortifications, and dilapidated adobe hovels, appear. We run out upon a long, low causeway, skirted by the arches of an aqueduct, over marshes. Other similar causeways are seen converging from a distance. One had not expected to find everything so unrelievedly flat. It is like climbing the mountain to find the Louisiana lowlands. A chain of yet higher mountains surrounds it, it is true; the snowy summits of Popocatepetl and its mate, the White Woman, always shine upon it from a distance, but Mexico itself is a basin. It has been under water, and would be yet, but for artificial works by which the lakes have been made to recede and left behind them these alkali-whitened margins.

It is a disillusionment very like that of approaching Venice at low tide.

IV.

THE CAPITAL.

I.

There was a custom-house at the Buena Vista station. Part of its profits are national, part municipal. The capital is in a Federal District, ruled by a governor, not unlike the District of Columbia. There is little inter-state comity as yet among the different parts of the republic. Each state still collects dues at its own frontiers, and the towns take tolls (the alcabalas) on merchandise and food entering their gates.

Mexico is not a cheap city of abode. Its hackney-coaches, as in European countries as well, are an exception to the general rule; but even these, with the various commissionaires, who zealously aid you in putting your baggage upon them, after getting it through the custom-house, are dear for the first time. Travelling is like so many other things in the world: you pay a bonus, or initiation fee, in the beginning, after which the charges are in a declining series. The particular hackney-coach which conveyed us, a travelling companion and myself, may have been a trifle dearer on account of a driver who aspired to a few words of English. Not that we greatly wanted it. The injury to one's feelings in these cases of the indifferent reception by the native of your first overtures in his own language (as if his own language were not good enough for him, forsooth), is sufficient, without a pecuniary burden added. But he charged for it, as I say.

"Well, good-night," he said, saluting us as patrons. "Wass you wants?" And, after having passed the long, shady strip of park called the Alameda, he even ventured upon a certain facetiousness, as, "Wills you to want a wiskey.?"

He had learned this proud acquirement in the military service on the frontiers of Texas.

A long, dark ride conveyed us to the principal hotel. As it was once the palace of the Emperor Iturbide, after whom it is named, it should have something stately about it, and so it has. There is a high, sculptured door-way, of an Aztec touch in the design, though not in the details, and long, grotesque water-spouts project into the street. Within is a large, dark, arcaded court, from which open *café* and billiard-room, the leading resort of the golden youth of the town.

The office is a dark little box of a place, with two serious functionaries, who seem to receive the visitor only with suspicion. The gorgeous and affable hotel clerk of northern latitudes is unknown. In the rear are more courts, not arcaded; and around all of these the rooms are ranged in several stories.

It is not so late on the evening of his arrival but that the traveller may, after dinner, still take a stroll. He will be apt to fancy at first, from the quietude, that his hotel is not on a principal street; but it is in the most central part of the city—on the street which, with three others running parallel for say half a mile, and the included cross-streets, contain the principal retail traffic.

It is an early discovery that Mexico is a grave and not a gay city. There are no crowds on the sidewalks, no eating of ices in public, no *cafés chantants*, nothing

Parisian. By nine or ten o'clock the people seem to have retired, perhaps to be up betimes in the morning for the work of the day. A military band plays three evenings in the week, but even these concerts, except on Sundays, are so sparsely attended that the men seem discoursing the music for their own amusement.

Policemen are stationed at short intervals apart in the quiet streets, with their lanterns set in the middle of the roadway. They are obliged, by regulation, to signal their whereabouts every quarter of an hour. The sound of their whistles, which have a shrill, doleful note, like that of a November wind, is heard repeated from one to another all the night through.

II.

As Mexico has not, until lately, at any rate, expected tourists, there are almost none of the usual appurtenances for their pleasure and information to be met with. While this may have its annoyances, if an ardent curiosity be baffled too long, on the other hand freedom from the sense of responsibility to exacting Baedekers and Murrays has advantages of its own. The visitor with an eye for the picturesque dips into a delicious feast of novelties, makes discoveries on every hand, and has the pleasure of testing the value of his own unaided conclusions. By daylight, with all its bright colors upon it, and its normal stir of life going on, the famous capital is a very different place from what it was at night. By little and little misapprehensions are shaken off. After the first moments of disappointment we like it always more instead of less, and in the end it takes a powerful hold.

Here at length is the great central plaza, in which events of such moment have been transacted. To actually sit down upon a bench in the midst of it, and gaze comfortably about—can it be possible?

The imposing cathedral makes a new pyramid on the spot where once stood the pyramid of the Aztec war-god. These stones should be ankle-deep with all the blood of various sorts that has been spilled upon them. For a moment one renews the pagan superstition. I would gladly see set up again, for a brief instant, old Hutzilopotchli, the war-god, aloft on his ancient terrace, hear the beat of the lugubrious war-drum, and see the mournful procession of captives winding up to the sacrifice, in charge of the sinister priests with their black locks flowing down upon their shoulders.

But not one instant too long. What! hideous priests, you will indeed lay them down on the sacrificial stone, and raise the knives of flint above their bared breasts for the monstrous slaughter? Not one hair of their heads shall be harmed. San Jago and Spain! When was Castilian ever known to turn his back upon a foe? Up the pyramid we go, leaping from step to step, though with no better weapon than a sun-umbrella in hand, to their deliverance. Ay, howl if you will, baffled miscreants, and rattle your spears and arrows like hail upon us! Down with your old Hutzilopotchli till he crashes in fragments below there. Your carven sacrificial stone shall be set up in the court-yard of the Academy of Fine Arts of San Carlos for this, and your great calendar-stone, a show-piece, against the side of the cathedral. It is a good day's work. I estimate that there were in that train of captives not less than a hundred souls!

But it is hard to conjure up images of desperate conflicts, though there have been so many, in this bright sunshine, with the multitude of pretty, novel sights. On one side of the square a beneficent institution, the National Loan Establishment, occupies what was once the site of the palace of Cortez; on another, the long, white, monotonous National Palace, the site of that of Montezuma. In the centre is a charming little garden, with benches, the Zocalo.

The cathedral, like most of the earlier architecture, is in the Renaissance style, far gone to the vagaries of rococo. It is saved from finicality, however, by its great size and massiveness, except in respect to the terminations of its towers, which are in the shape of immense bells. Adjoining, and forming a part of it, is a parish church, in a rich, dark-red volcanic stone, with carving that recalls the fantastic façades of Portuguese Belem. What a painting it would make, on one of the perfect moonlight nights, which bring out every line of the sculpture softly, and show the whole like a lovely vision!

There are little book-stalls in front, and gay booths devoted to the sale of refreshing drinks—*aguas nevadas*—from large, simple jars and pitchers of most noble and pleasing shapes. The drinks are dispensed by dusky Juanas and Josefas of Indian blood, with straight black braids of hair down their backs. With a characteristic taste the fronts of their booths are often wholly studded and banked up with flowers, and furnished with inscriptions formed in letters of carnation pinks and blue cornflowers.

Figures go by in blankets which one hankers to take from them for *portières* or rugs. The men of the poorer sort wear or carry, universally, the *serape*—a blanket with a slit in the centre for the insertion of the head. Apart from its artistic patterns, it is a useful garment in many emergencies. It is not the most improbable thing in the world that, in the course of the Mexican revival, we may yet see it introduced in the States, and running a course of popularity like the ulster. The corresponding garment of the women is the *rebozo*, a shawl or scarf, generally of blue cotton, which, crossed over the head and lower part of the face, gives a Moorish appearance. The background of life here seems more like opera than sober existence. Two other sides of the square are occupied by long arcades, among the merchants of which, protected from the sun and rain, one may wander by the hour, watching the shrewd devices of trade, and picking up those knickknacks, trifling in the country of their origin, which are certain to be curiosities elsewhere. From time to time pass across the view, dark and Egyptian-like, in a peculiar dress of bluish woollen, trudging under heavy burdens, Indians who have yet preserved the tradition of their race. Followed to their homes, they are found to dwell, among the ruined walls of the outskirts, in adobe huts which can have changed little since the time of the Conquest.

These genuine Aztecs have peculiarly soft, pleasant voices, in contrast with the Spanish voice, which is apt to be harsh. They are shiftless and squalid, but their manners are above their surroundings. It is a favorite way with the Mexican to say, " This is your house;" and I have had said to me on being introduced, " Well, now, remember! number so-and-so, such a street, is your house."

Having looked into one of these Indian abodes, and asked an elderly woman, by way of making talk, if it were hers, she replied, " Yes, Señor, and yours also."

Neither in the Zocalo nor the Alameda (a park, which holds somewhat the position of the Common, in Boston), are there trees with the hoary antiquity one might expect in such time-honored places. But it appears that the setting out of the trees, and the formation of the Zocalo

A FLOWER-SHOW IN THE ZOCALO.

entirely, is of modern date, the work of Maximilian, a monarch who, in his short, ill-fated reign, had many excellent projects.

The Zocalo is occasionally allowed to be enclosed, and an admission-fee charged, for select festivities. The orations were delivered there, for instance, on the national festival of the 5th of May. When I first arrived a flower-show was in progress. I have never seen anything more charming of the sort. Our florists might get a score of new ideas for the arrangement of bouquets. Strawberries were introduced into some for effects of color. Little streamers with gallant mottoes floated from others. There were lanterns, and birds in cages. A military band played, and people promenaded—dandies with silver-braided hats, stout duennas, and fathers of families, and slender, lithe señoritas, wearing the graceful mantilla instead of the Paris bonnet.

In front of the Zocalo a permanent flower market is held every morning, which is almost as pleasing.

Tramway cars run out of the plaza in numerous directions. The city early utilized this invention, and boasts of having one of the most complete systems existing. The inscriptions on them have an attractive look. One would like to take all the different routes at once. Patience! it is all accomplished in time. Shall we go to Guadalupe Hidalgo, with its treasures and its miraculous Virgin; to Tacubaya and San Angel, with their villas; Dolores, with its pensive cemetery, full of sculptures; La Viga, with its picturesque canal, giving access to the *chinampas* of flowers and vegetables; the gates of Belem and Niño Perdido, familiar in the story of the American conquest; Chapultepec? Yes, that shall be the very first—Chapultepec, theatre of exploits of American valor and of moving events in every historic epoch.

Mexico is extraordinarily flat, and laid out as regularly at right angles as our own symmetrical towns. At the ends of all the streets the view is closed by mountains. Its flatness, together with its position in reference to the adjoining lakes, are circumstances which have occasioned great solicitude in the past, and still call for almost as much, on a different ground. Formerly it was danger of inundation; now it is defective drainage. Bad odors offend the nostrils, and stagnant gutters and heaps of garbage the sight, of the wayfarer about the interesting streets.

COMPARATIVE LEVELS OF LAKES.

The drainage problem, divested of the mystery with which it has been surrounded in learned treatises, is simply this. When the vast slope from the sea has been surmounted, and the Valley of Mexico—as high as the Swiss pass of St. Gothard—is reached, it is found to be a shallow depression, containing six lakes. These are of many different levels—Texcoco the largest and lowest. On the edge of Texcoco, or in the midst of it, like another Venice, with canals for streets, was built ancient Mexico. This principal lake received the overflow of the others, and the city was subject to frequent inundations. It is even now, after a large shrinkage in the lakes, but a little more than six feet, at its central portion, above Texcoco. The waters of the three upper lakes—San Cristoval, Xaltocan, and Zumpango—were turned back as has been done with the Chicago River of late. A great Spanish drain in the early seventeenth century, the Tajo of Nochistongo, was cut through the mountains, and got rid of it in the direction of the Atlantic.

But Texcoco itself has no outlet, and, as experience has proved, even with only Chalco and Xochimilco to be taken care of, is still liable to overflow. With relief from this peril is inseparably bound up the drainage problem. The fall is so slight at best, that though Lake Texcoco be preserved at a normal level, and kept from backing up into the sewers, there is no destination for the sewage received by it, which lies festering in the stagnant water. With the rest is complicated also the irrigation of the valley. No end of plans have been offered to resolve these difficulties. Their history would make an interesting chapter by itself. Some have proposed to pump out the lake by steam; others, to intercept the waters running into it, and allow it to dry up naturally; another, to exhaust it by means of a great siphon of stone and cement. But the judgment of most is in favor of establishing a current, through a canal, to some point lower than the lake; and the mountains in the neighborhood have been searched for the most favorable point of exit for such a canal.

The plan was officially adopted, in fact, and a considerable beginning made, under the direction of an able engineer of foreign education, Don Francisco Garay. But the works were allowed to languish. Neither government nor community seemed more than half-hearted in the effort to get rid of evils to which they had so long been used. The problem still remains one of the most pressing of those to be resolved, and one of the most interesting to foreigners intending to make Mexico their home.

III.

Choosing any street at random where all are so attractive, and proceeding to its termination, in this direction or that, you arrive now at a mere *cul-de-sac*, now at a city gate, now at vestiges of adobe fortifications, with a moat. Few vehicles, apart from the hackney-coaches, are to be seen, but plenty of troops of laden donkeys, and everywhere the cotton-clad natives themselves bearing loads under which the regular beasts of burden might stagger. There is a story that when wheelbarrows were first introduced to their notice on the railroad works, the natives filled them in the usual way, and then carried them on their backs.

Each separate kind of business has its distinctive emblem. The butcher—elsewhere not a person noted for great taste in ornament—displays a crimson banner, and has his brass scales decked with rosettes. His supplies are brought him by a mule, trotting along with quarters of beef or carcasses of mutton on each side hung from hooks. But it is especially the *pulque* shops (corresponding to our corner liquor stores) which devote themselves to decoration in its most florid form. Not one so poor as to be without its great colored tumblers, and ambitious fresco of a battle scene, or subject from mythology or romance. They delight in such titles as "The Ancient Glories of Mexico," "The Famous St. Lorenzo," "The Sun For All," "The Terrestrial Paradise," and even "The Delirium," which often enough expresses the condition of customers who imbibe too freely.

On the tramways pass not only passenger-cars, but others for freight. They move the household goods of a family, for instance. There are also impressive cata-

THE CAPITAL. 49

THE HOMES OF THE POOR.

falques and mourning-cars, running smoothly along, with funeral processions. You may graduate from a hearse with six horses, driver, lackey, and four pall-bearers, all in livery, for $120, to one drawn by a single mule for $3; and there are cars for the mourners in the grand style at $12 and plain for $4.

Both these ideas, it would seem, might be advantageously adopted by suburban lines of our own.

Presently comes by a more economical funeral—a couple of *peons* (as the Indian laborers are called), at a jog-trot, bearing a pine coffin on their shoulders.

Battered old churches and convents on a great scale, and of a grand architecture, now for the most part devoted to other purposes, are extraordinarily frequent. Before the sequestration of Church property—in the war called of the Reform, under Juarez, in 1859—Mexico was well-nigh one great ecclesiastical estate. Without going into the religious question, and supposing only the operation of ordinary causes, it is easy to see how the Church corporations—repositories of the gifts of the faithful, moved by no feverish haste in speculation, and with no reckless heirs to spend their gains—must in course of time have become possessed of an enormous share of worldly goods.

There is no lack of sculptured old rococo palaces, of the conquerors and their successors, either. Many of these are of a peculiar, rich red stone, with carved escutcheons above their door-ways. There is one of which I was fond, in the Calle de Jesus, with immense water-spouts to its cornice, in the shape of field-pieces. Wheels and all project in high relief.

Only infinitesimal quantities of vacant land exist within the compass of the city. All is compactly built. The Continental system of *portes cochères* and interior court-

ENTRANCE TO A TENEMENT-HOUSE.

yards prevails. How many glimpses, both pleasing and curious, into these interiors! What a pity that the severity of our winters prevents building in a style which would be so admirably adapted to our summers! Over the entrances of some tenement-houses are placed pious dedicatory signs, as "Casa de la Santisima," "Casa de la Divina Providencia."

One day, as I made a hasty sketch of one of these, with a water-carrier lying asleep in the archway, the custodian came out and offered strenuous objections. "You are mapping the house" (*mappando la casa*), he said, "and I do not see how it can be for other than evil purposes."

One of the most charming of all the mansions I saw stood nearly opposite our hotel, and was faced up entirely with china tiles, chiefly blue and white, and set with old bronze balconies, as dainty and quaint as a dwelling in fairy-land. I examined the interior of this house also, and found it faced within as well with the same simple, Moorish-looking, tiles, in staircase walls, ceilings, and even the high, banked-up furnace, or range, in the kitchen. An affable major-domo occupied his leisure with painting, in a large library on the ground-floor. He was just now engaged in copying and enlarging, very poorly, the photograph of a lady, over which he held up his brush for criticism. A maroon carpet was laid up the centre of a grand staircase, and the same uniform color prevailed in the carpets throughout. The rooms were large and high, the principal ones opening both on the street, and, by means of light glass doors draped with lace, on the balconies running around the courts. These balconies are edged in the general practice with climbing vines and rows of handsome plants. In one of the rear courts could be heard and seen the family carriage-horses, together with others for the saddle, stabled according to custom under the common roof.

There was a large saloon, with divans, and old-fashioned mirrors, sloped forward from the walls, instead of pier-glasses; and a little boudoir, with furniture entirely in gilded wood and cane. There was a pretty family chapel, with two *prie-dieux* for the master and mistress, and a couple of benches for the use of the servants. In the bedrooms of such houses are usually religious pictures, copies of Murillo and the like; and there are also found quaint effigies of sacred things, as a representation of the Nativity; a Christ, with purple mantle and crown of thorns; a life-size Virgin, in raiment of tissue of silver, standing upon the globe and a serpent's head. The men of the country are very widely imbued with the sceptical spirit of the age, but the women, whose property these objects are, are still devoutly Catholic.

These rooms, in such interiors, though less lofty and impressively finished perhaps than those at Havana, have not the complexity of objects with which we, in an ill-understood passion for decoration, overload our own in the United States. They are large, and contain a few simple articles, with plenty of space around, and have an unmistakable dignity of effect. When we can make up our minds to do that, instead of depending upon a complication of costly rarities in little space, we shall begin to be palatial, and not merely *bon bourgeois*.

We do not know how republican we are, after all our travelling abroad and reverence for things European, till we come to where the stately old Continental traditions are actually in force.

One of the enthusiasts of the new progressive movement, writing of late of Monterey, a city of 40,000 people, in the north, already connected with us by the Mexican Central Railway, and coming into notice as a winter resort, notes, as one of the signs of improvement, that "the old Latin style of building, the square, flat-roofed house, with interior court, is giving place, in the new quarters, to American architecture." To which I reply, Heaven forbid! Let us never "improve" away with "American architecture" the Moorish-looking dwellings which, to lovers of the picturesque, should be one of the principal inducements for visiting the country.

V.

THE PROJECTORS.

I.

Meanwhile the court-yard of our hotel, the palace of the ancient Emperor Iturbide, is full of a curious group of English-speaking foreigners, discussing a multitude of projects. They sit usually in chairs on a little terrace at the left of the court, behind which is a modest little parlor, with a piano. As a general rule, the Mexican hotel is without parlor, reading-room, or any other of those appurtenances we are accustomed to look upon as an essential part of the composition of a hotel.

The guests take their meals at a restaurant, entered from the second court, or at other restaurants in the town where they please, there being no provision by the hotel itself. They look up wearily at their rooms around the circumscribing galleries, push their hats on the back of their heads, and pass their hands across their brows. The atmosphere, at this elevation of 7600 feet, is very rare, it will be remembered, and most are affected at first by a feeling of dizziness and loss of appetite. They do not find themselves quite right in health; and even the most athletic pause once or twice, and hold by the balusters, on their way up-stairs. The same amount of exercise cannot be taken, in fact, by either men or animals, as in a more dense atmosphere. The horses, for instance, though good and speedy, can only be run short distances, and then, as evaporation is rapid and draughts particularly dangerous, must not be let stand, but must be walked up and down till gradually cooled.

I recollect my first glimpse of my room, to which, after an interview with the sepulchral clerks below, I was shown by the barefooted boy, "Pancho," carrying a tallow dip. It was without windows or other opening except through a large transom above the door, and seemed hot and suffocating. This may have been the influence of imagination, however, for the climate is rarely either hot or cold, but noted for its remarkable evenness. There is no provision for heating during the winter. It is said that even after a very few minutes of fire, in stove or grate, the already thin air becomes so much farther expanded as to produce discomfort. Later, in my long stay at this hotel, I had a room higher up, on the sculptured front, looking down upon the life in the thoroughfare, which, taking a separate name at every block, is here the Calle de San Francisco. Again, I had one with a window commanding the shining, tile-covered dome and part of a garden approach to the lovely old convent of San Francisco, now devoted to the uses of an Episcopal mission, and beyond that the mountains, with the fair blue sky above them. Rising to begin the day, the mornings were found peaceful and lovely, the genial sunshine bathing the prospect, the blue sky but varied with the piled-up clouds out of which castles in the air are constructed. The visitor, having got over his temporary oppression, remarks upon this almost unbroken series with increasing wonder and admiration. It is hardly the custom to comment on the weather in Mexico, at least in the agreeable season, though the rainy season is a different matter.

"A pleasant day?" says the listener, with lifted eyebrows, should you do so. "Well, why not?"

OLD SPANISH PALACE IN THE CALLE DE JESUS.

Most familiar among the group of English-speaking foreigners in the court-yard during my stay was General Grant, who has lent a part of his great fame to the development of the resources of a much-suffering people. Did he ever reflect in these historic halls, one wondered, on the career of the Emperor Iturbide? Had all the talk on Cæsarism in the Press ever put the idea the least bit in his head? Rumors, mischievous to the cause of amity, ran at the very time that it was in Mexico, not the United States, that he proposed to found his empire. Certainly it would be difficult to imagine so unmelodramatic a figure in the robes and stars and crosses in which Iturbide has arrayed himself, after the pattern of Napoleon the Great, in his portrait at the National Palace.

Iturbide wrote in his memoirs—which, as a display of egotism, are highly interesting reading—one sagacious sentence. "Devotees of theories," he says, "are apt to forget that in the moral as in the physical order only a gradual progress can be expected."

This is very true; but the short-lived Emperor forgot, as have many of his republican successors, that despotism can never educate the citizen for the duties of freedom.

Only once before — namely, on the coming of Maximilian — has there been a stir that might be compared to the present in a country which the progress of the century has heretofore seemed to ignore. Could a secure government then have been established, much would have been done. But the new-comers arrived as masters, not as friends; and the conditions were wholly unfavorable. The real improvements, too, apart from those intended for the glitter and the comfort of the throne, were but the shadow of those proposed to-day.

SEMI-VILLA ON THE PASEO OF BUCARELLI.

Here the more efficient lighting of the city by electric light was heard discussed; there the opening of coal mines; here the establishment of sugar refineries, shoe factories, cotton mills. There were archæologists, constructors of telegraph lines, and engineers starting out or returning from reconnoissances. This person had come down to look into coffee-plantations; that, to establish a new line of steamers. This discourses of the improving tranquillity of the country, and asserts that three ploughs are now sold to one revolver. He names over prominent bandits who have become peaceable contractors and farmers.

Some will organize banks of issue, and rid us of the cumbrous silver dollar. Another is up from the interior with a scheme for a colony and mines—much too rose-colored, one would say—with which he will start back to New York to organize a syndicate. Mines of gold and silver are one of the specialties of the country; but they seem to present fully the uncertainties of mines elsewhere.

THE MODERN STYLE.

Some organized dinners, at which Mexican senators and deputies were enlisted for the cultivation of more friendly relations. These were held at the Concordia restaurant, or the Tivoli of Bucarelli, or of the Eliseo (summer gardens), with spacious banqueting halls. Much international good-feeling was manifested, and the Mexican national anthem and the "Star Spangled Banner" were played alternately after the speeches. Everything was to be made over anew. A few of the younger men were going and returning from expeditions of pleasure. They came back from a bull-fight; from the baths of Alberca Pane, where there is a fine tank for swimming, covered with an awning; or the theatre. They had many an amusing gibe, after our American way, on the backwardness of things, and the difference of manners and customs in the country.

But pleasure had as yet few votaries; the object of most was serious work. The business of railroad-building, and procuring of charters and subventions from government, threw all else into the shade. Five great lines, two of which had already made long strides, were to traverse the country from north to south, and more than twice as many from east to west, connecting the oceans. There were said to be six hundred American engineers in Mexico. They are often young graduates of Cornell and other polytechnic schools. In the capital the engineers and employés form set-

PORCELAIN HOUSE IN SAN FRANCISCO STREET.

tlements in boarding-houses of their own; make resorts of certain economical restaurants where little but English is spoken. They associate but little with the natives, but go about their work rather rough-and-ready in appearance, and seem to postpone adornment till the heat and burden of the campaign are over. There was a noticeable Southern element among them; and it will be found, generally, that the enterprises in Mexico have attracted a large representation from the Southern States. There is still, among the rest, a remnant of the ex-Confederate officers who came hither after the war, to engage —without great success, as it happened—in coffee-planting and the like.

Not a few of the young engineers, however, particularly those who have their field of operations in the provinces, have already found wives among the slender señoritas of the country. It seems another case of going after the women of Moab, as it were, for the rumor comes back that these exacting helpmeets have often made them change their religion, as a preliminary to naming the happy day.

II.

A leading point with the projectors, is whether or not Mexico is likely to become a large or metropolitan city. It seems difficult, when on the ground, to doubt it. Great cities have sprung up at a mere intersection of railroads. But here is one with a population of 250,000 people already, a seat of government and of schools, colleges, museums, and galleries of fine arts, with an admirable climate and extraordinary scenery, and three hundred and sixty years and traditions of great fascination behind it. There are to come into or connect with it, when all is complete, the Mexican Central, National, and International roads, from the north; the Mexican Oriental, on the eastern seaboard, and Occidental, on the western; and General Grant's road, the Mexican Southern, from the south—all to have interoceanic branches and feeders; the Morelos road, the Acapulco road, the English road to Vera Cruz; another, now constructing, to the same point by Puebla and Jalapa; and a number of short lines of less importance.

A small portion only of this would be sufficient to create a metropolis outright, while Mexico has grown to a certain greatness with no advantages at all—not even wagon-roads. It seems its manifest destiny, with its central position on transcontinental lines, and its established prestige, to become the chief depository and place of exchange for the whole country. It ought to be a favorable point, too, for manufactures, and to become the metropolitan residence of the wealthy from the interior. These have rarely come to the capital heretofore. Not even the senators and deputies bring their families, owing to the barbarous state of the roads. The existing difficulties of communication can hardly be conceived. There are perfectly authentic accounts of persons who have gone from Mexico to Vera Cruz, thence to New York, thence across to San Francisco, and thence by Pacific mail-steamer to Acapulco, rather than make the direct journey of three hundred miles on mule-back over the sierra.

It is fair to say, however, that there are those who think the future metropolis may be farther to the north, as at San Luis Potosi.

If Mexico, then, is to be a great city, whither is it to spread? It is compactly built within, and much of the land about it is low, traversed by causeways. There is no better place to think about it, nor to look down upon the capital as a whole, than Chapultepec.

My first visit there was made on the tramway, where I fell in with a Mexican colonel, who told me that he liked the Americans very well. He had spent some time in captivity among them, having been taken prisoner at San Jacinto, and had learned to know them as they are. They mean well, he said, and are enterprising and appreciative of the arts of life; and you can depend upon what they say. Most of his countrymen, he said, very sensibly, did not understand this, but were distrustful and jealous. Their idea of American character, in fact, is largely derived from foreign books in which it is conventionalized and caricatured in an unfriendly way. There is evidence of it on every hand. The American, as touched upon in the newspapers and current literature, is the "Yankee" of Dickens and followers of less intelligence on the Continent. He is a sordid person, exclusively wrapped up in "dollars," and can know but little of the chivalrous nature of those who thus superciliously disapprove of him.

There is nothing very warlike about Chapultepec at present. A glimpse is got, as you approach, of a light, oblong, colonnaded edifice, with a lookout on the top, which is now a part of the government observatory. The hill is not precipitously high, though of a good elevation. There is a monument at its foot to the memory of the pupils of the military school who fell in its defence in 1847, and in the grounds moss-grown cypresses and a tank of clear water. I found the main part of the building, when an upper terrace was reached, in a state of ruin. The light iron columns of an arcade had been coquettishly painted and gilded, and its walls decorated in the Pompeian style, under Maximilian, but all had been wrecked in the revolutions. There was a little garden, in which a small guide picked me some flowers. He answered, "*Quien sabe?*" in a childish lisp, to most inquiries, just as his father, the custodian, if he had been there, would

THE DRIVE TO CHAPULTEPEC.

have answered in his deeper base. "*Quien sabe?*" (Who knows?) is a more dreamy and speculative rendering of our own "Give it up," or perhaps "Dunno!"

The most prominent object, in the long line of the distant city against the bright gleam of Lake Texcoco behind it, is a sudden little volcanic hill—El Peñon—which rises out of it like a teocalli; and next to this the cathedral.

As the lay of the land is studied from here it seems rather natural that the city of the future, on grounds of good drainage, ease of access, and scenery, should advance in this direction to Chapultepec, ex-palace of the Montezumas and of viceroys, military school, fortress, and observatory, on the foremost spur of the foot-hills.

This was the intelligent forecast of Maximilian—a ruler, it must be admitted, much better fitted to cope with such pleasant matters than the ferocity of Mexican war and diplomacy. And such was the view of a rather wild-cat American Improvement Company, found among the projectors in the court-yard, which professed to intend a large purchase of land for building upon, to sell part of it, with houses, on the instalment plan, and to put up a mammoth hotel.

It seemed a little incongruous, this selling of the heritage of Montezuma on the instalment plan; but we are a people who do not stop even at the most venerable of traditions; and the scheme might not be a bad one in responsible hands.

Maximilian also made Chapultepec his summer palace, and laid out to it the handsome Paseo de la Reforma, the afternoon drive and promenade—the Bois and Central Park of fashionable Mexico. During Lent, however, fashion takes the caprice of changing to the Pasco de la Viga, along the canal by which vegetables and flowers are brought to the capital from the floating gardens. The Paseo de la Reforma is a wide, straight boulevard, nearly two miles long, starting from a certain equestrian statue of Charles IV. of Spain—the first bronze cast in this hemisphere, and fine and excellent work. It is two hundred feet wide, and has a double row of trees—eucalyptus and ash — shading its sidewalks. The Mexican equestrian dandy should be observed as he curvets his horse along it among the fine carriages. He wears now not only his weighty spurs and silver-braided sombrero, but a cutlass at his saddle-bow, and larger revolvers than ever. Not that there is need of them, since a couple of mounted carbineers—of whom there seems no great need either—are stationed at nearly every hundred yards; but they are a part of his peculiar display. Some of our young Americans, too, in the country, it must be said, almost out-Mexican the Mexicans themselves, carrying all their customs to an exaggerated extreme.

There are to be six circles, with statues, spaced at proper intervals along the way. The first, containing a fine Columbus, is finished; a Guatemozin, for the second, is in progress. The next, it is said, will contain Cortez. There at last will stand, face to face — their countrymen now one people—the heroic defender and the heroic conqueror, the two characters of such contradictory traits within themselves, who both acted according to their lights in their day and generation, and but followed the path of inevitable destiny.

The causeways of La Veronica and La Romita—containing ancient small-arched aqueducts, which bring water to the city—branch off from Chapultepec, and form two sides of an obtuse triangle, which the Paseo (or Calzada) de la Reforma bisects. It was along these causeways that the Americans ran, in that invasion of a very different character, in 1847. It is said that as Shields was charging on that to the right, after the fall of the castle, Scott, fearing his imprudent haste, sent to detain him. The aide had got as far as the preliminary "General Scott presents his compliments, and begs to say—" when Shields, apprehending the message, cut him short with, "I have no time for compliments now," and hurried on, and got into the city before he could be overtaken.

Do the Mexicans bear us a grudge for all that? They seem just now to have amiably forgotten it, and far be it from me to revive such memories in a boasting spirit. There is a behind-the-scenes to it, here, upon the ground. It is pathetic, and by no means calculated to produce complacency, to read in the small history studied in the schools the Mexican account of what took place. The almost unbroken series of defeats from which they went up, without hope of success, to the slaughter are frankly admitted. The country was torn by internal dissensions. The generals went back from the field to put down or sustain governments, refused to aid one another in their operations, and availed themselves of the troops given them to seize upon power, instead of fighting the Americans. There were not less than eleven changes of government, chiefly violent, during the short course of the war. In February and March of the year in which, in September, the invaders made their entry there had been fighting in the streets of the capital for well-nigh a month between two presidents, neither strong enough to put the other down. Want of courage is not a Mexican failing. It was want of leaders, unity, everything that gives steadiness in a great crisis.

The land ostensibly aimed at by the so-called Improvement Company follows the Calzada of the Reform for a considerable part of its length. It lies vacant, except for use as pasture. It has not been safe to live too far from the thickly-settled district till the establishment of law and order by the present administration, and the city itself has furnished room enough. But what new accommodations are to be needed in the great future, with the vision of which imaginations are regaling themselves, it is not an easy matter to determine.

Villas were spoken of, to be built with restricted rights, so as to preserve a select and park-like aspect. There were to be front lots enough on the Calzada alone to pay the cost. The grand hotel talked of was to surpass anything on the continent.

If somebody would but put up a hotel equal to our own of the second grade it would be a boon to American travellers. It might expect to draw, too, not a few of the Mexicans themselves, who are hardly slower than the rest of the world in recognizing a good thing when they see it. The magnates who shall have made fortunes in the new enterprises, and others who have them already, could, no doubt, be relied on for a liberal patronage.

III.

This project is of no farther importance than as a text for a mention of the Mexican tax and real estate laws, which have their features of decided interest. "In the moral as in the physical order," as our friend Iturbide tells us, "only a gradual progress can be expected." A nation of nine or ten millions, two-thirds of whom are of pure Indian blood, used only to the most primitive and poverty-stricken ways of life, cannot be too suddenly pushed forward. They must be allowed to go at a certain pace, even with the best of intentions, and slowly adapt themselves to the improvements designed for their good; for it is by them, the rank and file, after all, that these must be supported.

The country might seem, at first sight, the most glorious place for real estate speculation in the world. Real property is not taxed except upon such income as it produces. When not actually producing income, it may be idle indefinitely, and escape scot-free, however much it may enhance in value meanwhile. But there are embarrassing restrictions, devised through fear and jealousy of the foreigner, which make the prospect much less attractive. The traveller of means cannot follow his whim, as he might almost anywhere else in the world, of buying a pretty bit of land or house that attracts him and leaving it, to return to when he will, or do what he please with it.

By the Mexican Civil Code "no foreigner may, without previous permission of the President of the Republic, acquire real estate in the frontier states or territory within twenty leagues of the frontier." And "it is absolutely prohibited to foreigners to acquire rustic or urban property within five leagues of the coast."

This may be well enough, and is aimed principally at the United States, as a way of preventing any gradual encroachments from the borders; but farther, and more important: no foreigner may own real property at all, except on condition of remaining permanently and looking after it. If he be absent from the country for two years, his property may be denounced and entered by the first comer, the same as if it were a mine. He cannot even have an agent in the country to hold it for him. Nor, even should he comply with the rigid condition named, could he then sell it to another foreigner.

The transient foreigner, so far as he is concerned, cannot acquire real estate on any condition.

All this is set down in the Code in the most explicit terms. The most driving improvement company, therefore, could sell lots only to Mexicans. The class of wealthy Americans expected as winter residents would be ruled out of the calculation, though, of course, they may stop at the hotel.

There is also some ambiguity as to what commercial corporations, with one-third of their directors resident in the country, may or may not do, since the construction of the term "corporation" is not the same as with us. Some construing or explanatory enactments are needed to remedy the ambiguity last mentioned, and an entire sweeping away is needed of all the rest.

If there be sincerity in the manifestations of desire for progress, and aid from without, Mexico must sweep away narrow and benighted restrictions. If outside capital be demanded for works of amelioration and embellishment, how can it be expected at such a price?

And why, in the name of goodness, in this enlightened day, should not the foreigner be put upon the same footing as the native in these matters, and allowed to hold property wherever he will throughout the civilized world?

Let the foreigner bear in mind, too, that he must be matriculated at the Department of Foreign Affairs, through the Consul-general, in order to have any recognized standing in a court of justice, in cases of difficulty. Without this formality even his foreignness is not necessarily conceded to him as a protection.

VI.

THE FERRO-CARRILES.

I.

The *ferro-carriles*, the *caminos de fierro*, or railways, were the business of the hour. In speaking of the coming greatness of the capital I mentioned glibly the principal ones which are supposed to have a part in it. They are by no means all built. Far from it! It is not even certain that some of the most promising of them, on paper, ever will be built.

The matter of granting railroad charters in Mexico is by no means new. They have been granted for thirty years or so, to Europeans and natives, who did little or nothing with them. It was only when, under the adoption of a more enlightened policy, they came to be granted to Americans that the roads were built and the charters had a value. At once everybody who prided himself upon the necessary influence began to desire a charter also. He might not want to use it at once, but could keep it and see what turn things were to take. Or he might transfer it to some more powerful ownership to which it would be worth a consideration. This new ownership, too, might wait to see what was likely to happen. If railways promised to be profitable in the country, it was well for certain great corporations in the United States to have their feeders or extensions there; at any rate, they could keep others from the field till they should be satisfied of its character.

It is in this way, I surmise, that some of the present franchises have been got, and are reflectively held. There have been henchmen to procure them and turn them over to patrons, who wait a while before going to work, trusting to influence to procure the proper extensions and renewals of time, if needed.

Stories were afloat of practices employed in the obtaining of concessions and subsidies, which I should prefer to believe falsifications. I heard one or two of them, it is true, from somewhat inside sources, and such practices are not unknown elsewhere; yet I like much better to think that there are no persons of standing and influence in Mexico who could prostitute their high position, and put a shameless greed for gain before the public interest in a crisis like the present, as these stories seem to indicate.

"Why, in our great West," said an American visitor, settling himself back in his chair to complain vigorously of certain treatment he had received, "if an immigrant comes among us, we give him a lift. We help him build his house, or perhaps put him up a barn; and are glad to do it. If he has capital to start some kind of factory, we give him a piece of land free of charge. That is the American style. We put our hands in our pockets and pay out a little, knowing full well that we shall get it back in time in the greater prosperity of the town."

"Yes," I said, by way of sympathy with his aggrieved situation, and a proper pride in the American style of doing things, "and I am told that, in Chicago and St. Louis, they pay his hotel bills a while, and try to keep him, if not as a permanent resident, at least long enough to get out a new census, in which he may be included."

"But here," my interlocutor continued, "there is nothing of the kind. The first thing they ask about a new-comer is, 'How much can we make out of him?' They want pay for permitting him to do something for them. There is no public spirit, no local pride. What they want is exorbitant gains."

He went on to tell of an application for a charter by an American company, which was absolutely refused. They were afterward approached and told that the privilege would be granted to a committee of Mexican senators, who would in their turn transfer it to the company for a handsome consideration. The go-betweens in this negotiation declared that the personages who were to have the final voice in the granting of the charter, as well as themselves, would require to be paid, which might have been true, and might not. A liberal share of the subsidy to be voted for the railway was to be exhausted in this way.

I do not know whether this be anything more than political "striking," or black-mailing, with which we are familiar at Albany and elsewhere, and whether the corruption ever really reaches to head-quarters. At any rate, it was said that some part of the aid devoted to each several enterprise was diverted in this way to private benefit. The drainage of the valley had been offered in the United States at a reduction of forty per cent. from the amount voted by the appropriation bill, the difference to be retained by the purveyors of the opportunity. One hundred thousand dollars in cash was demanded, again, as a preliminary, for the opportunity to fill in the works of a certain harbor with stone at a reasonable rate. Such accounts may be worth looking into by Mexican authority, with the interest of good and economical work and the abatement of scandal at heart. There is probably no better form of patriotism for Mexico just now than a strict and uncompromising honesty of administration.

II.

There were entered in the convenient statistical handbook known as the "Annuario Universal," for the year, a list of forty-one railways as in *explotacion* (running), or under construction. But after many of those enumerated was inserted a note, to the effect that, owing to some unforeseen delay, the works were not yet begun. Taking out these, and a larger number on which, though technically begun, little or no labor had been expended, there was still an unlooked for array of constructed roads. Taking out the English road from Vera Cruz, and what had been done by the American companies, almost at the moment, these were found to consist of short bits of local line scattered throughout the country. There was not a through line among them; many were operated by animal traction only; they had been built by natives, been afflicted by bankruptcies and other troubles; and represented the railway situation of the country apart from outside assistance. You were even drawn a good part of the way by animals on the English branch from Vera Cruz to Jalapa; and in going from Mexico to the mines at Pachuca, after leaving the main line at Ometusco, we took first a diligence, and were then pulled by mules in a Philadelphia-built horse-car. The number of these isolated bits has not increased in the mean time, several of them having been bought up and incorporated in the larger enterprises.

In the mean time, however, the list of projected roads at least has been liberally increased. The Congressional session of 1881 was the most active ever known in the authorization of new enterprises on a great scale. The great Mexican Central, trunk line, had, however, been chartered in 1878, and the Mexican National in 1880. The first charter under the modern movement dates from October, 1867; and since then the Mexican Government has issued charters for over 20,000 miles of road, with subsidies probably to the amount of $200,000,000. Many of these, with their subsidies, have lapsed, of course. The Government is now held for about 15,000 miles of road, and subsidies of $90,000,000.

The enterprises on a great scale are all American, and the chief ones among them may be estimated roughly as follows:

	Miles.
Mexican Central (Boston Company)	2,000
Mexican National (Palmer-Sullivan)	2,000
Sonora (Boston Company)	500
Mexican Southern (General Grant, President)	1,000
Oriental (De Gress and Jay Gould)	1,200
Topolobampo (Senator Windom, President)	1,200
International (Frisbie and Huntington)	1,400
Pacific Coast (Frisbie)	3,000
Total	12,300

To these may be added the Sinaloa and Durango, from the city of Culiacan to the port of Altata, in Sinaloa; the Tehuantepec railway, and Captain Eads's ship railway across the same isthmus, to take the place of a ship canal. The privilege to build an American railway across Tehuantepec, it may be remembered, was secured (at the same time with the lower belt of Arizona) by the Gadsden treaty of 1853, supplementary to that of Guadalupe Hidalgo. The road was supposed to be needed for the consolidation of relations with our then newly acquired territory of California. The Pacific railroad filled its place, however, and the project, taken up and dropped from time to time, has since had but a lingering existence.

Captain Eads proposes to transport bodily ships of

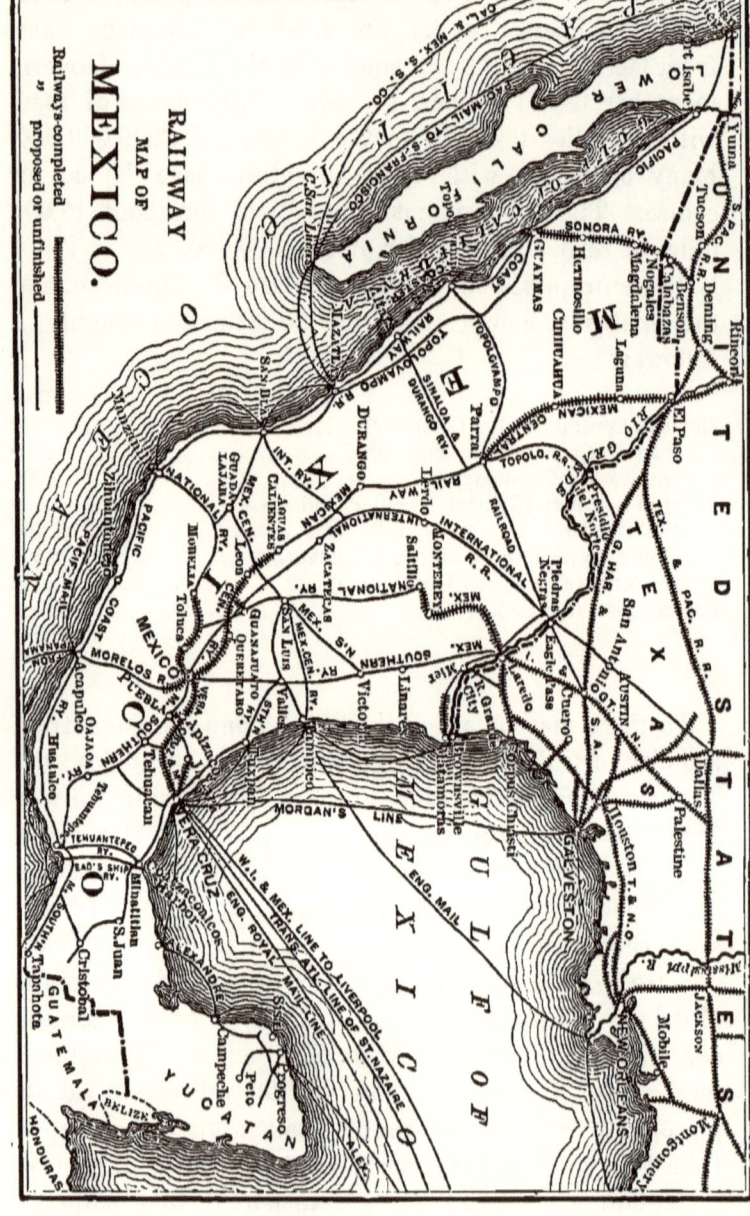

GENERAL RAILWAY SYSTEM OF MEXICO.

4000 tons, 190 miles, by land. He will have twelve lines of rails, and four locomotives at once; and, to avoid jarring in transit, changes of direction will be made by a series of turn-tables instead of curves. The scheme is a startling one, and meets with no little opposition. It is still only on paper; but its proposer, who has abundantly vindicated his sagacity in constructing the jetties of the Mississippi and the great St. Louis bridge, remains firm in his conviction that he will be able to sail ships across the isthmus on dry land.

III.

The several enterprises are succinctly divided into two classes—those on the ground, and those on paper. It is not necessarily a disparagement to the last that they are still in such a condition, for many of them are of very recent origin.

The original Mexican Southern road is to run south from Mexico, by Puebla and Oaxaca (capital of the populous state of the same name) and the frontier of Guatemala, with branches to the ports of Anton Lizardo, on the Gulf of Mexico, and Tehuantepec, on the Pacific. It is to connect also with the Tehuantepec railway. It relies, as a principal resource, upon the transport of the valuable productions of a rich tropical country, as cotton, sugar, coffee, rice, and the like. Oaxaca is an important small city of 28,000 people, birthplace of General Porfirio Diaz, the Mexican power behind the throne, and undoubtedly the weightiest person in the country. The route will be a rugged one to build. Much of the area is high and salubrious. The Oaxacan Indians are a sturdy race, who have followed their leader, Diaz, and others in many a hard-fought campaign.

This company, however, has lately effected a consolidation with the Mexican Oriental, and both will henceforth be known under the name of the Mexican Southern.

The Mexican Oriental sets out from Laredo, on the Texas frontier, and proceeds to the capital by way of Victoria, the capital of the state of Tamaulipas. It claims to have a bee-line, and to be 200 miles shorter than any other. Its mission is to occupy the district between the coast and the Mexican National. It throws out a branch from Victoria to San Luis Potosi; and has a coast-line connecting Tuxpan, Nautla, and Vera Cruz. It is fed by some 12,000 miles of road under control of Jay Gould in the United States.

The International is chartered to run from Eagle Pass, in Texas, to the city of Mexico, occupying a field left vacant between the Mexican Central and National; and is allowed to have also a cross-line to a point between Matamoras and Tampico, east, and between Mazatlan and Zihuataneso, west. The theory of each, it will be seen, is to have an interoceanic line as well as a main line north and south.

The Pacific Coast road covers the right to a vast stretch, beginning at a point below Fort Yuma, Arizona, and connecting the whole series of Pacific ports down to Guatemala. The Topolobampo has also a long extension southward, to touch at some of the same points.

The Topolobampo route (Texas, Topolobampo, and Pacific) crosses the northern border states. It professes to be a shorter transcontinental route to Australia and Asia than any other that can be laid down on the map. It claims to have at Topolobampo, just within the Gulf of California, the ancient Sea of Cortez, one of the few fine harbors of the Pacific coast.

These harbors are spaced at wide intervals apart.

That of the Columbia River of Oregon is the highest up. Then, 600 miles south, comes San Francisco; 441 miles below this is San Diego; 650 miles farther on, in a direct line, or 936, doubling Cape St. Lucas, is Topolobampo; and 740 miles south of this again is Acapulco. Between them all there is nothing worthy the name of harbor.

Topolobampo city, within the confines of the state of Sinaloa, exists only on paper as yet, but nothing is more impressive in its elegant regularity and finish than a paper city. It claims to be 800 miles nearer New York than San Francisco by railroad travel, and that a person coming from Liverpool to Sydney, Australia, would save 600 miles in laying out a course from Fernandina, Florida, by New Orleans and Topolobampo, which is indicated as a route of the future. If some of these representations be correct, no doubt it will be. We live in times of a ruthless commercial greed which is stopped by no sentimental considerations of vested rights and convenience. We have but to see a short, through line, with possible economies, to build it with all possible despatch.

The road in question is to start from Piedras Negras, on the frontier of Texas, and make for Topolobampo, across the states of Coahuila, Chihuahua, and Sonora, with branches to Presidio del Norte, also on the Texas frontier, and to Alamos, in Sonora, and the port of Mazatlan, down the coast. These routes pass near, and would greatly facilitate operations in some of the large silver-mining districts, of late entered with success by American capital and immigration. The reports of its surveys chronicle an engaging prospect in various other ways. It passes from belts of tropical products to those of white pine, oak, and cedar, and others fitted for cereals, grass, and cotton, with a rich iron mountain, and deposits of copper as well as silver.

The maxim is laid down that a railroad pays, in local traffic, in proportion as one section of its line supplies what another lacks. If the situation be as represented, Topolobampo seems provided with most of the essential conditions of success.

VII.

THE RAILWAYS AT WORK.

I.

The Sonora road is already built, and in operation as I write. It is a stretch of three hundred miles, from the Arizona frontier, to the port of Guaymas, near the centre of the shore line of the Gulf of California. Its United States connection is by a branch of the Atchison, Topeka, and Santa Fé, from Benson, through Calabasas, to the border at Nogales; and another is proposed, from the Southern Pacific at Tucson. The management of this enterprise, as well as of the Great Mexican Central, is practically that of the Atchison, Topeka, and Santa Fé.

Its course is across the state of Sonora. It abolishes the old system of ox-train transportation and the dusty stage-line from Tucson. It will be found fault with, among others, by the savage Apaches, whose refuge Northern Mexico has so long been. Their depredations, with their territory penetrated by railroads, must soon come to an end once for all. The other Indians of the state—Yaquis, Mayos, and Opatas—are docile, and a principal reliance for cheap labor. The road taps mines, and, by means of a branch, what is even more important for Mexico, the valuable Santa Clara coal-fields. It has the little city of Hermosillo, with its plantations, irrigated by aqueducts, in its course; and its port of Guaymas is commodious and sheltered.

II.

I have purposely reserved to the last—the better, perhaps, to present them to view—the two great trunk lines of principal importance, the Mexican Central and the Mexican National. These two represent the bulk of the entire movement as it is at present. Neither had many miles in actual operation during my stay; but the works, railway stations, city offices, and army of employés of both, were constantly in sight at the capital, and were the principal evidences by which the manner of the railway invasion of Mexico could be judged.

Energy of movement, ingenuity in planning, and an almost limitless expenditure, all indicated here conscientious work, and not simply railroad building on paper.

The Central begins at El Paso, the terminus of the Atchison, Topeka, and Santa Fé, as well as a station on the Southern Pacific, at the frontier of New Mexico. It extends to the capital, a distance of thirteen hundred miles, tapping on the way a long series of the leading cities of the republic, most of these as well capitals of states. It has also a great interoceanic cross-line, which is to pass from the port of Tampico, on the Gulf of Mexico, through the cities of San Luis Potosi, Lagos (the junction with the main line), and Guadalajara, to San Blas, on the Pacific. It is expected that the main line will be completed about July, 1884.

The first reached in the chain of leading cities is Chihuahua, with about eighteen thousand inhabitants. The line is already running to this point, and is completed in all three hundred and thirty-one miles southward from Paso del Norte. The visitor by rail may already have in Chihuahua a glimpse of a place presenting most of the typical Mexican features. It has Aztec remains, and a large cathedral, built out of a percentage of the proceeds of a silver-mine in bonanza. It is the scene where the patriot Hidalgo, who first raised the standard of insurrection against Spanish rule, was shot, having been treacherously betrayed by his friends. This story is, unhappily, of but too frequent repetition in Mexican annals.

Durango, three hundred miles farther, has twenty-eight thousand people. It has been spoken of as the *Ultima Thule* of civilized Mexico, the barren plains to the north—which are, indeed, very common in all these uppermost states—not having been considered worthy to be included with the country below. There are places where water is not to be had for two and three days at a time, but must be carried by the traveller. The inhabitants have had to depend considerably upon themselves for defence, as is seen in the occasional fort-like haciendas, with walls turreted and pierced for musketry.

Zacatecas, moving onward now into a country of recognized civilization, has 62,000 people; San Luis Potosi, 45,000; Aguas Calientes, 35,000; Lagos, 25,000; Leon, 100,000; handsome Guanajuato, capital of the state which is the richest of the whole interior, 63,000; Celaya, 30,000; Silao, 38,000; Irapuato, 21,000; Salamanca, 20,000; and luxurious Guadalajara, 94,000.

The mining of the precious metals is a leading industry over all the area thus described, which abounds also in the agricultural products of a gentle and temperate climate. The railroad is now running northward from the city of Mexico to Lagos, and is completed for three hundred and thirty-four miles from this lower end.

Lastly in the chain of cities may be mentioned Queretaro, which has a population of 48,000. It is the site of flourishing cotton-mills, an aqueduct which is compared with the works of the Romans, and it saw the final resistance and execution of Maximilian. Mexico itself has 200,000 inhabitants. I have summed up here nearly a million of people; and it would seem that a railroad along the line of which are scattered such communities as these, grown to their present dimensions without even tolerable means of approach, need not lack for support.

True, large numbers of the people are Indians and very poor; but I point to the example of Don Benito Juarez, the liberator of his country from the French, an Indian of the purest blood, and to numerous others accessible on every hand, to show that there is nothing inherent in the race itself to debar it from the highest development with increase of opportunities. And if any suppose that they do not like to travel, let him simply inspect the excursion trains where third-class cars are supplied to them in sufficient numbers.

III.

I made the trip over the section of the Central to the small city of Tula. Its principal feature is the passage through the great Spanish drainage cut, along one side of which it has been allowed to terrace its track. This cut—the Tajo of Nochistongo, before mentioned, designed for keeping the lakes from inundating the valley—was begun under the viceroys as far back as 1607, and continued for a couple of hundred years. Such mammoth earth-cutting—a ditch twelve miles long, a couple of hundred feet deep, and three hundred and sixty wide—was never seen elsewhere in the world; and it is said to have cost the lives of seventy thousand *peons*, or Indian laborers, in the course of construction. Why this should have been, and how they died—whether by slipping in and being buried, or under the exactions of cruel task-masters, and whether those who passed away simply of old age (for which it will be seen there was ample time) are included—does not appear.

I went partly by construction train, dining in their car with a group of jolly young engineers, and partly on horseback over the *terre-plaine* (the graded road-bed), which makes an excellent surface for riding. The peons, swarming on the work, in white cotton shirts and drawers, have reddish skins, bristly black hair, and a sudden, wild-eyed way of addressing you. They have an analogy to the Chinese type. They got at this time two and a half reals (thirty-one cents) a day. They are very suspicious, and have absolutely no idea of trust, or waiting over the appointed time. Dangerous strikes have resulted from some slight putting off of the pay-day, which usually takes place once a week. In other respects they are very tractable.

There were said to be thirty thousand of them at work on railroads at this date. The rate of wages, so favorable to the contractors at first, has been gradually rising under the active demand in the mean time, and I have heard, since my return, of a strike on one of the northern roads for as high as $1 a day. They buy gay clothes for Sunday, and *pulque*, and save nothing. Many will not even work steadily. Two such form a partnership to take a single place, and one works half the week and the other the rest. There were some who walked all Saturday night to spend Sunday at Queretaro, and returned Monday morning. On the haciendas they are generally in debt, and as they cannot leave when in debt, they are so far attached to the land, like serfs. Each gang has a *Cabo* (or head), who is simply an enterprising one of themselves, and gets an allowance of two cents extra for

each man he controls. The Cabo is a great man among the railway laborers, and out of cabos arise the Benito Juarezes, and hopes indefinite for the evolution of the race.

THE GREAT SPANISH DRAINAGE CUT.

I spent the night at Tula. It was the capital of the Toltecs before the day of the Aztecs. I climbed the Hill of the Treasure, to inspect some ruins over which archæologists have made a stir. There are no sculptures nor carved stones, nothing but some opened cellars and heavy walls, with patches of a red plaster, as at Pompeii, adhering to them. But we stayed our horses, and looked down, from a thicket of organ-cactus and nopal, upon a lovely sunset over the valley of Tula. It is a little pocket of fertility in the hills, and it does not seem at all wonderful that the Toltecs stopped there in their migrations southward.

My *mozo* pointed out a ruin in the thick woods, which he declared was Toltec, knowing that to be what I was in search of. It was picturesque enough, its walls having been split by an irrepressible vegetable growth; but it had the same style of battlements (a kind of Spanish horn of dominion) as the fortress-like church in the town, dating from 1553, and was much more modern.

I went into this cool old church—vast enough for a cathedral—next day, when the temperature was warm without. It was entirely vacant. Fatigued with my journeying, I sat on a comfortable old wooden bench, and dozed till awakened sharply by the striking of a little cuckoo-clock. I seem to have dreamed that the numerous quaint figures of saints, in dresses made of actual stuffs, had somehow an every-day existence there, in addition to their sacred character, and that they were taking notice of the intruder, and offering audible comments. This is one of the ways, I suppose, in which very good miracles have been wrought before now.

For the rest, the place consisted of a plaza, with two or three *pulque*-shops; a shop of general traps, with the ambitious title of "Los Leones;" a *botica* (or drug-shop), kept by one Perfecto Espinoza; a Hotel de las Diligencias; and a little jail, at one corner of the plaza, where a couple of soldiers walked up and down, and the prisoners peeped out through a large wooden, grated door.

And there was a good restaurant, kept by a little Frenchman, who moved on with it from time to time to the head of the line.

IV.

The Mexican National, or "Palmer-Sullivan," road is due to the same enterprise which established the successful Denver and Rio Grande system in Colorado and New Mexico. It is, like that, a narrow gauge, instead of a standard gauge, line, and a connection is to be ultimately established between the two. In some respects it may claim to be the pioneer in the modern movement, since its agent in Mexico, James Sullivan, had obtained a charter and begun to raise money in 1872, but was stopped in his project by the panic of the following year.

The National takes a much shorter line to the capital than the Central, say eight hundred miles, as against thirteen hundred. Its initial point is Laredo, on the Texas frontier. It is running already into Monterey, the capital of Nuevo Leon, and built below Saltillo. Of the charms of the little city of Monterey, which has medicinal springs beside it, travellers begin to speak in the warmest terms. It touches San Luis Potosi and Celaya as well as the Central, and has along or near its course other cities, well peopled, though less known to fame, as Matchuala, the population of which is 25,000. Its eastern port is Corpus Christi, Texas, though it will have a branch also to Matamoras. Its westward extension (only less important than the main line) winds round about, through the cities of Toluca, Maravatio, Morelia, Guadalajara, and Colima, down to the port of Manzanillo.

Four of these are capitals, and all are populous, and have wide, well-paved streets and handsome buildings, public and private. Toluca, at a great height, 8825 feet, above the sea, is often afflicted by a rather frigid temperature; Colima is distinctly in the tropics; but Morelia affords the happy medium, and its whole state of Michoacan has charms upon which the appreciative never have done expatiating. Humboldt speaks of the lake found at Patzcuaro as one of the loveliest on the globe. Madame Calderon de la Barca, in her journey here, could hardly refrain from regretting the lavishing by Nature of what seemed (so few were there then to enjoy it) almost a wasted beauty. "We are startled," she says, "by the conviction that this enchanting variety of hill and plain, wood and water, is for the most part unseen by human eye and untrod by human footstep."

The route winds, too, on its way to Guadalajara, around the great lake of Chapala. Truly, it seems they are to be happy travellers, those of the immediate future, to whom the simple device of the railway is to open up so much of the wildness and loveliness of nature, combined with the quaintness of an old Spanish civilization. We are apt to forget, in our preconceived impressions, what an important part Old Spain played in the country during three hundred years, what treasures she spent there. She had made a beginning of some of these solid, regular cities, which surprise one like enchantment on emerging upon them from forests and wastes, a hundred years before the Pilgrims landed at Plymouth Rock. Very little, in fact, has been added to what the Spanish domination left. The modern movement, since 1821, is to be credited with very little in the way of new buildings. Such compliments as are paid in the course of these descriptions to the architecture belong chiefly to that remaining from a much earlier date. The reputation of the republic is still to be made in all such matters when it shall have outgrown the ample legacies bequeathed it, and have need of farther accommodations peculiarly its own.

V.

In all, the National has completed four hundred and sixty miles. It is said of late to have been sold to an English company. We need not forego our American pride in its early achievements, even if this be so. Perhaps such a transfer might be of benefit, in allaying the dread of an overweening American influence.

It was not done even to Toluca in my time. It has to face its most arduous engineering difficulties at the very beginning, and fortunately goes far more smoothly afterward. No less than seventeen bridges, of solid construction, had to be thrown across the little stream of the Rio Hondo in two or three miles of its course.

A pay-train on horseback started out from the central office every Saturday, to convoy the silver coin for the wages of the army of hands employed on the first section of twenty miles.

"Ride with us!" its members often hospitably urged, and I more than once accepted the invitation.

It is an all-day adventure, and a fatiguing one. Behold us at early morning clattering out of the court-yard to ride up into the fastnesses of the mountains, a curious cavalcade. The treasure is packed upon the backs of a dozen mules, which are placed in the centre. A troop of *Rurales* (the efficient force organized by Porfirio Diaz for the better protection of the rural districts) takes the van. A numerous retinue of armed *mozos* of the company, with ourselves, bring up the rear. The young engineers, paymasters, and contractors, well mounted, with long boots and revolvers, present a handsome, half-military aspect.

We have presently lost sight of the city, and are upon

high rolling barrens, where the surface is volcanic and rent into an infinity of seams, and the only vegetation is that of nopal, or prickly-pear, as large as apple-trees with us. Here and there a cluster of white tents is seen at a distance, and cotton-clad peons delving in gulch or on mountain-side are like some strange species of white insects.

The whole expedition wears a most un-nineteenth-century air. We might be some band of marauders returned from an ancient foray. The Rurales have something in their cut—the buff leather jackets, crossed by ample sword-belts, and wide, gray felt hats—of the troopers of Cromwell. Each has a rifle in his holster at the saddle-bow, and a gray-and-scarlet blanket strapped behind him. Nothing could be more spirited, in color, than these costumes, dismounted beside a cactus-tree, or thrown out against the blue of distant mountains. On the harness of some of the mules are embroidered in red and blue their names, or that of some hacienda, as "Santa Lucia," to which they have belonged.

It is understood that an individual with a crimson handkerchief around the back of his head, under his silver-bordered sombrero, is the titular *cacique* of San Bartolito by descent from ancient chiefs. He precedes us, being employed by the company to look out for plots and ambuscades. When we have passed what he considers the dangerous points—these are generally in the neighborhood of elevations, whence an intending bandit could spy the road for a distance in both directions, and where are ravines on either side for concealment and escape—he rejoins the troop, and converses upon the propriety of his receiving more salary for his arduous duties. No molestation has ever yet been offered these caravans, and there is hardly likely to be. From a con-

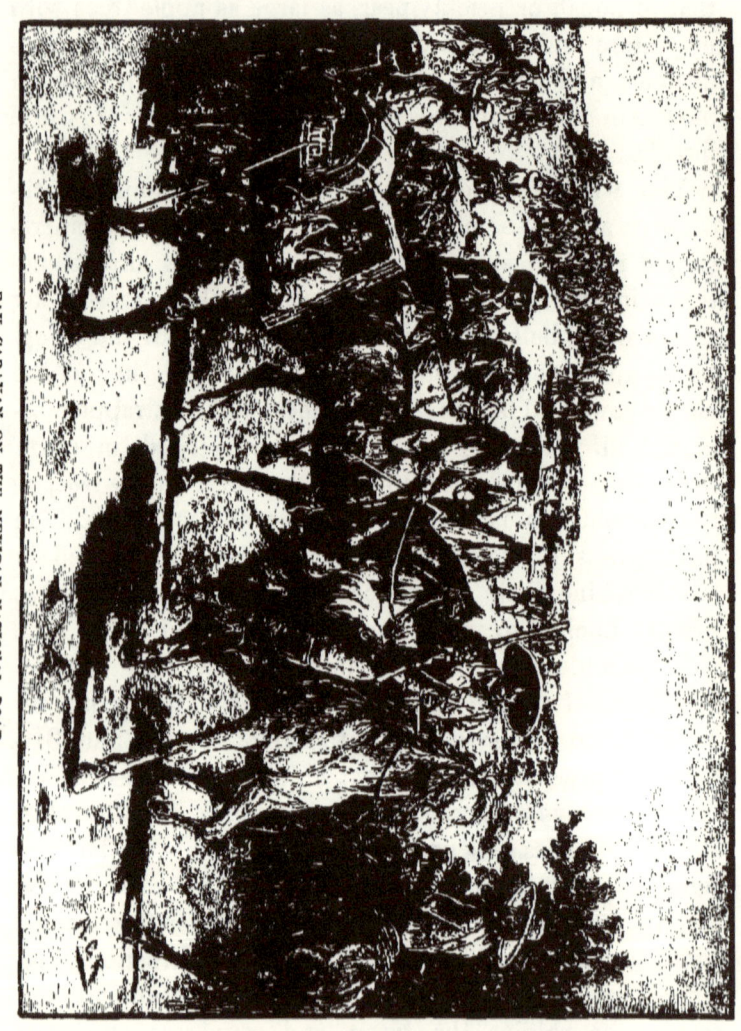

PAY CARAVAN ON THE MEXICAN NATIONAL ROAD.

siderable experience in remote parts of Mexico I am satisfied that, however prudent ample precautions may be in exceptional cases like this, the ordinary traveller runs little if any more danger of robbery than at home.

At the pay-stations we breast our way through crowds of the peons so thick that the horses can hardly be prevented from trampling upon them, always with their narrow foreheads, bristling hair, staring, wild eyes, and large, undecided mouths. Their money is jingled out to them through a pay-window into their shabby sombreros. Venders of small commodities and *pulque* wait for them, and profit by the new supply of funds.

At these stations the engineers lead a kind of barrack life. The interior contains some beds, a dining-table, and a safe; outside is a storehouse of picks, shovels, and barrows. Whether here, in their construction-car, or tents, they extend the stranger a cheery hospitality. They are hearty, robust fellows—"not here for their health," as their saying is. Many of them have seen service in war and in other climes, and their company is both amusing and instructive.

VI.

The right of way usually given in all the concessions is for a width of two hundred and thirty feet. Material and supplies for the road, and connected telegraph line, are exempted from duty generally for the period of twenty years. Neither the concession, property, nor shares can be alienated to any foreign government, nor can a foreign government be admitted as a shareholder. The fear of foreign domination crops out everywhere in Mexican legislation; and perhaps the weakness of the nation, and the sad experience of its seizure by Napoleon on the pretext of debt, are sufficient excuse for such nervousness. At any rate, all companies organized under its charters agree to be strictly Mexican, and to renounce all rights and exemptions as foreigners.

"NOT HERE FOR THEIR HEALTH."

There is no great vacant public domain, as with us, and the Government has not aided the new enterprises with land grants. Up to a recent period, however, it has attached to each concession a cash subsidy of $10,000 to $15,000 a mile. Both the Central and National are thus subsidized. In order that the burden may not fall too heavily upon an exchequer always weak, the payments are made to depend upon the pledge of six per cent. in the one case, and four in the other, of receipts at the custom-houses. Certificates for the several amounts as they become due are issued to the companies, which must wait for collection till there are funds to meet them.

The latest plan, affecting most of the great schemes still chiefly on paper, gives no subsidy with the charter, but gives, instead, certain privileges to atone for its absence. A less strict accountability to Government, with a much higher tariff of charges, is permitted. It has been questioned by some whether under these conditions a charter without the subsidy is not better than with it. It is to be borne in mind, however, so far as the matter of the higher rates is concerned, that between competing points the company which can afford to run at the cheapest rates gets the business. If but a tithe of the railroads now covering the map like a net-work be built, there need be no fear of the lack of a lively competition.

The stocks and bonds of railroads are not bought on the word of a desultory traveller mainly in search of the picturesque—though I will admit, too, that they are often bought upon less. I am not afraid, therefore, to express a certain enthusiasm about the *ferro-carriles* of Mexico, which are in everybody's mouth. It is the railways which have made the modern world elsewhere what it is, and why should they fail of the usual effect here?

They may be overdone, and there may be panics and shrinkages, such as have occurred elsewhere, though this is not extremely probable, owing to the reasons for wariness which lie very much on the surface. The conditions to be conformed to must not be sought in a parallel situation of things in the United States, but rather in such countries, perhaps, as Russia and India, with a large peasant population to be developed, instead of a new population to be created. We have built railroads in advance of settlement, and depended upon immigration to fill up in their wake. Mexico has but an infinitesimal immigration, and presents no great inducements to it at present. It must depend upon the local carrying trade and natural development of the industries and commerce of the country. It has a population per square mile but little less than that of the United States. These are of a natural intelligence, and capable of the stimulus of ambition when opportunities are opened. They are to be encouraged to be no longer satisfied with a bare subsistence for themselves, but to produce from their fertile lands a surplus, for which a market is now opened. They are to trade upon it and become amassers of wealth.

No less than 10,000 miles of railways are spread over what were once the old Mexican provinces of California, Arizona, New Mexico, Colorado, Wyoming, Nevada, Utah, and Texas. Railways have brought these out of the nothingness in which they recently lay so vast and desolate. What must they not inevitably do at last for Old Mexico itself, so fully peopled, and scattered with centres of trade and of the arts of civilized life?

VIII.

THE QUESTION OF MONEY, AND SHOPPING.

I.

It is perhaps thought that the work of improvement is to be effected entirely from without, the Mexican himself remaining passive, and allowing everything to be done for him. The view is supported by the extent to which the business of the country is already in the hands of foreigners. The bankers and manufacturers are English. The Germans control hardware and "fancy goods." French and Italians keep the hotels and restaurants; Spaniards the small groceries and pawn-shops, and deal in the products of the country. These latter have a repute for somewhat Jewish style of thrift. They are enterprising as administrators of haciendas, and often marry the proprietors' daughters, and possess themselves on their own account of the properties to which they were sent as agents. Whether it be due to such rivalry or not, it is to be noted that there are few Jews in Mexico. Finally, the Americans build the railroads.

The Mexican proper is a retail trader, an employé, or, if rich, draws his revenues from haciendas, which in many cases he never sees, and where his money is made for him. These are on an enormous scale. The chief part of the land is comprised in great estates, on which the peasants live in a semi-serfdom. Small farms are scarcely known. For his fine hacienda in the state of

Oaxaca ex-President Diaz is said to have paid over a million of dollars; on another the appliances alone cost a million. The revenues of Mexican proprietors have been heretofore devoted to the purchase of more real estate, or loaned out at interest; at any rate, "salted down" in some such way as to be of little avail in setting the wheels of industry in motion.

Before adopting, however, the conventional view that this state of things is due to inferiority of race or enervating climate, considerations on the other side are to be looked at. In the first place is the revolutionary condition of the country, which until a recent date subjected the citizen who ventured to place his property beyond his immediate recall to a thousand embarrassments from one or another of the contending parties. Such immunities and advantages as there were, were enjoyed by foreigners alone, under the protection of their diplomatic representatives.

Again, there have been peculiar inequalities of fortune, coming down from the old Spanish monarchical times. There has been at one extreme of society a class too abject, and at the other, one in too leisurely circumstances, to greatly aspire to farther improvement, and the middle class has been of slow formation. The difficulties in the way of travel and communication with foreign parts for the middle class, from the bosom of which financial success chiefly springs, have been of a repressive sort.

The climate, of the central table-land at least, must not be considered enervating. One must lay his ideas of climate, as depending upon latitude, aside, and comprehend that here it is a matter of elevation above the sea. Individual Mexicans are to be met with who, under the stimulus of the new feeling of security, have embarked their capital, put plenty of irons in the fire, and appear to handle them with skill. The street railways of the capital, an extensive and excellent system, are under native management exclusively. It is as successful in mining. It was only when the great Real del Monte Company at Pachuca, formerly English, passed into Mexican hands that its mines became profitable.

I should be strongly of the opinion that the backwardness of the Mexican is not the result of a native incapacity or lack of appetite for gain, but chiefly of the physical conformation of the country. The mule-path is traced like a vast hieroglyphic over the face of it, and in this is read the secret—lack of transportation.

But the zealous advocate of race and "Northern energy" objects: "How long is it since we had no railroads ourselves? And yet did we not reach a very pretty degree of civilization without them?"

But Mexico not only had no railways, but not even rivers nor ports. It was waterways which made the prosperity of nations before the day of steam. It is hardly credible, the completeness of the deprivations to which this interesting country has been so long subjected. The wonder is, to any experienced in the diligence travel, and the dreary slowness of the journeys, at a foot-pace, by beasts of burden, not that so little, but so very much, has been done. On the trail to the coast at Acapulco, for instance—in popular phrase a mere *camino de pajaros* (road for birds)—have grown up some charming towns, like Iguala, the scene of the Emperor Iturbide's famous Plan, which, it seems to me, the Anglo-Saxon race would hardly ever have originated under such circumstances.

Commerce and trade in such a land naturally have their peculiar aspects. There is, in the first place, the complicated tariff, already referred to. Americans should not let a new-born enthusiasm for a promising market hurry

MODERN SHOP-FRONTS AT MEXICO.

them into consignments without a thorough understanding of the premises. As to engaging in undertakings in the country itself, one who had done so held that the new-comer should make his residence there for six months or a year, and first acquaint himself with the people, their customs, and language.

"Better make it two years, on the whole," he said, reflectively, "and then he will go home again and let it alone altogether."

Without sharing this saturnine view, the importance of some preliminary acquaintance cannot be too strongly insisted upon. The great inertia of customs and ways of looking at things so different from our own is appreciated more and more as time goes on.

The most promising openings at present would seem to be, for capital, to work up into manufactures the raw material with which the country abounds. These opportunities will increase with the growth of transportation. Labor is cheap. The peons have little inventive but sufficient imitative talent, and make excellent mill-hands. They work for twenty-five and thirty-seven cents a day, and have no trades-unions nor strikes. There is little opening as yet for persons of small means. The government has taken but its first rudimentary steps toward the encouragement of immigration, and the path is beset with difficulties.

A commercial treaty is now in the hands of the Senate of the United States. It will be adopted in some form before long, and may result in the improvement of local business opportunities, as it must in the volume of trade, between the two countries. What we want is such a reduction of duties as to put us on the same footing at least as England (in favor of which there is a certain discrimination), so that our goods and machinery can be sold in the country on reasonable terms. It is predicted that a trade which is now about $30,000,000 per annum (including both exports and imports) can be made $100,000,000. The Mexicans, on their side, desire admission for their sugar and hemp. The treaty has met with its chief opposition thus far from our Southern sugar-planters. Their fear of competition is hardly reasonable at present. Our own product seems more likely to go to Mexico at first. It is a matter of note that sugar has been selling at eighteen cents a pound of late at old Monterey, in the country which professes to raise it.* The total

---

* Detailed figures of our trade with Mexico, and other useful matters, will be found in the "Border States of Mexico," by Leonidas Hamilton. Chicago, 1882.

value of the exports from Mexico for the past fiscal year has been $29,000,000. Of these $14,000,000 came to us, and $10,000,000 went to England. Our own exports to Mexico for 1881 were somewhat over $11,000,000.

II.

At present Mexico is perhaps the most difficult country in which to do business in the civilized world. A customer four or five hundred miles off, even on the best roads, is five or six days' journey distant. In preparing for it it is not long since he was accustomed to first make his will. The merchant has friendly as well as commercial relations with his customer. He is more or less his banker at the same time, not for the resulting profit, but because it is expected of him. If he does not offer such accommodation some other house will. Credits are long, and it is not expected that interest will be charged even on quite liberal overlaps of time.

Payment is made in the bulky silver currency of the country; and this is sent in large sums by guarded convoys, the *conductas*, which converge upon the capital four times a year—in January, April, August, and November. There were but two banks issuing bills at this time, and these to but a small amount, and receivable only at short distances from the capital. One of these was a private corporation, the other the National Monte de Piedad, or pawn-shop.

The visitor becomes early acquainted with the Mexican "dollar of the fathers," to his sorrow. Sixteen of them weigh a solid pound. It is obviously impossible to carry even a moderate quantity of this money concealed, or to carry it at all with comfort. The unavoidable exhibition of it, held in laps, chinking in valises, standing in bags, and poured out in prodigious streams at the banks and commercial houses, is one of the features of life.

Guadalajara, the supply from which unites with that from Zacatecas at Queretaro, is the northernmost point from which money is despatched by *conducta* to Mexico. A portion of that even from here is despatched to San Francisco, by the port of San Blas, just as a part of that from Zacatecas goes to Tampico through San Luis Potosi. The country north of San Luis to the east ships its funds to Matamoras; those of Durango are divided between Matamoras and Mazatlan; while Puebla, Oaxaca, and the rest of the south find their natural outlet at Vera Cruz.

THE "PORTALES" AT MEXICO.

The importance of the great *conducta* in these times is diminished by the growing safety of the transport of money by private hands. Its days are numbered with the progress of the railways, nearing so rapidly the central cluster of cities in which it has its origin. Even now it no longer came wholly to town, but took the Central train at the first feasible point, at Huehuetoca, the Spanish cut for the drainage of the valley. Its place as a spectacle is filled by the pay *conductas* of the railroads.

A revision of these accounts is needed almost from moment to moment as I write, to keep pace with the rapid changes in affairs. A National Bank and banks of foreign incorporators have been established in the mean time, with authority to issue large amounts of but inefficiently secured paper. The Mexican National Bank may now issue bills to the amount of $60,000,000, upon a capital of $20,000,000. They are legal tender from individuals to the government, but not from the government to individuals, nor between individuals. One of the arguments in favor of this bank, our minister was assured, was that it would counteract in some sort the influence of the United States: the usual patriotic leaven cropping up, it will be seen; though how it should accomplish the purpose in view it is by no means easy to understand. A flood of depreciated paper is driving the solid coin out of circulation; so that, while the traveller may be now able to carry his money comfortably about him, there may be much worse in store for the Mexicans themselves than the handling of bags of unwieldy dollars. It is not pleasant to see also that the government shows some unusual pecuniary embarrassment. Its expenditures for the last fiscal year exceeded its revenues by ten per cent., and a loan is talked of. Should a spirit of recklessness enter into the management of the finances, in all this whirl of novelties, complicated by the issues of paper, a crisis might be precipitated, which would, of course, have to be counted among the retarding influences on the railways.

III.

Shops and shopping in Mexico follow much more European than American traditions. A fanciful title over the door of the shop takes the place of the name of a firm or single proprietor. You have no Smith & Brown, but, instead—on the sign of a dry-goods store, for instance—"The Surprise," or "The Spring-time," or "The Explosion." A jeweller's is apt to be called "The Pearl," or "The Emerald;" a shoe-store, "The Foot of Venus," or "The Azure Boot."

The windows are tastefully draped, after the way of shop-windows. Within stand a large force of clerks, touching shoulder to shoulder. They seem democratic in their manners, even by an American standard. They shake hands over the counter with a patron with whom they have enjoyed a slight previous acquaintance; ask a mother of a family, perhaps, after the health of "Miss Lolita" and "Miss Soledad," her daughters, who may have accompanied her thither. One of them, they hear, is going to be married. Perhaps this is accounted for by the presence among the minor clerks of some of considerable social position—some of the class you meet with afterward at the select entertainments of the Minister of Guatemala, for instance. But a limited choice of occupations has been open to the youth of Mexico, and those who cared to work have had to take such places as they could. They apply now with great eagerness for the positions of every sort offering under the new enterprises.

It was not etiquette of late for ladies of the upper class to do shopping in public, except from their carriages, the goods being brought out to them at the curb-stone. Now they may enter shops. A considerable part of the buying, as of furniture and other household goods, is still done by the men of the family. Nor was it etiquette for ladies to be seen walking in the streets, even with a maid, except to and from mass in the morning.

The change in both respects is ascribed to the horse-cars. The point of ceremony, it appears, was founded somewhat upon the difficulty of getting about.

Americanism now appears in the streets with increasing frequency, in the signs of dealers in arms, sewing-machines, and other of our useful inventions. Our insurance companies, too, are a novel idea, to which the Mexicans seem to take with much readiness. The principal shopping hours are from four to six o'clock of the afternoon. From one till three, or even four, little is done. Even the horse-cars do not run in the middle of the day. There is a general stoppage of affairs for dinner. It is but a short time since that enterprising person, the commercial traveller, was unknown in the country, but now he begins to flourish here as elsewhere.

The profits of favorably situated houses, in the absence of keen competition, have been very large, and methods of doing business correspondingly loose. The Mexican merchant does not go into a fine calculation of the proportionate value of each item of a foreign invoice, but "lumps" the profit he thinks he ought to receive on the whole. Some articles, in consequence, can be bought at less than their real value, while others, in compensation, are exorbitantly advanced.

It is the smaller trade, and that most removed from metropolitan influences, which is the gayest and most entertaining as a spectacle. How many picturesque market scenes does not one linger in! Each community has its own market-day, not to interfere with others. The flags of the plaza and market-houses, which are commodious and well built, are hidden under fruits, grains, cocoa sacks and mats, striped blankets and *rebosos*, sprawling brown limbs, embroidered bodices and kirtles, as if spread with a thick, richly colored rug. A grade above the open market is the *Parian*, a bazaar of small shops, in which goods, sales-people, and customers alike might all be put upon canvas only with the most vivid of hues.

A "MERCERIA" AT PUEBLA.

I give some examples of the street architecture of the more important shops. The approach to many is under the welcome *portales*, shady in sunshine and dry in the wet. Not a few of the shops have been old Spanish palaces before being adapted to their present use. I transferred to my sketch-book a bit from the leading *merceria* (dry-goods store) of the important minor city of Puebla which I thought particularly interesting. It was called, after the prevailing fashion, "The City of Mexico." The entire front—upon which still remained the carved escutcheon, showing that it had been the residence of a family of rank—was faced up between carvings, in a gay pattern in tiles, the figures glazed, the rest an unglazed ground of red.

IX.

SOCIAL LIFE, AND SOME NOTABLE INSTITUTIONS.

I.

THE persons who once lived in these old Spanish palaces, and descendants of the titles of nobility existing before the Independance, are still much esteemed in a certain small circle in the country. There are pointed out to you those who should by right be marquises and counts, and the titles are occasionally given them. The Mexican nobles, from the time of Cortes down, lived in magnificent style in their day. The Count of Regla, who has left his trace after him in many directions, must have enjoyed almost the state of royalty. A single hacienda of his in Michoacan was thirty leagues in length by seventeen in breadth, and, sloping down from the temperate plateau to the tropic, comprised in its extent the products of almost every clime. He fitted out two ships of the largest size, building them of mahogany and cedar, and presented them to the King of Spain. Inviting his majesty to visit the country, he assured him that his horse should tread on nothing but ingots of silver from the coast to the capital.

A remnant of the old *noblesse* rallied around Maximilian when he came to assume the Emperor's crown. With this, and what remains of Maximilian's court, and some few other families of a peculiarly exclusive turn, a circle is constituted somewhat corresponding to the Parisian

Faubourg St. Germain. They are sometimes stigmatized as "Mochos," literally hypocrites. They are rich, pass much of their time abroad, protest against the sequestration of the Church property, and exhibit a refined horror at the vandalism of these later times.

"The government," they tell you, "is in the hands of the *populacho*, the rabble; the *gente honrada*, respectable society, has nothing to do with it."

In a novel which I have by a Mexican writer, Cuellar, a secretary of legation at Washington, the scene is laid in this faction or clique. "Chona," or Incarnacion, the heroine, or leading feminine character, "had been brought up from childhood more to abhor than admire. The conversations in the family continually turned upon the utter antipathy which the men and things of Mexico inspired."

"They had for visitors Church notables and those of the wealthy who still retained the parchments of their ancestry. If they made any new acquaintance it was some Spaniard lately come into relations with them through the business of their estates."

The fashionable men in the story have been educated at Paris, and become elegantly *blasé* there as well. In contrast to these is shown one Sanchez, a vulgar, pushing fellow, upheaved from the depths by the revolutions. He has the "gift of gab," which he has utilized to make himself a figure in politics; has enriched himself with the spoils of the Church establishment, and secured a good place under government. He more than hints, however, when he is found to have finally lost it, that he is ready to engage in upsetting "Don Benito"—it is now under the *régime* of President Juarez that the scene is laid—or in any other convulsion that may promise to again mend his fortunes.

II.

I do not quite know which side the writer himself is on, in this satirical work; it is so bitter all around. It is certainly interesting as showing two such boldly distinct types, one of them at least picturesque, evolved out of the peculiar conflicts of the country. Let us hope that there are few of the dangerous Sanchez pattern in the present juncture of affairs. The Mochos cannot now be numerous nor dangerous, with the wholesale victory of middle or lower class republicanism around them. They have taken little part, voluntarily, in the successive revolutions since their own overthrow, leaving them rather to be fought out by professional soldiers of fortune. They temporize a little; attend, perhaps, the wedding of some rich railway contractor's daughter, in order, as they say, not to draw upon themselves a direct enmity; but they do not open their own houses in return; they do not "entertain."

Don Sebastian Lerdo, spoken of as the most scholarly President the country ever had, is conceded to have been to a considerable extent "in society." He was expelled by Porfirio Diaz, and is now in retirement at New York. The political class since that time has either not been well received in the circle spoken of, or, perhaps too busy with other affairs, has not greatly cared for it.

Such being the case, there are few reunions, and these of an informal character. Nor do the officials give entertainments themselves. Social gayeties, as we understand them, can hardly be said to exist in Mexico. It is only under the neutral roofs of the foreign ministers that they take place with some satisfaction. I had the good fortune to be at the capital during the visit of General Grant, and to see a social movement which, by the general testimony, was quite phenomenal. There was, among the rest, a fashionable wedding, attended by the President and his cabinet. A "reception" and banquet were given in the evening on the occasion of the signing of a civil contract between the parties. The religious ceremony took place at church next day. The interior courts of the house were wreathed with flowers, and lent themselves palatially to the festivity, as they always do. The banquet was spread along the bases of the columns of the arcade.

The young Mexican women are still kept apart from the other sex, and made love to chiefly on their balconies in the good old-fashioned, romantic style. Their manners when met with in public, however, are not so unusual as might be expected. They seem neither more nor less diffident than elsewhere. They are allowed to take part at balls in a slow waltz called the *danza*—so slow as hardly to be a dance at all—which is chiefly an opportunity for conversation.

The high-contracting parties to the marriage abovementioned were by no means young, and in general the exceeding precocity of development and early age of entering into the marriage relation supposed to be characteristic of the tropics were not apparent. It was said that mercenary considerations were not frequent, and claim was laid to a good deal of simplicity and honest affection in the settlement of these matters; though how the parties get at each other, under the restrictive system, sufficiently to enter upon a simple and honest affection, is one of those things that remain a mystery. It is said that the young woman who remains single is not stigmatized for it in the common way as "old maid." They say very charmingly instead: "She is difficult. She is hard to suit."

In the country the match-making is often taken charge

SOCIAL LIFE, AND SOME NOTABLE INSTITUTIONS. 111

INTERIOR COURT-YARD OF MEXICAN RESIDENCE.

of by the village priest, who brings the parties together finally at dinner.

As a general remark, the manners of the lower class of the country are much better than ours, and those of the upper are not as good—not as often based upon real kindliness of heart and genuine desire to be of service. The Mexican promises a hundred things which he has no intention, often no ability, of performing. The American is not without his faults—the more's the pity—but in a general way he aims to do as he agrees. He will often make against the Mexican the reproach of a certain slipperiness—a lack of appreciation of the importance of adhering to his word.

III.

Each considerable group of foreign residents, as the French, Germans, and Spaniards, has its handsome casino, or club-house, which is a standing resource for the diversion of members.

A French traveller as far back as 1838 complains of the unsociable conduct of the Mexicans. If something of the kind be still observed, therefore, it is not new. "They abound," he says, "in a superfluity of fine phrases, and it is in this easy way that they discharge themselves of their obligations."

All who know European life, however, are aware that the theatre and the café, with people of the Latin race, largely take the place of the social visiting and entertaining at home prevailing among Anglo-Saxons. Our next-door neighbors, after all, may only have followed, making a little more severe, the traditions of Old Spain. Ladies do not often appear at the cafés, but they are often at their boxes at the theatres, to which they subscribe by the season; and they would go more frequently yet,

MEXICAN COURTSHIP.

no doubt, were the pieces as a rule better worth their consideration. There are three large, well-built theatres, the Nacional, Principal, and Arbeu, and minor ones for the working-class.

The entertainments esteemed of chief importance are those of the French opera companies which come over from Havana, on their rounds. A native Spanish opera-bouffe and ballet, called *zarzuela*, is much given at other times. For the rest, the theatrical pieces presented are the works, in prose and verse, of the Spanish dramatists current at home, or occasionally of some native dramatist, announced with an extra flourish which his production does not usually justify. They are all announced with a sufficient flourish, so far as that is concerned. There is always going on some especially *Gran Funcion*, as, for example:

"The grand Drama of Customs, Entirely New, in three acts and verse, by the distinguished poet, D. Leopoldo Cano, author of the precious comedy, 'La Mariposa,' entitled 'LA OPINION PUBLICA.'

"This sublime work of the distinguished poet, D. Leopoldo Cano," the bill goes on to say, "was received at Madrid with an astounding acclaim. The Spanish Press has lavished upon it a thousand eulogies. * * * In choosing it for the second subscription night, we feel that the public will know how to value it as it truly merits, and to value at the same time the skill of the Company in their most finished studies and essays."

I do not recollect any of this as very novel, or likely to be of interest if translated, apart from some portions depending upon such a difference of manners and customs as to be hardly intelligible to an American audience. My acquaintance with the theatre began with a piece at the Nacional, called "The First Patient." There was a young doctor on the stage, and an acquaintance of his had fallen in love with his wife, and put a note in her work-basket by way of telling her so. The note was conveyed to the husband, who, instead of shooting the imprudent writer, took occasion presently to assume a look of horror, and pretend that the latter had gone blind. Before the Lothario could protest, a bandage was clapped over his eyes, medicaments given to make him believe in his own misfortune, and he was put under a course of onerous treatment.

After a series of absurd situations he was finally released, persuaded by degrees that he was cured. The patient raised the bandage. "*Veo! veo!*"—"I see!"—he exclaimed, in wild delight.

"Very well, then—see that!" said the husband, thrusting the offending letter under his nose.

This was amusing enough, but I was quite as much amused all the time with the studious efforts of a companion who had come with me—the French engineer sent out to examine mines, before mentioned—who proposed to turn the theatre into a school of languages. He grasped at every word a semblance of which he seemed to catch, and dived for verifications of it into his grammar and dictionary. He resented in his ambition any interpretation of passages which he did not himself originate, and constructed such a theory of the play as its author would by no means have recognized. When the *dénouement* came, in the bold "*Veo!*" he seized upon it with avidity.

"'*Veo*,' c'est bien trouvé ça—'*veo*,'" he said, reflectively, digesting it at his leisure. "*Je vais le retenir ce 'veo;' vous-allez voir.*"

And so he did, and proceeded to use it vigorously in the restaurants and the like on the following day.

IV.

Though so much more be still proposed, there are certainly some reasons for self-complacency in the country even from the American point of view. Education is found to be provided for in a manner that awakens admiration and surprise. The primary schools are least looked after, but the pupils who pass through these with a disposition to go farther have an array of advantages open to them at the capital superior to anything of a parallel sort in the United States. The Government maintains national schools respectively of engineering, law, medicine, agriculture, mechanic arts, and trades (for both sexes), a conservatory of music, an academy of fine arts, and a library, provided with an edifice that New York well might envy. It maintains a museum, institutions for blind, deaf and dumb, and insane, for orphans, and young criminals, and a long list besides of the usual charities of enlightened communities. The schools are open without money and without price to all, and there are even funds to provide board, lodging, and pocket-money for students from a distance, who are selected on certain easy conditions.

The students in agriculture pass some months of the year at the haciendas to observe different crops and climates. The graduates of the School of Arts and Measures go out into the world prepared to make their living as carpenters, masons, photographers, electro-platers, and at numerous other trades. Before an opinion is passed upon Mexican civilization the accommodations and neat uniforms of the pupils of the blind institute should be seen; the noble building erected in the last century for the School of Mines; the beautifully clean, wide corridors, sunny class-rooms, embroidery-rooms, dormitories, and drawing-rooms of the *Viscaynas*, the national college for girls; and the arcades and charming central garden of the National Preparatory School (in the professions) for young men.

There was a fountain spouting among tropical plants in the garden of the Preparatory School the day I went there, and by the fountain was a young panther, or lion, of the country, as they call it, confined in a cage. The students, young fellows, who did not differ so greatly from Yale and Harvard undergraduates in aspect, except for the dusky Indian complexions among them, came now and then and stirred up the lion a little, making him play with a ball in his cage. They seemed to prepare their recitations walking around the garden or sitting in the ample corridors.

The principal text-books are studied in French or English, in which languages they are apt to be written, and the recitations are conducted in the same languages; so that, what is so rare with us, graduates emerge from these schools very tolerable linguists without ever having been out of their own country.

All these institutions are housed for the most part in the vast ancient convent edifices, which furnish ample quarters to whatever is in need of them—to barracks, hospitals, post-offices, prisons, railway stations, iron founderies, and cotton-mills.

Each state of the republic, again, has its free college. Judging from that of the state of Hidalgo, however, which I saw at Pachuca—its internal arrangements in a very filthy condition—all do not follow very closely the example of the capital.

In the department of jails, unhappily, there is a deficiency. As at present arranged, they can present but moderate terrors to evil-doers. The really fine penitentiary at Guadalaxara is the only one in which modern ideas of penal discipline are followed. There is by law no death penalty at present. The number of nefarious criminals is kept down by semi-official lynchings, shooting on capture, into which nobody ever inquires. Others are transported to Yucatan. There still remain enough, however, to make one look with uneasiness on the slightness of the means of restraint employed. The bolts and bars are often only lattices of wood instead of iron. At the city prison of Belen some two thousand persons are confined. It seemed to me that a large part of them must be much more comfortable than at their own squalid homes. They made a strange spectacle indeed, looked down upon in their large courts. Of all ages, and for sentences of all durations, they eat, sleep, and work at various light occupations together. No attempt is made to prevent their communicating or staring about. They have good air, light, and food, and are allowed a part of their own earnings. They take a siesta at noon, play checkers, gossip, and even bathe luxuriously in a central tank.

The liberality toward education spoken of is the more creditable since the Mexican treasury is not flourishing, and a yearly deficit is more common than a surplus. These expenses appear to be regarded as essential, whatever else may suffer. It is the more creditable, too, since the heads of the government do not indulge themselves in expensive surroundings. The American legislator is not himself without his marble colonnades and his furniture of black walnut upholstered in Russia leather; but President and Cabinet ministers here walk upon threadbare carpets in the National Palace. The chamber of the Senate is a modest little hall; and the Deputies sit in shabby quarters in another part of town, which were once simply a place of amusement, the Theatre Iturbide.

The museum, chiefly of Aztec antiquities, to which one turns with interest, is not of the extent or informing character that may have been expected, and is under by no means brilliant management. Its greatest attraction is the arrangement of some of the larger fragments, particularly the great sacrificial stone from the ancient temple of the war-god, in the court-yard. There is a setting of shrubbery and vines about them, and the sunlight striking in among these upon the gray old remains, produces some charming effects.

X.

THE FINE ARTS AND LITERATURE.

I.

THE school of fine arts, on the other hand, the Academy of San Carlos—which was to celebrate with a special exhibition the one hundredth anniversary of its foundation—produces, both in its collections and the ability of its directing professors, a most satisfactory and agreeable impression. You enter galleries which carry you back again to the Louvre and Uffizi. They used a great deal of bitumen, the old painters here. In its darkening it has left now and then only isolated lights upon a face or bits of drapery to glimmer out of a midnight gloom. It is an artificial taste, no doubt, to like it, and "caviare to the general;" but like it one does, at its most artificial, after a long absence from anything of the kind.

The walls recall such galleries as that of Bologna in the liberal scale of the works displayed. With such models before them, there is no reason why students should fall into a niggling and petty style. As a matter of fact, they do not. They seem to excel in a bold, large composition and the rendering of grandiose ideas. This, rather than color, is their strong point. If our New York schools of art are able to equal the portfolio of drawings I saw as the result of a fortnightly exercise, they are certainly not in the habit of doing so. Nor were they at all equalled by those of the prize competition of the students of the British Royal Academy which I saw in the first year of the presidency of Sir Frederick Leighton. This devotion to large academical ideas—the fortunes of Orestes, Regulus, and Belisarius — it is true, is a source of weakness rather than strength from the money point of view. The market of the time demands a domestic, *genre*, realistic, and not a grandiose art. The market for art of any kind in Mexico is extremely small. There are no government commissions farther than an occasional portrait or two, and enlightened patrons hardly exist. There are no pictures of consequence in the best Mexican houses. The predictions at Havana were not verified. The abundance of native talent receives little encouragement. Many a bright genius is forced to paint his inventions on the walls of *pulque* shops, and finally to quit the profession for lack of support.

The subjects are, for the most part, severely religious, in consonance with the taste of the wealthy convents, the patrons of art for whom they were originally painted. The series is in a declining order of merit chronologically. The earliest Mexican masters are the best. They came from Europe, contemporaries of Murillo, Ribera, the Caracci, trained in the splendid Renaissance period at its acme, and they left here works which do it no discredit. Mexico was a hundred years old already, and it was high time that art should arise when Baltazar Echave began, somewhat after the year 1600. There is a romantic tradition that it was his wife who first taught him to paint.

The genius of this early school is very decorative, and marked at once by refinement of sentiment, breadth, and vigor. It delights in rich stuffs and patterns, in the glitter of plate and weapons. It fills up all portions of the canvas symmetrically, and colors with a subdued richness. I recall a St. Ildefonso, by Luis Juarez, as an exquisite work. The saint, in a rich red mantle, by a praying-desk and chair, both draped in the same color, is receiving from angels the paraphernalia of a bishop. The mantle of the nearest angel is in burnt sienna, and these warm red hues, relieved by cool whites, are repeated throughout. There is a group of six angel heads composed in an ellipse, and, in the air, a Virgin, with that bevy of fluttering angels about that take the place of clouds in landscape. The minor heads, painted chiefly from the same model, are full of sweetness and intelligence.

Arteaga has a noble St. Thomas; José Juarez, a quaint couple of child martyrs, Saints Justo and Pastor, who trudge along hand-in-hand like a pair of burgomaster's children (the scenes of their martyrdom shown in the background), while angels rain down upon them single pinks, roses, and forget-me-nots, carefully painted. A younger Baltazar Echave, and Juan and Nicolas Rodriguez, are of almost equal force.

A second period begins with Ibarra and Cabrera—the latter very much the better—at the end of the same century. They are without the same distinction. Their figures have a bourgeois air. They aim to be pictorial instead of decorative. The crude red and blue garments with which we are monotonously familiar in religious art come in with them; and the draperies, in smooth, large folds, are apparently made up out of their heads.

The foreign gallery boasts many excellent works of the school of Murillo, and an original each of Murillo, Ribera, Carreño, Leonardo da Vinci, Teniers the elder, and Ingres, with also probable Vandycks and Rembrandts.

A collection has also been formed of works of merit, contributed to the regular biennial exhibitions, and purchased by the Academy to illustrate modern Mexican

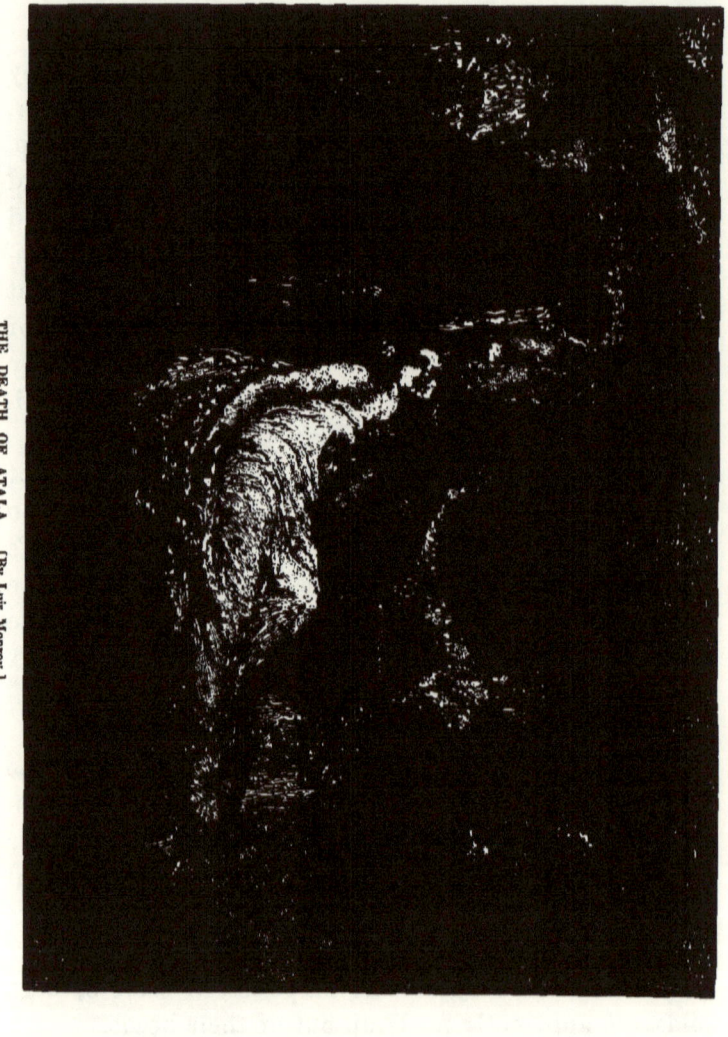

THE DEATH OF ATALA. [By Luis Monroy.]

art. The religious tradition still prevails to a large extent, though the subjects are now taken from the Scriptures instead of the Bollandists. They are Hagar and Ishmael, the good Samaritan, the Hebrews by the waters of Babylon, and Noah receiving the olive-branch, and the like.

There is in this contemporary work the general fault of an over-delicacy and smoothness of painting, and a lack of realism, while the design is excellent. These voyagers in the ark have not experienced the woes of a deluge, and the shepherds have the complexion of Lady Vere de Vere. Rebull, who studied at Rome under Overbeck, repeats here the dove-colors, violets, and lemon-yellows of the modern decorations of the Vatican done under that school.

The works of the latest period, under the able direction of Señor Salome Pina, a pupil of Gleyre, are much more virile, and the subjects more secular. We have now Bacchus and Ariadne; the death of Atala; the slaying of the sons of Niobe; an arch and dainty Cupid poisoning a flower, by Ocaranza; a charming fisher-boy, by Gutierrez. Some of the artists have had the advantage of study also abroad. The strongest of them all, Felix Parra, now enjoying a grand prize of Rome, produced the masterpiece, a great canvas representing the friar Las Casas protecting the Aztecs (from slaughter by the Spaniards)—a work in sentiment, drawing, and color worthy to hang in any exhibition in the world—before he had seen any other country than his own.

Velasco has set a powerful lead in landscape. He is especially a master of great distance. His favorite theme is the curious, sienna-colored Valley of Mexico, which he paints to the life.

There are some scattered works of the early school, besides, in the houses of a few *dilettanti* at the capital and Puebla; and some few in the cathedrals of the same places, though scarcely to be seen, from their disadvantageous positions. Good pictures need not be looked for in the churches. No doubt they were once numerous, but they have been sacked from the country by invaders and others, and found a profitable market abroad.

II.

In sculpture there is talent corresponding to that in painting. The stately system of burial, in the *panteons*, lends itself to sculpture and furnishes opportunities which with us are relegated to the commonplace tombstone-makers. The *panteon* is a solid city of the dead, walled in, paved, and with courts and arcades like a city of the living. The monument of greatest note is that, by Manuel Islas, at the Pantheon of San Fernando, to Benito Juarez, "the second Washington" of his country, old Padre Hidalgo having been the first. His effigy in marble, so realistic and corpse-like that it seems to have been modelled from an actual cast in plaster, lies upon a mausoleum, with a figure of Fame bending over it. The realism of the principal figure is almost repulsive, but it is redeemed by the grace of the angel, and nobody can deny to this large work great vigor and dignity.

The bodies are not buried, but sealed up in mausolea, or in niches in a wall, which present somewhat the aspect of a Roman columbarium. Some of the monuments are of the lovely Mexican onyx, with letters in gilt. I noted one bearing only the initials M. M. They were alluring to the curiosity, and on inquiring I found that it was that of Miramon, general-in-chief of Maximilian, who fell by the executioners' bullets, with his master, and General Mejia, at Queretero.

There were no flowers on this one to-day, but the tombs of the patriots were elaborately decked, for it was the great festival of the Cinco de Mayo.

I walked out and stood in the round-point by the colossal bronze statue of Charles IV. The Paseo de la Reforma and the causeways glittered with bayonets; the cadets were coming down from the Military School back of Chapultepec, and the garrison from the Citadel, to join in the procession. The troops were reviewed in front of the National Palace—as troops in smaller numbers seem always being reviewed there. They are mainly of Indian blood, and small in stature. The cavalry especially had a rusty look in their outfit, and did not compare with the dashing *Rurales*. The officers, on the other hand, are trimly uniformed and quite French in aspect. There were patriotic speeches in the Zocalo; the main thoroughfare was strung with lanterns; and our Iturbide hotel was very picturesque, with its three tiers of balconies draped in the national colors—green, white, and red.

From time to time, as the procession moved, cannon were fired in the Plaza, and the bells of the cathedral turned over and over, like the wheels of machinery. I never saw a better-conducted crowd. There was no fighting, no inconvenient elbowing, no drunkenness. In the evening the lanterns were lighted, and the great square was filled with venders of fruits and knickknacks, around little bonfires of sticks, where they would bivouac for the night. Later, red lights were kindled in the towers of the cathedral, and every detail within stood out upon a lurid ground as if they were burning. One could imagine the camped venders in the square to be the ancient Aztecs resting upon their arms, in order to attack Cortez in his quarters on the morrow.

III.

Scarcely the same improvement is to be got from Mexican literature as from Mexican art, but it is not without its interest, both in itself and as an aid to knowledge of the people. Journals are very numerous. They are started upon slight provocation, and as easily disappear. They attain, as a rule, but a circulation of a few hundred copies. It is thought that the *Monitor Republicano*, by far the most important, may circulate from six to eight thousand. The problem of existence for many of them would be difficult without government aid. Subventions are given, without public objection, so far as I have observed, to the greater part of those managed with ability. The system of subventions to the press was begun by our old friend of school history, Santa Anna, and has been continued ever since by governments which could not afford to have anything more than the truth told about them, at any rate. It is an encouraging sign, however, that the *Monitor* is not a subventioned organ, yet speaks its mind temperately and without apparent malice.

There is no efficacious law of libel, since extreme violence of language is often indulged in by the periodicals in their controversies with each other and outsiders. The duel, which still survives, is somewhat of a corrective upon this. The newspaper is about such a one in appearance as at Paris, and includes a daily section of a serial story. A Sunday edition is published, with literary selections, and particularly poems, in large supply.

Actual literature as such is poorly paid. The reading public is small. A thousand copies is a good edition even for a popular book. The chief literary lights are found, as a rule, not of the shy, scholastic order, but possessed of talent for oratory and bustling affairs. They take posts in Congress, and are appointed as cabinet ministers. General Riva Palacio, Juan Mateos, Prieto, Paz, Altimirano, Justo Sierra, Peza, are deputies; Payno, a senator; Cuellar, who wrote under the pseudonym of "Facundo," a secretary of legation. These are the native writers whose works are more frequently in the hands of the public than any others.

Prieto, who is chiefly a poet, however, has written a book of his travels in the United States, in which some amusing things will be discovered. He finds that with us "the totality [*lo colectivo*] is grand and admirable, but the individual egoistic and vulgar." He saw Booth's Theatre, which is all of white marble (*el Teatro de Both, todo de marmol blanco*); and, besides our hotels, the establishment which we call a "Boarding" (*el Boarding*). The Hudson and East rivers, he says, are two arms of the sea, which freeze in winter, and even the immense quantity of ice collected from these does not suffice for the demands of the summer.

The poetical talent, of which we had a premonition in Cuba, is that which principally abounds. There is plentiful skill in versifying, with here and there a strain of something very much higher, in the volumes of the numerous authors. Prieto, above-mentioned, is found principally a poet of "occasions." He writes for the unveiling of statues, to steam, electricity, and the like. Juan Mateos strikes a fierce patriotic note. Altimirano, a fiery Indian orator, who models himself in Congress rather after Mirabeau, chooses as his themes for poetry bees, oranges, poppies, morn, the pleasures of rural life. They are excellent subjects in themselves, but it is an artificial, and not a real, existence he describes. He would like to be Horatian, summons nymphs to disport with him in the shade, and abounds in florid terms, without thought.

Carpio is inspired more or less by Biblical subjects, as Pharaoh and Belshazzar. In De Castro, Zaragoza, Gustave Baz, and Cuenca are found charming conceits, of pensive cast, and bits of description of a limpid purity. Jewellers in words they may be called at their best, affiliated to the Venetian school.

The argument of Zaragoza's "Armonias" (Harmonies) is briefly as follows: "When the flowers are dead, and spring is over, the swallows take their flight; and when again the flowers of spring adorn the mead, they, too, return, bringing blessings on their wings.

"But when the illusions depart and leave behind them only the thorns of the passions, in vain we invoke and wait for them to return. The illusions, the swallows of the heart, return, alas! never."

So Gustave Baz, brooding in the sere winter over some heavy sorrow, reflects upon the return of spring. But the very contrast of its joyousness, the fresh rippling of the brooks and melody of the birds, will but render his sadness the heavier. "Then most keenly," he laments, "will break forth my grief. Then weightiest will the air be laden with my sighs."

The gem of the Lyra Mexicana is undoubtedly a certain fugitive sonnet, "A Rosario," by an unfortunate young man, Acuña, who ended by taking his own life. The poem expresses the charming ideals in love and the bitterness of its disappointment, in a youth of fine and sensitive nature. It has a poignancy and realism which have, perhaps, never been surpassed. He returned from a long journey, as the story is told, and found his betrothed the wife of another. The shock proving unendurable, he committed suicide, leaving to the faithless one the poem, a part of which may be thus rendered:

"Well, then, I have to say that I love you still, that I worship you with all my being. I comprehend that your kisses are never to be mine, that into your dear eyes I am never to look. . . . Sometimes I try to sink you into oblivion, to execrate you. . . . But alas, how vain it is! my soul will not forget you. What will you, then, that I should do, oh, part of my life? What will you that I should do with such a heart? . . . Oh, figure to yourself how beautiful might have been our existence together! . . . But now that to the entrancing dream succeeds the black gulf that has opened between us—farewell! love of my loves, light of my darkness, perfume of all flowers that bloomed for me! my poet's lyre, my youth, farewell!"

IV.

If one try to select the most obvious trait in the native fiction it is undoubtedly patriotism. This patriotism is rampant in the press, and in the forms of official life. The authorities are Citizen President, Citizen General, and the like, as in the first French Republic, and they conclude their official documents with the formula: "Liberty In The Constitution." The usurpation of Maximilian served to bind the country into a certain unity and awake this feeling to its utmost.

Two romancers, General Riva Palacio, and Juan Mateos, have made use of the events of the French invasion in a curious class of bulky novels, to call them so, which have scored a popular success. "The Hill of Las Campañas," and "The Sun of May," of Mateos, are respectively more or less authentic accounts of the final defeat and execution of Maximilian, and the defence of

Puebla, slightly disguised. The "Calvary and Tabor," Riva Palacio, treats of the career of the Army of the Centre in the same wars. Numbers of the characters therefore are persons actually living, to be met with every day, which gives to this fiction a singular effect.

Thus, in "El Sol de Mayo," Manuel Payno, Altamirano, and Riva Palacio himself are mentioned and their manners described in the debate on the financial measure which brought on the Intervention. Lerdo, long since an exile, resident in New York, was at that time "*el profeta inspirada de nuestra nacionalidad*" (the inspired prophet of our nationality).

I pick out from the same book this paragraphic mention of our own civil war: "And Edmundo Lee shone like a star in the victories of Springfield and Bull Run." Perhaps the friends of General Robert E. Lee would have some difficulty in recognizing him under such a description.

These novels are printed with each sentence as a separate paragraph, for easier reading. They first began to rival somewhat the popular Fernandez y Gonzalez, by some called "the Spanish Dumas," whose works are printed in the journals, together with translations of those of Gaboriau and Dickens. Another flimsy series, in covers of green, white, and red, called "*Episodios Nacionales*," aim to sugar-coat a didactic exhibition of the events of the War of Independance. One individual after another tells a long, dreary narrative about what happened; these fall in with somebody else who tells more, and so it goes.

These stories are read chiefly by the middle and lower classes, the upper class, as in most provincial states of society, preferring books from abroad. Their favorable reception may be accounted for in part by the lack of regular histories and of newspaper intelligence, so that the populace may to some extent be getting their information for the first time.

Riva Palacio has written also, with Manuel Payno, a large work appropriately called *El Libro Rojo* (The Red Book). It gives an account (and graphic illustrations) of the heroes and other notables in Mexican history who have come to violent ends. This is a fate that has overtaken aspirants to distinction quite regularly, and the plates from the book, hung up at the book-stalls in the Portales, are a ghastly chamber of horrors. The three fighting curates of the early insurrection, Hidalgo, Morelos, and Matamoras begin the series; and Maximilian, Mejia, and Miramon, standing with bandaged eyes at the Hill of las Campañas, for the present conclude it.

Several minor writers have feebly essayed the Aztec material for fiction. Riva Palacio has availed himself also of the picturesque life under the Spanish viceroys. Of him it is to be said that, though of the sensational school, and careless in plan, he has, not unfrequently, passages of genuine force, and unhackneyed incidents that enchain the attention.

XI.

SOME TRAITS OF PECULIAR HISTORY, AND THE MEXICAN "WARWICK."

I.

It would seem that history in Mexico might be a somewhat confusing study; and so, in fact, it is. There have been fifty-four Presidents, one regency, and one Emperor, in fifty-six years, and a violent change of government with nearly every one.

Picking up the little volume by Manuel Payno, used in the schools, and opening it at random, I find—

"*Question.*—What events followed?

"*Answer.*—Truly imagination is lost, and memory confounds itself, among so many plans and *pronunciamentos;* but we will follow the thread as best we can."

The period referred to is that of the revolt of Texas, which proceeded to constitute itself "The Lone Star Republic." Looking a little farther with interest to see how this is accounted for, we find:

"The settlers were North Americans, a portion, as we have said, colonized by Stephen Austin. They set up the pretext that they were not permitted to sell their lands, and, later, that the Federal Constitution had been violated; and they rose against the Government. The latter felt it necessary to put down the rebellion, and took measures to assail that remote and sterile State."

These dispositions, as we know, ended in the defeat and capture of Santa Anna at San Jacinto. There is always a fascination in being behind the scenes, and I confess that this little opportunity of finding out what was thought of itself by a country which has jarred so much with our own was one of the attractions of being in Mexico. The American war is accounted for as a wicked attempt to sustain and annex the revolted province of Texas; and equally good solutions are found for the various other invasions by foreign powers.

What! is there no absolute right? Are all combatants alike striking for their altars and their fires, and resisting wanton aggression? Will not these Mexicans even yet admit, though beaten, and though it has passed into history, that they terrorized our frontier, and oppressed an industrious and enterprising province? Why, then, perhaps both sides were wrong; and let us aspire for the day when all such quarrels may be settled by an international arbitration.

II.

The young Mexican learns first about his Aztec ancestry, the mild semi-civilized aborigines, who built cities and temples, and were ruled by luxurious Montezuma and scholarly Nezhualcoyotl. The latter, at Texcoco, was a maker of verses and stoical maxims like another Marcus Aurelius.

Cortez conquered the Aztecs in 1519. Then followed a government of nearly three hundred years by sixty-four Spanish viceroys. A rebellion, of eleven years' duration, marked by many of the features of a servile uprising, drove out the Spaniards in 1821. Grasping and inconsiderate in their colonial management as their way has always been, the Spaniards had probably only themselves to thank for it.

Iturbide, who commanded the revolt at the end, made

himself briefly Emperor. His generals, notably the irrepressible Santa Anna, who first here comes into view, rose against him, and proclaimed a Federal Republic. Santa Anna, when the opportunity offered, made himself Dictator, and changed the Federal Republic to a centralized republic, and the states to departments. Santa Anna had numberless ups and downs, having obtained possession of the supreme power no less than six times, with intervals of overthrow and banishment.

The Federal Republic was reconstituted in time, with twenty-seven states, one territory and a federal district, pretty much on the model of our own, and it still retains this form, as it is likely to. There is no doubt about the democratic tendency of the people, but perhaps it is something in the impulsive blood of the Latin race which has prevented the leaders from conceiving a republic on the Anglo-Saxon plan. They have been inspired almost without exception by a craving for the sweets of power. Their rampant patriotism has been like the religion of those persons who would die for a cause, but will not live in accordance with the least of its dictates. There seems to have been no conception until lately of that larger patriotism which educates the people in their duties, and constitutes a state of society where the rights of all are guaranteed and people go about their avocations without interference.

III.

Would you recall, by-the-way, what became of Santa Anna? He, who had so indignantly shaken off the yoke of Iturbide, wrote a missive of congratulation, while living in banishment in the West Indies, to Maximilian, and endeavored to take service under him. His aid was rejected, whereupon he turned to Juarez, only to be repulsed again. In a rage at both sides, he fitted out an expedition on his own account, landed in the country, and was well-nigh being shot, after the model, and almost on the same ground, as that Iturbide whom he had pronounced against forty-two years before. The court-martial, however, spared his life, "in consideration of the ancient services done to his country in Texas, at Tampico, and Vera Cruz," and sent him again, superannuated and poor (for he had squandered an ample fortune in this attempt), to finish his days in banishment.

I cannot forbear going a little farther into the questions and answers of the little history. Of the gallant generals who fought so well for the Independence, Victoria was the first President. Bravo pronounced against him, and was exiled to South America. Guerrero, defeated as a candidate for the succession by Pedraza, took up arms and seized it by force. He repelled, while in office, a new attempt by the Spaniards to recover the country.

"*Question.*—I suppose that with this triumph the government of Guerrero was firmly established?

"*Answer.*—This was to have been hoped, but that happened which always happens in Mexico—just the contrary."

Bustamente, in fact, pronounced against Guerrero; and when the latter would have returned to the capital from an expedition designed to put down the revolt, he found it closed against him, and in favor of Bustamente also.

" *Q.*—What end had this revolution?

" *A.*—The most terrible that can be imagined. The Government at Mexico, feeling that it could not overcome Guerrero . . . bought over, for $70,000, a Genoese named Picaluga, who commanded a vessel anchored in the harbor of Acapulco. Picaluga invited Guerrero to dine on board, and this manifestation of hospitality was accepted in good faith. When they had dined the Genoese signified to Guerrero that he was a prisoner, and set sail with him to the port of Huatulco and delivered him into the hands of his enemies. This great and good man, valiant and worthy of the respect and gratitude of the nation . . . was shot in the puebla of Cuilapa, on the 15th of February, 1831."

It was not till 1848, for the first time, that the Presidency was transferred without violence, and under the law. The incumbent was General Herrera, and he was succeeded peaceably by General Arista. These two administrations "will forever place themselves before historians, both Mexican and foreign," says the history, "as models of honor, economy, and order." But Arista was deposed in two years, and in the next three months there were four Presidents, the last of them Santa Anna, on one of his periodic returns.

Thus the turmoil of revolutions has continued down to recent times. A certain Don Jose Maria Gutierrez Estrada directed a letter to the authorities in 1840, proposing, as a measure of relief, that a monarchical government should be established in Mexico; and the idea, in the distracting state of things we have seen, cannot be considered wholly without reason. It caused great scandal nevertheless, but Gutierrez Estrada stuck to it tenaciously, and, by a very singular coincidence, he was one of those who, twenty-four years after, went to Miramar to present the imperial crown to the Archduke Maximilian.

If I cite a number of such events from the past it is not for the purpose of being disagreeable or arguing that the same state of things is to last. It is partly because they are amusing, and partly to obtain a more encouraging point of view for the present. It will be seen that the later administrations, though not without their faults, are a vast improvement upon their predecessors, and do not constitute a declining ratio.

GENERAL PORFIRIO DIAZ, EX-PRESIDENT OF MEXICO.

General Porfirio Diaz occupied unmolested a full term, from 1876 to 1880, and handed over the place to General Manuel Gonzales, who holds it at present in the same security. Diaz began the current career of improvement by his liberal chartering of railroads, and Gonzales follows in his track. Both must be considered to have made a most exemplary and promising use of their powers. But, since we have arrived at "Don Porfirio," let us see how he entered upon office in the beginning.

IV.

Since he is, by general admission, the power behind the throne, the Mexican "Warwick," the President who has been, is, and is to be, let us inquire a little also who he was. "His influence in the country," says the *Monitor*, "is decisive, incontestable. Something more than Benitez in the past, he is not only the great commoner, but the one man of the present."

Porfirio Diaz was born in Oaxaca, in 1830. His family destined him for the law, but he took to soldiering instead. Beginning as a private, he entered the city of Mexico as general-in-chief of the forces which wrested it from the French. Once in these wars, when a prisoner at Puebla, he let himself down by a rope from a tower and made his escape. His career is studded with romantic incidents, but the career of what Mexican leader is not?

The Latin race admires the military type, and "Don Porfirio," or more familiarly "Porfirio," as the people delight to call him, bethought him to turn his prestige in the field to account. He offered himself for the Presidency against Juarez, on the platform of no re-election, in 1871. Lerdo de Tejada, Chief Justice of the Supreme Court, was also in the field as a third candidate. Let the figures in this remarkable election be noted, as an indication of the acute interest the Mexican voters take in their own balloting. In a population of 8,836,411 a total of only 12,361 votes were cast. Juarez received 5837, Diaz 3555, Lerdo 2874, and 95 are recorded as "scattering."

"*Q.*—Relate to me what happened thereafter.

"*A.*—General Porfirio Diaz issued, from his hacienda of La Noria, a manifesto, hence called the *Plan of La*

Noria, repudiating the existing powers, and proposing to retain military command until the establishment of a new order of things."

A bloody war of more than a year followed, in which the Porfiristas were utterly routed. Diaz, amnestied, presented himself at the capital, and was affably received by Lerdo, who assured him, on the part of the Government, that he might live tranquil without fear of persecution or harm. "Nothing," breaks forth our historian, in enthusiasm about these times, "gives a better idea of the constancy and elevation of the Mexican character, a heritage from its Spanish ancestry, than what passes in our wars, both civil and foreign. It appears that defeats but serve as stimulus and fresh aliment to the fray."

Upon what possible theory these ambitious chiefs have always made their partisans so ready to be slaughtered for them, is a speculation which I shall not go into. Porfirio now remained quiet till 1876, when he issued the *Plan of Palo Blanco,* and rose against Lerdo, who had succeeded Juarez. He captured Matamoras by a bold stroke of strategy; was himself captured on shipboard; and escaped from the Lerdists by leaping into the sea, through the connivance of the French captain, whom he afterward made consul to St. Nazaire. After a series of suchlike adventures his persistence won the day, and Lerdo took to flight. "Don Sebastian" Lerdo is spoken of as probably the most scholarly and accomplished President the republic ever had. He had been a school-master, however, and tried to govern the country in the pedagogue spirit to which he had been used. He lost favor, too, by his lack of military talent, and fled when his fortunes were by no means desperate. The country people were strongly on his side at first, but this singular thing happened — that, finding him unable to protect them against the roving bands of revolutionists favoring Diaz, they joined them in disgust, and went on with them to the capital.

It is upon such original guarantees that the authority which Porfirio has devoted to the extension of law and order and the benefits of civilization reposes.

V.

The subject of these remarks is a person neither talkative nor taciturn. He is of commanding height, a swarthy, half-Indian complexion, a figure stalwart but not heavy, and of a military yet somewhat nonchalant bearing, all of which may form a part of his attraction. He knows how to utilize the arts of peace as well as war. Perhaps he believes a little in the motto, "Let me make the songs of a nation, and I care not who makes its laws;" for the ballad-singers at Santa Anita, on the Viga Canal, whither the populace swarm on Sundays to indulge in dancing, *pulque, tamales*, and flowers from the floating gardens, have many a long-drawn refrain to the praises of Don Porfirio Di-i-i-az. It is hardly fair, perhaps, to suggest that these are subsidized, since they may rest upon pure admiration of his merits, after all.

The Mexican law prohibits re-election, except after an interval of four years, and Porfirio Diaz was too ardent a one-termer to be able to overstep this prohibition with any consistency. He has placed his friend and fellow-soldier Gonzales in office as his *locum tenens*. He will assume it himself for the next term, dating from 1884. After that—so the plan is supposed to be arranged—he will give it to General Treviño, his companion in arms and strong auxiliary in his pronunciamentos. Treviño has married the daughter of an American general, Ord, and it may be supposed that American interests will not suffer in his hands.

Porfirio is romantic even in his Machiavellianism. The only source from which he might have had anything to fear was perhaps a lingering Lerdist sentiment.

GENERAL MANUEL GONZALES, PRESIDENT OF MEXICO.

It represents, or represented, a conservative element, of better social position than the rude democratic force in power. He set to work to conciliate this Lerdist sentiment. He has been able to take of late the effectual means of marrying into the very midst of it, having chosen for his third wife the daughter of Senator Romero Rubio. Romero Rubio was the right-hand man of Lerdo, and his companion in exile. He is now president of the Senate, and the official who is empowered by law to call and control a new election, in case of a vacancy in the Presidency of the nation. Gonzales suffers from an old wound, received at Puebla, and it has been thought by some that Diaz might need to be called to the chair even before the appointed limit of time.

Nor could he have had any personal repugnance to overcome in this match. His usual good-fortune attends him. The young lady is under twenty, accomplished, and of a high-bred air. She will be recollected by Americans as among the prettiest of the belles who took part in the round of festivities given in honor of General Grant at his last visit. This, too, will be pleasing to the people. Don Porfirio means that the people shall be pleased. When General Grant, on his first visit to the country in his tour around the world, was the curiosity and hero of the hour, Porfirio was his inseparable attendant and courteous host. A certain resemblance was traced between them. Both had been illustrious generals, both presidents. When Grant returned a second time, and was now less popular, on account of his interest in the railway concessions, and a jealousy which had meantime arisen of American aggression, Don Porfirio was unfortunately obliged to be far distant, distributing charity to sufferers on the northern confines of the republic.

The work of conciliation has long been going on. Old functionaries have been reinstated in place; veteran army officers have been approached and offered new commands. One of these latter told me that President Gonzales had sent for him, after having kept an espionage on his conduct for some time, and asked him, in a bluff way,

"Why do you continue to talk against the Government, and pass your time in idleness—you who were once so good a soldier?"

"Sir," he replied, "you know my sentiments, and the

cause for which I fought. I cannot deny that I hold them still. I take the consequences. I have pawned my valuables and clothing for food. If I rust in idleness it is because I have no occupation to turn to."

"I admire your manliness," the President replied. "Here is your appointment to the command of a regiment. Your cause is dead, as you know, and cannot be revived. I ask of you no political services. I ask of you only to be as before—a soldier."

It is needless to say that after this there was at least one Lerdist the less.

I do not wish to be understood as finding fault with this policy of astute conciliation; far from it. The hammer-and-tongs method has been so long in vogue that it is a delightful relief. The chicanery of matrimonial alliances, and assumption of frank and soldierly manners, will be welcomed by all the foreign capital in the country as a great improvement upon throat-cutting.

From vast estates in Oaxaca, which with a commendable economy he has amassed meantime, the Mexican Warwick, controls the destinies of his country with an ease like moving one's little finger. He pleases himself in the interim to be governor, and commander of the forces, of this fighting state. In the absence of any efficient electoral system the country is under his absolute dictatorship; while, with the ostensible division of powers, there is no way of tracing the responsibility to its source.

Not that there is the least danger of anybody's trying to do so. There are apparent Brutuses in both Houses of Congress, orators and poets who have turned off many a diatribe and many an ode to freedom on the best classic and French republican models, but they have nothing to say against this Cæsar. They are not very free agents, to tell the truth. They are really sent by the governors of the respective states, and these governors have been manipulated in advance. Porfirio can undoubtedly make threats as well as promises; and an unlucky representative, if content to forego a better place, may even lose the one he has. He cannot depend upon adequate support, either, should he have a notion to resist. The "boys" are much given to "going back" on one another in Mexican history.

I shall be found fault with by some persons, as likely as not, for undue severity. He is a beneficent Cæsar, after all, compared with former times; he has brought back something like a Golden Age; he oppresses nobody, at least, not the foreigners, and gives a stimulus to every worthy enterprise.

So be it; and probably there is no more genial government than a Cæsarism of the beneficent sort, fairly established. But it is too full of dangers. Porfirio is doing nothing to educate the nation. "In effect," one of his own papers says to him, "it is not alone with railways that a nation so disorganized as ours can reconstitute itself; not alone the locomotive and the telegraph that can make us happy. There should emanate from the regions of power something like an impulse of obedience to the law and observance of the institutions upon which the social and political well-being of the country rests."

It is not probable that there will soon again be serious disturbances. "All the grabbers have got places," say some critics of a cynical turn, "and there will be no more revolutions." A better saying, however, is current: "A bad government is preferable to a good revolution." There is a weariness of fighting. The country seems to savor the little-known luxury of peace with a positive gusto. The railways diminish the chance of trouble by for the first time furnishing ample employment to the idle, who formerly occupied themselves in plunder and were ready to follow the banners of insurgent chiefs. They will be a potent military engine in enabling the Government to mass its forces at points of danger. The fear, too, may be present of interference by foreign governments, should the enterprises of their citizens be threatened with serious damage by new upheavals.

Still, there are great administrative abuses. The civil service is notoriously corrupt. Opportunities for galling oppression are open to the governments, both federal and state, and, most ominous of trouble, redress by the ballot is not possible. The anomaly is presented of a republic in which there is no census nor registration of voters, no scrutiny of the ballot-box except by the party in power. There is hardly a ray of interest in the political machine by the people themselves. The number of votes cast at elections is pitifully small, as we have seen. It is not considered worth while to vote. The lower classes read no informing journals, have no public speakers. No organized opposition exists. Such opposition as there is is purely personal. All contests for office are personal, and not a matter of principles. The Government—that of the centre influencing the states, and these in turn the communities—sustains and counts in what candidates it pleases. There are no data for objection, since nobody can point to the real number of voters in a given place, nor their names.

When this is understood it seems to account for almost all that has happened. There is absolutely no remedy for oppressive domination but in rebellion. With the best of dispositions, the most entire patience, what has happened in the past may happen again.

If there be any statesmanship in Mexico, may we not hope to see some champion arise to remedy this, instruct the masses in their rights, enumerate and register them, and insure them the first essential of a free government —an accurate and unfettered suffrage?

XII.

CUATITLAN, AND AROUND LAKES XOCHIMILCO AND CHALCO.

I.

THE saying is current that "Outside of Mexico all is Cuatitlan."

It shows that the capital entertains a true Parisian esteem for itself, and a corresponding contempt for the rest of the country. Cuatitlan is a little village twenty-five miles to the northward, reached by a narrow-gauge railroad, built by Mexicans, but purchased by the Mexican Central. It was at Cuatitlan that I saw my first bullfight. It is one of the two places in the vicinity where the capital thus amuses itself, the sport being prohibited in town. In some states, as Zacatecas, it is abolished entirely.

There were five bulls killed that day, and three horses, but no men—unfortunately, the novice in these cowardly and disagreeable representations is inclined to think. Each bull came in ignorant of the fate of his predecessor, and ran at the streamers with a playful air. You felt like scratching his back and calling him "good old fellow," instead of waiting to see presently his pained astonishment and torture, his glazing eye and staggering step, and death like that of an actor in melodrama. The horses were wretched hacks, allowed to be gored purposely as a part of the spectacle. They were driven around the ring

150   OLD MEXICO AND HER LOST PROVINCES.

ENVIRONS OF MEXICO.

afterward till they dropped, and their life-blood poured with an audible noise, like the spatter of a rivulet. Upon which the boisterous youth of Mexico, of the lower class, cried "*Bello!*" "*Bellissimo!*" in frenzied delight.

The gray old walls of the parish church, immense, and of excellent design (as they all are), rise above the amphitheatre. Within are figures of saints grotesquely adorned, or realistically horrible, in the usual style. The devout Indians are not archæologists, and have no idea of paying honor other than as they understand it. I have it on authority that when left to themselves they have been known to equip the Saviour of the World in a twenty-dollar hat, *chaparreras* (a kind of riding breeches), spurs, sabre, and revolver, sparing no expense to make him a cavalier of the first fashion.

The houses of the town, built of concrete or adobe, sometimes plastered and tinted, are of one story. There are some small portals for the use of out-of-door merchants, a few *pulquerias*, and thread-needle shops, and a *meson*, or inn, "of the Divine Providence," where enormous-wheeled wagons are corralled in line, and muleteers sleep upon their packs, as in the times of *Don Quixote*.

This is Cuatitlan, this the Mexican village, which can be dreary enough to one who does not look at it with the fresh interest of a new-comer. You cannot take as much comfort in the lower class of people as you would like, on account of their habits. There is no denying that in the neighborhood of Mexico at least they are very dirty. They do not clean up even for their festivals. I saw them dancing at a public ball at the Theatre Hidalgo, which, among other amusements, the municipality provided for them free, on the national festival of the 5th of May. There were charcoal dealers and such persons, with their women, and they had not taken the pains to remove a single smudge of their working-day condition.

Cuatitlan was the birth-place of the simple peon Juan Diego, who in 1531 saw the miraculous apparition of the Virgin of Guadalupe. He was passing the barren hill where her elaborate pilgrimage church now stands, and she gave him roses which had flowered where no flower had ever been seen before. A banner with the image of this miraculous Virgin was carried all through the wars of the Independence. Guadalupe is still one of the spots to be visited, and you buy such sacred knick-knacks there as at Lourdes or Einsiedlen, but the church is stripped of its treasures now, and the surroundings have a shabby aspect.

II.

At San Angel, Tlalpam, and other similar points in the vicinity of the capital, there was formerly an extensive villa life. It has curiously decayed, even while the security of living in such a way has increased. There are no fierce heats, however, to drive people to the country. It is always comfortable in town. No watering-places nor summer resorts in our sense of the word exist. People who go to their haciendas visit them more to look after their business interests than in need or love of country life. Bills are up in the grated windows of the long, low, one-storied villas at San Angel, and the fruits fall untasted in the orange and myrtle gardens. The villagers endeavor to atone for this neglect of them by feasts of flowers, and little fairs, which last a week at a time. On these occasions, among other attractions, existing ordinances against gambling are set aside, and their small plazas are filled with games of hazard.

The Viga Canal, as far as Santa Anita, is a livelier and

SUNDAY DIVERSIONS AT SANTA ANITA.

more unique resort. Santa Anita is the St. Cloud or Bougival of Mexico. Thither go, especially on Sundays, lively persons to disport themselves on the water and pass a day of the picnic order, taking lunch with them, or depending on such cheap viands as the place offers. The wide yellow canal is more Venetian than French at first. A mouldering red villa or two on its banks, with private water-gates, might belong to the Brenta. Afterward lines of willows and poplars are reflected in the water, and then it is French again.

Flat-boats coming on, piled up with bales of hay and wood, echo each other peacefully from distance to distance. Swift, small *chalupas* (dug-outs) follow, managed by the Indian master in poses for a sculptor, while his wife—or it is as often an Indian woman alone—is ensconced among flowers and vegetables, with which it overflows. This is the region of the *chinampas*, the gardens from which the markets of Mexico are most liberally supplied. They are formed by the division of what was once a marsh, by narrow branch canals, into small oblong patches. The patches are so small that the owner passes around the borders in his canoe, and keeps all portions moist with water, which he throws out upon them with a calabash. By this care, and the rich character of the redeemed soil, luxuriant crops are produced.

The houses of the village are generally of bamboo, and without windows, sufficient light penetrating through the interstices. The first business of the participants in the Sunday festivities here is to provide themselves with large, thick wreaths of lovely poppies and blue and white cornflowers, which are sold for the merest trifle. They wear these upon their heads, in their caperings, with a highly classic effect. A general frizzling sound is heard, where eatables, of which peppers form a large ingredient, are prepared on little charcoal furnaces without and primitive fire-places within. "Come in!" the busy venders cry; "come in, señors, señoras, and señoritas, and be seated! *Aqui los niños!* Here is the place for the children! Here is the place where they are appreciated, and by no means considered a nuisance!"

"*Tamales calientitos!* dear little *tamales,* very nice and hot!" they cry. In the same caressing way a cabman in want of a job will call you *patroncito,* "dear little patron," though you may be as large as a grenadier.

They decorate their little stands with turnips and radishes cut into ingenious shapes of flowers, and with a profusion of little birds in wax, and the Mexican Goddess of Liberty astride of an eagle. A swarm of flat-boat men cluster at the edge of the canal, bidding for your patronage. Dancing is going on in almost every court-yard; the ballad-singers strike up lazy refrains; and in the Carcel, in a dirty little plaza, by a fountain, a single prisoner monotonously rattles his wooden grating, and glares out at the gayety like a madman. No self-respecting American prisoner could be induced to stay in a place so easy to escape from. But there is no accounting for tastes.

III.

But are there no real *chinampas,* no gardens that actually float, according to the tradition? Was all that, then, a myth?

Not at all. The soil hereabouts is solidified now, anchored down, as it were; but it has in its time floated, and in that condition borne crops. Farther on whole expanses are found only kept in position by stakes, with four feet of water below, and yet strong enough to sustain grazing cattle. An expedition was organized, in which I was privileged to set off, under the hospitable guidance of the Director of the Drainage of the Valley, to witness these marvels in person. We had a large row-boat, rowed by five oarsmen; and in our party was an amiable English traveller, who has written a book about Mexico,* and described, among others, this very expedition.

We started about seven o'clock in the morning from the garita of La Viga, an old Spanish water-gate, at which toll is taken from the market boats. The current was against us. The canal of La Viga, a stretch of about sixteen miles, is the outlet of Lake Xochimilco into Texcoco. Chalco and Xochimilco are practically the same lake, being separated only by a narrow causeway of ancient date, which is open at the centre and spanned by a little bridge.

There are numerous hamlets along the way, built like Santa Anita, and each with a few venerable palm-trees in its plaza. The Jefe Politico of one embraced our Director of the Desagüe and kissed his hand. At another a solid little bridge had lately been thrown across the canal, and we heard of a banquet that had been given on the occasion. The orator of the day had delivered a resounding address on human progress, and declared that he was proud to be a resident of a village which could accomplish such a feat. We lunched at a fort-like hacienda at Ixtapalapa, the point where the canal issues from the lake, and there found horses awaiting to take us to the top of the Hill of the Star. Upon this eminence, according to Prescott, were rekindled the extinguished fires and the beautiful captive sacrificed at the end of each of the cycles of fifty years, when the Aztecs thought the existence of the world was to be terminated.

---

* Brocklehurst's "Mexico To-day." John Murray: London, 1883.

We found nothing on the summit but a few heavy foundation stones, possibly remains of a sacrificial altar. Our horses had to be walked actively about, to prevent their taking serious cold from the rapid evaporation. It is chiefly memories that are found on such places. I plucked there, however, to send in a letter, a dark-red common flower, and pleased myself with the fancy that it might have drawn its sanguinary hue from the ground so steeped in slaughter.

Though at the entrance of the lake, no shining expanse of water was visible. The greater part of the surface, in fact, is covered with a singular growth of entwined roots and *débris*, supporting a verdant meadow. Passage through it is effected by canals and shifting natural channels, which change with the wind.

Two of our men after a time got out and towed the boat. The ostensible *terra firma* sank under their weight like the undulations of "benders" in thin ice. Now and then one floundered and went in waist-deep, whereat the others laughed. The margins are kept in place along the permanent channels by pinning them down with long stakes.

We fell in with wandering strips of growing verdure, called *cintas* (ribbons), and larger ones, *bandoleros* (bandits), drifting about at their own sweet will. Our host told us, though this he would not guarantee as of his own experience, that in the earlier times a garden of flowers and vegetables was now and then wrecked along-shore after a gale of wind, as if it had been a bark. Contrabandists, robbers who occasionally beset the market-boats, and political refugees have sometimes found this a favorable place of refuge, and escaped pursuit by diving under the illusive area and coming up elsewhere.

We dined *al fresco* at Mas Arriba, a place named quite

in the American style, literally Farther On. The margins were full of yellow water-lilies, and the clear spaces reflected distant mountains. Evening drew on, and then night. The frogs and crickets waked up their lonesome refrain, and fire-flies twinkled brightly in the morass. A few drops of rain fell, which increased in time to a shower.

IV.

We reached the long causeway between the two lakes late at night, in pitch darkness and torrents of rain, and screened ourselves a while under the little bridge, which barely accommodated the boat. Here was Tlahuac, an ancient island town or village, at the centre of the causeway. Waiting was useless. We landed in the rain, bought candles at a wretched *tienda* kept by Indians as solemn as statues, and set out in search of a lodging. A mozo preceded us, like a great fire-bug, sheltering a burning candle under a straw mat as best he could, to aid us in keeping out of the deeper puddles.

We were recommended to the Padre, as the only person capable of entertaining visitors of our distinction, and found him in an ancient Dominican convent looming up in the darkness. He received us with many apologies, gave us a good supper, manifested an interest in the late gossip of Mexico, and put us to sleep on the church carpets on the floor of a vast, bare room, provided with a few old religious pictures and bits of furniture.

Any temporary discomforts of this night of adventure were amply atoned for by the beautiful bright morning of the next day. We found Tlahuac a kind of Venetian island, a Torcello, as it were, on which some population of New Zealanders might have put up their thatched huts. The church rising in the centre had one of the usual shining tiled domes, and was preceded by a court and arched gateway. Its outer walls were covered with a large pattern of quatre-foils in red and yellow. I do not recollect just such a design again till I came later to the old Spanish mission of San Juan Capistrano, in Southern California. The island has sunk, or rather the lake has risen, in course of time, and the bases of the columns in the church are some four feet below the level of the ground.

Near by was the village school, and, as we got under way, we heard the shrill little voices of the children reciting their spelling in concert. All the shock-headed adult residents, in their garments of white cotton, looked as stupid as possible; but it is not always safe to judge by appearances.

From here the view of the two great snow-clad volcanoes is uninterrupted and glorious. We were told to feel with the oars at one place in the canal the pavements of a submerged Aztec city. Cortez mentions such a one in his letters. In 1855 the rumor of a new Pompeii spread abroad, based upon the finding of a few submerged Aztec huts in Lake Chalco, but no remains of any real importance have ever come to light.

V.

On this day, in Lake Chalco, we took our mid-day meal at the base of Xico, a little island volcano now extinct. It is of solid granite, without so much as a blade of grass externally, and the ascent is smooth and difficult. The boatmen sometimes see "Will-o'-the-wisps" on its summit, which, they say, are kindled by the witches. We climbed it, notwithstanding, and found a gently sloping crater, filled with maize-fields, which could easily have been approached from the other side.

The water began to be charmingly clear, and the bottom was full of a red weed like coral. We gathered ferns, lilies, the fragrant little white flower of St. John—*flor de San Juan*, sold in large bunches in the market—and other flowers, yellow, purple, and vivid scarlet, of unknown names.

The clouds still hung threateningly about, and gave us now and then a slight sprinkle of rain. But as we drew near to Chalco and the end of our two days' voyage they cleared away.

The prospect from this point is the subject for a landscape painting of the grand order. The town of Chalco, with an ancient and noble church edifice, supplies the element of human interest. In front is the blue water in spaces, with their reflection, and a wealth of marsh plants, arrow and lance heads, ferns, and flowers. In the distance is the great snow-clad mountains, upon which wreathing mists throw changing lights and shadows. Ixtacihuatl, the White Woman, though the lesser, I continually find the more picturesque of the two, in its sharp and rugged outline. Popocatepetl, in the more perfect symmetry of its cone, is a little monotonous, like Orizaba.

We came, by a short branch canal, to the station of La Compañia, on the Morelos railway, and took the train back to town. We were just in time to hear of a disturbance near by by General Tiburcio Montiel, and his arrest by the Government forces. It was said that he had headed a communistic uprising of Indians for the recovery of their lands. He declared through the press afterward that he had but gathered a posse to aid him in the execution of some legal process. Quaint risings of a communistic sort, however, have not been uncommon. Demagogues have more than once told the simple-minded peons that the lands of the country were theirs—had been wrested from their ancestors by the Spanish conquerors —and it was high time to get them back. An ingenious hacendado, waited upon by such a delegation, admitted their view, but met it with another.

"Yes," said he, "the Spaniards took your lands, it is true; but before that you Aztecs took them from the Toltecs. Find me first, therefore, some Toltecs; I will yield my title only to them."

XIII.

TO OLD TEXCOCO.

I.

My next journey was by lake across Texcoco to the old capital of that name. I had hoped to take *El Nezhualcoyotl*, which lay in the mud by the Garita of San Lazaro, when I went to make preliminary inquiries. There would have been a certain fitness in approaching the ancient capital in a boat named after the sovereign who made it illustrious; but it was not its day for sailing.

The *Nezhualcoyotl* was clipper-built, as it were, a long, rusty, gondola-like scow, devoted exclusively to passenger traffic. We took instead a freight-boat of much larger and heavier build, *La Ninfa Encantadora*, or "the Enchanting Nymph." She would have been called the *Mary Ann* or *Betsy Jane* elsewhere, but such is the difference in the tropical imagination.

A cabin sheltered the passengers and some budgets of goods which were done up in the inevitable *petates*, rush mats, and included two bags of silver. There were a couple of young women going to *pasear*—take a little vacation—at Texcoco. "It will be *triste*, of course," they said, "like everything out of Mexico; still, we are going to try it for a while." They offered a part of their lunch, as travelling companions were continually doing wherever I went, and the skipper offered us *pulque*. Two older women, in blue rebosas, sat like statues, holding their parcels and an Indian baby in their laps, from one end of the long journey to the other.

The canal of San Lazaro on this side extends about a league to the lake. It is very much less attractive than that of Chalco. Its terminus in the city is the point of a most animated and Venetian-like market scene, but one earns his pleasure in dealing with this canal at the expense of many a bad odor. Six men put a sort of harness on themselves and dragged us along, plodding on the tow-path, as Russian peasants drag their boats in some of their rivers. A man on horseback with a towrope also assisted, on the other side.

The water, shoal in the beginning, shoaled more as we went on, till we were aground on flats in the edge of the lake. The city sewage was aground with us. Still, the situation was relieved by the striking prospect. The teocalli-like Peñol, where there are warm baths, was close at hand. Sky and water were of an identical blue; the shallow expanse reflected the circuit of dark and purplish foot-hills and great snow-peaks beyond as perfectly as if it had been as deep as they were high.

Our crew walked for an hour in the mud, pushing against long poles projected from the sides, before we could be said to be fairly afloat. Then they came aboard and poled the rest of the way. They walked up an inclined plane, carrying the poles over their heads, and came down, pushing, with them supported against their shoulders, in a bold and striking motion. It was eight o'clock when we set out, and four when we reached the mouth of the short branch canal which makes up to Texcoco. The distance must be about thirty miles. A cross arose out of the lake half way over, and our polemen stopped at it and shouted three times, with startling effect, "*Alabo al gran poder de Dios! Ave Maria pu-*

rissima!"—"Hail to the almighty power of God! Hail, Mary the purest!"

Unexpectant of anything of the sort, I hurried out from the cabin, taking it to be some defiance at enemies, or disturbance among ourselves. We met other packets like our own, loaded with people. A considerable part of the cargoes was the fine large red earthen jars and dishes we saw at Mexico, which are made at Texcoco. The piled-up bales and pottery, the strange figures, and the flashing poles of one of these craft, coming on, make it a highly original and spirited subject.

Then we fell in with one of the curiosities of the lake — disbelieved in by some — swarms of the *mosca*, a little water-fly, so thickly settled on the water that we took them for flats and reefs. They resemble mosquitoes, but neither sting nor even alight on the boat. They are taken in fine nets and carried to Mexico, as food for the birds; and they have eggs, which are sold in the market and made into tortillas, which are said to be very palatable.

The shores are encrusted with native alkali, which has its share in the production of the disagreeable odors. Peasants gather the crude product and load it upon donkeys, to carry to a salt and soda works, and a manufactory of glass, situated at Texcoco.

Was it in this same branch canal that Cortez launched his brigantines for the destruction of the naval power of the Aztecs? There is water in but a part of it now; and traces of substantial locks are found, where grass is growing and cows feeding.

II.

I spent nearly a week at Texcoco assimilating the quiet interior life of the country. I dined at the Restaurante

CREW OF "LA NINFA ENCANTADORA."

Universo, both cheaply and better as a rule than at Mexico, and found a chamber with the keeper of the principal *tienda*, there being no inn. I even became something of an expert in *pulque*. The true connoisseur takes it *mitad y mitad:* half of *agua miel* newly from the maguey field, and half the stronger beverage of longer standing. I made the acquaintance of the Jefe Politico, a polite, youngish man, said to be a terror to evil-doers. He had made the roads safe. He had a way of shooting at brief notice, and transporting to Yucatan, or if he contented himself with a mere fine it was a sounding one. The *pulquerias* must be closed at six o'clock, and other shops at nine. One day the Deputy returned from his seat in Congress, and was given a characteristic reception. A troop of twenty or so of his constituents mounted on horseback, and preceded the omnibus in which he was drawn, from the railway station back into the town, at the top of their speed, shouting and firing pistols. Crackers and pistols were fired also from the omnibus.

I made the acquaintance also of the local druggist, an intelligent person, who had a collection of antiquities. He was of the pure Indian race, and professed himself proud of being an Indian, and proud of being a Texcocan. He had lately brought out a very strong distillation of *pulque*, a kind of patent medicine, and asked my advice about introducing it in the United States. He evidently thought we were made of money, for I am sure we never should have been willing to pay so much a bottle.

The place has now about six thousand people. Its churches are immense. It has a long, shabby plaza, with a market arcade on one side, and an Alameda, also in poor condition. The Jefe Politico might extend his protection next to a few internal improvements. Hamlets cluster near together in a fertile area round about. I noted one day two peons soberly carrying on their shoulders, among the magueys, what appeared to be a dead body. It proved to be instead the saint of the village church, which they were quaintly conveying, as a loan, to one of the others, to assist in a festival of the morrow.

In the hamlet of Santa Cruz the population are potters. Each has a little round tower of a furnace attached to his house, works on his own account, and sets out the large, ruddy jars on his roof to dry. He could acquire a competence if persevering, but the moment he has a dollar ahead he stops work till it is spent. In other houses persons were seen at looms weaving blue cotton stuffs for apparel.

Numbers of ancient carven stones occur, let into the church walls and pavement, and set up in the Alameda. Remains of teocallis are also numerous, as they might well be in a place once the seat of the Augustinian age of Aztec culture. They are treated with no respect at all. They are worn down into mere knolls, and planted with crops. From the site of one now levelled a proprietor was said to have taken out a treasure. What with its age, the destruction of haciendas in the wars, and the practice of the Indians, still prevailing, of burying their money in the ground, there ought to be treasure-trove in Mexico, if anywhere. Certain it is that my host at the *tienda*, Señor Macedonia, had in his till some beautiful old Spanish coins, which he displayed to the gossips who came in the evening to sip beverages and play dominos.

Among the gossips thus sociably *tomando copas* (taking cups) at the *tienda* there was one, a certain "Don Santiago," who told me that he was pulling down, in his garden, the largest pyramid of the place, to sell the material for building purposes. This was of real interest.

Going thither, his pyramid was found to be indeed of imposing size. It was laid up in regular courses of sun-dried brick, and there were vestiges of a facing and superposed pavements of cement, as at San Juan Teotihuacan. There was present in the place with me an archæologist—a newspaper archæologist, I should call him. He termed himself an "expedition;" he had an omnivorous taste for unearthing things, without knowledge of the language, or apparent acquaintance with any previous researches or theories; and his discoveries were intended principally to redound to the fame of a journal which had sent him out. Between us we brought to light a section of a great bass-relief which now occupies a place in the National Museum at Mexico. It was probably seven feet in its longest dimension and five in the other, and must have been a quarter or so of the whole work. It contained a calendar circle, no doubt establishing the date, and part of the figure of a warrior in elaborate regalia, possibly that of old Nezhualcoyotl himself. The archæologist, whom perhaps I unfairly disparage for the auspices under which he appeared, set to work with a will, and soon had half a dozen natives taking the surface off the rest of the soil in the vicinity, for the remaining fragments, but without success. It was the fierce practice of the Spaniards to break the religious emblems of the conquered pagans, to prevent them, as far as possible, from returning to their idolatrous practices, and most likely they rolled down one fragment of the great stone one way, and another another, to separate them as widely as possible; so that they will be found on different sides of the pyramid. All day long it was "Don Santiago!" here, and "Don Santiago!" there, as the excavators plied their labors; while I spent some part of it, shaded by an impromptu awning of mats, noting

down in a drawing the peculiarities of the "find" we
had made. I do not profess myself an archæologist,
except from the picturesque point of view. It is my
private surmise that a great deal of good investigation is
lavished upon these matters which had much better be

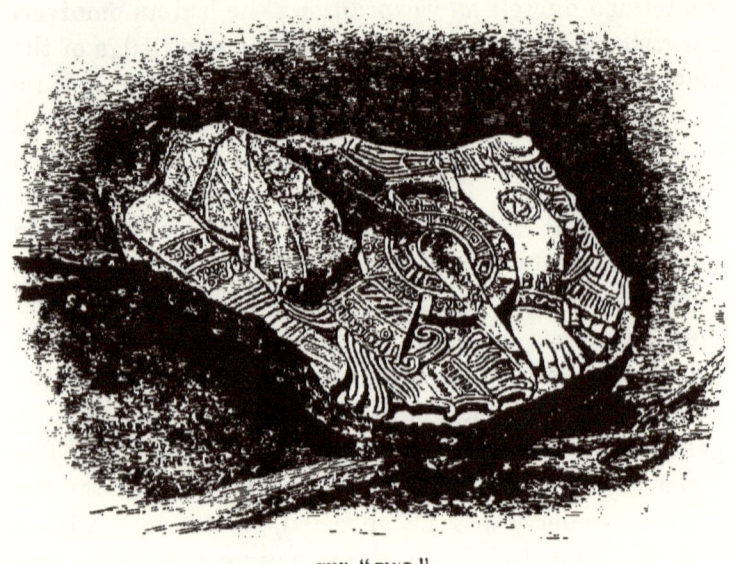

THE "FIND."

spent upon the present; but here was a case in which the
sentiment of the picturesque was amply gratified. There
was a genuine pleasure in being one of the first to salute
this interesting fragment of antiquity after its long sleep,
to tenderly brush the dirt from it and trace its enigmatic
lines.

III.

There is a decided resemblance, to this day, in looks
and habits, between the Mexican peon and the Chinaman. Writers on the subject have generally represented

America as originally peopled from Asia, the Asiatics having crossed over, perhaps, at Behring's Straits, and made their way south. One Mexican writer stoutly maintains that Mexico was the cradle of the race, and the migration was in the opposite sense. This accords, at any rate, with Buckle's general theory, that the thickly settled portions of the earth were at first those where climate and a natural food-supply made the maintenance of life easy. In these places, too, civilization began. The warm and fertile area of Central America, therefore, would have teemed with humanity before the waste North was peopled. There may have been sculptured cities, one upon another, long before even Uxmal and Palenque, the origin of which was lost in obscurity to the Aztecs.

However this may be, the Aztecs themselves, whether descendants of a race expatriated from the South and become rugged in the North, or having crossed over from Asia, came down from the colder regions, like the Goths and Vandals upon Italy. The tradition on this point is clear. One day two leading personages, Huitziton and Tecpultzin, in their far-off northern regions, wherever they were, heard a small bird singing in the branches *ti-hui! ti-hui!*—let us go! They listened intently and took counsel together. "This is really very singular," we may suppose Huitziton saying, while Tecpultzin sagely laid a finger beside his nose and listened again. One would like a historic picture by some competent humorist of these two simple worthies deciding the fate of their nation. *Ti-hui! ti-hui!* piped the little songster inexorably, and that there seemed nothing for it but that the Aztec people should move southward, which they proceeded to do.

They overwhelmed the civilized Toltec capital at Tula

in their progress. They had a farther oracle saying that they were to stop when they should arrive where an eagle was sitting on a nopal plant; and this they found at Mexico, on the very spot which now is the plaza of San Domingo. The whole district became filled in time with small kings and princes tributary to the Montezumas. The most refined and peaceable type of them all arose at Texcoco.

In the Cerro of Texcocingo, some ten or twelve miles back of the town, remain extensive vestiges of an architectural magnificence which show that the accounts of the historians are not made of whole cloth. We had a trooper appointed us, as an escort and guide, by the Jefe Politico, and rode out to visit them.

Ascending the hill, of perhaps two thousand feet in height, overgrown with hardy nopal and maguey, you come to excellent flights of steps cut in the solid rock, giving access to aqueducts, bathing tanks, cisterns, and caverns, heavily sculptured within and without, which are remains of temples and palaces.

Our trooper had little ambition in these matters, and after showing us a part declared that there was no more, and went comfortably to sleep. It was only by climbing alone to the top that I found the principal display. Here the philosophic Nezhualcoyotl, in his retirement, hung in the air, above the wide prospect of his capital, the lake, and his rival of Mexico. And here, in the deserted mountain, with a guide who had gone fast asleep below, his ghost might be half expected to be met with wandering in the still sunshine, but unfortunately it was not. He wrote poems of a pensive cast. He reflected even in his time as to whether life is worth living, and his general theme was the vanity of all things mortal.

"Where is Chalchintmet, the Chicameca?" he asks.

"Mitl, the venerator of the gods; Tolpiltzin, last of the Toltecs; and the beautiful Xinlitzal — where are they?"

These no doubt once famous personages can be the better spared now, on account of their unpronounceable names, but to the writer they represented something very tangible and solid.

"Very brief is the realm of flowers," he continues, "and brief is human life. . . . Our careers are like the streams, which but run on to excavate their own graves the more surely. . . . Let us look, then, to the immortal life. . . . The stars that now so puzzle us are but the lamps that light the palaces of the heavens."

Such, if he be properly presented by Spanish adapters, were the sentiments of this early monarch. Truly the latent capacities even of the natural man are not so far below the surface; and it may be that no agency will be found so potent to awaken them with a rush as the modern facility in railway transportation.

IV.

On the return we visited a country residence, combined with large mills for making paper and grinding grain. It was called the Molino del Flores, and belonged to the wealthy Cervantes family of Mexico. One of this Cervantes family was the subject, in 1872, of a celebrated exploit by the *plagiarios*, or kidnappers. He was seized while coming out of the theatre at night, a cloak was thrown over his head, and he was bundled into a cab. He was buried a long time under the floor of a house, just enough food being given him to sustain life. The *plagiarios* did not secure the large ransom they demanded, after all, but were finally apprehended, and shot—three of them—against the wall of the house, the Callejon Zacate, No. 8, where they had detained their victim.

The Molino del Flores was not only charming in itself, but may serve as a text for mentioning the very different sentiment thrown around anything in the shape of a manufactory from that prevailing with us. Mills, residence, granaries, and chapel, terraced up into a steep hill-side from a little entrance court, are constructed upon the same *motif*, and form a single establishment. It is set in a striking little gorge. The water-power, after turning the mills, is utilized for lovely gardens, in which there are a hundred fantastic jets and surprises. There is an out-of-door bathing tank, for instance, at the end of a secluded walk, screened by shrubbery. The disrobing seat is managed in a small cave in the cliff, and the shower, on pulling a ring, falls from the summit, forty feet above. It is a place that might have served for such an adventure as that of Susannah and the Elders.

In the novel of "Maria," one of the most charming of stories, with which I first made acquaintance in Mexico, though its scene is laid among similar customs in South America, the heroine is represented as preparing the bath for the hero in such a tank by scattering fresh roses into it with her own fair hands.

A rustic bridge, on which La Sonnambula might have walked, is thrown across the cataract to a quaintly frescoed, rock-cut mortuary chapel, where, among others, the last titled ancestor of the house lies buried. He had ten distinct surnames—was Marques de Flores, a General of Brigade, signer of the Declaration of Independance, Captain in Iturbide's Guard, Cavalier of the Order of Guadalupe, Regidor, Governor, *Notabile* under Maximilian, and more; from which it will be seen that the pomp of the hidalgos well survived in Mexico.

The same caressing way of looking at industrial establishments here noticed is universal, and is, in part, no doubt, due to their rarity and a thorough appreciation of their usefulness. I recollect everywhere the sugar haciendas, "beneficiating" haciendas, or ore-reducing works, and cotton-mills treated in similar fashion.

One voyage across Lake Texcoco was quite sufficient of its kind, and I returned by diligencia to the junction point of the since completed railway, and thence by rail to the capital. The pulling-gear of our diligencia was a thing of shreds and patches. A boy ran beside the mules all the way to mend the broken ropes and supplement, with whistling and flapping, the exertions of the driver. The houses in the villages are of unwhitewashed adobe, with palings of organ-cactus. It was like riding through a brick-yard. Fine irrigating canals, fed from the mountains, frequently crossed our course, indicating the substantial scale on which agricultural works are conducted. More than one monumental ruined hacienda, too, showed that they had formerly been on even a more elaborate scale than now.

XIV.

POPOCATEPETL ASCENDED.

I.

I do not know whether I advise everybody to climb Popocatepetl. There it is always on the horizon, the highest mountain in North America, and one of the few highest in the world—a standing inducement to the adventurous. Few accept it, however, though among those who have done so are said to be ladies. I should somewhat doubt this, but, even if so, there seem to be some features of this ascent which make it uncertain whether the effort "pays" quite as well as Alpine mountaineering.

At any rate, if one will go, let him have all the particulars and the necessary outfit in advance, at the capital itself. Little aid or comfort will be found elsewhere on his way. The proper preliminary for ascending Popocatepetl is to find some one who has been there and knows all about it, and to bear in mind besides the few following points, for his informant will be sure to have forgotten them.

The feet are to be kept dry and warm, for there are hours of climbing in wet snow. This is, perhaps, best accomplished by superposed pairs of stout woollen stockings. The guides usually recommend strips of coarse cotton cloth, to be bound around in Italian contadino fashion; but this is a delusion and a snare, and they mean it to be so. They consider, very justly, that if the traveller can be made so uncomfortable as to quit the ascent before it is half accomplished they shall collect the price agreed upon and be saved a great part of their trouble.

There should be shoes provided with some arrangement of spikes in the soles, against the painful slipping backward. There should be a supply of food and warm covering for camping-out, since absolutely nothing is to be had, and the temperature is very cold at the shelter of Tlamaca, where probably two nights will have to be passed.

I accomplished the ascent with two companions. We had in the beginning such assurances of special assistance that it seemed about to be robbed of all its terrors. The volcano is regularly owned, and worked as a sulphur mine, by General Sanchez Ochoa, Governor of the Military School. We were put in charge of one of his superintendents, who was to see that we had every convenience, and that the *malacate*, or windlass, was put in order for us to descend into the crater. I surmise that this particular superintendent did not greatly care to encounter the needed hardships on his own account, for certain it is that in the sequel we were left short of many elementary necessities, and there was no *malacate* for the descent, nor any reference to it.

You arrive at Amecameca, forty miles from Mexico, by train. Everybody should go there. It is one of the loveliest of places, and has inns for the accommodation of visitors. Amecameca will one day be frequented from many climes, if I am not much mistaken. It has features like Interlaken. Cool airs are wafted down to it from the mountains, and its site resembles an Alpine vale. There are points of view in the vicinity whence a sharp minor peak separates itself from the main snow mass of

Popocatepetl, like the Silberhorn from the Jungfrau, at Interlaken. The streets are clean, and the houses almost all neatly lime-washed in white or colors. The marketplace is a scene for an opera—a long arcade, full of bright figures; behind this is a group of churches and courtyards; behind these the vast snow mountains, as at Chalco, but nearer. A little hill at the left, across a strip of maize-fields, is called the Sacro Monte, and has a sacred chapel of some kind. I climbed thither while the negotiations for horses and guides were in their first tedious stage, and found a quaint Christ in the chapel, and a most engaging view from its terrace.

II.

We set off with a captain, or chief guide, who called himself Domingo Tenario; a peon guide, Marcellino Cardoba, who had worked for three years at sulphur-mining in the volcano. He also acted as muleteer. We had four horses and a mule—the whole for eight dollars a day. Domingo Tenario would also ascend the mountain for a dollar more. We were to be gone three days, the greater part of which the expedition consumes.

The first part of the way wound among softly undulating slopes, yellow with barley, out of which projected here and there an ancient pyramid, planted with a crop also. By the roadside grew charming white thistles, tall blue lupines, and columbines. We crossed *arroyos*, brooks, and *barrancas*, gorges. The aspect changed to that of an Alpine pasture. There were bunch grass, tender flowering mosses, and cattle feeding. An eccentric dog, who was attached, it seemed, to one of the horses, and had the ambition to ascend the mountain also, instead of saving his strength for it, here ran up and down and

S*

bit at the heels of the herds in the most wasteful manner. It seems a small detail of an enterprise of pith and moment to mention, but "Perro," as we called him, for want of acquaintance with his name, if he had one, contrived a score of sage and amusing devices to attract an attention to himself beyond his deserts. The horses were frescoed on the flanks with a kind of Eastlake decoration made up of the brands of successive owners.

The English landed proprietor in our small party occupied himself with collecting specimens, and soon had a kind of geological and botanical pudding in his satchel. The American engineer took observations with his barometer and thermometer. Crosses are set up at intervals along the way. These indicate places where a death by violence has occurred, but not always a death by the hand of man. Did the custom prevail of setting up a cross in New York, for instance, wherever a violent death had occurred, we too should have a liberal share of these emblems.

We entered the deep, solemn pine-woods; the night came on, and a sharp cold seemed to penetrate to the marrow. Buildings appeared in the gloom, with red flames dancing merrily through the windows. Aha! the rancho of Tlamaca, with hospitable fires made up, no doubt, expressly for our reception!

What a disappointment! The buildings proved to be but some shelters of rough boards, with plentiful interstices, and not a whole pane of glass. The cabin devoted to the uses of the superintendent contained but a single cot. The dancing flames were those from the process of smelting the crude sulphur, which is done in brick furnaces in the principal structure. Two Indian boys stirred the fires, and coughed in a distressing way all night long. We threw ourselves down to sleep among the sulphur-sacks. One was choked by the fumes, if near the furnaces, and penetrated by the draughts through crevice and broken window-pane, if remote. Tlamaca is itself 12,500 feet above the sea, and its thermometer ranges about 40° Fahrenheit. Without other covering than a light rubber overcoat—for I had not been instructed to bring other—it was impossible to sleep. I went out and paced the yard, sentry fashion, at three o'clock in the morning, as the only resource for keeping the blood in circulation. It was moonlight, and I had the partial compensation of studying the volcano, bathed in a lovely silver radiance.

Mountains are rather given to making their poorest possible figure. Here we are, at this point, already 12,500 feet above the sea, and this is to be subtracted from the total. Shall we ever meet with a good, honest mountain rising its whole 19,673 feet at once, without these shuffling evasions? I fear not. They are only to be found in the designs of tyro pictorial art.

I say 19,673 feet, because so much General Ochoa insists that Popocatepetl is, by a late measurement with the barometer of Gay-Lussac. He even estimates 1700 feet more for the upper rim of the crater, which has never been scaled. I do not know that this has ever passed into any official form, but I had it from his own lips. The latest Mexican atlas makes it but 5400 metres, or 17,884 feet, which coincides with the measurement of Humboldt. I much prefer to rally to General Ochoa, for my part, and to believe that I have climbed a mountain of 21,373 feet, instead of one of a mere 17,884.

The barometer of our own expedition, unfortunately, stopped at 17,000 feet, the limit for which it was set—a limit which barometers are not often called upon to surpass.

III.

We left the Rancho, at six in the morning, on horseback, and rode three hours toilsomely over rocks of basalt, and black sand. The poor animals suffered painfully, but we needed all our own strength for the later work, and could not spare them. They were left at a point called Las Cruces, where a cross tops a ledge of black, jaggedly-projecting volcanic rock. The lines of composition in this part of the ascent were noble and magnificent, the contrasts startling. Across the vast, black undulations, on which our shadows fell purple-black, appeared and disappeared in turn the rich red castellated Pico del Fraile, and the dazzling white breadths of the greater mountain engaging our efforts.

Backward from Las Cruces lay a dizzy view of the world below. Across was the height of Ixtacihuatl, the White Woman, keeping us company in our ascent. The valley of Mexico could be seen in one direction, the valley of Puebla, and even the peak of Orizaba, 150 miles away, in the other. Against the mysterious vastness stood the figures of our men and horses on the ledge of volcanic rock, as if in trackless space.

It was here that "Perro" charged down the slope after crows, which tantalized him and drifted lazily out of his reach, and so wasted his forces that he was obliged to abandon the expedition. Las Cruces was 14,150 feet up. The climb now began on foot, in a soft black sand. One of the leading difficulties of the climb is said to arise from the exceeding thinness of the air, which makes breathing difficult. I cannot say that I discriminated between this and the shortness of breath due to the natural fatigue.

Isolated pinnacles of snow stood up like monuments in the black sand, as precursors of the permanent snow-line. The cool snow-line was a luxury for the first few moments. We sat down and lunched by it, and from there took our last views backward. Cumulus clouds presently filled up the valley with a symmetrical arrangement like pavement. Such bits as appeared through furtive openings recalled the charming lines of Holmes's, in which a spirit, "homesick in heaven," looks back on the earth it has left:

> "To catch perchance some flashing glimpse of green,
> Or breathe some wild-wood fragrance, wafted through
> The opening gates of pearl."

Up to this point—a little higher, let us say—the effort is rewarded. A view of "the kingdoms of the world and the glory thereof" has been had which could not be got elsewhere. But above this it has little more reward than that of being able to boast of it to your friends. A few steps in the snow, and imperfectly protected feet were sodden, numb with cold, and not to be dried again till the final descent. There was a painful slipping and falling in the snow, and blood-marks were left by ungloved hands. The grade is excessive, the top invisible. Who can estimate when he shall attain it? The prospect consists of jagged snow-pinnacles without cessation, an endless staircase of them reaching up into the sky. Sometimes, in the sun, all the pinnacles glitter; again, thick fogs, like a gray smoke, gather round. There is no more casting yourself down now in warm scoriæ and sand. If you sit you are chilled. Yet rest you must continually. Every step is a calculation and an achievement. You calculate that you will allow yourself a rest after ten, after twenty more. The snow is not dangerous; there are no crevasses to fall into, as in the Alps; it is only monotonous and fatiguing. I seem to have gone on for an hour after farther endurance was intolerable. The guides encourage you—when they find that you really mean to go up—with the adjuration, "*Poco á poco*" (little by little); so that we paraphrased our mountain as "Poco-a-poco-catepetl."

Finally, with sighs and groans of labored effort, instead of the lightness with which one might be expected to salute a point of so extreme high heaven, we staggered over the edge of the crater at about two o'clock in the afternoon. I had doubted at one time whether the English landed proprietor would be able to reach it. He had grown purple in the face. Perhaps I had even hoped that he might need a friendly arm to assist him down again on the instant; but he said, with the true British tenacity,

"Oh, *bless* you, I am going to the *top*, you know."

And so he did.

IV.

It was a supreme moment. One seemed very near to eternity. It seemed easy to topple through the ice minarets guarding the brink, and down into the terrific chasm.

There is no comfort at the top when reached. It is frigidly cold. None of the expected heat comes up from the interior. An elemental war rages around, and it is no place for human beings. There is a kind of fearful exaltation. A slope of black sand descends some fifty feet to an inner edge, broken by rocks of porphyry and flint, which the imagination tortures into fantastic shapes. Hence a sheer precipice drops two thousand feet, a vast ellipse in plan. There was snow in the bottom of the crater. Jets of steam spouted from ten *sulfataras*, or sources, from which the native sulphur is extracted. The hands who work there are said to live in the shelter of caves, and remain for a month at a time without exit. They are lowered down by windlass, on a primitive contrivance they call a *caballo de minas*—horse of the mines. The sulphur is hoisted in bags and slid down a long groove in the snow to the neighborhood of the rancho. It takes the palm in purity over all sulphurs in the world. A company has been formed, it is said, for the purpose of working the deposits more effectually and utilizing the steam-power in the bottom for improved hoisting machinery.

The men were on strike at the time, as it happened, and the windlass was not in place, and was not adjusted. If it had been, and we had descended, we might have found the warmth for which we were well-nigh perishing. Snow began to drive from the heavy cloud-banks. When it snows the crater within is darkened, roarings are said to be heard, and strange-colored globules and flames play above the sulfataras.

"What if there should be an eruption?" suggested the alarmist of the party, as we began to beat our retreat from the untenable position.

"There has not been an eruption for at least seven thousand years," said the scientific member, with contempt. "A certain kind of lignite in the bottom, requiring that length of time to form, establishes it."

"So much the more reason, then," said the alarmist: "it is high time there was another."

With that we slipped and floundered down the snow-mountain with the same celerity with which Vesuvius is descended. We crossed again the black volcanic fields, mounted our horses, and spent once more the night at Tlamaca, having learned by experience how to make it slightly more comfortable than the other. The next day we rode back to Amecameca.

When Señor Llandesio, Professor of the Fine Arts at Mexico, made this ascent, as he did in 1866, he says that he found two attempts necessary before he succeeded. I have the pamphlet in which he describes it. "The guide and peon whispered together continually," he says, "which made me think they were going to play us some trick."

Sure enough, they did. After a good way up they represented that it was perilous, impossible, to go farther. He descended, and had taken his seat in the diligencia to return to Mexico, when he met another party, with more honest guides, and, turning back with them, this time succeeded. He describes a young man so fatigued on the mountain that he desired, with tears in his eyes, to be left to die. Another succumbed owing to the singular cause, that he had fancied that ardent spirits would have no effect in the peculiarly attenuated atmosphere, and had emptied nearly a whole bottle of brandy.

Señor Llandesio was told by the Indians that they believed in a genius of the mountain, whom they called Cuantelpostle. He was a queer little man, who dwelt about the Pico del Fraile, helped the workmen at their labors when in a good humor, and embarrassed them as much as possible when in a bad. They said, also, that presents were offered by some to propitiate the volcano, for the purpose of obtaining rain, and the like. These were buried in the sand, and the places marked by a flat stone. This practice may account for some of the discoveries of Charnay, who unearthed about the foot of the mountain much interesting pottery.

XV.

A BANQUET, AND A TRAGEDY, AT CUAUTLA-MORELOS.

I.

WHEN I saw Amecameca again it was to pass it on board a gala train going down to celebrate the completion of the Morelos railway to Cuautla, in *Tierra Caliente*. The Morelos railway is a native Mexican work. It was built under the auspices of Delfin Sanchez, a son-in-law of President Juarez, was rushed forward with great expedition, in order to secure valuable premiums, added to the regular subsidy by Government, and there was much defective work in its construction. It is laid to the narrow gauge, and projected ultimately to reach Acapulco, but this latter need hardly be looked for in any predicable time. At present it reaches about seventy-five miles—to Cuautla-Morelos, capital of the state of Morelos.

All official and distinguished Mexico was aboard that day—the President, the justices of the Supreme Court, generals, senators, *littérateurs*, and, greatest of all, Porfirio Diaz. "Porfirio" wore a felt hat with a tall top, and his manner with his friends was easy and unpretentious. Had the accident of a week later happened that day instead, the Republic of Mexico would have needed to be reconstructed from the bottom upward.

A locomotive *exploradora*, a look-out engine, went on ahead of us to see that all was safe. Every little place had its music and firing of crackers, and the local detach-

IN TIERRA CALIENTE.

ment of *Rurales* reined up at the station. At Amecameca there were as many as fifty of the latter, with drawn swords, all on white horses, which the firing made plunge with great spirit. At Ozumba was a battalion of mounted riflemen, under command of a handsome young officer in an eye-glass, who might have come fresh from the military school of Saint Cyr. The Indian populations, who could never have seen the locomotive before, maintained nevertheless, as their way is, a certain stoicism. There were no wild manifestations of surprise, no shouts; they even fired off their crackers with a serious air.

The line is a congeries of curves without end, to overcome the three-quarters of a mile grade perpendicular from Amecameca to Cuautla. Cuautla has seven thousand people. For the ten years, up to this time, there had not been even diligence communication with it, and the railway was an event indeed. The enterprise was carried through chiefly by the exertions of a Señor Mendoza Cortina, who has great sugar estates in the neighborhood.

The streets were decorated with triumphal arches, and borders of tall banana-plants. They were shabby, and the place more squalid than is the rule in the temperate climates above. The Indians had an apathetic look. Few young and interesting faces were seen among them, but an extraordinary number of hags. I found in use some very pretty pottery, which I was told was made at Cuernavaca, forty miles away. Simple bits of stone and shell were impasted in the common earthenware with an effect like that of old Roman mosaic. There was a distinctly Indian Christ in the parish church. In the plaza in front stands a great tree, somehow connected with a *noche triste* of the patriot Morelos. Like Cortez at Mexico, he was forced to retreat one night in 1812, after a gallant resistance of sixty-two days to a siege by the Spaniards.

II.

The extremely civilized company pouring down to this shabby little place had a grand banquet in an old convent now adapted to the uses of a railway station, and plentiful speech-making afterward. There were a number of merry young journalists of the party, and they comported themselves as merry young journalists are apt to. They rapped on the table and called "otro!" "otro!"—another!—with pretended enthusiasm, even after the dullest speeches. It seemed typical of something curiously illogical in the Mexican mind that in festoons about the banqueting hall were set impartially the names of the presidents and other great men of the past, from Iturbide down to Manuel Gonzales. Iturbide adjoined Bravo and Guerrero, by whom he was shot as a usurper and enemy of the public peace; and Lerdo Porfirio Diaz, by whom he was ousted as traitor and tyrant. In the same way these personages, alternately one another's Cæsars and Brutuses, are honored impartially in the series of portraits in the long gallery of the National Palace.

There was naturally prominent here the portrait of the Padre Morelos, with the usual handkerchief around his head, and bold air of bandit chief. It is curious that priests should have taken such a share in the early insurrection. They recall those warrior ecclesiastics of the Middle Ages, who used to put on quite as often the secular as the spiritual armor. Probably the oppressions of the Spaniards were often too intolerable even for ecclesiastical endurance. Morelos, strangely enough, when the revolt broke out, was curate under Hidalgo at Valladolid, in Michoacan, and followed him to the field. He came, in his turn, to be generalissimo of the Mexican forces, and to have the name of Valladolid changed to Morelia in his honor. He had undoubtedly the military gift. His defence of Cuautla is considered one of the most glorious deeds of Mexican history. It was the third in the trio of priests, Matamoras, his intimate and lieutenant, who broke the siege with a hundred horse and aided his retreat when it finally became necessary.

Matamoras in due course was taken and shot, at Valladolid, by no other than Iturbide, the future liberator. Iturbide, then in the Spanish forces, "had signalized himself," to quote our history again, "by his repeated victories over the insurgents, and the excessive cruelty of which he made use on frequent occasions." He routed Matamoras at Puruapan, took him prisoner, and put him to death; as has been said. To repay this, Morelos butchered two hundred Spanish prisoners in cold blood. So the strife of incarnate cruelty went on. Morelos himself was made prisoner by an act of treachery, and shot, after the customary fate of Mexican leaders, at San Cristobal Ecatapec, at four o'clock in the afternoon of the 21st of December, 1815.

Iturbide's account, in his minutes, of the insurgent chiefs whom he was so active in exterminating is very far from flattering. And here they are all apotheosized together. Verily it seems as if some high court of inquiry and review should be constituted for apportioning out a little the relative merits and defects of the past. The Mexican national anthem, a stirring and martial air, invokes among other things the sacred memory of Iturbide. But if Iturbide really deserved to be shot on setting foot on shore after his banishment, it seems much as if Americans should invoke the sacred name of Benedict Arnold. Arnold, too, rendered excellent services to his country.

Nobody was a braver or better soldier than he before he attempted to betray it to the British.

Well, I suppose the Mexicans understand it, but I don't. Are they content with such a mixed ideal of good? Can a person have been such a patriot at one time that no subsequent crimes can weigh against him? One very simple lesson from it all would seem to be a less impatience with the ruling powers, on the one hand, and much less haste with powder and shot, on the other.

III.

I stayed a couple of days at Cuautla, to visit the sugar haciendas. The sugar product is large, and the district one of the most convenient sources of supply for central Mexico. A week afterward the newly inaugurated road was the scene of an accident unequalled, I think, in the annals of railway horrors. Five hundred lives were lost, in a little barranca, an insecure bridge over which had been washed out by the rain. A regiment in garrison at Cuautla was ordered to Mexico, and started in a train of open "flat" cars, there not having been passenger cars sufficient for the purpose. On other flat cars was a freight of barrels of *aguardiente*. The start was made in the afternoon. There was delay on the track. The shower came on, the night fell, and the men, pelted by the storm, without protection, broke open the *aguardiente*, and drank their fill. Some say that the engineer reported the road unsafe, but was forced by an exasperated officer to go on with a pistol at his head. They came to the broken bridge, and the train went through. The soldiers who were not mangled and incapacitated outright—drunk, and crazed with excitement—stabbed and shot one another. The barrels of *aguardiente* burst and took fire; the cartridges in the belts exploded; the swollen torrent claimed its own; and the fury of a tropical storm, in a night as black as Erebus, beat down upon the writhing mass of horror.

It was at this price that the extra subventions for speedy completion of the work were earned. A whitewashing report was made afterward, I believe, but the Government caused the road to be put in order before it was again opened; and the case may serve as a needed lesson to all railway builders in Mexico.

XVI.

SAN JUAN, ORIZABA, AND CORDOBA REVISITED.

I.

The impressions of the first journey upward from the coast are too vague to satisfy, yet it is better to push on to the capital and not take off the edge of the novelty by dallying on the way. The intervening places are returned to afterward.

How different the feeling now! The things that had seemed so formidable are harmless enough. You take now with gusto the *pulque*, handed up at Apam. You understand the motley figures, the interiors, the flavors of the strange fruits and cakes, the proper expressions to use, and prices to pay. The helpless feeling of standing in need of continual directions is got rid of, and travel has become a matter of confidence and pleasure. Our Mexicans of the lower class are not over-quick in the matter of directions, to tell the truth. I recollect, as an example, asking a small shop-keeper, one day, the way to a neighboring street.

"There it is," he said; "but" (insisting, in a flustered way, on being puzzled by my accent, though he had comprehended what I meant) "*no hablamos Americano aqui*"—"We don't speak American here."

I found a lodging at a tienda at San Juan Teotihuacan, the ancient city of the dead. The owner had before entertained Americans. He had a dog to which he had given, in pleasant recollection of one of them, as he said, the remarkable name of "Lovis," which afterward proved to be "Lewis." Adjoining was a barracks of *Rurales*, whose bugles sounded a cheerful *réveille* in the morning. The central plaza is perhaps three miles from the station. On the way you cross a handsome stone bridge built by Maximilian. The river San Juan had vanished from under it and left a mere gulch, as is the way with most of the streams in the dry season.

The inhabitants have their houses, gardens, and all, often above the cement floors left by the extinct race, and the edges of these floors crop out beside the road, worn down through them. Nobody has framed a satisfactory theory of the place, but it is supposed to have been a great pantheon, or burial-place, for the dead of importance. Maximilian encouraged excavations, and a great Egyptian-looking head, unearthed in his time, is seen. Charnay dug there later, and so did my friend of the newspaper expedition. Probably a commission ought to be issued by the Government for tunnelling, without impairing their form, the two pyramids, to ascertain if there be not something of importance within. It is at present both conservative and apathetic in such matters. The larger pyramid, that of the Sun, has an excellent zig-zag plane approaching its summit. A long road, called the "Street of the Dead," strewn on both sides with heaps of weather-worn stones, indicating constructions, extends from it to that of the Moon. Both are now grown with scrubby nopals and pepper-trees.

A couple of children ran out from a cottage at the foot of the Pyramid of the Sun, to sell "*caritas*," the little antiquities, the day I approached to climb it. From the top you see other villages, as San Francisco, Santa Maria Cuatlan, San Martin. The inhabitants of San Francisco have erected a cross here, where an idol, with a burnished shield, once stood to catch the first rays of the rising sun, and come in procession each year, on the 3d of May, to conduct a religious ceremonial and drape it with flowers. The white summit of Popocatepetl barely shows itself above the intervening range of the Rio Frio. The officiators at the pagan altar may have hailed it sparkling afar, like another sacrificial fire. The country round about is garden-like, abounding in maize and maguey, sheep and cattle. I observed some large straw-ricks, fashioned by leisurely employés, in the prevailing taste for adornment, into the form of houses, with a figure of a saint chopped out in bass-relief. It was a calm, lovely Sunday. A fresh breeze played, though the sun was warm; cumulus clouds piled themselves up magnificently; and the tinkle of the church-bells came up from the surrounding villages.

The clouds—"luminous Andes of the air," as a poet has aptly called them—are of especial impressiveness, I think, above this great plain. I noted them again with great pleasure at Huamantla, in the state of Tlaxcala. It is a shabby place of unpainted adobe, out of which rise the fine domes and belfries of a dozen churches, as if they were enclosed in a brick-yard. Thither Santa Anna retired for his last futile resistance, after the Americans under Scott had taken the capital; and there, according to the school history, "the terrible Amerian guerilla, Walker, was killed in personal combat by an intrepid Mexican officer, Eulalio Villaseñor." Near by is Malinche, a mountain dubbed with a nickname given by the Aztecs to Cortez, which is a feature of all this part of the country. It is not of great height, but of peculiar, volcanic shape. It is a long slope, made up of knobs and jags, reaching to a central point as sharp as an arrow-head. Peons are ploughing, with oxen and the primitive wooden plough, in fertile ground around its base, and its dark mass is thrown out boldly against dazzling banks of cloud.

II.

At Orizaba you are down in the tropics again, but not tropics of too oppressive a kind. A young friend from Mexico was making a visit there in a family to which I was admitted, and I was glad to see something of the place in a domestic way. It has, say, fifteen thousand inhabitants. The Alameda, with its two fountains, stone seats, orange-trees, and other shrubberies, is very charming; so is the little Zocalo, by the Cathedral. There grows in the gardens here the splendid tulipan, a shrub in size like the oleander, the large flowers of which glow from a distance like scarlet lanterns. Tall bananas bend over the neatly whitened houses. My Hotel de Diligencias was white and attractive. Next to it a torrent tumbled down a wild little gorge, amid a growth of bananas, and, passing under a bridge, turned flouring and paper mills. I had this under my eyes from my window; and I had also an expanse of red-tiled roofs, gray belfries and domes, and the bold hill of El Borrego beyond. The city is enclosed by a rim of hills. It was now the season when the rains were growing frequent; and a humid atmosphere, and wet clouds, dragging low and occasionally dropping their contents, kept the vegetation of a fresh, vivid green.

At the hotel *table d'hôte* a couple of young men of very Indian physiognomy—lawyers, I should judge, by profession—talked pantheism and such-like subjects in the tone of Victor Hugo's students. A lady whose husband was a general officer told me that she had been in

THE HILL OF EL BORREGO, AT ORIZABA.

the United States—at New Orleans—accounting thus for a little knowledge of English. That meant that she had shared her husband's exile there. One comes to understand and smile at it after a while. "*Tomo el rumbo á la costa, y salio de la Republica, embarcandose para Orleans*"—" He took the road to the coast and sallied from the Republic, embarking himself for New Orleans"—has passed almost into a formula in the accounts of public. men, New Orleans having always been a notable place of temporary refuge and plotting for their return.

There was a gay party, of station, who had come down to *pasear* a little, in a private car, and were taking back with them a great supply of the flowers and fruits of the tropics. Shall I reluctantly admit that they all ate with their knives, and with the sharp edge foremost? Our waiter gave us, smilingly, soup without a spoon, this and that other dish without a fork, and hastened off for long absences; or he would apathetically say, "*No hay*"— "There is none"—of a dish, but would bring it if it were insisted on with decision. A fellow-guest informed me at dessert that he had been in New York, and that the American fruits and *dulces*—sweets—were all alike and insipid. This shows that there is a natural equilibrium in things, for it is precisely the complaint that visitors from the North first make of those of the tropics.

My acquaintances in the place were the family of the Licenciado—let us say—Herrera y Arroyo. The names of both masculine and feminine progenitors are thus usually linked together by the "*y*"—and. They told me that there was very little formal entertaining done. They occupied themselves with embroidery, studying English, and domestic matters. Their house was roomy, but had little furniture. The rocking-chair can never again be called a peculiarly Yankee feature by anybody who has seen it in the lower latitudes. The typical Mexican parlor, or living-room, has, like the one here, a mat spread down in the centre, on a brick floor, and two cane rocking-chairs on one side and two on the other, in which the inmates spend much of their time.

We had a kind of picnic one day to the Barrio Nuevo, a very pretty coffee-and-milk-like cascade of the Rio Orizaba. Boys ran out from thatched cottages in the edge of town to pick flowers and offer them to the señoritas, expecting to be rewarded, of course, with a little consideration. There is another cascade, even prettier — the Rincon Grande.

The next day we went to the sugar *ingenio* of Jalapilla. A fine wide avenue of trees stretched up to it. The locusts were singing in them. The grass and trees were exquisitely green. The snow-peak of Orizaba, hidden at the town itself, here rises above intervening hills. There were arcades, and monumental gateways, and a massive aqueduct on arches, which brings the water from a fine torrent. In the sunless green archways of the old aqueduct the señoritas found with rapture specimens of rare and delicate ferns growing. Ox-wains brought the cane to the mills. We watched it through the processes of crushing in the machinery, and tasted the pleasant sap when first expressed, and later at some of the stages of boiling down. *Aguardiente* is also made on a large scale. The peasants along the road sell you a draught of it in its unfermented state, with tamales. The residence attached is a large, two-story white house, with a high iron gate between white posts. It was loaned to Maximilian as a country retreat by the conservative owners at one time. At present it is shabby and unfurnished, but a single room being occupied by the proprietor, who has the rough-and-ready tastes of a ranchero, and little taste for display.

III.

At one of the theatres at this time was playing, by a Zarazuela, or "variety" company, "La Torre de Neslo ó Margarita de Borgogno;" at the other, by a juvenile company, "La Fille de Madame Angot."

Whoever would thoroughly enjoy Mexico must have the taste for old architecture. There is no end to it, and it is often the only resource. It is of that fantastic rococo into which the Renaissance fell, in the luxury and florid invention of its later stages; but even where least defensible, from the point of view of logic and fitness, it is redeemed now by its mouldering, its time-stains, and superposed layers of half-obliterated colors. Little can be said, except in this way, for the carvings and various detail, but the masses are invariably of a grand and noble simplicity. The material is generally rubble-stone and cement, and cannot be very expensive. The principal lines of the style are horizontal. The dome, semi-circular in shape, plays a great part in it. I have counted not less than eight, like those of St. Mark's, at Venice, on a single church. The dome is built, if I mistake not, of rubble and cement also, on a centring of regular masonry, perhaps even of wood. It is a reminiscence of the Moors. These edifices were put up three hundred years ago, by builders in the flush of the Byzantine influence, which radiated from Granada, then lately conquered. I know of no school in which the niggling, petty, and expensive character of our own efforts in this line could be better corrected. *Vamenos!* Will not some of our leisurely young architects with a taste for the picturesque travel here, with their sketch-books, and bring us back plans and suggestions from this impressive work, for use among ourselves?

Some of the old churches take an added interest from their present fate. It would have been monotonous to have them all alike in full ceremonial, and now they are pathetic. I used to linger to hear the buglers practise in the cloistered church of Carmen, used as a barracks. It is stripped of everything, the pavement broken, the walls full of bullet-holes, and painted with the names of detachments, as 18° *de Infanteria,* 7° *Compaña de Grenaderos,* which have occupied it. In the smoke-stains, the damp, to which patches of gilding still adhere, and the vestiges of scaling fresco, dim, mysterious visions are made out. The bare chancel daïs, still surviving, gives to the interior the aspect of some noble throne-room. In our own country such a monument would be inestimably prized, and would become a pilgrimage-place from far and near; but here it is simply one of a great number.

In the little public plaza outside a few convicts were repairing the paths. A pair of them would bring some dirt, about an ordinary wheelbarrow full, on a stretcher, dump it in a leisurely way, and go back for more, all with plentiful deliberation. They might have been laborers, engaged by the city aldermen, on a New York boulevard. A couple of soldiers with muskets lounged on the stone benches to guard them as they worked. The punishment of the prisoners could hardly have been in what they did, but principally in the exposure—unless, indeed, they were taken from a different part of the country. I wondered if their friends came here sometimes and watched them; and what a pain it must have been for the sensitive to work thus, hedged round by an invulnerable restraint and infamy, in sight of the homes where they had lived and all the ordinary avocations of life in which they had engaged.

An important cotton-factory at Orizaba has a fine architectural gateway, and a statue of the founder, Manuel Escandon (1807 to 1862), in the court, after the practice heretofore adverted to. Paper is also made here. A series of fines is prescribed, in printed rules, for the hands coming late in the morning and falling into other misdemeanors. The sum of these makes up a fund for charitable use among themselves. A savings-bank department is also conducted for the benefit of the operatives. To encourage savings an extra liberal interest is paid when the amount on deposit has reached fifty dollars. To avoid in part the interruption of the frequent church holidays, a dispensation had been obtained from the ecclesiastical authorities, allowing work to go on, on most of them, as usual.

IV.

From Orizaba the next stage was to Cordoba. Cordoba is in the full tropics, and there I first made acquaintance with the coffee culture, the leading industry of the place. The plant is less striking in aspect than I had expected. It is a bush, with small, dark, glossy leaves, its stem never over six or seven inches in diameter, even at an age of fifty years. It is twelve feet high at most, but usually topped and kept lower for greater convenience in harvesting the product. It bears a little axillary white flower, fragrant like jasmine, and the green berries at the same time. A coffee plantation has not the breadth of the *platanaras*, the fields of towering bananas; but it needs shade, and large oaks are left distributed through it which accomplish this purpose. If left to the sun wholly it yields large crops at first, then dies. The coffee plant should bear after the fourth or fifth year, and yield a half-pound yearly for fifty or sixty years. It should have cost, up to the time of beginning to bear, about twenty-five cents. This is supposing a high cultivation. By the more shiftless method commonly found in use here it costs but half as much, but, on the other hand, yields no more than three ounces on an average.

Some few Americans, and other foreigners, have established themselves at Cordoba, and lead a dreamy existence in the shade. At one time it was the scene of an extensive coffee-planting by ex-Confederate generals, but these attempts were not successful. I was fortunate enough to be conducted about by an old gentleman, of German birth, who had lived here forty years. He had the tastes of a naturalist and farmer, and the existence pleased him. He took in his hand a *machete* from the wall, and we set forth for a walk, with much improving discourse by the way, in the fields and plantations. The *machete*, a long half cleaver, half sword, opens you a path through a thicket, cuts you a coffee or an orange stick, lops an orchid from its high perch on the rugged tree-bark, or brings down a tall banana, and splits open its covering to serve as a protection to a budget of botanical specimens. Some small grandchildren of the house begged to accompany us. They had hardy, out-of-door habits, and ran by our sides with merry clamor, finding a hundred things to interest them along the way.

My genial guide had planted coffee himself. Much money has been lost at it, it seems, and it cannot be very profitable except under economical processes and an improved market. When transportation becomes cheaper we shall have introduced into the United States from Mexico also many choice fruits, notably the fine Manilla mango, not now known. The fruits of the country grow on you with experience. To my taste the juicy mango, which at its best combines something of the melon, pine-apple, peach, and pear, is the most delicious of them all. Other fruits are the chirimoya, guava, mamé, granadita (or pomegranate), zapote, chazapote, tuna, aguacate, and many more, the distinctive peculiarities of which I could not describe in a week.

The best soil for the coffee is that of virgin slopes, capable of being well manured. It should be manured once in two years. The planting takes place in the rainy season, and the principal harvest is in November and December. Women and children cut off the berries, which are then dried five or six weeks, and barked; or are barked earlier by a machine. The chief labor consists in destroying the weeds, which must be done from two to six times a year. The plants are set in squares, at a distance of about seven feet apart. The trees recommended for shade are the fresno, or ash, cedro (cedar), the huisache, aguacate, maxcatle, cajiniquil, and tepehnajé, the characteristics of which I could hardly explain, more than those of the fruits, except that they are generally dark and glossy-leaved, and many of them as large as our elms. There is a theory, too, in favor of shading by bananas, and plantations are found where the two grow together.

But a native proprietor with whom I talked objects to this. "The platano is a selfish and grasping plant," he says, indignantly. "It draws twice and thrice its proportionate amount of nourishment from the soil. Is it not beaten down, too, in every storm? And the ravaging hedgehog comes in search of it, and, while he is about it, destroys the coffee as well. No, indeed, no combination of platano and coffee for me!"

The poor platano! However, it can stand abuse. How quickly it grows! Its great leaves, more or less tattered by friction, flap and rustle above your head like banners and sails as you walk about in the tropical plantation. It is called the "bread of the tropics." An acre of land will produce enough of it to support fifty people, whereas an acre in wheat will support only two. If the tropics had had a good deal harder time in getting their bread, by-the-way, they would not have been in so down-trodden and slipshod a condition.

I will not say that we had the better coffee at our hotel for being in its own country. It is the old story of "shoemaker's children" again, I suppose. On the contrary, I recollect it as especially poor. The hotel—possibly it has improved by this time—was wretchedly kept and served. They gave us half a dozen kinds of meat in succession, without ever a vegetable, in such a luxuriance of them. The waiters were sunk in apathy, the management even more so. They seem often to say to you, with an ill-concealed aversion, at a Mexican hotel, "If you *will* stay, if you will insist on bringing your traps in, we will do what we can for you, but we are not at all anxious for it."

Pack-mules were kept in the court, and under a cloister at one side women and girls were stripping tobacco. Your room, at a provincial hotel, opens upon a gallery in which mocking-birds are hung in wooden cages—always one at least. It is the practice of the Mexican mocking-bird to sleep continuously throughout the day, so as to be in health and spirits for the exercise of the night. He begins at midnight, and continues his dulcet ingenuity of torture till daybreak. Naturalists have had much to say of the mocking-bird, comparing him to a whole forest full of songsters, and the like. It may be unwise to set up in opposition to so much praise, but there are times when a planing-mill in the vicinity, or a whole foundery full of trip-hammers, would be a blessing and relief in comparison.

Should the mocking-bird have injudiciously impaired his strength during the day, so as to allow of a brief respite, the interval is filled in by the shrill, quavering whistles of the street watchmen, who blow to each other every quarter of an hour during the night, to show that they are awake and vigilant.

You leave Cordoba at 4.30 in the morning; that is, if you go by the up-train. I was awakened an hour too soon at my hotel, which, having to call me, wanted it over as soon as possible. I had leisure while waiting to collect the views of one of these watchmen. He showed me the Remington rifle with which he was armed. He said that he went on duty at 7 P.M. and finished at 5.30 A.M., and received three and a half reals—forty-two cents—a day, which he did not think enough. There are no cabs at Cordoba. It is a tram-car, making a total of two trips a day, that takes you, bag and baggage, two dark miles or so to the station.

V.

But I did not leave before first visiting the Indian village of Amatlan. I do not insist that erudition of incalculable value has been brought to light in these travels, but they were a succession of excursions into the actual heart of things. I was pleased when I could find something unmodified by the innovations of railway travel, and witness the familiar, every-day life of the people. Perhaps we never thoroughly understand anybody until we learn his routine. A stimulus to what we usually neglect, and take as a matter of course, is aroused abroad. Law-making, education, buying and selling, eating and drinking, marriage, and the burial of the dead, all yield entertainment. The traveller who spreads before us only the *outré* and startling that he has seen may still leave us very much in the dark about where he has been. In Mexico, however, almost everything is *outré*.

To Amatlan and back is a comfortable day's excursion. We found saddle-horses for hire, and a young Indian as a guide, and set off. My companion on this excursion was a commercial traveller, a sprightly young American of Spanish origin. Commercial traveller in machetes and other cutlery: such was his profession. The machetes were of American make. I have one hanging in my room at this writing which came from Water Street, in New York. This agent had taken his last order (having canvassed the little store-keepers in the plaza under my own view, as if they had been those of Kalamazoo, Aurora, or Freeport), and was awaiting the sailing of his steamer from Vera Cruz. Having nothing more to do, he entered into the examination of manners and customs for their own sake with a certain zest, though perhaps comprehending for the first time that such things could be worth anybody's notice.

Amatlan is the richest Indian village in—well, one of the richest of Indian villages. Its plantations of pine-apples are the finest in the state of Vera Cruz, to which all this territory from Orizaba down belongs, Orizaba being its capital. The pines grow about sixteen inches in height, and should last ten years. They are set in narrow lines, and the general aspect of the field from a little distance is that of large sedge-grass. You will buy three of them sometimes for a *tlaco*, one cent and a half. We met natives driving donkey-loads of them to market. There were some fields of tobacco, of fine quality, in flower. The Peak of Orizaba is magnificently seen from all this district. It is lovelier and bolder than at first upon familiar acquaintance. Church, the painter, finds the preferable point of view farther up the railroad, using the wild gorges of Fortin as a foreground. The village proved to be composed chiefly of wooden and cane huts, shingled or thatched, and the population to be exclusively Indian. They do not wish any others to join them. They display everywhere the same clannish disposition. If persons of European origin who might come to remain could not be got rid of by churlishness, it is thought that severer means would be resorted to.

The Indian race, as a rule, is patient and untiring in

certain minor directions. They make long, swift journeys, for instance, acting as beasts of burden or messengers, so that, seeing their performances, the words of Buffon come forcibly to mind: "The civilized man knows not half his powers." But in the greater concerns of life, those requiring forethought for a permanent future, they are very improvident. Perhaps, however, those of Amatlan differ from others, or perhaps the general reputation may not be wholly deserved, for the Cordobans tell you that Amatlan is even richer than Cordoba.

There are said to be a number of native residents worth from $50,000 to $80,000 each. They buy land, and bury their surplus cash in the ground. It may well enough be that the lack of savings-banks, or any more secure place of deposit for money than the ground, has something to do with the improvidence complained of. The alcalde, the chief of them, was estimated as worth a million, though this I should very much doubt. He had no large ways of using his wealth, but was said to incline to avarice and delight in simply piling it up. There was a project at one time to build a tram-road hence to Cordoba, the capital to be supplied in part by the Indians, but it fell through. Some of the well-to-do send their sons to good schools, and even to Mexico, to take the degree of licentiate. These favored scions, on their return, must put on the usual dress, and live in no way differently from the rest. The daughters, on the other hand, are never educated, but set, without exception, to rolling tortillas and the other domestic drudgery.

VI.

We dined at an open-air shanty posada, with dogs and pigs running freely about under our feet. Coffee, without milk, sugar, and pine-apples were all supplied by the fields about. Some few spectators were interested, but not very much, in a slight sketch I made of their buildings and costume. My commercial traveller, by way of arousing greater enthusiasm in this, represented that it was to be "put in a machine" afterward, and showed, by a dexterous chuckle and twist of the thumb, how it would then be so improved that you would never know it. But even this stirred them only indifferently.

We visited the alcalde in his quarters. He was bristly-haired, clad in cotton shirt and drawers, and bare-legged, like the rest. Official business for the day was over, but he showed us the cell in which on occasion he locked up evil-doers. He was said to administer justice impartially to the rich and poor alike, and with a natural good-sense. But for occasional perversions of justice effected by a Spanish secretary he was obliged to employ, he himself being illiterate, it was thought that his court averaged well with the more pretentious tribunals of the country.

We rode back by a different way, through a large, cool wood. It abounded in interesting orchids, and there was an undergrowth of coffee run wild, the glossy green of its leaves as shining as if just wet by rain. There was not that excessive tangle and luxuriance supposed to be characteristic of the tropics; our own woods are quite as rampant. All that is found, you learn, in Tehuantepec, for instance, and Central America. There tree-growths seize upon a dwelling, crunch its bones, as it were, and bear up part of the walls into the air; and it is vegetable more than animal life that is feared. We forded three pretty brooks, and came to an upland where cows were pasturing, and the steeples of Cordoba were again in sight. Our young guide lassoed a cow, led her to a shed where tobacco was drying, and offered us the refreshment of a draught of new milk.

Being asked if this were quite regular and correct, he answered that the cows were there at pasturage in charge of his uncle. I trust that this was so.

XVII.

PUEBLA, CHOLULA, TLAXCALA.

I.

You turn off from the junction of Apizaco, on the Vera Cruz railway, to go to the large, fine city of Puebla. It is the capital of the state of the same name, and has a population of about seventy-seven thousand. Many prosperous *fabricas* (factories) are seen along the fertile valley of approach; then the forts, attacked and defended on the great Cinco de Mayo, appear on the hills, looking down, like Mont Valerien and Charenton above Paris.

Certainly everything out of Mexico is not Cuatitlan. Puebla is very clean, well paved, and well drained. The streets are not too wide, as many of them are at the capital. I thought our hotel, De Diligencias, which was very well kept, by a Frenchman, much better than the Iturbide. It had been a palace in its day, and had traces yet of armorial sculptures. Our rooms opened upon a wide upper colonnade, where the table was spread. It was full of flowers, which shut out whatever might have been disagreeable to the eye below. I am bound to admit that the remorseless mocking-bird sang all night among them. I have mentioned heretofore the tiled front of a shop, "La Ciudad de Mexico." A picturesque mosaic-work in tiles of earthenware and china upon a ground of blood-red stone abounds. Sometimes it is a diagonal pattern, covering a whole surface; again only a broad wainscot or frieze. Plaques, representing saints, which you take at first for hand-bills, are let into walls. These tiles are made at Puebla, where there are as many as ten *fabricas* of them, the best in the country. I visited one of these, found the manufacture cheap, and brought away some specimens. The workmanship is rude and hasty, but the effect artistic and adapted to its purpose. The most liberal example of their use, and one of the most charming interiors I have ever seen, was that of what is now the *Casa de Dementes*, or lunatic asylum for men, of the state of Puebla. It was formerly a convent of the nuns of Santa Rosa, and was decorated after their taste. Entrance, vestibule, stairs, central court, and cloisters, with fountain in the centre; balustrade, benches, tanks and bath-tubs, kitchen furnace, and numberless little garden courts, are all encrusted with quaint ceramics. It is like walking about in some magnified piece of jewelry. The blue-and-yellow fountain in its court is as Moorish as anything in Morocco.

There are forty-two patients in this institution, with an attendant appointed to each ten. The rich among them pay $16 a month, the rest nothing. Another one, San Roque, contains thirty-two women, also maintained by the state. The general hospital, of San Pedro, another large ex-convent, with a nice garden, was clean, cool, and well ordered; and—curious feature to note—departments for allopath and homœopath arranged impartially side by side. These governments take, officially, no sides with either, but give them both a showing.

The Cathedral at Puebla is equal in magnificence to that at Mexico. There is the usual Zocalo, full of charming plants, before it. The large theatre, "De Guerrero," entered by a passage from the portales, had but a scant audience on the evening of our attendance, but was itself worthy of inspection. It had four tiers of boxes and a pit; the decoration was in white and gold, upon a ground of blue-and-white wall-paper, the whole of a chaste and elegant effect. The peasant costumes of women in each of the provinces vary in colors and material, though the same general shapes are preserved. At Cordoba, white and striped cotton stuffs were in order; at Mexico, Egyptian-looking blue-and-black woollen goods. Those in all this part of the country I thought particularly pleasing; and the great market and gay Parian, or bazaar, where they are principally displayed, were not soon exhausted as a spectacle. The men are usually barelegged, and in white cotton. In the warm part of the day they carry their bright-colored serapes folded over one shoulder, and when it is cooler put them on, by simply inserting their heads through the slit.

Now comes by a woman in white, with a red cap and girdle; now two girls of fourteen, all in white, hurrying swiftly along under heavy burdens. Here are women in embroidered jackets, others in chemises, with profuse bands of colored beads, or rebosos of rayed stuff, like the Algerian burnous. Skirts are of white blanket material, with borders of blue, or blue with white, or yellow. The principal garment is a mere skirt of uncut goods, wrapped around the hips and kept in place by a bright girdle. Above this is whatever fantastic waist one pleases, or a garment with an opening for the head, after the fashion of the serape. To all this is added a profusion of necklaces of large beads, amber, blue, and green, and large silver ear-rings, or others of glass, in the Mexican national colors, green, white, and red. There is a universal carrying of burdens. The men accommodate theirs in a large wooden cage divided into compartments. The women tie over their backs budgets done up in a rug of coarse maguey fibre. Often they carry a child or an earthen jar in it; or, when full, pile a large green or red water-jar on the top.

Affording so abundant material for the artist, they were excessively suspicious of any attempt to turn it to account. There were traditions among them that bad luck would be encountered should they allow pictures to be taken. It was to take away something from themselves, and they would be left incomplete—probably to waste and die. Nor could their costumes be bought from them except with great difficulty. Much as still remains, there has been a great change, and disappearance, since the close of Maximilian's empire, of local peculiarities in dress. There has been a disappearance, too, with the advent of machinery and imported notions, of many pretty hand-made articles that formerly adorned the markets. Among these were carvings in charcoal, once of a peculiar excellence. Of those that remain still of great interest are life-like puppets, in wax and wood, of figures of the country, costumed after their several types.

On the evening of May 19th, as we sat at dinner in the hotel corridor, down came the rain in the court. In a few moments a row of long gargoyles were spouting streams which were white against the blackness, and crossed one another like a set display. "*Va!* for the rainy season!" said the host. It usually begins by the 15th. "*Voilà!* ten months past in which we have had scarcely a drop!"

As almost any desired climate can be had by varying more or less the altitude, the rainy season is of variable date in different parts of the country. At Mexico it is very much later. I did not find it, either here or elsewhere, so incommoding as might be fancied. It rains principally at night, and the succeeding day is bright and clear.

In Mexico, as in California, the rainy season means that in which rain falls about as with us, while the dry season is that in which there is none at all.

II.

Have any forgotten the tragic advent, and preliminary agitations, of the entry of Cortez into the sacred city of Cholula? He assembled the caciques and notables in the great square, and, at a given signal, turned his arms upon them and slew them, to the number of three thousand. He had discovered an artful plot among them for the destruction of his army, and it was his aim in this way to strike such a terror into the country that he should have done with such things once for all. The god worshipped at Cholula was a far milder one than the bloody war god at Mexico—the peaceful Quetzalcoatl, God of the Air. He instructed the people in agriculture and the arts. His reign was a golden age. Cotton grew already tinted with gorgeous dyes, and a single ear of maize was as much as a man could carry. To his honor the largest of all the teocallis and temples was erected. He was represented with painted shield, jewelled sceptre, and plumes of fire. Could Cortez have waited till now (such are the changes of time) he might have gone into Cholula from Puebla, to the foot of this very pyramid, in a beautiful horse-car. A tram-way, ultimately to be extended, and operated by steam, reached to this point, a distance of six miles, and our conveyance was a horse-car with a glass front (New York built) which I have never seen equalled elsewhere. The driver of it was a Tennessee negro, who had married an Indian maid and settled, much respected, in the country. He had formerly been body-servant of a Mexican general, had travelled with him in the United

States and Europe, and picked up several languages. He called upon us afterward at our hotel, to politely inquire our impressions of his tram-way.

The principal features of the trip were exquisite views of Popocatepetl and Ixtacihuatl across yellow grain-fields; a dilapidated convent turned to an iron foundery; an old aqueduct crossing the plain; a Spanish bridge, sculptured with armorial bearings, across the river Atoyac; and a fine grist-mill; and farther on a cotton-mill, turned by the water-power of the same river.

There has been a controversy as to whether the great mound was natural or artificial in origin. I do not see how there can be doubt about it now, for where numerous deep cuts have been made in it, for roads or cultivation, the artificial structure of adobe bricks is plainly visible. Such a place as it is to lie upon at ease and dream and go back to the traditions of the past! You may cast yourself down under large trees growing on the now ragged slopes, or by the pilgrimage chapel on the crest, where the God of the Air once reared his grotesque bulk. There is a sculptured cross, dated 1666, at the edge of the terrace, and rose-bushes grow out of the pavement. I know of no prospect of fertile hill and dale, scattered with quaint villages, in any country that surpasses it. An American was there that day with the purpose of buying a hacienda, if he could find one suitable, and I for one thought there were many plans much less sensible.

Cholula had four hundred towers in its pagan times, and it may have had round about it almost as many spires when the Christian domination succeeded. Let me recite the names of a few of the villages seen from the top of the great pyramid, all with their churches, by twos and threes, or more: San Juan; San Andres; Santiago; Chicotengo; La Santissima; La Soledad; San Rafael;

San Pablo Mexicalcingo; San Diego; La Madalena; Santa Marta; Santa Maria; San Isidoro; San Juan Calvario; San Juan Tlanutla; San Mateo; San Miguelito (Little Saint Michael); Jesus; San Sebastian.

One of the old churches lying deserted in the fields might be purchased, no doubt, and utilized for the basis of a picturesque manor-house. Suppose we should take yonder one, for instance, down by the Haciendita de Cruce Vivo—the Little Hacienda of the Living Cross? A cloud is just now passing over, marking the place with a dark patch. A brook is leaping white through the meadow, trees stretch back from the walls, and the rest lying in strong light is divided by patches of an exquisite cultivation with the regularity of market-gardens.

We dined, at Cholula, at the clean Fonda de la Reforma, in a large, brick-floored room, invaded by flowers from a court-yard garden. No people can fashion such charming homes without excellent traits; so much is positive beyond dispute. We were admitted, I think, to the residence portion of the house, the owner of which was a doctor, and we examined, while waiting for our repast, a lot of his antiquated medical books, some dating from 1700.

The plaza is as large as at Mexico, but grass-grown—for the place is of but modest pretensions now—and lonely, except on market-day, when the scene is as gay and the costumes even prettier than at Puebla itself. In the centre is a Zocalo; at one side a vast array of battlemented churches. That of the Capilla Real, consisting of three in one, is now decayed and abandoned. On the other is a fine colonnade devoted to the Ayuntamienta, or town council, with the jail. What a pity it is that we have so scant accounts left us of the life of Mexico when all this feudal magnificence was in full blast!

PRISONERS WEAVING SASHES AT CHOLULA.

I cannot say just why I visited so many prisons. Perhaps because they were always under the eye, adjoining the public offices, and the prisoners were a cheerful lot, who did what they could to attract attention. At Cholula we found them weaving, on a primitive kind of hand-loom, bright sashes of red and blue, which are sold in part for their own benefit. Their accommodations compared favorably with the barracks along-side. When we asked questions about them they stopped work and listened attentively. The guards, I fancy, thought we were trying to identify some persons who had robbed us —not conceiving of such a visit for the pure pleasure of it.

III.

When I inquired the way to Tlaxcala there was such an ignorance on the subject at my hotel, at Puebla, that it almost seemed as if I was the first person who could ever have been there. A luxurious Englishman abandoned me at this part of the expedition, claiming that nobody knew whether there were conveyances from the junction, whether there were even inns. It seemed to him a case of sitting on a Tlaxcalan door-step and perishing of hunger, or being washed away by the torrents of the rainy season. I found, however, that there was a choice of two trains a day, and went on alone. What then? I suppose Cortez did rather more than that. Tlaxcala was the most undaunted and terrible of all his enemies. He made his way to it after insuperable obstacles, and it was only by the alliance of the warlike Tlaxcalans, when he had finally won them over to his cause, that he effected the conquest of Mexico.

The recollection had involuntarily given me rather dark and depressing ideas of Tlaxcala, as a place of gloomy forests and gorges suited for martial resistance. Who that has not seen it, I wonder, has the proper conception of Tlaxcala?

IV.

It is not gloomy; there are no forests; the country is open and rolling; and the name "Tlaxcala," it now appears, is fertility, the "Land of Bread." I left at 11 A.M., and arrived at the village of Santa Ana, on the railroad to Apizaco, in a couple of hours. After a time a conveyance was to be had, in the shape of a dilapidated hack drawn by three horses, in the lead, and two mules. This was run as a stage-line to Tlaxcala; and in an hour more, largely of floundering over ruts and following the beds of swollen brooks—for nobody ever thinks of mending a road in Mexico—we were there. We met, on the way, the carriage of the state Governor, an ancient coupé, improved by the addition of a boot, and drawn by two horses and two mules. I was deposited on the sidewalk at the upper side of a plaza, and scrutinized keenly when there by the shop-keepers of the surrounding arcades and loungers on comfortable stone benches.

Tlaxcalan allies, in the shape of a small boy and a larger assistant, seized upon my satchel, and we set out for a personal inspection of such houses of entertainment as were to be heard of. The Posada of Genius was altogether too wretched and shabby, as is apt to be the way with genius. The Meson of the—I have forgotten its name—was too full to offer accommodation, and had a morose landlord, who seemed to rejoice in the fact. I came at last to a house where simply chambers were to be let. It was highly commended by my smaller Tlaxcalan ally, a very rapid-talking small boy, with the air of one much in the habit of dodging missiles.

"It will be two reals" (twenty-five cents) "the night, as you see it," said the proprietor, waving a hand in an interior bare of furniture.

"Ah! two reals the night!"

"But perhaps the gentleman would desire also a bed, a wash-stand, and a looking-glass?"

"Yes, let us say a bed, wash-stand, and looking-glass."

"Then it will be four reals the night."

The larger Tlaxcalan ally, who had had nothing to do, established a claim for services by offering praise of each successive article of furniture as it was brought in, as, "*Muy buena cama, señor!*" "*Muy bonito espejo!*"—"A very fine bed, señor!" "A very charming mirror, señor!" —and the like.

V.

Now, all this is all exactly as it happened, and one should hardly be compelled to spoil a good story by adding to it. Yet this appearance of amusing stupidity is dissipated, after all, by remembering the methods of travel in the country. Many, or most, journeys are made on horseback, and the guest is likely to want only a room where he can lock up his saddle and saddle-bags and sleep on his own blankets, or, if luxurious, on a light cot, carried with other baggage on a pack-mule. This is all the accommodation provided at the general run of the mesones.

At the Fonda y Cafe de la Sociedad I supped, by the light of two candles, with a gentleman in long riding-boots, who had a paper-mill in the neighborhood. He told me that he had learned the business at Philadelphia. He was of a friendly disposition, and declared that I was to consider him henceforth my correspondent, so far as I might have need of one, on all matters, commercial and otherwise, at Tlaxcala. And to that extent I may say I do so consider him to this day.

My room had, first, a pair of glass doors, then a pair of heavy wooden ones, and opened on a damp little court, in which the rain was falling. There were no windows nor transom, positively no other opening than a couple of diminutive holes in the wooden door, like

"The fiery eyes of Pauguk glaring at him through the darkness,"

as one awoke to them in the early morning. Another streak under the door figured as a sort of mouth. There was a clashing of swords in a corner of the shady and handsome Zocalo when I went out, and I fancied at first a duel, but it was only a couple of *Rurales* going through their sabre exercise under direction of an officer. The morning was bright and beautiful. Hucksters were putting up their stands in the arcades for the day's business. A new market elsewhere, consisting of a series of light, open pavilions, was one of the best in arrangement I have ever seen.

Tlaxcala recalls some such provincial Italian place as Este, seat of the famous historic house of that name. It has once been more important than now. The persons of principal consideration are the state employés. It is the capital of the smallest of the states, the Rhode Island or Delaware of the Mexican federation. I entered the quarters of the Legislature, and found there the Governor, a small, fat, Indian-looking man, scarred with a deep cut on his cheek, conferring with a committee of his law-makers. There are eight of these in all, and they receive an annual stipend of $1000 each. In the legislative hall a space is railed off for the president and two secretaries. There is a little tribune at this rail, from which the speeches are made. The members face each other, in two rows, and comfortably smoke during their sessions, after the custom of the Congress at Mexico also. The rest is reserved for spectators. On the walls are four quaint old portraits of the earliest chiefs converted to Christianity, all with "Don" before their names.

The secretary of the Ayuntamienta has in a glass case in his office some few idols, the early charter of the city and regulations of the province, and the tattered silken banner carried by Cortez in the conquest. This last, once a rich crimson, is faded to a shabby coffee-color, and the silver has vanished from its spear-head, showing copper beneath. Tossed into corners were two large heaps of old, vellum-bound books from the convents. This is a common enough sight in Mexico. Treasures are abundant here which our own connoisseurs would delight to treat with the greatest respect. Apart from this there is no other museum nor especial display of antiquity. The town, kept nicely whitewashed, looks rather new. It contains, however, the oldest church in Mexico. The chapel of San Francisco, part of a dismantled convent, now used as a barracks, bears the date of 1529, and within it are the first baptismal font (the same in which the Tlaxcalan chiefs above-mentioned were baptized by Cortez) and the first Christian pulpit in America. The ceiling is of panelled cedar, picked out with gilded suns and the like. The approach is up an inclined plane, shaded with ash-trees. Through three large arches of an entrance gate-way, flanked by a tower, the town below appears as through a series of frames. A massive church in the

OLD FONT AT TLAXCALA.

town plaza was cracked and unfitted for use by an earthquake in the year 1800, and its ruins stand untouched, with the bells still hanging in the steeple.

THE FIRST CHRISTIAN PULPIT IN AMERICA. TLAXCALA.

To counterbalance this a modern church, very white, and a landmark to all the country round about, has been put up on the high hill of Ocatlan, a couple of miles back. I climbed there and looked down upon the prospect. Women and girls were going up to the sanctuary with bunches of roses, on some religious errand. There were wild pinks by the wayside, the air was full of the twittering of birds, and the chimes rang musically. Looked down upon from the height, Tlaxcala was seen

PART OF CONVENT OF SAN FRANCISCO. TLAXCALA.

to be a compact little place, flat-roofed, low, almost exactly square. The wide bed of the Zatuapan River, now very shallow, wound by it. The opposite hills, hung over by vapors and rain-clouds with changing lights among them, were now purplish and now indigo black.

VI.

On the floor above me at my lodging resided, in a comfortable way, a doctor. He had with him a friend, French by nationality but long resident at Mexico, who was at present *paseando* a little here for his health. This gentleman confided to me, mysteriously, that, since spending some time here, he had reason to believe that there were mines of silver and gold in the vicinity. In fact, he knew of some. "An Indian, some years ago," he said, "brought to the padre of one of the churches two papers containing a fine dust. It was *poudre d'or*—gold-dust—nothing less. What do you think of that?"

I thought highly of it—as I always do of treasure stories; nothing is more entertaining.

"There are indications, in reading history," he went on, "that much of the supply of the precious metals in the time of the Conquerors was taken from here. You are aware that most of the valuable mines were abandoned by the Spaniards in the terrors of the War of Independence, and have never since been worked. Often their very location has been forgotten. I have a friend here who has certain knowledge of a place where *poudre d'or* can be found."

He paused, perhaps to allow an offer to be made for an interest in the attractive enterprise, but none was made.

He continued, alluringly: "It is my intention to enter into thorough explorations, now that I have leisure, as soon as my health is slightly more restored."

I took the seat beside the driver on the ancient conveyance, going back to Santa Ana. We went along sandy lanes, in which the rain of the night before was almost dry, and between hedges of maguey. Maize on the right—tall but slender, and without the large ears we are accustomed to; barley and wheat on the left. All the country fertile. Malinche boldly in sight, and a sky of rolling clouds, as in Holland. Shock-headed Indian children, with a Chinese look, holding babies, and peering at us out of rifts in palisades of organ-cactus. Bright skeins of wool in door-yards, and glimpses of peasants weaving serapes in interiors. I recollect that morning as one of a few of unalloyed content. Perhaps it was because, in being at Tlaxcala, I had gratified a curiosity of an exceptional eagerness.

XVIII.

MINES AND MINING TRAITS, AT PACHUCA AND REGLA.

I.

We bought tickets for Pachuca at the Hotel Gillow, in Mexico. Pachuca, one of the earliest, and richest, of the mining districts in the country, notable for both its earlier and later history, is, fortunately, also one of the most accessible to the traveller from the capital.

We took the train, from Buena Vista Station, at six in the morning. At Omeltusco, forty miles down the Vera Cruz Line, a group of diligences stood in waiting. Our own proved to be drawn by eight mules—two wheelers, four in the centre, and two leaders. We jolted along execrable roads, turned out where the mud-holes threatened to engulf us, and rode instead over high maguey stumps which threatened to hurl us back into them. The country was covered with magueys. The driver, by whom I sat, on the box-seat, for the better view of what was passing, asked me, in a patronizing way,

"Have the Norte Americanos also *pulque?* and do they *se borrachau* (get drunk) with it, like people here?"

We reached San Agostin, a shabby adobe hamlet, at eleven o'clock, waited there a while for the Philadelphia-built horse-car on the tramway, of which I have before spoken, and were at Pachuca about sundown. As to scenery, historically, and from the point of view of its returns, Pachuca is rivalled among mining districts perhaps only by Guanajuato; but the place itself is shabby, and, lying nine thousand feet above the sea, its atmosphere is raw and penetrating even in July. Regularly every afternoon blow up a breeze and a dust like those which have attained celebrity at San Francisco.

There were said to be ten thousand miners at work in the district. Perhaps five hundred are British subjects, originally from the tin mines of Cornwall. They manifest in their new surroundings a rude independence of character amounting to surliness. I heard here of my French engineer who had been sent over to examine mining property. He had eccentrically given his left hand, after a way some Frenchmen have, to the captain of one of the mines, on his descent, and the colony talked of nothing but this. They had banded together to guy and mislead him in his inquiries as much as possible, and one of them told me, with a bitterness the trivial circumstance hardly seemed to warrant, that if he came again, with his supercilious way of treating people, they would try to tumble him into some pit. Our poor friend, I fear, went away, if he believed what was told him, with some very singular items of information.

II.

Pachuca has become a good-sized city within a comparatively modern period, while Real del Monte, adjoining, once more important, still remains a village. The English element is not new in either. There was probably more of it toward 1827 than even now. On the close of the War of Independence an impression went abroad of most brilliant profits awaiting whoever would furnish capital to reopen and work the old Spanish mines abandoned and ruined in the disasters of the long struggle.

The idea was seized upon with especial avidity in England. It was represented that but two simple things were needed: the pumping-out of the water which had accumulated in the disused shafts, and improved machinery for working at lower levels, than those which had been within the reach of the primitive appliances of the country. Seven great English companies were formed, which proceeded to pour out millions upon millions of pounds, distributing the money among the several mining districts of chief repute; and these half depopulated Cornwall for laborers for the new interests. The idea was in itself a good one. Mexico had produced in three hundred years of mining, according to the estimate of Humboldt, $1,767,952,000 of value in the precious metals. The yield had been going on before the Revolution at the rate of $30,000,000 yearly. It was an industry of the greatest regularity. From 3000 to 5000 mines were in operation, and constituted its chief wealth. Its towns were mining towns; its great families mining families. The funds from this source had built the churches, the dams for irrigation by which the great agricultural estates were brought under cultivation, and had supplied the gifts and loans to the King by which the nobility secured their titles. By the Revolution this source of wealth was exhausted and dried up. The new Congress of the country felt the imperative need of doing something to reopen it, and encouraged the advent of foreign capital by a legislation which is still felt as a liberalizing influence in mining matters.

The idea was a good one, as I say, but the foreign investors did not sufficiently estimate the difficulties of their undertaking, the novelty of the country, language, persons, and processes, and the physical obstacles with which they had to deal. Almost without exception they lost money. The "boom" of 1824 was followed by a panic in 1826, a general depression at home, and, in course of time, the transfer of the interests to cheaper hands.

Among the English companies mentioned was the Real del Monte Company, which bought up, among others, all the mines of the Count of Regla, at Real del Monte and Pachuca. These had produced in fifty years $26,500,000. The history of the growth of the Count's magnificence is briefly this. His principal vein, the Biscaina, had been worked continuously from the middle of the sixteenth century. Its yield in 1726 was nearly $4,500,000. In the beginning of the eighteenth century it was abandoned in consequence of the impossibility of drainage with the defective appliances of that day. A shrewd individual took up these mines anew in later years, and associated with him Don Pedro Tereros, a small capitalist, who became his heir. In 1762 Tereros struck a bonanza, and in twelve years took out $6,000,000. He procured the title of Count of Regla by his munificent gifts to Charles III., and, investing his money judiciously, entered upon the career of splendor to which reference has heretofore been made.

By 1801, however, he found himself at such a depth with his levels that the yield was insufficient to pay the expenses of extraction, and the mines were again disused. It was in this condition that the English company took them, knowing full well that there was treasure in the deeper levels, and proposing to bring it out with its improved machinery and Cornish labor.

The director took a salary of $40,000 a year, built himself a castellated palace, and rode out with a body-guard of fifty horsemen. A magnificent road was built to Regla, six leagues away. The only access thither, for the six hundred mules of the Count of Regla, had been by a dangerous bridle-path. Five large steam-engines and lesser machinery were dragged up from the coast at Vera Cruz, occupying the labor of a hundred men and seven hundred mules for five months.

In all this probably a million pounds was consumed. Treasure was not found as expected—what there was appearing instead in new mines. After struggling hopelessly a while the management passed into other hands. The parade was dispensed with, and the costly machinery sold out, to a Mexican company, for about its value as old iron, and then the property began to pay.

An English "Anglo-Mexican Company" also owned mines at Pachuca, and in like manner came to grief. There was an element of luck in all this, too, it must be admitted. Less than a hundred feet from where work was stopped in the Rosario, for instance, one of the mines of the latter, the new company struck a bonanza, which has been paying munificently ever since.

The present director, Señor Llandero y Cos, a brother of the Secretary of State, lives in the same castellated palace, but on a simpler scale. I had reason to know that even he had had not a little to suffer from the fierce independence of his surrounding Cornishmen. I descended into two of the richest mines, Santa Gertrudis and San Rosario. Of these Santa Gertrudis has paid in a brief space thirty-nine dividends of $20,000 each.

III.

The interior, even of the richest Mexican silver-mine, is hardly what the novice might expect. You put a candle, pasted by a lump of mud, on the top of your hat and crawl through all sorts of dark and dripping holes. Now and then a guide flashes his light on some black and grayish discolorations with a look of professional pride, but you do not exactly fall down in ecstasy over these. There are no forks and spoons hanging ready to your hand, no presentation plate, nor even ingots. The heaps of ore about the shafts do not glitter, and seem good for little but to mend the roads. The principal shafts are about sixteen feet in diameter, the galleries five by eight, and spaced about eighty feet apart. At the San Pedro mine the pumping-engine was of one hundred and fifty horsepower, and another of the same power drew up the malacate, or skip, full of ore in bags of maguey fibre. In some of the old mines, at Guanajuato and San Luis Potosi, they tell us, peons still tote the ore up the interminable ladders on their backs; but this, I think, must be rare. The depth of the Santa Gertrudis is about six hundred feet. The material is marl, limestone, and quartz, all of a soft character and easy to work, but requiring a heavy timbering-up. The clothing of the laborers is ransacked for nuggets by three separate searchers in turn, as they emerge from their work.

There is a Government School of Practical Mining at Pachuca, to which students are sent after finishing the theoretical course at the Mineria, or school of technology, in Mexico. The director, an affable man, showed us the process of beneficiating, or extracting the metal from the rough ore, in miniature. You see the rock first crushed and reduced, with water, to a paste, then mingled with sulphate of copper, common salt, and quicksilver, which get hold of the metal. The quicksilver is afterward withdrawn and reserved for continued use. He gave me, also, a pamphlet of his on a new form of application of "La Accion Mechanica del Viento"—the mechanical action of the wind. A large wind-mill was moving in the court-yard made in accordance with his principle, which substituted large zinc cones for the ordinary sails and slats.

The extracting processes were more entertainingly seen, however, at the beneficiating haciendas themselves. The "Loreto" is one of the principal. The ore is crushed either by the Cornish stamp, which drops a succession of iron-shod beams upon it; the Chilean mill, which grinds it by means of superposed revolving stones; or the *arastra*. The last is the most primitive, cheapest, and still most in use. The crushing is done by common stones, hung to the arms of a horizontal cross, dragged round and round in a circular bed by mule-power.

Then follows the making of *tortas*, "the patio system," which had its origin here in 1557. Numerous large mud-pies of the powdered ore and water are laid out on a vast open court floored with wood. The chemicals mentioned are thrown in in successive stages, and troops of broken-down horses are driven around in the mass for from two to three weeks in succession, thoroughly mingling it together. It is then brought in wheel-barrow loads to washing-tanks, where men and boys puddle it bare-legged till the metal falls to the bottom and the detritus runs away. "Rebellious" ores are treated by first calcining, then separating with mercury by "the barrel process." This last is done chiefly at the hacienda of Velasco, on the way to Regla.

Of the two hundred and sixty-seven mines in the district, seven are worked by the Real del Monte Company. The paying mines are comparatively new, discovered within the last twenty or thirty years. The old Spanish mines do not pay, and are, in fact, little worked. The stories of old Spanish mines, abandoned, perforce, at the date of the Independence, and ready to yield splendid returns to whoever will reopen them, serves very well as romance; but it must be remembered that sixty years have elapsed since the Independence, and there have been plenty of prospectors with a shrewd eye for gain in the country in the mean time. The Mexicans themselves are good miners. It will not do to look on with amused contempt even where very primitive processes are largely retained, for these are often better adapted to the peculiar conditions than any others. Thus the puddling of the *tortas* by mules and human legs, with labor at but thirty cents a day, is deliberately preferred to machinery.

Whoever might care to make purchases in such a place would do well to buy among the newly discovered mines. Or one may yet prospect for himself, for the district appears by no means exhausted. Robbers in the state of Hidalgo long served as an impediment to freedom of prospecting in out-of-the-way places, and it is only of late that their power has been broken. The last Governor is said to have shot three hundred of them. Wild-cat properties and pitfalls of the usual sort await the unwary here. That perversity which, by some natural law, seems to take hold upon dealers in mines as well as in horses possesses them in Mexico not less than elsewhere.

The Mexican mine is divided into twenty-four imaginary equal parts, *barras*, and fractional parts of these are bought and sold as its stock.

IV.

As to the mining laws of the country, I have heard them described by some Americans as better than our own. In certain respects this is true. The reprehensible looseness with which our American "district recorders" receive conflicting claims covering the same property many times over is unknown. An official goes to the field and settles the equity of the case at once, and never records but one title. Litigation about the original title of a Mexican mine is almost unknown, while that of an American mine of any value is invariably in litigation.

On the other hand, there are some drawbacks. While a foreigner may hold property in mines in Mexico without being subject to the obligation of residence, as in respect to other real estate, provided he have a resident partner, nobody in Mexico, foreigner or otherwise, can acquire a mine outright and in absolute ownership. He cannot own it in fee, no matter what sum he pays for it. The legal theory is that the title to a mine is only that of "conditional possession," and in the nature of usufruct, which is "the right of using and enjoying a thing of which the owner is another." On violation of the conditions the title reverts to the sovereignty—formerly the King of Spain, now the Republic of Mexico. The body of the Ordinances as at present followed was promulgated by the King of Spain in the year 1783. To allow a mine to stand idle is assumed to be an injury to those who might otherwise work and extract profit from it. It is enacted, therefore, as follows:

"I (the King) order and command that any one who shall for four consecutive months fail to work a mine, with four operatives, regularly employed, and occupied in some interior or exterior work of real utility and advantage, shall thereby forfeit the right which he may have to the mine, and it shall belong to the denouncer who proves its desertion."

The method of acquiring title to a new and original mine is to go before the proper officer in the district in which it has been discovered and register a claim. Ninety days is then allowed to any other persons who may advance pretensions to it also, to appear, after which it is confirmed to him whose case is best established. Abandoned and forfeited properties are "denounced" by a similar formality. Veins or mines may be denounced not only on common lands, but those of any private individual, on paying for the surface occupied. In order, however, to obviate malicious or idle destruction, the searcher may be made to give security, before beginning his trial, for any damage he may occasion to the owner of the ground. Sites and waters for reducing works are included in the same permission.

The denouncer must take possession and begin the prescribed work within sixty days. The discoverer may have three *pertenencias*, or claims, continuous or interrupted, on any principal vein which is absolutely new. The *pertenencia* consists of two hundred mètres along the line of the vein and one hundred on each side (or as the miner may desire), as measured on a level. A person, not the discoverer, can denounce two contiguous mines, on the same vein, but one may acquire as many others as he likes by purchase.

The ancient code created a General Tribunal of Mining for New Spain, and gave it cognizance of all mining matters. It was composed of a President, Director-general, and three Deputies-general, elected by the *Reales*, or mining districts, and two Deputies besides, elected by each *Real*. The *Real* had to be a place containing a church, six mines, and four reducing establishments, in actual operation. The qualifications for holding office were, that one should have been engaged in practical mining for ten years, that he should be an American, or European Spaniard, free from all inferior blood, and that he should agree to "defend the mystery of the Immaculate Conception of Our Lady."

It would seem that offices were not always in as active

demand as in our days, for heavy fines are enacted for non-acceptance on election, besides being compelled to serve afterward. An honest and straightforward purpose appears in the rules of procedure quite worthy of imitation elsewhere. Let us cite some examples.

"As said classes of causes and suits," says the King, "ought to be determined between the parties briefly and summarily, according to manifest truth and good faith, as in commercial transactions, without allowing delays, declarations, or writings of lawyers, it is my will that whenever any persons appear in said Royal Tribunals . . . to institute any action, they (the tribunals) shall not admit any complaint or petition in writing until after they have cited the parties before them, if it be possible, so that, hearing orally their complaints and answers, they may settle with the greatest despatch the suits or dispute between them; and not being able to succeed in this, and the matter in question exceeding the value of two hundred dollars, petitions in writing will be admitted, provided they be not drawn up, arranged, or signed by lawyers. . . . In the judgments which may be pronounced no consideration shall be paid to any default in observing the minute formalities of the law, or to inaccuracies or other defects; but, in whatever stage of the proceedings the truth may be ascertained, the causes shall be decided and adjudged."

The legal fraternity had secured a repute for sometimes misleading justice, it is seen, even so far back as this. There appears to have been a *Consulado*, or Tribunal of Commerce, upon pretty much the same plan. This ancient system has been swept away by various stages. Since the day of the republic the power once vested in the old tribunal has been lodged with the ordinary civil courts and political authorities.

It is doubtful whether mining has ever been pursued to better advantage, made more productive and regular, and more effectively freed from the element of wild-cat speculation, than in New Spain of the period considered.

There were decrees to prevent miners, especially those of affluence, from wasting their substance. Negligence in tunnelling, imperfect ventilation, and the like, by which life and health are endangered, were severely punished.

Criminals and vagabonds were made to labor in the mines, but the main bulk of laborers in early times consisted of the Indians, apportioned to proprietors as *repartamientos*, and held in a kind of slavery.

V.

The gorgeous Count of Regla was a great mine-owner here in his day. It was hence that he would have taken the ingots for the King of Spain to ride upon from the coast to the capital, should they have been called for by an actual acceptance of his splendid invitation before mentioned.

His ancient beneficiating hacienda of Regla, say eighteen miles from Pachuca, is of great interest. A most excellent wagon-road, constructed by the Real del Monte Company, at large expense, leads to it. As many as eighty heavily loaded ore-wagons, each drawn by from eight to a dozen mules, traverse it in a single day.

Señor Llandero y Cos kindly provided us, for this and the remaining part of our expedition, with horses and a mozo, to be kept at our convenience. White posts of substantial masonry dotted the abrupt slopes, by way of locating the various claims. Some lonesome-looking wooden structures, not unlike Swiss chalets, generally marked the shafts of the smaller mines as we went onward, while a small *arrastra* or two was turned by mule-power in the neighborhood. One, called the Fortune, if what was said were true, should rather have been the Misfortune or the Ill-fortune, for it had never produced a tlaco of profit.

Convolvuli and fragrant *flor de San Juan* touched with a trace of beauty the sterile hills. Real del Monte, embowered in rich woods, presented a scene like a fine landscape in Pennsylvania. We stopped first at the old *Presidio*, above the Tereros Mine, where the convicts drafted for mining labor were formerly kept; then dismounted and went down a ravine, to see the mouth of a tunnel, seven thousand yards in length, built to drain the works of the original Real del Monte Company.

Hamlets were set near together along the road, and the country continued bold and generously wooded. At the abandoned Moran Mine, one of the Count of Regla's principal treasure-stores in its time, we found picturesque remains of walls and columns, with a round tower, which had once contained a hoisting drum. It was obliged to be abandoned, like the Sanchez, in the vicinity, for lack of water. Near the Sanchez is the mouth of the general drainage tunnel constructed by the Count. Esteemed very important in its day, it has been wholly eclipsed by works on a larger scale prevailing in the mean time. Velasco, where "rebellious" ores are treated, is presided over by an English superintendent. He had in use a crushing-machine of still a different pattern from those described. Heavy iron rockers, driven by steam-power, were worked back and forth upon the ore in a bath of water. It was claimed that one-fourth more work could be done with this at an equal expenditure of power than by the Chilean mill. Attached to the establishment in the usual way were a charming villa and gardens. The superintendent at Pachuca sometimes came there to pass a fortnight's vacation.

The immediate approach to Regla is along the side of a deep tropical barranca. Bananas grow generously within it, and a palm-thatched Indian village crowns its opposite verge. The hacienda itself is set down in a most impressive natural formation. It is encompassed by grand columniated cliffs of basalt, like those of the Giant's Causeway. The columns are hexagonal in shape, with an average diameter approaching three feet. At places whole areas of them have been distorted and twisted hither and thither in the cooling, with a most wild and singular effect.

A cascade like a little Niagara tumbles roaring down among them, and furnishes the strong water-power for the works. The hacienda belongs to the Real del Monte Company, and it is chiefly ores of that company which are brought to this strangely attractive scene to be treated. Troops of horses were going round in the usual way in a great walled patio, making the tortas. Connected with this were smelting-furnaces and kindred buildings of many sorts. Madame Calderon de la Barca, who also visited Regla, found it such a place as might have been conjured up by magic, by some giant enchanter, for his own purposes. Mediæval-looking towers, gateways, terraces, a chapel, and prison garnish it. Opposite the chapel is a pretty residence, Moorish in aspect, surrounded by vines and flowers. The whole is said to have cost some two millions of dollars.

We spent a night here with the superintendent, Don Ramon Torres, a youngish man, who had learned his avocation in the mines at Guanajuato. He seemed but too delighted, in his comparative isolation, to entertain company and honor the introduction of his chief, Señor

Llandero. He dwelt in his talk upon the lack of ambition among the Indian laborers. He said, among other things, that in the Tierra Caliente the women were better workers than the men.

SUPERINTENDENT'S HOUSE AT REGLA.

Our next stage from here was to be the hacienda of Tepenacasco, near Tulancingo, where Mr. Brocklehurst and myself had been invited to visit, in order to witness the manner of life on one of the great country estates. Regla is rather famous for thunder-storms, and on the day of our departure we had one of the traditional sort. Within a few minutes after its commencement the cascade was blood-red with soil torn out by the swollen stream. The storm abated at first, but we encountered it in renewed fury on wide green uplands like an Illinois prairie, known as the Plains of Mata. As we galloped in the midst of it, the rain pouring in torrents from our rubber blankets, the lightnings (*rayos*) darted into the ground, now on this side, now on that, in a way which I can only compare—perhaps too trivially—to spearing for olives in a jar with a fork. The *rayos* are dangerous in this region, as naturally on open plains everywhere, and crosses mark places where herdsmen have been stricken down among their flocks. One of these victims had been found recently, with his animals gathered around in a circle at close quarters staring at him curiously, while he lay stark on his face.

The rain had its lulls and relapses, and twice in succession we took shelter under the sheds of isolated *ranchitos* which we fell in with. We were joined here by an occasional ploughman, wearing the long cloak of coarse woven grass, which diverts the water from the wearer. We were joined, too, by all the domestic animals of the neighborhood. The wait at the last retreat seemed as if it would never end. At last a pig ventured forth, and we said, idly, that if he should return we would accept it as an augury that the deluge was over and the waters had ceased upon the face of the earth. Sure enough, he came back presently, munching a green carrot-top; and, receiving this like the olive-branch brought to Noah, we sallied forth. Our confidence proved well justified. A lovely prismatic bow of promise was presently set in the sky, the clouds rolled away, scattering their last lingering drops, the rills babbled merrily, and the face of the country sparkled with an enchanting freshness. We paused again briefly at a hacienda which belonged to the Governor of the state. The main building was large, plain, and yellow-

PLOUGHMAN IN GRASS CLOAK.

washed, and had before it an enclosed threshing-floor, on which grain is tramped out by the feet of horses. A young American girl had been employed as governess here up to a recent date.

It was now toward evening. The sunset glowed warm upon the little hamlet of Acatlan, through which our road was seen winding below. In its midst lay a dismantled convent, with belfries still standing, which from a distance resembled an English ruined abbey. It was found on being reached, however, unlike the latter, to be built of bricks and adobe. I had at first taken this for our hacienda itself, but the hacienda proved equally attractive in a different way. After a couple of miles farther on we sent back our horses and guide with a warm missive of thanks to their owner, and were hospitably installed at Tepenacasco.

XIX.

A WEEK AT A MEXICAN COUNTRY-HOUSE.

I.

WITH a taste for country life, so novel a domain to explore, and constantly agreeable weather, I found a week's stay at the hacienda one of the most agreeable of experiences. From a distance the extensive habitation has a stately air, like some ducal residence. In approaching it you pass first through fields of maguey and blossoming alfalfa, then by a long stone corral for cattle, extensive barracks and huts of laborers, and a pond bordered with weeping willows. It is built of rubble-masonry and plaster, whitewashed, and consists of a single liberal story. The dwelling, with numerous connected buildings, makes in all a façade of about six hundred feet. A belfry, with two tiers of bronze bells hung in arches, sets off the centre. The large windows are defended by cage-like iron gratings. A door, flanked by holy-water fonts, at the left of that forming the main entrance, opens into a family chapel. In a gable above the main entrance is inscribed this motto—which has not, however, prevented the hacienda from being the scene of more than one sack by revolutionary forces:

"*En aqueste destierro y soledad disfruto del tesoro de la paz*"—"In this retirement and solitude I enjoy the treasure of peace."

Immediately in front of the buildings is laid out, after

THE HACIENDA OF TEPENACASCO.

a usual custom, a substantially paved and enclosed area, semicircular at one end, used as a threshing-floor. Troops of running horses are driven around here upon the grain, like those in the *patio* process, only in a very much livelier fashion. The long façade was made up in part of massive *trojes*, or granaries, comprised under the same roof as the house. Each *troje* has a special name of its own inscribed upon it. There were, for instance, the "*Troje de la Espigero*" ("Corn in the Ear"), the "*Troje de la Teja*" ("Tiled Roof"); and the "*Troje de Limbo*" and "*Troje de Nuestro Señor del Pilar*." The walls of these granaries were of great thickness, in order to preserve the contents cool and at an even temperature. Heavily buttressed, and with their long lines of piers, a yard square, extending down the dim interiors, they are more like basilicas of the early Christian era than simple barns. The central cluster of buildings alone, not counting those detached, covers perhaps from four to five acres. Mounting to the roof and looking over its expanse, broken by the openings of numerous courts, you seem to be contemplating, as it were, some agricultural Louvre or Escorial. Its rear wall is washed by a *presa*, or artificial pond for irrigation, which stretches away like a lake. Beyond this rises a charming grassy hill, called the Cerro. We climbed the Cerro, and lounged away more than one afternoon there in sketching, and contemplating the beautiful level valley of Tulancingo, spread out below.

The white hacienda with red roofs lay in front, reflected clearly in its pond. Tulancingo was a white patch at a distance, and other white patches nearer by were the hamlets of Jaltepec, Amatlan, and Zupitlan—the latter in ruins. Straight, lane-like roads led from one to another. The mountains on the horizon afforded glimpses of basaltic cliffs of the same formation as those at Regla, and of the white smoke of charcoal-burners rising from their forests. Cattle wandered in fine herds in the grassy pasture, each tended by its herdsman and dog. We saw a troop of them at twilight come to drink at the pond, and the complication of all their moving forms was curiously picked out in silhouette against the gleaming brightness of the water.

At evening there returned to the court-yard of the hacienda, to disband after their day's labor, sometimes as many as forty ploughmen. If it had rained they wore their barbaric-looking grass cloaks. They drove yokes of oxen and bulls harnessed to the primitive Egyptian plough, and carried long goads to prod their animals. After them rode in now and then an armed horseman, wrapped in his serape, who overlooked and guarded them at work. At the same time came troops and droves of the other animals needing to be housed: black swine from the grassy slopes of the Cerro; mules released from harness; young horses and mules not yet put to work; milch-cows, and young steers and heifers, each wending its way sedately to its own department.

Most of the cattle, I observed, were hornless. This is brought about by a practice of paring the young horns when first sprouting. It would seem that this might be desirable among ourselves, both on the farm and especially in transporting cattle in the cars ordinarily in use. Milking-time came only once a day—in the morning—and not, as with us, twice. The hind-legs of the cows are lassoed together when being milked. The calves of tender age are also lassoed to the side of the mother, and it is a quaint and amusing sight to see their impatient demonstrations while awaiting the conclusion of the process.

THE THRESHING-FLOOR.

I sat down one day with "Don Rafael," the administrador, or salaried manager, of the estate, to make a rough map of its general distribution and extent. The property proved to be some eighteen miles in length by twelve in its greatest width, and of very irregular pattern It had no less than eleven large *presas*, formed by dams at convenient points for irrigation. The principal dam was a mile in length, and by means of it had been formed a lake of two miles in its principal dimension. On the borders of this stands the feudal-looking ruined hamlet, with church and hacienda, of Zupitlan, before mentioned. The bulk of the estate was in grass, but irregular patches of ground had been taken out here and there for various crops, and to each was given its special name. Thus the field of San Pablo was devoted to maize and alfalfa; Las Animas, San Antonio the Greater, and San Antonio the Less were given up to maize; Del Monte and San Ignacio el Grande to barley.

The *magueyales*, or maguey fields, were of considerable extent. The making of the *pulque* from their product was confided to a special functionary called the tlachiquero. The heart of the maguey is cut out at a certain stage of its growth and a bowl thus formed, into which a quantity of sweet sap continues to run regularly for several months. By the end of that time the plant is dead, and is uprooted and replaced by another. The sap is at first called *agua miel*, or honey-water, which it resembles. The tlachiquero makes a daily pilgrimage to the fields, and draws off the *agua miel* by means of a bulky siphon formed of a gourd. Sometimes he bears simply a bag, made of undressed sheepskin, like the wine-skins of Old Spain, on his back; again, he is accompanied by a donkey loaded with a number of these skins. He transfers the sap to these bags, and returns with it to a department of

THE TLACHIQUERO.

his own, called the Tinecal. There he pours it into shallow vats of undressed skin, where it is allowed to ferment. Without describing the process farther in detail, in a fortnight it is ready for sale or for home consumption.

The pasture fields have their distinctive titles also. There were, for instance, San Gaetano, San Ysidro, and San Dionysio; and, again, the corrals of San Ricardo, San Gaetano, and Las Palmas, where cattle were enclosed at various times. Dairy-farming was the principal industry of the estate. Its neat cattle numbered seventeen hundred head. The pay-roll showed a total for the week of eight hundred and fifty men and boys.

The living apartments of the dwelling were set along two sides of an arcaded court-yard, which had a dismantled fountain in the centre. Offices and store-rooms occupied the other two sides. A department for the butter and cheese making had a special court to itself in the rear. One of the store-rooms contained an ample supply of agricultural implements. Those of the slighter sort, I learned, such as ploughs, spades, picks, hammers, and the *coa*, a peculiar cutting-hoe, are made in the country, at Apulco, not far distant, where are also iron-works. An iron plough made at Apulco costs $7, while the imported American plough costs $10. There are wooden pitch-forks and spades among the implements. The wooden, or Egyptian, plough is much more in use than that of iron. It consists simply of a wooden beam shod with an iron point, and has an adjustable cross-piece for service in case the furrow needs to be made wider. The purpose to which it is most applied is that of turning shallow furrows between rows of corn, and for this it appears well enough adapted. At Pensacola, in the state of Puebla, such larger pieces of agricultural machinery as reapers, mowers, and separators are manufactured.

II.

We happened, among other accommodations, in our exploration of the corridors, upon a prison, described as for use in locking up the refractory peons when they will not work.

"Can you do that? Have you, then, such an absolute power over them?" I asked our host, in some surprise.

"Why, no," he replied, in effect, deprecatingly, "I suppose not; but, you see, now and then it is the only way to manage them, and we have to. It is not civilizated, that people," he continued, in an English which left something to be desired, "and we do the best what we can."

This seems something very like a feudal control on the part of the hacendado, but his numerous dependents do not seem to complain of it. Cases of protest before the magistrates are rarely known, and should they be made it is not likely, since the magistrates are friends of their masters, and of the same social station, that they would meet with any great attention.

We found this laboring population living in squalid stone huts, often six and eight persons in a room. The floors were simply the dirt of the ground, and there was sometimes not even so much as the usual straw mat to sleep or sit upon. We were told here again that the peons are avaricious. They are believers in a general way, but not greatly given to religion. Few attend the services at the chapel, even on Sunday. They summon the priest when about to die, but not otherwise. But few of the children go to school. As a whole, they seemed about as wretched as the poor Irish, except for the advantage over the latter in climate. In every interior is seen a woman on her knees, rolling or spatting the interminable tortillas.

The laborers on the pay-roll were of two classes: those employed by the week, and those employed by the year. The former "found themselves;" the latter were "found" by the estate, and paid a certain sum at the end of the year. Wages ran from six cents a day for the boys to thirty-seven for the best class of adults.

III.

The administrador was assisted, in the management of the hacienda, by the *mayor-domo* and the *sobre-saliente*, who acted as his first and second lieutenants; a *caporal*, who had general charge of the stock; and a *pastero*, who had charge of the pastures. The *pastero* it was who indicated the condition of the various areas of pasturage, that the animals might be moved to one after another of them in turn. These minor officers were of the native Indian race. They were dark, swarthy men, very bandit-looking when armed and mounted on horseback, but in reality, when you came to know them, as mild and amible persons as need be wished for.

One, "Don Daniel," supervised the butter and cheese making interest. A book-keeper, "Don Angel," kept an account of all the property of the estate—receipts, and disbursements, and an inventory of stock—upon a system which seemed a model of commercial accuracy. Every week a report was forwarded to the owners, at Mexico, upon a printed blank filled out in the most exhaustive detail, so that they could see at a glance how they stood.

The administrador, Don Rafael, was a steady-going man of middle age, a native of San Luis Potosi. He had land and *casitas*, little houses, of his own, which he rented. He had also a house in the city of Tulancingo, near by, occupied by his family, whom he visited once a week. His salary reached about $1000 a year, and he could be called a person of substance. A conspicuous scar on his forehead led it to be supposed that he might have seen service in the field; but he spoke with contempt of the wars of his country when questioned about it, and said that he had got his scar in breaking a horse.

"A sensible man can always find better occupation than fighting," he said. "I have busied myself with regular industry. The North Americans, now, understand that. They have good ideas. There everybody works and gets a little ahead in the world. Without money in his pocket what is a man good for? He might as well take himself over to the cemetery yonder at once and have done with it."

Don Angel was young, mild, taciturn, painstaking, and a native of Old Spain. His handwriting was small and neat, and he had a great head for details. His salary was the sum of $400 a year. The revenues of the estate which it was his province to cast up amounted, I was told, to $20,000 a year.

Don Daniel, the butter and cheese maker, was young also, but large, handsome, rosy, and had excellent teeth, with coal-black hair and beard. He was a model of robust health and lively spirits. He too had a wife at Tulancingo, whom he visited every Sunday, returning before daylight on Monday morning, to be in time for the milking. He was given to strumming on a guitar in the evening, and assembled around him in his room such convivial spirits as the hacienda afforded. Nonsensical refrains like

"Amarillo si, amarillo no,
Amarillo y verde, me ho pinto,"

were heard proceeding from there long after more staid and decorous persons were in bed.

Another member of the household was, let us say, "Manuel," a boy of eighteen, looking younger, who had formerly been a cadet at the national military school. He was here learning the business of a hacienda, or, as some said, he was a young scapegrace whom it was designed to keep out of mischief. At any rate, he was an aide-de-camp to Don Rafael, and took his orders about on horseback. He dressed, like Don Rafael, in a substantial suit of buff leather. He was a very garrulous and communicative person, and, as our attendant and guide—in which capacity he offered himself, I think, somewhat as an excuse for escaping more onerous labors—he furnished us much useful information. His elders took a tone of raillery with him, representing him as a very callow youth, whose views were of no consequence, and who should be seen but not heard from. They ridiculed his French, which he had learned at the military school, even affecting not to believe that it was French at all. Our visit was the occasion for a strenuous effort on his part to set himself right on this point.

"*N'ai-je pas bien dit?*" he cried to us, across the generous dining-table where we sat together, stretching at the same time a bony, school-boy arm for aid in putting the scoffers down.

One day we mounted to go to a beautiful clear spring of water, which was admired even as early as by Humboldt in his travels. On others we visited the adjacent hamlets, or Tulancingo, from which, later, we were to take the diligence homeward. Again, we made our objective points the various crops, a dam undergoing repairs, or the remoter pastures and corrals.

The herdsman and a boy-assistant at these corrals slept at night in their blankets under a mere pile of stones. The upper irrigating dams are discharged of their waters, when it is desired, by the primitive device of lifting up one cross-beam after another from a narrow gate in the centre. In some of the maize-fields are look-out boxes, aloft on high poles, as a device against crows and other marauders. The general surface over which we rode was the grassy plain, affording a delightful footing for the horses. It was of a fresh, soft green, and enamelled besides with flowers, like violets, the blue maravilla, and many varieties of a yellow flower resembling the dandelion, but prettier.

IV.

The room first entered from the main corridor in the house itself was devoted to the uses of a *despacho*, or office. Here was the department of Don Angel, and the master himself sometimes took his place behind the long, baize-covered table, strewn with matters of business detail, to hold audience with the peons of the estate, who came, with wide-brimmed hats humbly doffed, to make known various wants and complaints. In the corners stood rifles, spades, and the long branding-iron, which is heated in the month of August to brand the young cattle with the device of their owner.

A fat dark peon enters, and proffers a request for an allowance to be made him for a baptism in his family.

"A baptism?" says the master, briskly. "Well, now, come on! Speak up; don't stand mumbling there! Let us see what your ideas are."

The man suggests, deferentially, to begin with, the sum of $3 for a *guajolote*, or turkey, as a *pièce de résistance* for his feast.

"You are always wanting a *guajolote*, you people. You don't need anything of the kind. However, let us say $1.50—twelve reals—for the *guajolote*. What next?"

"The *pulque*—about forty *cuartillas* of *pulque.*"

"Twenty *cuartillas* of *pulque*," says the master, ruthlessly cutting down the estimate by half. "Well, what next? Speak up!"

The peasant, one of the laborers by the year, perseveres, in his humble, soft voice, regularly making his estimate for each article twice the real figure, and having it as regularly cut down. He caps the whole by demanding four reals for a sombrero, well knowing—and knowing perfectly well that his master knows also—that the kind of sombrero he would be likely to want costs but one real.

We had proposed to witness the festivities of this christening, but unfortunately delayed too long at table on the evening of its occurrence, and lost it. But the sky was gloriously full of stars as we went out among the huts and barracks. A woman came out of one of the tenements and made a complaint of a neighbor with whom she had had a row, but got no great sympathy, and hardly seemed to expect any. They are admirably polite, these poor rustics—nobody can deny them that. As we sat by the road one day at Amatlan, sketching, some of the women called to us as they went by:

"*Buenas dias, señores! Como han pasado, ustedes, la noche? Adios, señores!*"—"Good-day, sirs! How did you pass the night? Good-bye, sirs!"

We had not in any way first addressed them, and they did not stop, but went swiftly onward, scarcely turning their heads to look. These and many more of the sort are but their ordinary salutations.

The immediate family at the hacienda consisted of one of the several heirs, "Don Eduardo," his wife, mother, and two small children, and their Indian nurses. They were in the habit of spending but a small portion of the year here, and, when they came, lived in quite informal style. Servants and employés, equally with her intimates, called the young mistress "Cholita," a diminutive of her name Soledad. There was little or no receiving or paying of visits, owing to the great distances to be traversed and the scarcity of neighbors.

V.

Social life in the country is hardly known. We had piano music and singing in the evening in a stately, dimly-lighted *salon* of the style of the First Empire. One day a large farm vehicle, gayly decorated with boughs, was brought around, all hands got into it, and we proceeded to the lake at Zupitlan for a picnic. The provisions were carried on a litter by a couple of men, and a guard on horseback, with his rifle, rode along-side for our protection. Such a precaution was not absolutely needed, perhaps, but there had been a time—before the Governor of Hidalgo had taken his summary measures—when the brigands would have swooped down from the adjacent hills and seized upon such a procession with little ceremony. After dining *al fresco* we amused ourselves with shooting some of the ducks and cranes which abound on the lake.

We had chocolate and buns on rising in the morning, and two over-liberal repasts, resembling each other in character, at noon and nine in the evening. The dogs swarmed in and out over the house, which presented the aspect of a generous farm rather than a villa.

It was designed in its day for much greater state. The furniture, though battered and ruined now, was of the charming artistic pattern of the First Empire, and all the rooms were large and of fine proportions. In one of

NURSE AND CHILDREN AT THE HACIENDA.

the two principal bedrooms the bed is raised upon a daïs, ascended by steps. In the other the corners are cut off by columns, so as to give it an octagon shape. In three of these corners the beds are regularly built in between the columns; the fourth is taken for a door. It so happened that I had not read Madame de la Barca before leaving home. Perhaps I had but a rather disparaging idea of a work descriptive of Mexico coming down no later than 1839. On taking it up after my return I had an opportunity to find how little the country had changed. She too visited this hacienda of Tepenacasco. She noted, among other items, a quaint wall-paper, of a Swiss pattern, on the octagon room. That very paper is there to this day.

The proprietor was of quite a different sort in those times. He used to give bull-fights in the court before his portal, which is now a threshing-floor, and is said to have entertained half the population of Tulancingo at his table. He finally ruined himself by his extravagance. It is said, among other things, that if he took a sudden notion to go to Mexico, a hundred and twenty miles away, he rode his horses so hard that they sometimes dropped dead under him.

XX.

ON HORSEBACK AND MULEBACK TO ACAPULCO.

I.

THE time came at length—all too soon—for my final Mexican journey—to the Pacific coast at Acapulco, where I was to take the steamer for San Francisco.

I was advised not to go to Acapulco. There are always persons ready to advise you not to do perfectly feasible things. It was now August, and the rainy season had begun in town itself. It began one afternoon with a rush. I had been reading at the National Library, and, coming out at four o'clock, found the streets a couple of feet deep in water. The cabs, now at a premium, and some few men on horseback, who could give a friend a lift, served as impromptu gondolas upon these impromptu canals. There were also *cargadores*, who, for a medio, carried you on their backs from corner to corner. I was told that ladies in the balconies, watching the animated sight, now and then slyly held up a real, in consideration of which the *cargador* dropped some gallant in the water, presenting a ridiculous sight. Such inundations last several hours before the sluggish sewers can carry off the surplus water, and they leave the ground-floor habitations of the poor in but a cheerless condition, as may be imagined.

If this were to be added to the other embarrassments of life every afternoon, it was not interesting to think of remaining longer at the capital. And yet, with Macbeth, there seemed "nor flying hence, nor tarrying here." The journey to Acapulco was represented as very difficult and dangerous. The route was a mere trail or foot-path, a *buen camino de pajaros*—a good road for birds. No wheeled vehicle ever had passed or ever could pass over it. All this was, indeed, the case. Three large rivers were to be crossed, and these unbridged.

"Suppose," said the advisers, putting the case in that bold and alarming way in which advisers delight, "that these should be swollen by the floods, as is naturally to be expected now in the rainy season. You would then be delayed so long on their banks as to miss your steamer, which touches at Acapulco only once a fortnight. Again, the road lies, for days at a time, in ravines and the beds of streams; but when the waters occupy their channels what room is there for travellers?"

If to this were added the natural reflections of the novice on the score of danger to property and person in entering upon so wild a section, the prospect was not at all a pleasing one. Nevertheless it would be almost too much to expect that a person bound for California should come back to the United States again in order to go there, and I had a firm conviction that the Acapulco trip could be made.

II.

I had negotiated a little already with an *arriero*, or muleteer, named Vincente Lopez, in a street called Parque del Conde. He would furnish a horse to ride, and a mule to transport my baggage, each for $20—all other expenses to be defrayed personally along the way—which makes the three hundred miles come a good deal higher than so much railway travel. I had thus dallied with the idea, and my decision was precipitated by the sudden coming down of the rain. I hurried to Parque del Conde Street, and closed with Vincente Lopez. I was glad to learn from him that he had also another patron who was going, in the person of a colonel of the army. The journey, under the most favorable auspices, consumes ten days on horseback, besides the day occupied in going down by stage-coach to the provincial city of Cuernavaca, where the bridle-path begins. Considering all the circumstances as stated, there were many companions one would much less prefer to have than so presumably bold and well-informed a person as a Mexican regular officer.

He proved to be a veritable military man, a colonel who had seen twenty years' service in different wars of his country, and bore bullet-holes in his body as the result of them. He had begun in the War of the Reform, which overthrew the Church and aristocratic party; he had fought against the French and Maximilian in the second War of Independence; and, lastly, for the government of Lerdo against Porfirio Diaz. To the party of the latter he was, however, now reconciled, and he was going to take a command on the disturbed northern frontier. If more were needed, he had lately fought a duel, as he told me, in which the weapons were sabres, and had so slashed his opponent, a brother officer, that the latter was laid up in a grievous state at the hospital. A vacant barracks had been set apart, by the War Department, for this proceeding. Army duelling, as on the Continent, is connived at. The case seems to be that, if you fight, you are afterward reprimanded; but if you do not, you are likely to be cashiered as pusillanimous.

Not that the colonel was in all respects the most agreeable of travelling companions. He was much wrapped up in his own affairs at first, and later displayed some traits of a certain childish selfishness.

Vincente Lopez collected our baggage at the appointed time. He was a plausible person, and when he desired the full amount of his bill in advance I had well-nigh yielded to him. I submitted, however, as more equitable, that one-half should be paid down and the remainder on the completion of the journey according to contract.

"That would be equitable, indeed, for ordinary *arrieros*," said Vincente Lopez, "but I am one of especial probity. It is my habit to watch over the persons who confide themselves to my care with a tender solicitude, and in the present instance I have intended to multiply even my usual pains. I am one of those who have never known what it is to encounter on the way the slightest delay or annoyance."

He seemed wounded in his finest sensibilities by an appearance of mistrust, which was to him hitherto unknown. There were considerations in his favor. He said that the colonel, at another hotel, had paid the full sum in advance, and this proved true. Whatever money was to be taken, besides, must be in the heavy silver coinage of the country, $16 to the pound, and to be rid of the weight and jingling of even a part of it was desirable. Still, on the whole, the contract was drawn in my way, by the advice of the dark secretary of the Iturbide Hotel. Though it seemed almost cruel at the time to act in this formal manner with so good a man, the precaution proved in the sequel to be very useful.

III.

My colonel was accompanied down to Cuernavaca in the *diligencia*—in which we were all extremely jolted,

THE "DILIGENCIA."

dusty, and uncomfortable together — by two generals. They had apparently come to give him parting directions about his mission. One of them was a thick-set, black-bearded man, with a husky voice, and a conspicuous scar upon his face. I must not branch off too much into side issues, but the history of the scar was that, while commanding in Yucatan, he had ordered to be shot, on some of the ordinary revolutionary pretexts, a member of the powerful family of Gutierrez Estrada, a family with commercial houses in Paris, Mexico, and Merida, and noted, among other things, for the beauty and intelligence of its women. A brother of the victim came over from Paris as an avenger, sought out the general in question, met him in a duel, and left this mark, which, at the time of its infliction, brought the recipient to death's door.

The city of Mexico is some 7500 feet above the sea, and, having come up, we now followed a great downward slope. It abounds in bold points of view, from which the prospects spread vision-like at vast distances below. Cuernavaca presents one of the most thrilling of these. What is yonder singular detail in the valley? A hacienda set in the open side of an extinct volcanic crater, of which the whole interior has been brought under smiling cultivation. And yonder yellowish spot? The sugar-cane fields of the Duke of Monteleone. He is an Italian nobleman of Naples, who inherits, by right of descent, a part of the estates reserved here for himself by Cortez. The Conqueror was made "Marquis of the Valley," with his port at Tehuantepec, and an estate comprising twenty large towns and villages, and 23,000 vassals.

Nowhere is there a quainter group of old rococo churches than that in this solid little city. They have flying buttresses, of two arches in width, descending quite to the ground, domes, and other inlay in colored porcelain tiles; and they are all clustered together, with tombs and a battlemented wall about them. A student of architecture coming this way with his sketch-book in his hand could find material here for a month. I am not sure that the trip could not be made enjoyably, as it certainly could economically, on foot, with an attendant to carry a knapsack, as we met some German naturalists and prospectors making it farther on. Close by is a garden on a great scale—the Jardin Borda—to which one obtains admittance for a fee. It has a stone fish-pond as large as a lake, terraces, urns, and statues worthy of the most luxurious prince in Europe. I was told that it could be bought for $5000. I asked the custodian about the owner—what he had been remarkable for.

"He had *altos pesos*," replied the man, which is Spanish for "a pile of money." Bushels of delicious mangoes were rotting untouched along the walks. From the outer terrace you look down into the barranca which Alvarado crossed by a fallen tree when sent by his indefatigable general against the disaffected Gonzalo Pizarro. Here are guava, mango, pine-apple, banana, and plenty of other fruits, but not yet the cocoa-nut, which only flourishes lower down.

Behold us ready to set forth on the trail! Vincente Lopez is not present, strange to say, to cast about us the fostering care he has promised. On the contrary, he has quietly sold out his contract and gone back to the Parque del Conde with his profits. We are in the hands of a new muleteer, "Don Marcos," who has never made the journey to Acapulco before, and a fourteen-year-old boy, "Vincente," who is depended upon to find the way. Every cavalcade in Mexico is bizarre, and ours, ordinary enough there, would attract attention elsewhere. First, upon the mule "Venado" rides the colonel, a tall, spare man, in military boots, wide hat with silver braid, and a linen blouse, through which project the handles of huge revolvers. He is aiming, not at display, but comfort. Of myself I shall say nothing. It is a privilege of the narrator to let it be supposed that he is always gallant and imposing in appearance, and exactly adapted to the circumstances of the case. I rode the rather large bay horse "Pajaro." Don Marcos, a deprecating, tricky person, with a purpose, soon evident, of making up from us his bad bargain, wore a crimson poncho and cotton drawers, and bestrode the small white horse "Palomito" ("Little Dove"). Thus appreciatively had he thought fit to name all the animals, though he had but on the instant come into possession of them. The trunks, first securely sewn up in cocoa-mats, were tied, the colonel's upon the back of the mule "Niña," and mine upon "Aceituna." Vincente, the boy, ran barefoot most of the way to Acapulco behind the mules, crying, "*Eh! machos!*" and cracking at them with a combination whip and blinder. With this same blinder their eyes were covered while their loads were being put on and taken off, at morning, noon, and night.

There was a bit of wagon-road at first, as there is outside of each of the more important places along the way. This soon merged in the trail, which was of increasing wildness. The huts and hamlets we fell in with were of cane, well thatched. There were fields of cane, trains of mules laden with sugar-loaves, and an occasional stately sugar hacienda. Now and then there were the remains of one ruined in the wars. At noon the mules were unpacked at some favorable point, and the expedition rested for several hours. It was the custom to take a siesta during the extreme heat of the day. At night there were occasional *mesons*, or rude inns, but generally our stopping-place was such accommodation as could be offered by the inhabitants of the villages. The baggage was piled up under a thatched pavilion. Beds, consisting of mats of stiff canes resting upon trestles, were arranged for us along-side, or in open piazzas. These, in the warm nights, were more agreeable than might be supposed. *A la guerre comme à la guerre!* Sleeping almost under the *belle étoile*, you could study the constellations, the outlines of strange, dark hills, your own thoughts, and hear the dogs bark, down at remote Sacocoyuca, Rincon, and Dos Arroyos, and there was not a little pleasant novelty in the situation. At the gray of dawn we were off.

The people, all of Aztec blood, were gentle with us, honest, and not much less comfortable in their circumstances than farmers newly established at the West. The predicted difficulties of the undertaking largely melted away. It rained chiefly at night; there were but one or two showers in the daytime, though of these one was very hard. The food obtained along the way was of rustic quality, and occasionally scanty, but, on the other hand, it was often excellent. Chickens were generally to be had, with fried bananas as the most frequent vegetable accompaniment. The national dish of *frijoles* (black beans) was always palatable. There was milk in the morning, but not at night, the cows being milked but once a day. We foraged more or less for ourselves. The colonel would demand a couple of eggs under the off-hand formula of *un par de blanquillos*, which can hardly be translated, but is as much as to say, "A pair of little white 'uns." He declared it "a miserable population" where they were not to be had.

On the very first day out Don Marcos came to say that he had no money with which to buy feed for the animals. It was with the reserve I had retained, doled out little by little, that this necessary purpose was thereafter accomplished, and the *arriero* perhaps kept from leaving us in the lurch.

It was *à propos* of this incident that my first glimpse into the peculiar nature and inclinations of the colonel was obtained. It was now evident that it would have been better not to have paid the man in advance. But the colonel refused either to regret that he had done so or to regard it as a lesson for the future.

"I am a philosopher," he said. "The philosopher makes no account of such things."

These views he professed also on other occasions, and seemed, with a bravado of stoicism, almost to go in search of inconveniences.

"But is it not rather philosophy," I argued, "to avoid such inconveniences as one can by a little exercise of forethought, and then endure the inevitable with equanimity?"

"No; that is the civilian's, not the soldier's, point of view," he persisted, with obstinacy.

IV.

This route, probably no better, and certainly no worse, was travelled, as now, nearly a hundred years before the Pilgrims landed at Plymouth Rock. It was the sole highway between Acapulco, the only really excellent port on the Pacific Coast, and the capital. It has seen the transit of convoys of treasure, slaves, silks, and spices from the Indies, bound in part for Old Spain. A regular galleon used to sail from Acapulco for supplies of Oriental goods. It has seen the march of royalist troops, under the sixty-four viceroys, and of many a wild insurgent troop. Morelos operated here, with his bandit handkerchief round his head, and kept the district clear of Spaniards down to the sea at Acapulco. By one of the rivers still lies the massive stone-work for a bridge, the construction of which was abandoned in the War of Independence, seventy years ago.

Most momentous of all the processions it has seen, however, must be counted that of Iturbide, who returned along it, with his new tri-colored flag of the three guarantees—Religion, Union, and Independence—to the capital, to make himself, for a brief season, Emperor. This brilliant figure, of such an ignominious end, is still greatly honored in Mexico, and there is something rather typical of Mexico, or of Spanish America generally, in his history. Taking the position which would have been that of a Tory here, he fought against the earlier insurrection of his country, from its outbreak, in 1808, till 1820. Sent in command of an army against the rebel chief Guerrero in the latter year, he united with instead of attacking him, seized a convoy of treasure to serve as sinews of war, and drew up at Iguala—a charming little city on the route—a plan of independence of his own. The Viceroy, in despair, tried to buy him back with promises of pardon, money, and higher command, but without success. He made a triumphal entry into the capital in September, 1821. In May of the following year a sedition, which he had without doubt artfully set on foot, roused him at his hotel at night, with a clamor that he should become Emperor. He appeared upon his balcony and affected to reluctantly consent to the popular will.

He modelled himself after Napoleon, nearly his contemporary. There is a portrait of him at the National Palace, in the same gorgeous coronation robes affected by the latter, though in his own whiskered countenance he is more like the English Prince Regent of the same date.

In August he imprisoned some Deputies, and in October, still following his illustrious prototype, put his troublesome Congress out-of-doors. But in October also the country rose against him, and he was obliged to leave it and take refuge in England. He returned again in July of the next year—another Napoleon from Elba; but, instead of sweeping the country with enthusiasm, he was seized upon landing, and ordered to prepare for death within two hours. Four days of grace were finally given him, and then he was shot.

Iturbide was a person of a highly politic turn, as has been seen. A thorough devotee of expediency, he maintained (and there was not a little truth in this) that a people made up so largely of Indian serfs suddenly released from tyranny was not ready for self-government. He said that he had meant the Empire to be only temporary. He had shown no personal valor in the service of his country, as there had been no occasion for it; all his actual fighting had been against it. Yet he is commemorated in the national anthem,* and a certain hold, in the Napoleonic way, which he had upon the popular imagination, was relied upon by the French when they endeavored to establish Maximilian in Mexico. A grandson of Iturbide still lives who was adopted by Maximilian, in order to give his dynasty a more indigenous effect, and made heir to the succession. The boy's mother, who at first acquiesced in the usurping order of things, later repented, and endeavored to get him away. This was finally effected through the mediations of Secretary Seward and Mr. John Bigelow, then Minister to France.

---

* "Si á lo lid contra hueste enemiga
Nos convoca la trompa guerrera,
De Iturbide la sacra bandera,
Mexicanos valientes, seguid !"

XXI.

CONVERSATIONS BY THE WAY WITH A COLONEL.

I.

ITURBIDE was the subject of confab between the colonel and myself as we jogged along the way; and this led naturally up to Maximilian. My companion had served under Escobedo in the campaign in which Maximilian was overthrown, and had witnessed his execution at the tragic Cerro de las Campanas.

"He died like a true soldier," said the colonel. "He was not afraid; though he deserved his fate, and I would not have had it otherwise."

It seems to be the general verdict that this ill-starred ruler was not without the physical fortitude which is esteemed a part of the heritage of princes. But he was better fitted for many other things than the task of fastening a monarchy upon belligerent Mexico. I drew the conversation, when an opening appeared, to the present novel relations of Mexico with our own country.

"Had I the authority," said the colonel, frankly, "I would never have granted the railroad charters which are making this great bustle. I fear the aggressions of the Americans. The conservative Mexican policy is to grant you such privileges only when they are balanced by others to Europeans. This was the consistent policy of Juarez and Lerdo. It was Porfirio Diaz, during his presidency, who first broke it down and brought this invasion upon us."

"We, on the contrary, incline to make it one of his merits," I said—"a proof of his superior enlightenment. He stepped over the boundaries of narrow prejudice and jealousy, and allowed a beginning to be made of developing the country by those who were ready to do it, without waiting farther for those who would not."

"His enemies say he was bought," rejoined the colonel, who had evidently no great love for Porfirio. "He has not been wholly above corruption in his time. He made fabulous sums out of the liquidation of the military arrears, for instance. He paid a million dollars for his magnificent hacienda in the state of Oaxaca. Where did that come from? That is a great weakness among us for official corruption. There are too many examples of it. A defaulting person in a high place is rarely punished. When I see a case of that kind treated with severity I shall begin to conceive new hopes."

"But," I argued, "the Americans certainly have no other designs than that of commercial profit. They do not want your country. What Americans have anything to gain by taking it? Who would put his hand in his pocket to pay the expenses of a war of annexation? We look out for ourselves as individuals, and we fail to see where the profit comes in. We are large enough now to gratify our own vanity on that score. Love of glory and territorial aggrandizement is not one of our national traits. Spoliation might rather be feared at the hands of some ambitious prince, if you had any such for a neighbor, who could turn it to personal account."

"You will not annex us with bayonets," he returned; "you will annex us with dollars. I feel it; I know it. Your great commercial enterprises will insensibly get hold of the vitals of our country, and the rest will follow. Perhaps there may be disturbances, and your government called in to protect the property of investors. There will naturally be sympathy for them at home, and they will move heaven and earth rather than lose. A thousand times better that our country were not developed at all than at such a price."

As I still insisted upon the unreasonableness of this notion, the colonel continued: "Even granting that you are sincere in what you say of the wishes of your people, I feel that it is the manifest destiny of Mexico to be taken by the United States. In former times the Latin races ruled the world, but in this and the coming ages the Saxon race will do it. You are a strong, commercial people, and commerce is the breath of the nostrils of modern civilization. Look at what you have done in California since it ceased to be a Spanish province. I have been at San Francisco—a great, splendid city; I looked upon it with amazement. 'This was once Mexican,' I said to myself. 'Ah, what a different genius from that of Mexico!' Yes, you will get us. It will be the amelioration of many abuses, and our greater prosperity, without doubt; but I hope I shall never live to see the day. As a patriot, as a soldier, I would give my life fifty times over rather than consent to it."

"But, since you concede such benefits as probable," I ventured to say, "what is this patriotism upon which you so strongly insist? We do not want you, and have no designs upon you, but—purely for the sake of argument, and talking as enlightened persons—is it not rather fantastic? Is a boundary-line such an object in itself? May not a good deal that has stood for patriotism in the past be a mere provincial narrowness? Supposing that Mexico, or Canada, without force, but in its own judgment of what was for the good of its people, should desire to become a part of the Union, maintaining its organization in states and its local self-government as now, and merely sending delegates to Washington to represent it in national affairs, would you, as a Mexican citizen, feel bound to resist, as if it were the consummation of something scandalous and recreant? Is not the enjoyment of life, liberty, and the pursuit of happiness to the greatest advantage, the object of a rational being? Is there any virtue in an essential Mexicanism, Americanism, or Anglicism, that it should be preserved at all hazards?

And, having asked many such-like questions, I endeavored, farther, to explain a view that we may be all approaching a great cosmopolitan period, when we shall be members of a republic of nations, and foreigners, as such, shall nowhere any longer be either dreaded or despised.

"That is all very well," said the colonel, stubbornly, "since the advantage is to fall on your side; but I tell you I would give my heart's blood rather than see it."

As to the value of his prognostication I have no opinion; but this seriousness of conviction about the plans of the Americans from such a source was full of interest. It is held by the bulk of the Mexican people, and it means trouble ahead for the enterprises, since it must increase with their very success.

"Has any party ever been heard of, with you, in favor of annexation?" I went on to ask.

"There is no such party," he replied. "There are none who could favor it — unless, singularly enough, it might be the Church party. Protestant country though you are, with you they could enjoy a greater freedom than here. Since their suppression under the War of the Reform there can be no convents, religious orders, nor monastic schools; but in the United States, I understand, they could have as many as they wished."

The colonel was rather fond, as stated, of dwelling upon the soldier's point of view. One day, when he had been writing, as he said, to his mother, he declared, in a gloomy mood, not without its pathos: "That is the only tie that binds me to life. At forty-four, as you see me, I have passed through many disappointments and chagrins. I have little pleasure in the present and no great hopes for the future. Well, that is a proper state of mind for the soldier.

"The soldier," he went on to say, "should be one who either sets little value upon life, and looks to death as a release, or one having a supreme sense of honor, of pride in his profession, and duty to his government. He makes a contract, as it were, with authority. He is well paid and highly considered; in return, he must be ready to spill his blood whenever his employer demands it."

II.

The display of childish selfishness on my companion's part to which I have adverted consisted in getting up one morning and riding off on my horse, without saying so much as "By your leave." He had cast eyes on it as we went along, judged it to be on the whole preferable to his mule, and in this direct way took possession. The matter was adjusted, but not till it had assumed at one time an almost international aspect. It was in the coolness resulting from this incident that I rode on alone and first saw Iguala.

The expedition had stopped, after its usual day's march, before sunset, at the tropical hamlet of Platanillo. I was anxious, however, to pass the night instead in the notable city named. The twilight shuts down very rapidly here, and from the estimates of casual informants I had miscalculated the distance. "*Adelantito, señor*," they said, after the inaccurate way of such informants— "Just a little way ahead;" "*Aca bajito, no mas*"—"Right down there; a mere trifle, that is all." I had a distant glimpse or two of it from the pass, while the sun glowed like a beacon-fire on the crests of vast mountains encompassing its little valley. A small lake sparkled in its vicinity, and plantations of cane near it showed a brighter green. Of the town itself, which might have been a mammoth hacienda, only a dome and a few white spots appeared out of the midst of a quadrangle of foliage marked off on all sides to an even line. Then night came on, a dark and cloudy one, though without rain. My horse slipped with me on the steep over rolling stones. It was no longer safe to ride after that, and I led him most of the way, picking out the path in the dark. The view had been very deceptive, and we had many miles to go.

Lonely gulches, brooks, and bits of wood were passed. Cows had gone to sleep in upland pastures, and one occasionally loomed up, a mysterious shape, in the path and took herself out of the way. The rays of a clouded moon gleamed now and then on a white patch of the lake, but the city seemed to have vanished out of existence. At last, however, a dim light in a dome, then a barking of dogs, and audible human voices. All this time there had been neither house nor hut. It was after nine o'clock. I came close up to one of the formal lines of trees, opened a gate in it, and was in the midst of Iguala.

I do not know whether the place has quite advantages enough to offset so much discomfort. What there is to be seen could easily have been taken in the next day on the march. There is no other vestige of Iturbide yielded to inquiry than the house in which the Plan of Iguala is

OUR CAVALCADE AT IGUALA.

said to have been signed—the oldest, as it is one of the shabbiest, in the place. It is of one story, like most provincial Mexican houses, with the whitewash badly rubbed off its adobes, and is now a poor *fonda*, or restaurant, without so much as a sign.

But Iguala is charming. A row of clean, white colonnades, made up of square pillars of masonry, supporting red-tiled roofs, extends around a central plaza. The windows of the better residences are closed, not with glass, but projecting wooden gratings of turned posts, painted green. The market, a little paved plaza, opening from the other, consists of a series of double colonnades, light, commodious, and very attractive. The church, of a noble, massive form, made gay by an azure belfry and clock, stands in a grassy enclosure surrounded by posts and chains. Across the way is the zocalo, with brick benches, deep, grateful shade of *tamarindos*, as large as elms, and arbors draped with sweet-peas in blossom. Such a park, such a church, and such a market could be conscientiously recommended as worthy of any populace in the world. The heads of palm-trees star the heavier, Northern-looking foliage. Grass sprouts plentifully between the cobble-stones, and gives a rural air. A band played in the zocalo in the evening, though there was but a small scattering of persons to hear it.

As I was making a sketch of the zocalo from a portal some very well-dressed young men and a professor came out. It proved that this house was a school, and a pleasant one it seemed.

"*Amigo*"—friend—they said, in a rather patronizing tone, "what is your interest in this place? What is your picturing designed for?"

Three days farther on is Chilpancingo, to which also complimentary terms—in a lesser measure than Iguala—

may be applied. It is the capital of this rugged Guerrero, a state named after the patriot general, who was once, like our own Marcos and Vincente Lopez, a muleteer. It contains an ornate Government-house, a zocalo with a music-stand; and we met here a colonel of the detachment of cavalry guarding the country, gotten up in such dapper civilian riding-dress as if for a promenade in Central Park. Population—but populations are hard to get at in Mexico. I should say, at random, for either place, about three thousand people.

At Chilpancingo you see the place in which the original Declaration of Independence of Mexico was proclaimed, in 1813. It had to be fought for many a long year till the day of Iturbide. This is merely a white house with a tablet, and not of farther interest. It was a wild and problematic cause, truly, when remote Chilpancingo was resorted to by the first constituent Congress, assembled by Padre Morelos, to throw off the yoke of Spain.

But how has all this been done? These little bits of ornate civilization are like enchanted places which we happen upon in penetrating the fastnesses of the mountains. Perhaps we had better take out at once some such commission as that of the Adelantado of the Seven Cities; and yet greater discoveries may await us, never before heard of by man. Each lies in its miniature valley, smiling and fertile, with wagon-roads for a little space around; but their inhabitants can hardly be conceived as going over the wild trail to supply themselves with the fashions and comforts they possess.

Candid judges from without would pronounce it impassable, and think it a practical joke that they were asked to consider it a road. We crossed and recrossed swift, small streams, the water reaching to the animals' shoulders. The colonel had a way of dangling his military boots on such occasions in the water, to let me see how excellently they were made; but one night, I observed, he could not get them off, and the next morning he could not get them on. All of one day we traversed the *cañada*, or gorge, of Cholitea, over a sandy bed of which the flood had not yet taken possession; another day, the Cañada del Zopilote. Our old friend of the North, the ailanthus, was common where other natural features were dreariest, and often filled the air insufferably with its odor. The three rivers crossing our way were swollen indeed, as had been predicted. When we came down to the wide Mescala it was opaque with red soil, and tearing past at twenty miles an hour. We were transported across it in a flat skiff guided by an oar. There was no plank to aid in the embarking of the horses, and one of them fell into such a panic as caused a terrific combat of well-nigh half an hour. He was finally thrown on board, more dead than alive, with lassoed legs.

"Ah, what a soul you have!" (*Ah, que alma tienes!*) cried Marcos fervently to his animal, which had well-nigh kicked us all into the river; and losing all policy in his rage, he begged to borrow my revolver, that he might despatch such a brute, of the ownership of which he was ashamed.

The Papagallo River succeeding, we crossed in a dugout, and the animals swam. I asked the colonel, in my simplicity, if this were not more or less like war, meaning the manner of travel, our foraging, half open-air way of sleeping, and the like. He smiled in disdain, and gave me a sketch of his campaigns in the day of the French usurpation. The rightful government had had at one time so little foothold in the country that it was called the Government of Paso del Norte, from the farthest town on the northern frontier, to which it was driven. Eating and sleeping seem hardly to have been the custom at all till, by an unremitting guerilla warfare, the tide was turned.

When we came to "the Cajones," however, he admitted that this was a little like war. We slipped and slid all one day down the Cajones—natural, or rather most wofully unnatural, steps in the solid rock, in the midst of a dark forest. The perpendiculars are three and four feet at a time, and often there are mud-holes at the bottom; and besides, there are vines that aim to take you under the chin. The sagacious steadiness of the pack-mules, picking their steps unaided in the most critical situations, was wonderful to see.

We met peons, in white cotton, coming up with barrels of ardent spirits on their shoulders, and we came to a full stop to allow the passage of jingling mule-trains of goods. The water ran in the path with us, courteously sharing its right of way. At one place it increased and converged from every side, and the wood was full of its murmurs, as if another universal deluge were coming to overwhelm us. It was full, also, of patches of pale-green light upon moss-covered stones, and limpid pools, and delicate ferns, like snow crystals turned vegetable. Now and then some white cascade stood out of the semi-obscurity like a beckoning Undine.

Among vegetable growths on the way was the gum-copal, not unlike our white birch. There was a tree, the *cuahuete*—if I may trust the pronunciation of Marcos—smooth, bronze-colored, and often of a repulsive red, as if full of blood. We saw a good many charming red-and-yellow flowers on a high bush, like butterflies alighted, and once or twice a sprig of heliotrope and a calla-lily. The *amape*, found in the villages, and somewhat like the chestnut, was the finest shade-tree. There was a notable absence throughout the journey of what we are accustomed to deem the essentially tropical features. Very often one might have been riding in the woods of Connecticut. There was not even a rank luxuriance of growth, just as there were no serpents nor the swarms of pestiferous insects (other than a few gnats) to have been expected. We saw once a couple of coyote wolves trotting demurely along, and, again, a large *iguana*, a harmless reptile, one of which I also noted later, gliding around an old bronze gun at the fort of Acapulco.

Birds I hardly recollect at all, except a white heron or two, charmingly reflected in an upland pool one early morning, and the *tecuses*, a kind of black-bird. Vincente pelted at these latter with small stones, by way of trying his aim. The organ-cactus, however, should be exempted from the complaint of a want of tropicality. It abounds thickly about the gorges and on the mountain slopes. Rising twenty-five feet and more in height, the plants are like seven-branched candlesticks of the Mosaic law, or spears of the gods hurled down and yet quivering in the earth. The fan-palm, too, must be excepted. It crops out on the bleak hill-sides as common as mullein-stalks with us. I can never respect it, in the conservatories, again. To see it thus was a kind of shock: it was like seeing some exotic belle of society masquerading as a kitchen wench. For one day before reaching the coast we had the cocoa-nut-palms. Nobody in the hamlets would get the fruit down for us except on a wholesale order, for munificent prices, which brought the cost above what it is in New York. There was often a shortage of the other fruits and commodities, as sugar, in the same way, in or near the very places where they grew.

Toward the concluding stages of the march we fell in

with another travelling-companion, an officer in the Customs service. When he learned that the colonel was going to the frontier, with a view, among other things, to suppress the extensive smuggling carried on there, he said, "You had better make your little $20,000 or $30,000 by protecting it. That will be much less trouble. The smugglers will buy up your soldiers, anyway; so it amounts to the same thing."

I must not represent that the colonel was always of an oppressively serious carriage. On the contrary, he developed a vein of humor, the more amusing from the simple good-faith of those at whose expense it was generally exercised.

"Do you charge no more than this to persons of our consideration, my good woman?" he said to a peasant, whose bill was modest, though but in keeping with the primitive nature of the accommodations. "It is a species of affront, as one might say. Do you comprehend that I am a colonel in the army, and this gentleman a learned traveller, noting down the manners and customs of foreign lands? When strangers of our position come this way again understand that double what you have demanded is the least that you should take."

The woman, abashed, received double her fee, and replied that she would bear the lesson in mind for the benefit of future comers.

Again, meeting three honest-faced Indian maids, with pitchers on their heads, going to the spring, he said, "Good-day, Marias!" and turning to me, in an aside, "Not that I know, from Adam, whether one of them is Maria or not."

He praised glaringly, to her face, as of exceeding comeliness, a servant-maid who wore gold ear-rings and necklace, and was, perhaps, not of more than average dumpiness and plainness. She waited on us at table at Tierra Colorada. The colonel desired to know her name.

"Victoria."

"Well are you named Victoria!" he cried, in simulated enthusiasm. "*Que cara simpatica!*" ("What a sympathetic face!") he repeated at intervals.

Meekly, and with no suspicion of raillery, she replied, each time, "*Mil gracias* ("A thousand thanks"), *señor.*"

"Give thanks rather to Heaven, which made you so, and not us, who do but recognize it," rejoined the colonel, piously.

At La Venta de Peregrino the night was hot, and it still rained, after having rained all day. A garden of bananas twenty feet tall grew next the basket-like house of canes where we stopped. We hung up our wet garments and properties on the poles of the thatched porch, or pavilion, till it resembled one of those very numerous national establishments, the *empeños*, or pawn-shops. Dogs, cats, donkeys, horses, pigs and fowls—"shooed" out, when they became too familiar, with an emphatic *Ooch-t!*—gathered under the same shelter, as if it had been a Noah's ark. We supped on pepper-sauce, tough chicken, frijoles, tortillas, cream-cheese, and coffee without milk, spread out upon a mat on the ground. The proprietor in person—a man in an embroidered shirt and cotton drawers, whose talk was not of the wisest sort—held pitch-pine splints to light the feast.

"Now, how does it happen, hombre," inquired the colonel, as if in a speculative way, "that a person of your fine appearance; a person of manners, intelligence, education, hospitality; a statesman, as one might say, who goes to Dos Arroyos to see who is going to be elected mayor" (the man had been there that day, as he told us), "with a fine house like this—how does it happen, I say, that you have not a table of any sort to serve two travellers a supper upon?"

"*Pos bien*," said the illiterate host, both pleased and flustered, scratching his head. "Tables? Yes, tables, now, to be sure. All that you say is very true, but there is a great scarcity of carpenters in this part of the country. *Si, escasen muncho* (Yes, they are mighty scarce), I can tell you."

III.

Two days after this we came down to Acapulco. It is a town for the most part of straggling huts, with a straggling thirty-five hundred of people. It has no vestiges of its antiquity but an old Spanish fort, after the order of Morro Castle, dismantled by Maximilian's French on their abandonment of the place.

Near the fort lay a couple of rusted rails in position on a bit of washed-out embankment, the beginning of a railroad inaugurated here with a flourish on the 5th of May, 1881. Having passed over the line, one would judge that it might be much more than dread of American aggressions which would prevent its speedy completion.

There was no small pleasure in discovering at last, like another Balboa, the Pacific Ocean, in boarding the fine steamer of the Pacific Mail Company, the *City of Grenada*, which had come her long jaunt from Panama northward, and re-establishing connection with the outer world.

With this, too, began an acquaintance with the western ports of Mexico. One of the semi-monthly steamers, rightly chosen, each month puts into them all. An idea of the country can thus be got which would not be possible otherwise without much greater fatigue and expense, but it is not at all as favorable as that presented by the interior.

Neither of the three lower ports is of great size. Acapulco has the most complete and charming harbor. Manzanillo is a small strip of a place, on the beach, built of wood, with quite an American look. The volcano of Colima appears inland, with a light cloud of smoke above it.

THE BELLS OF SAN BLAS.

San Blas is larger, but still hardly more than an extensive thatched village. On the bluff beside it exist the ruins of an ancient, substantial San Blas, shaken to pieces by an earthquake. Some old bronze bells from its church have been brought down and set up on some rude wooden trestles, on the ground in front of the poor chapel, without a belfry, which now fills the ecclesiastical needs of the place. This arrangement is sometimes referred to satirically as *la torre de San Blas*—the steeple of San

Blas. My slight sketch of these bells, made on a fly-leaf of my note-book in the first instance, came to have an importance far beyond its own merits. I have the gratification of knowing that it proved to be the source of nothing less than the last inspiration of Longfellow. The great and good poet died on the 24th of March, 1882. In his portfolio was found his final work, "The Bells of San Blas," dated March 15, which afterward appeared in the *Atlantic Monthly*. His memorandum-book contained a reference, as a suggestion for a poem, to the number and page of *Harper's Magazine* of the same month, in which the sketch was published.

At Mazatlan we are in a bustling harbor, and a well and handsomely built little city, with improvements and shops of the better sort, which other countries than Mexico might be satisfied with. It seems surprising, until we comprehend the extensive back country which is tributary to it, how a city of but fourteen thousand people can be justified in maintaining so elaborate a stock of goods.

We steam finally across the Gulf of California and up the coast of that peninsula which seems one of the remotest points of the globe. The days are calm and blue; the bold outlines of the shores offer constant novelty. An arbitrary line is passed: we have lost Mexico, but gained California—the richest and most marvellous of her provinces.

It is remarkable now to recall that, upon the accession of the Emperor Iturbide, Mexico boasted of being, with the exception of Russia and China, the most extensive empire in the world.

PART II.
THE LOST PROVINCES.

THE LOST PROVINCES.

XXII.

SAN FRANCISCO.

I.

It is the way of sea-coasts, as observed from the water, to maintain a close reserve. If they allow us a cliff or two, a suggestion of green forests, or a mountain in the background, it is as much as they do. All their natural projections, from a steamer's deck, retire into a straight line. "You have chosen your element," they seem to say, "and you shall not enjoy at once the pleasures of both. If you can do without me, so can I without you, and until you take the pains to disembark you shall know nothing of the attractions I purposely keep out of sight just over the surf-whitened margin."

The coast of California seems of even an especial moroseness in this respect. You pass some few islands, inlets at San Diego and Wilmington, the Santa Barbara Channel, and the bays of Santa Monica, San Luis, and Monterey; but for the most part the coast of the land of gold stretches on unbroken, low, brown, and bare. Search is vain for any suggestion of orange-grove or palm. It is foreign-looking to one who arrives from the east of the United States. Lions might come prowling down such slopes. It might be Morocco, and we, on our travels, some new Crusoe escaped in the long-boat, with Xury, from the Rover of Sallee, and afraid to land for the howlings of wild creatures.

If, in our Pacific Mail steamer, we were discovering the country for the first time—as every traveller does discover a new country for the first time, no matter what accounts he may have heard of it—we should try along without finding a single good harbor for four hundred and fifty miles, from San Diego, at the Mexican frontier, to San Francisco.

Then all at once comes an opening through bold Coast Range at the water's edge, and we are in the far-famed "Golden Gate." It is a mere eyelet—a strait, giving access to a wide expanse of bay. So happy is the opening, and commodious the shelter afforded, that the reversal of the churlishness prevailing up to this point seems miraculous.

There is no doubt, when once the site is understood, as to why San Francisco is located just where it is. It has the only natural harbor between Astoria, Oregon, to the north, and San Diego, to the south. It bears, besides, with this advantage, such a relation to the resources of the back country, that it could not escape a destiny of greatness.

It is not simply a bay upon which we have entered, but an inland sea, with a great commerce of its own. Immediately in front rise round-backed Goat Island and Angel Island, resembling monsters asleep; and terraced Alcatraz, with its citadel, as picturesque as a bit of Malta. Vistas open beyond on many sides, with gleams of light falling on white cities under lowering atmospheres of smoke. San Francisco, close at hand, piles up impressively on steep hills, its bristling structures covering their undulations sharply from numerous hills. The water-

ALCATRAZ ISLAND.

front is full of shipping. French and Russian and British frigates, and a Mexican gun-boat, are lying at anchor. Craft of all shapes and sizes cross one another's wakes in the harbor. The lateen-sails of Genoese and Maltese fishermen and the junks of Chinese shrimp-catchers are among them. Large ferry-boats, superior, as a rule, to those we are familiar with at the East, ply to Oakland, the Brooklyn of the scene—a city already of fifty thousand people; Alameda, with its esplanade of bathing pavilions; Berkeley, with its handsome university and institution for blind, deaf, and dumb; San Quentin, with its prison; and rustic Saucelito and San Rafael, under the dark shadow of Mount Tamalpais.

From Oakland projects an interminable pier, built by the Central Pacific Railway. A mile in length as it is, it was to have gone on to a junction with vacant Goat Island, which would then have been made a city also, and become the terminus of all transcontinental journeys. This project was stopped by violent opposition from property-holders on shore.

Patches of yellow, under the Presidio, are taken by our novices on the steamer for the "Sand-lots," famous in the Kearneyite agitations. The Presidio is a barracks, which was a fort and mission in the time of the first settlement by the Spaniards—to what slight extent they ever settled the place—in the year 1776. The man who has "been here before" plants himself squarely on the deck, pulls down a silk cap over his eyes, and explains that the Sand-lots are not the Presidio, but nothing less than the large yard of the new, unfinished City-hall, in the centre of town. But Kearneyism is dead and buried, he says—as the case proved—and there will be no chance to see one of these traditional assemblages.

He names for us the various hills, and points out the

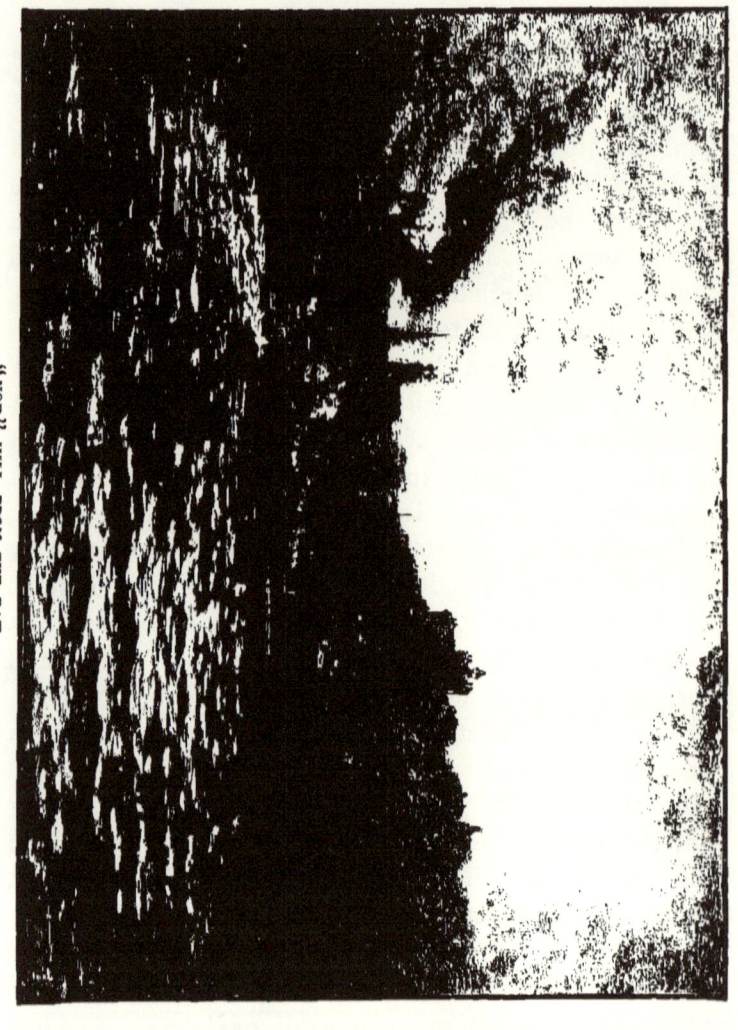
"NOB" HILL, FROM THE BAY.

Palace Hotel, the Market Street shot-tower, and the homes of some of the great millionnaires who have made such a stir in their day and generation. Three or four of these latter top California, or "Nob," Hill, with a prominence in keeping with their owners' station. They are those of the railroad kings, Crocker, Stanford, and Hopkins—the mining kings having up to this time expended their principal building efforts in the country. "Nob" Hill is three hundred feet high, plebeian Telegraph Hill nearly as much, and Russian Hill, to the west—the latest precinct taken into favor for fine residences—three hundred and sixty. Murray Hill, New York, be it noted, is but seventy-eight. The riff-raff of Telegraph Hill climb, as is seen, by a multitude of wooden stairways; but how in the world do the Crœsuses get up to their habitations, which cut the sky-line so imposingly? We shall see.

The city does not begin directly at the ocean, but a mile or two within. It follows the inner shore of a long, narrow peninsula which comes from the south to meet one coming from the north, and forms with it the strait and bay.

It is, indeed, an inland sea, this bay. You go southward upon it thirty miles, northward as far, and thirty miles north-eastward to the Straits of Carquinez—which has Benicia on one side, and Martinez, the point of departure for ascent of the peak of Mount Diablo, on the other. Through these straits you pass, again, into Suisun Bay, which receives the waters of the Sacramento and San Joaquin rivers, and is itself some twenty miles in extent.

II.

You are struck, on coming ashore from Mexico, with the excessive thinness of everything American. Our belongings seem all of a piece with our light-running machinery, with the spider lines of you American buggy waiting for its owner. We evade Nature by a deft trick, and do not obstinately oppose her. There the old walls were as solid yet as the everlasting hills; here we seemed to be living in flying-machines.

How strange, arriving from the other side of the world, to find people lining the dock dressed in the common way, and chattering the common speech, even to the latest bits of slang! A China steamer, however, had come in along-side just before us, and supplied a novel element of foreignness. Almond-eyed Celestials, in blue blouses, swarmed her decks and poured down her sides. Groups were loaded into express-wagons, and driven away uptown in charge of friends come down to meet them. Others trudged stoutly on foot, with their effects deposited in a pair of wicker baskets, at the ends of a long bamboo on their shoulders. This way of carrying burdens is constantly met with. The vegetable dealers hawk thus their wares from house to house, and present the aspect of the figures in cuts of the tea-fields. It is poor travelling when the curiosity alone and not the imagination is gratified, and San Francisco promises ample material for both.

Had we come in the gold days of '49 we should have landed some half-dozen blocks farther inland than to-day. By so much has the water-front since been extended and built into a solid commercial quarter. The 'Forty-niners found but a scanty strip of sand at the base of the steep hills.

Why, then, did they stop here, and build their city at such infinite pains and expense, instead of seeking a more convenient site elsewhere? There is, or was, some even more serious objection to all other locations. At Oakland, insufficient depth of water; at Saucelito, where whalers, Russian and other, had been accustomed to refit, Tamalpais, 2700 feet high, as against Telegraph Hill, but 300. Distant Benicia and Vallejo—the latter now the naval station of the Pacific Coast, and once briefly the capital of the State—were much too far away. Steam was little in use. The greater part of the ships came under sail, and there were no tugs to pull them. They must be able to get in and out with all greatest attainable expedition.

Such ships as these were, according to the accounts we have of them! The most antiquated and dangerous hulks were furbished up once more for this last voyage. The eager humanity they carried took little heed of perils and discomforts so they were but on the way to the goal to which all adventurous spirits turned. When the port was still but a beggarly scattering of huts and tents it could muster two hundred sail, good and bad, at once. Many of them never got out again. It was not on account of nautical difficulties, but partly because they had no return cargoes, and principally because their crews ran away from them to the mines the moment foot touched shore. Certain craft were beached and converted into dwellings; others, utilized for a time as warehouses, rotted at their moorings, and to-day form "made ground." The remarkable city to which they came, which had eight hundred and fifty souls in 1848, and twenty thousand in '49, has now, in an existence of thirty-four years, three hundred thousand.

The buildings on the level made ground stand generally on foundations of piling. The practice prevails, too, of tying them well together with iron rods, against the jar of the occasional earthquake, which is among San Francisco's idiosyncrasies. It is proposed to improve the water-front with a continuous, massive sea-wall, and a portion of this is already built. Extensive yards of attractive redwood lumber, which resembles cedar, and warehouses for grain, are seen. The elevator system, owing to lack of ships for properly carrying grain in bulk, is nowhere in use throughout California.

We reach next an area given up to heavy traffic in the fruits and produce of the country. Battery and Sansome streets succeeding are lined with large wholesale drygoods houses similar to those in the greater Eastern cities. Montgomery Street shows stately office buildings, exchanges, and hotels. Kearney Street has been hitherto the chief site of the more elegant retail trade. Its prestige is passing, however, to Market Street, a wide thoroughfare which recalls State Street, Chicago. Having unlimited room for extension in the north and south direction of the peninsula, whereas the others named are contracted, Market Street is to be San Francisco's Broadway of the future.

The financial centre is contained in the area of two blocks, between California and Bush, Sansome and Montgomery Streets. Here are those institutions whose great transactions and singular history are unknown now to but few parts of the world.

The Nevada Bank, financial lever of the Bonanza kings, and point from which has been supposed to emanate all the weightiest influences connected with mining matters, is a four-story and Mansard iron building, with the usual classic "orders." The Bank of California, whence the brilliant Ralston rushed forth from his troubles to drown himself in the bay, is two stories, of "blue stone," of a pleasant color, and exceedingly sharp, agreeable cutting. The Merchants' Exchange, erected so long ago as 1867, is a very ornate, town-hall-looking

CALIFORNIA STREET, SAN FRANCISCO.

building, of iron and stone, dark-colored, with a clocktower in the centre. It is adjoined by the Safe Deposit Company, in a similar style, in the basement of which a glimpse is to be had of a splendid steel treasure-chamber, with a dozen life-size men in armor, gilded.

The large and agreeably proportioned Stock Exchange, on Pine Street, is of gray granite, with numerous polished columns. The board-room within is an amphitheatre, and a bronze railing protects the circle of seats. With its agreeable illumination and neat furniture, including Axminster rugs, it presents a much more homelike aspect than is the rule with such places. Mining stocks exclusively are dealt in.

It is quiet enough now. We have fallen upon evil days. Capitalists have withdrawn their millions to the East; ships come only in ballast, for grain, instead of with valuable exchange cargoes, and charge rates almost prohibitory; there is not one "turn-out" now on the Cliff House road where there were formerly a dozen; and real estate has shrunk fifty per cent.—if in some places it have any value at all.

This board was once the theatre of a speculative movement which took hold upon the community like madness. The aggregate value of the mining stocks on the list, at the period of highest prices, in the year 1875, was, in round numbers, $282,000,000. The aggregate value of the same stocks in the summer of 1881 was but $17,000,-000. There had occurred a shrinkage of $265,000,000, or more than fifteen times the total value surviving.

What had happened? The "bottom had dropped out" of the famous "Comstocks," perhaps the richest mines known to history. "Consolidated Virginia," valued at $75,000,000, was now worth less than $1,000,000. "Sierra Nevada" fell from $27,000,000 to $825,000. But the greatest shrinkage of all was in "California." This unhappy stock shrank from $84,000,000 to $351,000.

These figures explain a depression the vestiges of which, though the ruinous crisis has long passed, still remain. The stock-gambling mania possessed the community without distinction of station, and hardly of age or sex, and when the bubble broke there was reason enough for gloom with all who had laid up their treasure in such unstable form.

Some of the earlier buildings, now flat, thin, and unornamental, were obtained at expense quite out of proportion. The stone for the old City Hall was brought expressly from Australia; that of the Wells-Fargo building, and the Union Club, from China. The granite of the Branch Mint, a fine, classic design, was dressed in Oregon. The newer structures exhibit all the varieties of form and color in which the modern decorative taste delights. The material for most is procured in the State itself.

The idea of being in a remote part of the world is kept before you in many ways. Here is a sign of the "New Zealand Insurance Company." Fancy New Zealand, where a cannibal population was lately eating missionaries, sending us over its insurance companies! Here is the Alaska Commercial Company, the Bank of British Columbia; and here, its inscription gilded in Chinese as well as English, the Hong-Kong and Shanghai Banking Company. An occasional building is without the usual entrance-doors, its staircase, in the comparative mildness of the climate, left as open as the street.

A system of alleys passes among the colossal structures, and these abound in refreshment resorts—"The Dividend Saloon," "Our Jacob," "The Comstock Exchange," and "The New Idea"—to which the hastening business men repair in intervals of their labors. The San Francisco boot-blacks, a model to their class, are neatly uniformed men instead of ragged urchins. Favored by the climate, they establish their rows of easy-chairs on platforms under a canvas awning, have a newspaper and the gossip for you while you wait, and somewhat usurp the place so long sacred to the barber.

LONE MOUNTAIN.

The corner of California and Montgomery Streets may be considered one of two focal points in San Francisco; the "Lotta Fountain" is the other.

The Lotta Fountain—a tawdry, little, cast-iron affair, presented to the city by the actress after whom it is named—has been given a place of distinguished honor. Five important streets radiate from it. Its pedestal is a place where the timid seek refuge when entangled in the throng of vehicles. Market Street extends to the Oakland Ferry one way, and past the Mechanics' Institute and pleasure resort of Woodward's Garden to the distant Mission Hills in the other. Geary Street takes you, by a "cable road," westward to Lone Mountain, around which all the cemeteries are grouped, and Golden Gate Park, stretching to the ocean. On the top of Lone Mountain stands up to view from far and wide a dark cross, which weirdly recalls that of Calvary. Third Street, a thoroughfare of working-people, abounding in small restaurants, markets, and "tin-type" galleries, leads to the water at a different angle from Market. Finally, Kearney Street debouches also at the Lotta Fountain, and Montgomery terminates but a few steps below.

The Palace Hotel, vast, drab-colored, of iron and stuccoed brick, looms up nine stories in height on Market Street, and closes the vista from Montgomery. Studded with bay-windows, it has the air of a mammoth bird-cage. The San Franciscan, wherever met with, never fails to boast of it as the most stupendous thing of its kind in the world. With the conviction that size is not always the particular in which our hotels, like some of our communities, most need improvement, I should say that perfection had hardly yet been reached.

Within it is more satisfactory. At night an electric light strikes upon many tiers of columns, as white as paint can make them, in a large glass-roofed court, with an effect quite fairy-like and Parisian. Twice a week a band plays there, and the guests promenade up and down their galleries or look over the balustrade. In the bottom there are flowers, people sitting in chairs, and carriages stand in a circular, asphalt-paved driveway.

Though the resident of San Francisco feels called upon

to complain of its present stagnation, the bare existence of such a place strikes the new-comer with amazement.

Its air is not ephemeral, but of a fine, massive gravity. Its shops are filled with costly goods, its streets with comely, beautifully dressed women. It has an art and literature. Private galleries contain foreign modern pictures of the best class. Some local artists have made for themselves a more than local reputation. There is a well-attended "School of Design," which has already graduated several pupils whose talent has been recognized abroad. The "Mercantile Library" is the most handsome and complete in its appointments of any American city.

San Francisco "society," though a trifle bizarre in the use of its newly acquired wealth, has an under-stratum of unexceptionable refinement. Its most bizarre side, too, is certainly approved of in Europe, where its magnates entertain kings and give their daughters in marriage to lofty titles.

The European traveller who visits "the land of Barnum" and "of Washington" with literary intent must be cruelly broken up by what he will find here. Such a place should be a vast, motley camp, as it is known to European travellers that most American cities should be. With its thirty-three years, and its heterogeneous elements, it should exhibit a combination of squalor and mushroom splendor. The wretched shanty should elbow the vulgar palace, a democratic boorishness of manners, blazing in diamonds, the faint, refined natures that by any chance have ventured into such a Babel. But, alas! we live in an age of expedition, of labor-saving inventions. With unlimited means, such as here enjoyed, the work of years is condensed into months. Camp there is none, but a luxurious city, presenting all the ordinary characteristics of civilization.

An association comprising in a genial way most of the best elements of San Francisco is the Bohemian Club. It is found taking a very creditable interest in literature and the arts—it numbering the professionals and amateurs in these branches in its membership—and entertains and welcomes distinguished strangers. A monthly entertainment of a light, composite character is held, known as a "Jinks." The grand festival of the year, however, is a "High Jinks," which takes the form of an excursion into the country. The principal ceremonial of the High Jinks has sometimes been held at night, in masquerade costume, among the Big Trees, the enormous redwoods of Sonoma County, to the northward. It may well be believed that the doings on these occasions are as fantastic and amusing as the merry inventions of a couple of hundred bright social spirits can make them.

III.

A population of three hundred thousand souls is not extraordinary now, as populations go, but there are certain things which make San Francisco cosmopolitan beyond its actual size. An entirely new commercial situation gives rise to a new *milieu*. San Francisco faces toward Asia, the great English-speaking colonies of Oceanica, and the islands of the sea, as New York faces Europe. It enjoys already a trade with the Orient amounting to ten millions per annum in imports and eight millions in exports. The possibilities of this trade, extended among the teeming populations in the cradle of the human race, seem almost limitless. A way will be found sooner or later out of the imbroglio into which our inexperience has plunged us on the Chinese question, and communication will flow unimpeded. In countries sepa-

"HIGH JINKS" OF THE BOHEMIAN CLUB AMONG THE BIG TREES.

rated by water, and demanding each other's productions, cities arise at the places of transfer, and proportioned to its volume; and for all this San Francisco has one of the most remarkable of situations.

The Oriental trade is but a small item in the total. It has ships, besides those bound for the Eastern and European ports, going out to the British and Russian possessions in the North, Mexico, Central and South America, Tahiti, Feejee, Manila, the Sandwich and Friendly Islands—to all those far-off points in the South Pacific which now in their turn promise to shine with the light of civilization and become powers of the earth.

Coals are burned at firesides—not of the most desirable quality, it must be confessed—which come from the coast once characterized by the poet in the line—

"The wolf's long howl on Oonalaska's shore."

Seventy millions pounds of sugar a year are brought from those Sandwich Islands which slew Captain Cook, now a civilized, modern state. But it is particularly Australasia, and our coming relations with it, that awaken admiring speculations. Melbourne, Australia, has already more than 280,000 people, Sydney 225,000, while along the coasts of that once cannibal New Zealand, now sending us its insurance companies, scatter also a line of flourishing cities: Dunedin, with its 43,000 people; Auckland, with 40,000; Christchurch, 32,000; Wellington, 22,000; and I know not how many others.

Astoria and Portland, in Oregon, San Diego, and, no doubt, ports to be created in time along the Mexican shores, will receive a share of these new influences in the world, but at San Francisco they touch us first and nearest.

There is a definite fascination in coming to the "jumping-off place," the final verge of the latest of the continents. An excellent situation in which to feel it is to lie on the brown heather at the point above the Golden Gate —though it is a raw and gusty place in which to lie too long—or to look down from the parapeted road or piazza of the Cliff House.

Here practically nothing intervenes between you and Japan, except we make mention of the clump of Seal Rocks, upon which the grouty sea-lions are floundering and roaring, down there in the surf in front.

"Ah! when a man has travelled," says Thoreau, "when he has robbed the horizon of his native fields of its mystery, tarnished the blue of distant mountains with his feet, he may begin to think of another world."

Very well. Perhaps it may do a man no harm to think of another world now and then, if not upon one pretext, on another. At evening the Golden Gate is the way to the sunset. The orb of day settles into the sea at the end of the gleaming strait, precisely in that East where we always figure it to ourselves as rising in the morning. The great circle is at last complete; and, as the extremes of every kind, even of love and hate, are said to be identical, the old, quiescent East has become the bound of the new, impetuous West.

"What is a world to do," you idly ask, "when it has no longer a West? How is it to get on without that vague open region on its borders, always the safety-valve and outlet for surplus population and uneasy spirits?"

"But when the race has quite arrived at this farther shore, will it stop here? or will it possibly start round the world again? Will it go on yet many times more, always beginning with the highest perfection yet attained, weaker types dying out in front to make room, till it shall become in its march a dazzling army of light?

GOLDEN GATE, FROM GOAT ISLAND.

Is a millennium, perchance, to be reached in this cumulative way, as the power of a magnet is increased by the number of turns of the helix?"

"The sentiment of gain," I say, continuing these wise speculations, "has been the leading factor in drawing the nations around the globe. Gold has been dangled as a bait: first, the hope of it by conquest; later, in mines of the precious metals. It has danced, Ariel-like, will-o'-the-wisp-like, before them. Tantalized, disappointed, after floundering on a ways, they have paused to develop the lands upon which they found themselves.

"But now at length, when the vacant spaces are full, and the need of subterfuge exhausted, the bait is cast down, to be gorged upon by those who find it. Never before, till '49, were its followers rewarded with such unstinted liberality. The treasure of the earth seemed piled up in the fastnesses of the far Pacific."

I recall that their yield since the year 1848 has reached the sum of $2,100,000,000, and is still going on at $80,000,000 a year. Gold, scattered at first in the very sands, was later washed out of the gravel-banks, by the hydraulic process, and later yet got by crushing the quartz rock. When gold began to diminish it was followed by silver. The great "Bonanza" mines of Nevada were discovered. "Consolidated Virginia" alone produced $65,000,000 in seven years.

IV.

What fabulous sums besides—to go back to town—the managers made by the ingenious process of "milking the market" I do not undertake to compute. The prices of this celebrated stock at successive dates, not far apart, were: first, $17 a share; then $1; $110; $42; $700; and then, in the final collapse, in 1875, little or nothing at all.

I have seen a poor saloon called the "Auction Lunch," on Washington Street, near the Post-office, said to have been kept by the once barkeepers, Flood and O'Brien, who attained such a splendid prosperity. There is no historic tablet over the door, but one naturally looks with reverence at the place where the beginning of such things could be. The proprietors of the "Auction Lunch" were in the habit of taking gold-dust occasionally in a friendly way from miners, for safe-keeping while the owners were enjoying themselves about town. It was from such persons that they obtained the "points" which resulted in their getting possession first of "Hale and Norcross," and then of the greater part of the properties of the Comstock lode.

I fell in with a professed friend of theirs of early times, whose fortunes had not mended at all at the same pace. He descanted on the inequalities of fate, and what he termed "bull-dog" luck.

He could prove that Flood and O'Brien were not even good business men—"though Jimmy Flood does go about with a wise air," he said, "and Billy O'Brien left, at his death, half a million dollars to each of eight or ten nieces."

There is hardly a limit to the exceptional characters and exceptional doings to be heard of in San Francisco. Though the city affect—or has been driven into—a quiescent air now, it has hardly ever done anything like any other place. It began with the wild Argonauts of '49, whom Bret Harte has so strikingly portrayed. It had had six great fires, which destroyed property to the amount of $23,000,000, when yet less than three years of age. It was ruled for months, in the year 1856, by a vigilance committee, which rid it of eight hundred evil-doers of one sort and another, the worst by summary execution, the rest by banishment.

The politics of the State before the war were Democratic, with a rather strong Southern bias. There was a long feud between the two great Senatorial paladins, Broderick and Gwin, which resulted in the death of Broderick by the duelling-pistol of one of the partisans of the latter. There was the long fight and a final deliverance from an incubus of forged Spanish land titles, the manufacture of which "had become a business and a trade," and which covered the area of the city many times over. Then came the war, and the peculiarities growing out of the retention of a solid currency, while the rest of the country was deluged with a depreciated paper.

The brilliant period, later, when the Bonanza mines were pouring out their floods of riches, and the favorite stocks were running delightfully up and down the gamut from $1 to $700 a share, was followed, as I have said, by a depression of the deepest dye. In the unbearable disappointment of their losses, and the stagnation of trade, a part of the community snatched at a theory held out to them by demagogues, that it was their political institutions which were somehow to blame. Upon this basis a singular new party, wild and half-communistic in character, arose, and met with a brief success. The truckman, Denis Kearney, was its Caius Gracchus or Watt Tyler, and set it in motion with blasphemous mouthings from an improvised tribune in the Sand-lots. It elected a mayor who was at the same time a Baptist preacher. This mayor's son—preacher, too—rode up one day and assassinated at his own door an editor who had passed strictures on their course. The party voted a new constitution, which was thought to be a prelude to universal confiscation, and capitalists fled before it in alarm.

And, finally, this remarkable city, having become the

recipient of a Chinese immigration which has given to a part of it the aspect of a portion of the Flowery Kingdom, has been agitated by fears of complete subversion under Orientalism, and has originated new problems for political economy and international law.

After but a tithe of such violent and novel experiences any city would be glad to rest awhile. San Francisco seems entering upon a new period, and likely to do things henceforth more in the normal way. There has been a time of contemplation, and the lessons of the past have struck in. As things have slowly improved the gloom of the reaction has disappeared after the unhealthy inflation that gave it birth. The new political craze was of but short duration. I never saw anywhere so quietly conducted an election as that of the last autumn, which dismissed the Kearney-Kalloch faction from power. A special provision prevents the approach of any person but the voter immediately engaged within one hundred feet of a polling-place. I had rather expected to see dead and maimed Chinamen lying at every corner, or fleeing before infuriated crowds. But though San Franciscans entertain beliefs of their own as to the undesirability of a great Chinese immigration, during a long stay I neither saw nor heard of an attempt to molest any individual on account of it.

The new constitution itself proved a harmless bugaboo. It is a gratifying tribute, in fact, to native common-sense and Anglo-Saxon ideas that this instrument, produced in a time of great excitement, and, as was charged, with the most subversive intentions, should not only contain so little that is dangerous, but so much in a high degree commendable. It does not harm property. Frightened capital may return with entire safety. I profess myself so far a person of incendiary opinions as to hold that an honest directness of purpose in this new constitution, its effort to simplify legislation and sweep away embarrassments, often maintained much more in the interest of legislator and lawyer than the public good, is well worthy of imitation elsewhere.

Physical and commercial conditions are also changing. Life hereafter will depend less upon spasmodic "finds," and more on the humdrum and legitimate industries. Mining, though the supply of treasure, with improved machinery, still holds out in a uniform way, takes a lesser rank. Agriculture and manufactures come every day more to the front. California produces an annual wheat crop of $50,000,000, a wool crop of $10,000,000, wines to the amount of $4,000,000, and fruits worth as much more, though these last two branches are but in their infancy. Of the greater part of all this San Francisco is the *entrepôt*.

The smoke of the soft coals of Alaska, Oregon, and Australia too may be allowed to thicken the air to some purpose, since it produces manufactures to the amount of $75,000,000 per annum.

XXIII.

SAN FRANCISCO (Continued).

I.

KEARNEY STREET (sharing its distinction now with Market Street) is, in sunshiny weather, the promenade of all the leisurely and well-dressed. It abounds in jewellers, who often combine the business of pawnbroking with the other, and are fond of prefixing "Uncle" to their names. Thus, "Uncle Johnson," "Uncle Jackson," or "Uncle Thompson," all along the way, make a genial proffer of their hospitable service. There are shops of Chinese and Japanese goods, though this is not the regular quarter, and "Assiamull and Wassiamull" invite us to inspect the goods of the East Indies.

Perhaps European foreigners of distinction—English lords, M.P.'s, and younger sons, German barons and Russian princes—on their way round the world, are not more numerous than in New York, but they seem more numerous in proportion. The books of the Palace Hotel are seldom free of them, and they are detected, at a glance, strolling on the streets or gazing at the large photographs of the Yosemite Valley and the Big Trees which hang at prominent corners.

There is a genial feeling about Kearney Street, which arises, I think, from its being level—at the foot of the steep hills. The temptation is to linger there as long as possible. The instant you leave it for the residence portion of town you have to begin a back-breaking climb. The ascent is like going up-stairs, and nothing less.

The San Francisco householder of means is "like the herald Mercury new-lighted on a heaven-kissing hill." How in the world, I have asked, does he get up there? Well, by the Cable road. I consider the Cable road one of the very foremost in the list of curiosities, though I have refrained from bringing it forward till now. It is a peculiar kind of tramway, useful also on a level, but invented for the purpose of overcoming steep elevations.

Two cars, coupled, are seen moving, at a high rate of speed, without jar and in perfect safety, up and down all these extraordinary undulations of ground. There is no horse, no steam, no vestige of machinery, no ostensible means of locomotion of any kind. The astonished comment of the Chinaman, observing this marvel for the first time, may be worth repeating once more, old as it is:

"Melican man's wagon, no pushee, no pullee; go topside hill like flashee."

The solution of the mystery is an endless wire cable hidden in a box in the road-bed, and turning over a great wheel in an engine-house at the top of the hill. The foremost of the two cars is provided with a grip, or pincers, running underneath in a continuous crevice in the box with the cable. When the conductor wishes to go on he clutches with his grip the cable; when he wishes to stop he lets go and puts on a brake. There is no snow and ice to clog the central crevice, which, by the necessities of the case, must be open. The system has been applied, however, with emendations, in Chicago, and is about to be on the great Brooklyn Bridge, at New York.

The great houses on the hill, like almost all the residences of the city, are of wood. It seems a pity, considering the money spent, that this should be so. It is attributed to the superior warmth and dryness of wood in so moist and cool a climate, and also to its security against the shock of earthquakes. Whatever be the reason, the San Francisco Crœsuses have reared for themselves palaces which might be swept off at a breath and leave no trace of their existence. Their architecture has nothing to commend it to favor. They are large, rather over-ornate, and of no particular style.

The Hopkins residence—a costly Gothic château, carried out also in wood—may be excepted from this description. The basement stories, however, are of stone, and there is enough work in these and foundations to build many a first-class Eastern mansion. To prepare sites for habitations on the steep hills has been an enormous labor and expense. The part played by retaining-walls, terraces, and staircases is extraordinary. The merest wooden cottage is often prefaced by works which outweigh its own importance a dozen to one.

When a peerage is drawn up for San Francisco, the grader will follow in rank the railroad-builder and the miner. To hardly anybody else has such an amount of lucrative employment been open. What a cutting and filling! what gravelling and paving!

Striking freaks of surface and arrangement result. The city might have been terraced up, like Genoa, or Naples above the Chiaja. It is picturesque still, in the thin, American way, through the absolute force of circumstances. You enter the retaining-walls of stone or plank through door-ways or grated archways like the postern-gates of castles. You pass up stone steps in tunnels or vine-covered arbors within these; or zigzag from landing to landing of long, wooden stairways, without. Odd little terrace streets and "places," as Charles Place, with bits of gardens, are found sandwiched between the regular formation. A wide thoroughfare, Second Street —cut through Rincon Hill, the Nob Hill of a former day, to afford access to water for vehicles—has been the occasion of leaving isolated, high and dry, some few old houses, with cypress-trees about them, approached by wooden staircases almost interminable. Dark at sunset against a red sky, for instance, they present effects to delight the heart of an etcher.

HIGH-GRADE RESIDENCES.

In this line, however, nothing is equal to Telegraph Hill, which bristles with the make-shift contrivances of a much humbler population. Bret Harte lived there at one time, and asserts that the goats used to browse on his pots of geranium in the second-story windows. They also pranced on the roof at night in such a way that a new-comer thought there had been a fine thunder-storm. Elsewhere, instead of precipices, you meet with chasms.

Looking down from the roadway, you will see some poor figure of a woman sewing in a bay-window which was once filled with air and sunshine, but now commands only a patch of mildewed wall.

The views from the hills are of no common order. As you rise on the Cable road you hang in the air above the body of the city, and above the harbor and its environment. The Clay Street road, one of the steepest, passes through the Chinese quarter. Half-way up an ensign, of a blue-and-crimson dragon on an orange field, on the Chinese Consulate-general, flies, a bright bit of color in the foreground. The bay, far below the eye, has an opaque look. On some rare days it is very blue in color, but oftener it is of slate or greenish gray. Passing vessels criss-cross their wakes in white upon the green like pencils on a slate.

The atmosphere above it is rarely clear. Some lurking wisp of fog at best is generally stealing in at the Golden Gate, or under dark Tamalpais, watching to rush over and seize upon the city. An obscurity, part of fog and part of smoke, hovers in areas, now enveloping only the town, again the prospect, so that nothing can be seen, though the town itself be free. Now it lifts momentarily from the horizon for glimpses of distant islands and cities, and the peak of Mount Diablo, thirty miles away, and shuts down as suddenly as if these were but figments of a vision.

The view down upon the lights at night is particularly striking. Set in constellations, or radiating in formal lines, they are like the bivouac of a great army. It might be the hosts of Armageddon were encamped round about awaiting the dawn. For several days, from California Street Hill, there was the spectacle of a devastating fire in the woods of Mount Tamalpais. Its dark smoke rendered the sunsets lurid and ominous, and at night the burning mountain, reflected in the bay, was a more terrible Vesuvius or Hecla.

II.

One is hardly supposed to "travel" as yet in America as in Europe. We make our journeys here for definite objects, chiefly on business. No doubt, if we could bring ourselves to the same receptive frame of mind, the same readiness to be amused by odds-and-ends of experience, a good deal the same kind of pleasure could be got out of it as there. San Francisco at least appears to afford a few of exactly the same details which receive the attention of the leisurely abroad.

Italian fishermen eat macaroni, and drink red wine, and wait upon the tides, about the vicinity of Broadway and Front Streets. The Italian colony, for the rest, is pretty numerous. The part that remains on shore is chiefly composed of grocers, butchers, and restaurateurs. Chinese shrimp-catchers are found in the cove at Potrero, behind the large new manufacturing buildings of that quarter, and again at San Bruno Point, twelve miles down the bay. Their boats and junks are not on a large scale, but display the usual peculiarities of their nautical architecture.

The French colony is also numerous, and the language heard continually on the street. Taking advantage of the variety and excellence of supplies in the markets, French restaurants furnish repasts—including a half-bottle of wine of the country—of extraordinary cheapness. A considerable Mexican and Spanish contingent mingles also with the Italians, along Upper Dupont, Vallejo, and Green Streets. Shops with such titles as

La Sorpresa and the *Tienda Mexicana* adjoin the *Unità d'Italia* and the *Roma* saloon. A Mexican militia company turns out, under the green, white, and red tricolor, on every anniversary of the national independence, the 16th of September. During the Carnival season a form of entertainment known as "Cascarone parties" prevails among the Spanish residents. The participants pelt one another with egg-shells filled with gilt and colored papers. Sometimes a canvas fort is erected in the street, and attacked and defended by means of these missiles and handfuls of flour. Such Spanish life as there is can hardly be said to have remained from the early days, since the Spanish settlement at best was infinitesimal. It has been attracted here in the mean time like other immigration. A dusky mother, smoking a cigarette, in a hammock, in a palm-thatched hut, on the Acapulco trail, told me of a son who had gone to San Francisco twenty years before and become a carpenter there. He had forgotten now, she heard, even how to speak his native language.

The Latin race seems to have been especially attracted to the country of a mild climate and original traditions like their own. But German and Scandinavian names too on the sign-boards—Russian Ivanovich and Abramovich, and Hungarian Haraszthy—show that no one blood or influence has exclusive sway. There appears to be an unusually free intermingling and giving in marriage among these various components. They are less clannish than with us. Lady Wortley Montagu remarked, at Constantinople, some hundred years ago, a similar fusion, and believed it a reason for a debased and mongrel race. But a very different class of blood mingles here from that of Orientals at Constantinople. Our much more cheerful theory is, that we are to combine the best qual-

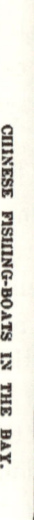

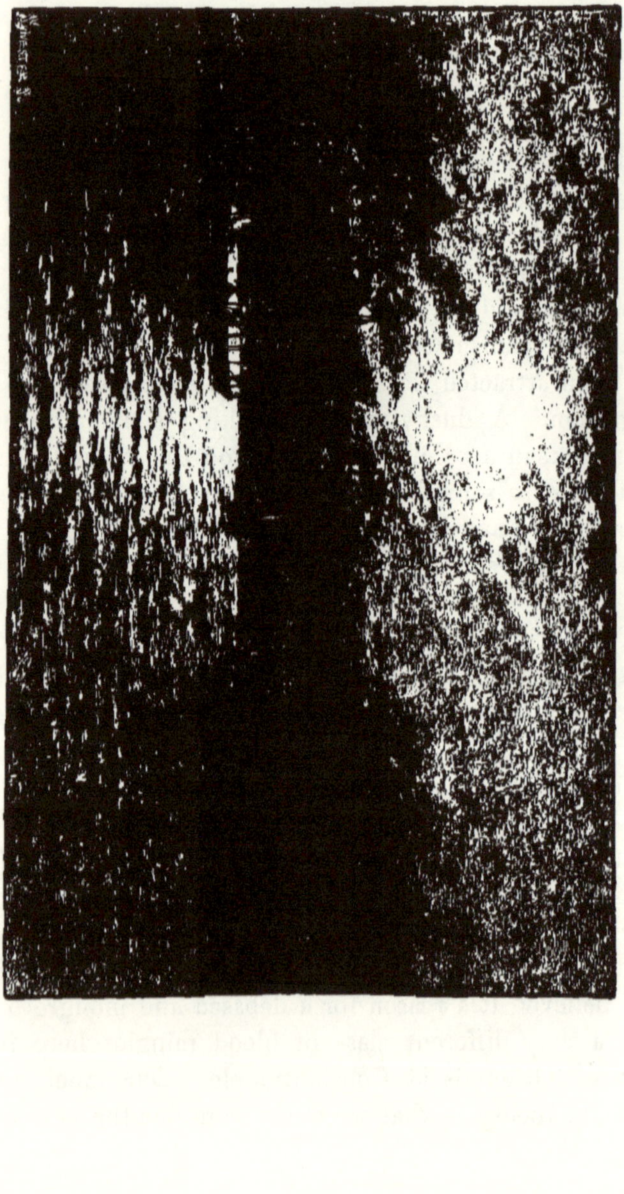

CHINESE FISHING-BOATS IN THE BAY.

ities, the hardihood and good looks of all, while eliminating their defects. Certainly the bright, intelligent aspect of the children of San Francisco does nothing as yet to discredit such a theory.

Such vestiges of '49 as yet remain are extremely few. I confess to surprise as well at the slightness of the historic records at the Pioneer Society. I make little doubt that they could be easily paralleled in many other libraries of the country. "North Beach," under Telegraph Hill, may be visited both for its memories and present aspect of picturesque ruin. It is where the pioneer ships landed. Hence, also, the ill-fated Ralston swam out into the bay, and here are the remains of "Harry Meigs's Wharf." Harry Meigs was a famous prototype of Ralston's in the Fifties. Defeated in brilliant financial schemes, and having endeavored to save his defeat by forgery, he was obliged to take flight. He chartered a schooner to take him to the South Sea Islands, which lay off the wharf for him at midnight.

"This is hell," he is reported to have said as he stepped on board, expressing thus his Lucifer-like sense of humiliation and downfall.

He did not remain long at the South Sea Islands, but sailed for Peru. There he began the world again, built all the railways of that republic, became a great millionaire, sent back and paid all his debts, and was divested, by act of Legislature, so far as legislation could do it, of the stigma of his crimes. His story is by no means a good one to hold up to the emulation of youth, but it is romantic, and in some sense characteristic of California.

The blackened old pier is a dumping-place for city refuse now, and swarms of *chiffoniers* gather around it to pick out such scraps of value as they may before they are washed away by the daily tides.

The leading streets of San Francisco commemorate the pioneers of State or place. A newer series adopts the names of the States of the Union, and simple numbers, which are carried already to Forty-fifth, for avenues, and Thirtieth for streets. The fast-growing, tough, fragrant, but scrawny, eucalyptus is much in use as a shade-tree. In the door-yards grow cypresses, the Spanish-bayonet, and the ordinary flowers, needing a great deal of sprinkling to keep them in good order.

The San Francisco school of writers, developed in the successful days of the *Overland Monthly*, have not made much use of the city itself in their literature. Bret Harte confined his local range to the doings of certain small boys, some "Sidewalkings," and the disagreeable features of the climate, in "Neighborhoods I Have Moved From." It was from Folsom Street that the adventurous Master Charles Summerton, aged five, set out for his great expedition to Van Dieman's Land, by way of the Second and Market Street cars. I had occasion to visit Folsom Street sometimes, and even this slight incident—such is the potency of the literary touch—has given it a genial interest which many others, as good in appearance, and even stately Van Ness Avenue, on the other side of town— very much better—by no means share.

III.

San Francisco offers, in my view, the advantage of saving a trip around the world. Whoever, having seen Europe, shrinks from farther wanderings may derive here from a compact Chinese city of 30,000 souls such an idea of the life and doings of the Celestial Empire as may appease curiosity and take the place of a voyage to the Orient.

The Chinese immigrants, it is true, rarely erect buildings of their own, but fit themselves to what they find. They fit themselves in with all their peculiar industries, their smells of tobacco and cooking-oil, their red and yellow signs and hand-bills, opium pipes, high-soled slippers, sticks of India ink, silver pins, and packets of face-powder, their fruits and fish, their curious groceries and more curious butcher's meat—they have fitted all this into the Yankee buildings, and taken such absolute possession that we are no longer in America, but Shanghai or Hong-Kong. The restaurants make the nearest approach to the national façades, but this is brought about by adding highly-decorated balconies, lanterns, and inscriptions, and not building outright.

I had the curiosity to try one of the best of the restaurants—quite a gorgeous affair, at the head of Commercial Street—and found the fare both neatly served and palatable. There was a certain monotony in the bill, which I ascribed to a desire to give us dishes as near the American style as possible. We had chicken-soup, with flour paste resembling macaroni; a very tender chicken, sliced, through bones and all, in a bowl; a bowl of duck; a pewter chafing-dish of quail with spinach. All the food is set out in bowls, and each helps himself, with ebony chopsticks, to such morsels as he desires. The chopsticks, held in the fingers of the right hand, somewhat after the manner of castanets, are about as convenient to the novice as a pair of lead-pencils. We drank *saki*, or rice brandy, in infinitesimal cups, during the dinner, and at dessert very fine tea.

The upper story of these places is reserved for guests of the better class. Those of slender purses are accommodated below. To these is served a second drawing of the same tea which has been used, and such meats as re-

CHINESE QUARTER, SAN FRANCISCO.

main in a tolerable state. The upper story is decorated with carved work, painted scarlet, and heavily gilded, and screens, lanterns, and teak-wood tables and stools; while below pine-wood tables are deemed good enough.

A BALCONY IN THE CHINESE QUARTER.

Dropping in late one evening for a cup of tea, I had the fortune to witness a supper-party—a novel, *genre* picture, glowing with color. There were a dozen dignified-looking men, dressed in handsome silk clothing—black, blue, and purple. With them were as many women— young, slender, and pretty, of their type, while the women seen walking about the streets are very coarse and clumsy.

Their black hair was carefully smoothed, and looped up with silver pins, and their complexions were daintily made of pink and white and vermilion, realizing exactly the heads painted on their silken fans. The most interesting girl was of Fellah or Hebrew aspect, and was probably not without an admixture of other blood in her veins. The men occupied carved teak-wood stools about a large table, spread with a white cloth, and covered with charming china. The women stood by and served them. Now and then one of the latter rested momentarily on a corner of a stool, in a laughing way, and took a morsel also. The whole was a bit of bright *Chinoiserie* worth a long journey to witness.

They were very merry, and played, among other amusements, a game like the Italian *mora*. In this one would hold up fingers in rapid succession, while the others shouted the probable number at the tops of their voices. What with this, their laughter, drumming on the table, and general hubbub, besides an orchestra of their peculiar music adding its din from behind a screen, they were not very unlike a party of Parisian *canotiers* and *grisettes* supping at Bougival.

The temple and the theatre of the Chinese emigrant have an identical character wherever he goes. I found here the same scenes in both I had witnessed in Havana at the beginning of my journey. The temple, economically set up in some upper rear room, abounds in gandy signs and some good bronzes, but is little frequented. The theatre is far more popular. The dresses used here are rich and interesting. The performers are continually marching, fighting, spinning about, pretending to be dead and jumping up again, and singing in high, cracked voices like the whine of a bagpipe. A doughty warrior, who may be Gengis Khan or Timour the Tartar, and bear

IN A CHINESE THEATRE.

himself with the "most haughty stride and withering pride," will sing you his lines in this same puny, whining voice, and no other. The slightness of the means of illusion is a naïve feature of interest in the Chinese drama. As one of the simple rustics in the *Midsummer Night's Dream* holds up an arm to represent a wall, across which Pyramus and Thisbe are supposed to talk, so here, if it be designed, for instance, to represent the march of an army through the woods, a screen is put up at one side of the stage, bearing an inscription which no doubt says "Woods," and around this the military betake themselves.

The cemetery is more curious even than the theatre of Chinadom in San Francisco. I came upon it in the course of a long stroll one afternoon, and was almost the only spectator of some peculiar ceremonial rites in propitiation of the dead. It is not grouped in the general Golgotha at Lone Mountain, but adjoins that devoted to the city paupers, out among the melancholy sand-dunes by the ocean. It is parcelled off by white fences into a large number of enclosures for separate burial guilds, or *tongs*. These have large signs upon them—" Fook Yam Tong," "Tung Sen Tong," "Ye On Tong," etc. One has almost difficulty to persuade himself that he is awake witnessing such doings as here take place in the broad sunlight of Yankeeland.

It is the practice to convey the bones of their dead to China, but there are preliminary funerals in regular form. All the "hacks" in San Francisco are often engaged. The bones are left in the ground a year or more before removal.

Toward three in the afternoon a number of expresswagons of the common sort drove up with freights of Chinamen and Chinawomen, and curiously assorted provisions. The "hoodlum" drivers conducted themselves peaceably enough, but seemed to have a certain sardonic air at the idea of having to draw their profits from patrons of such a class. The provisions were unloaded, taken up and laid on small wooden altars, of which there is one at the front of each *tong*. Most conspicuous were whole roast pigs, decorated with ribbons and colored papers. There were next roast fowls, rice, salads, sweetmeats, fruits, cigars, and rice brandy. The participants set to work to fire revolvers, bombs, and crackers, kindle packages of colored paper, make profound genuflections before the graves, and scatter libations upon them of food and liquors. Only the roast pigs were reserved and taken home again; all the rest was scattered about. The din and smoke increased apace; the strange-garbed figures pranced about like sorcerers, and the decorated pigs loomed out with a goblin air. It seemed a veritable witches' Sabbath. Some of the fruits and cigars were hospitably offered to me as I looked on; and I will say that parsimony does not seem a vice of the Chinaman, though he lives upon so little, and is content with moderate returns.

Coming back the same way in the evening, I noted prowling figures of white men among the graves, gathering up the fragments cast down by the improvident heathen.

I am glad, on the whole, not to have the mooted Chinese question to settle in person. On the one hand, a great law of political economy—the natural right of man to seek happiness where he will; on the other, a view that the best good of a community does not necessarily consist in mere size and value of "improvements." The reflective mind will find it rather in the greatest average distribution of comfort. I should say that there have been no evils of consequence experienced from the presence of the Chinese population as yet. Without them the railroads could not have been built, nor the agricultural nor mining interests developed. With all the complaint, too, of competition, the wages of white labor are better here than at the East, and the cost of living is certainly not more.

A proper male costume for San Francisco is humorously said to be a linen duster with a fur collar. The variability of the climate within brief spaces of time is thus indicated. It varies largely, in fact, in different parts of the same day, though the mean for the year is remarkably even. The mean for January—the coldest month—is but fifty degrees, and for September—the warmest—fifty-eight. It is a famous climate for work, but the average temperature, as is seen, is pretty low for comfort. People go away for warmth in the summer quite as much as for coolness. The rainy season—the winter—is really the pleasantest of the year. The air is clearer then, while the prospects are verdant and best worthy to be seen. At other times fogs prevail, or bleak winds arise in the afternoon, and blow dust, in a dreary way, into the eyes of all whose misfortune calls them to be then in the streets.

We return to town from our Chinese ceremony along wide Point Lobos Avenue, the drive to the Cliff House. It is skirted on one side by the public pleasure-ground, Golden Gate Park, an area of half a mile by three miles and a half, which is being redeemed from an original condition of drifting sand in a wonderful way. All the outer tract near the ocean is as desert and yellow as Sahara. A few scattered dwellings appear in the sands, each with its water-tank and wind-mill, a yucca-plant or two, and some knots of tough grass about it. The city appears on the edge of the steep, as if it were looking over in surprise.

XXIV.

THE VILLAS OF THE BONANZA KINGS.

I.

I HAD marked out as a field of travel Southern California.

It is not easy to decide on the instant just what Southern California should be deemed to comprehend. Most of the State, leaving out the mining and lumbering districts, displays some of those tropical features in which the idea of Southernness to the imagination of the temperate climates consists. You see orange, fig, and pomegranate trees surrounding pleasant homes at Sonoma, well to the north of San Francisco. One of the most important districts for raisin-culture is near Sacramento and Marysville, north-west. At the springs of Calistoga, seventy-five miles north, is found a group of the finest palm-trees in California. It is safe to assume, however, that all this will be found in the greater perfection as the low latitudes are approached.

San Francisco lies not far from midway of the State, and Southern California may conveniently be taken as all that part south of the seaport and metropolis. It was upon the area just below, around the Bay, that the Rev. Starr King lavished his most polished eulogies, describing the "flowers by the acre, flowers by the square mile," which he saw there, in the spring. To the vicinity of San José, fifty miles down, Bayard Taylor proposed (if he should live to be old, and note his faculties failing) to retire in order to renew his youth. And but seventy-five miles farther south are the summer resorts—and winter resorts as well—of Santa Cruz and Monterey.

I set out in mid-autumn, the time of the county fairs, when the products of an agricultural country should be seen to particular advantage. There was held at San José the combined fair of the counties of Santa Clara and Santa Cruz, and that I made my first objective point.

There are no means of exit from San Francisco by land except to the southward, the long, narrow peninsula on which it lies being surrounded on all other sides by water. One may cross, however, by ferry to Oakland—the Jersey City and Hoboken, as well as Brooklyn, of the place—and go around the bay on that side by a road which reaches San José also. In doing so you traverse Alameda County, which raises nearly a million bushels of wheat a year from a single township, together with tons of sugar-beets, and more hay than any other county in the State. It comes third also in rank for grape-vines, and has tropical pretensions of its own, making an exhibit of orange and lemon trees in certain favored nooks. But the more direct way is the coast division of the Southern Pacific Railway, down the peninsula.

Let us glance at topography a moment. California is fenced off into valleys by two long north and south ranges—the Sierra Nevadas, immensely high, and the lower Coast Range. These meet in acute points, north at Shasta, and south at the Tejon Pass, and become one. They enclose between them the vast central space known in its upper portion as the Sacramento Valley, and its lower as the San Joaquin Valley, from the two main rivers by which it is drained. The granite Sierra Nevadas

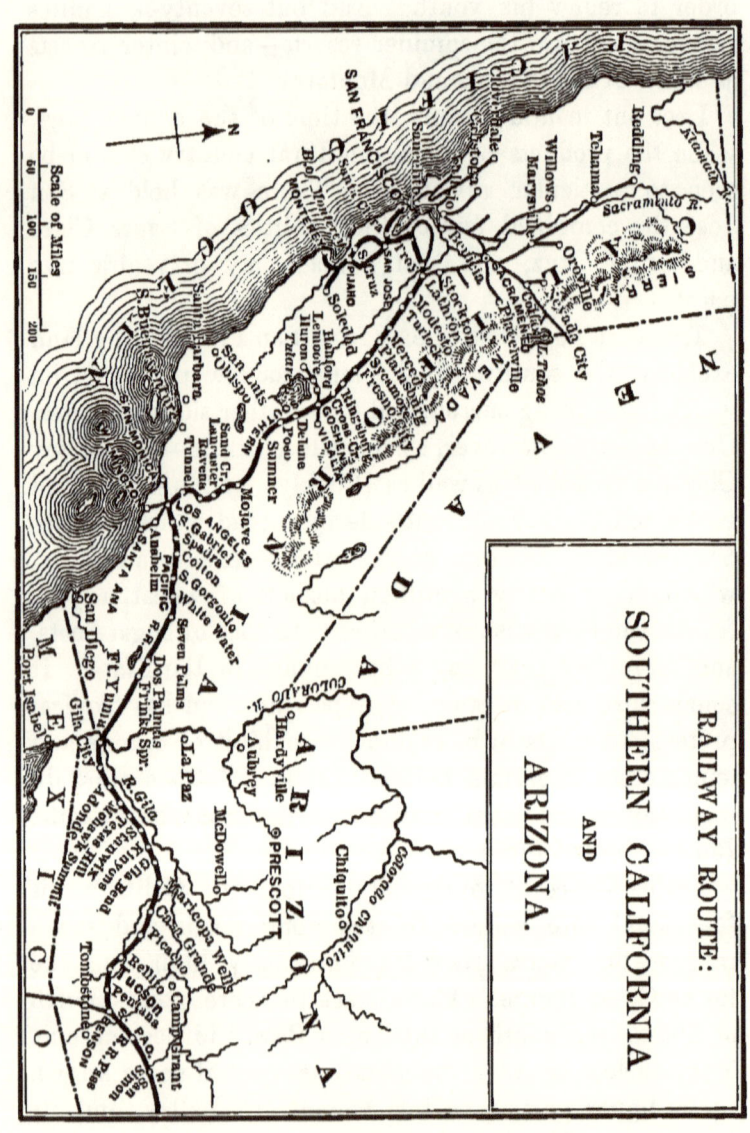

contain the peaks of from thirteen to fifteen thousand feet elevation which have obtained an extensive fame in the world. The Coast Range, of softer materials, averages only from two to six thousand feet.

The Sierra Nevadas do not greatly divide their strength, but the Coast Range throws out frequent spurs parallel to itself. These take separate names, as Sierra Morena, Santa Clara, and Santa Cruz mountains, and form numerous long, narrow valleys and benches of table-land between themselves and the Pacific Ocean.

Down the large Santa Clara Valley, one of those formed in this way in the midst of a diversified region, our first excursion takes us.

By the time the files of freight-cars constituting the immediate environs of all American cities are passed we find ourselves running through a tract of small vegetable gardens and windmills. Clusters of buildings in white enclosures, that looked from town, on their hills, like Mexican haciendas, are "institutions" of various sorts. A long arm of San Francisco Bay accompanies us thirty miles south, and is seen gleaming to the left, with a wide stretch of marsh between. Ark-like structures on piles, at intervals along the water's edge, are guard-houses, keeping watch over beds of the small California oyster, which has never yet been either coaxed or driven into a grandeur commensurate with the pretensions of everything else about it.

The conception that has gone out about Southern California is that it is an earthly Paradise. I will say at once that it is very charming, even in the dry season, but it is an earthly Paradise very different from the best idea of it one has been able to get by previous investigation. I found myself there, in short, in the dry season, and most writers have spoken of it only as viewed in the season of rains and verdure.

The guide-book promises, "after a few minutes' ride, orchards, vineyards, elegant farm-houses, prospects to charm all who love the beauties of nature." But, really —one rubs his eyes—where are they? The ground is mournfully bare and brown. Hardly a tree or a bush is seen; not a green blade of grass. At length some small trees, a variety of scrub-oaks, at a little distance resembling the olive! Farm-houses are few, and not at all "elegant." The hills are of the color of camel's hide, and not unlike the camel's humps.

At Millbrae, finally, there is a glimpse of the wooden towers, in the American style, of a villa, and a large dairy barn. At Belmont the low hills are close at hand. At Menlo Park a charming flower-bed is cared for, by the track, as at foreign railway-stations. We are in the chosen site for villa residences of the San Francisco millionnaires. The surface is flat, and with its growth of oaks recalls the outskirts of Chicago, as at Hyde Park or Riverside.

The valley widens till the hills are distant and veiled in blue, with tawny grain-fields between; but still no verdure! And where are the wild flowers? One hardly expects them now "by the acre and by the square mile," it is true, since it is autumn; but of all the primroses, the larkspur, the lupin, the poppies of tradition, not one! Not a narcissus! not a chrysanthemum! Oh, my predecessors! what shall I think of you?

In the spring the flowers bloom and carpet the earth as grass carpets it elsewhere. Speaking of the spring the eulogists do not say a word too much. But it is my originality to have seen Southern California in the autumn and winter—as it is for seven months of every year, and as it may be, in exceptional seasons, the whole year through.

Not to make a great deal of this bareness and dryness would be to neglect a most essential feature. The annual rains begin in December, January, or February, and continue till June, diminishing in May, which is sometimes itself a dry month. In the autumn the leaves fall —what comparatively few there are to fall—as elsewhere, and are not renewed.

"But you set up to be a land of perpetual summer, you know," one argues with the Californian, in the first state of surprise.

"So we are," he replies; "but that does not necessarily mean perpetual verdure. Look at the thermometer! look at the fertility of the land! You have but to run water on it by irrigation, and it will do whatever you please. Contrast this brown season with your own white one. The land is dry and easy to get about on, and the sky above is uniformly pleasant. Do you prefer your fields of sheeted snow, under the howling blasts? your quagmires of mud and slush, alternately freezing and thawing?"

"Very true," I admit, accepting this different point of view.

Then, perhaps, by way of finishing touch, he adds, rising to a dignity well justified by the facts, "California sets up to be a land of relations, commercial, agricultural, mineral, and social, which have made it a power in the world. It has revolutionized values, struck the key-note of new social conditions, and begun a new commercial era. California has arrived at a point where she takes her place in the Union on the ordinary terms. We no longer depend upon a repute for astounding beauties and eccentricities—though of these, too, there is no lack, as you will find."

II.

San José, a city of twenty thousand people, contests with Sacramento the honor of being third in importance in the State. You alight there at the small station. In the vicinity are a waiting horse-car, a blacksmith's shop, and rail-fences painted with advertisements. These have a very American look, to begin with, for a place with a romantic Spanish name—a place to which you are recommended to come in search of the elixir of life. And so have the small picket-fences an American look, and the comfortable little clapboarded wooden houses behind them, with scroll-sawed ornaments in their piazzas. With the exception of an unusual number of French and Italian names on the sign-boards, and some large, clean tuns in front of the shops of dealers in native wines, it is as downright a little Yankee town as ever was. There is much shade in the streets, and in a public green, but the trees are yet too small and low.

It is a clean, prosperous city, the centre of a rich agricultural district. It has excellent schools and all the other conveniences of life. A good deal of money has been spent on the principal business buildings. As in most other provincial towns throughout the State, they are much covered with bay-windows, in what might be described as the San Francisco style of architecture. An iron trestle-work tower was going up at the intersection of the two main streets, to rise to a height of two hundred feet, to contain an electric light and illuminate the town. The white Court-house, in the classic style, though not large, is agreeably proportioned, and quite a model of its kind.

The week's doings at the Fair Grounds resolved themselves chiefly into trotting-matches. I was told that the combined display of the two counties was poorer this year than either was in the habit of making alone. There was racing and ornamental riding, one day, by young women, and those who took premiums were girls of but fourteen and sixteen. Another popular feature of these county fairs was "firemen's tournaments," in which different companies held contests of speed, equipped with all their paraphernalia.

There was but a scattering display of live-stock, and little or no fruit. The two-hundred-pound squash, the twenty-six-pound turnip, the beet five feet in length and a foot through, the apples and pears commensurate with these, were not shown. I had seen them before, and did not much regret their absence. I have a lurking suspicion that there is a standard of the vegetable as of the human race, and that the Tom Thumbs and General Bateses of the one are not more fortunate in their departure from it than those of the other.

The capacity of the country to produce fruits, not simply of abnormal size, but fine quality—excepting the apple, which requires extremes of heat and cold, and remains insipid—has, perhaps, been too well tested to need competitive exhibitions. What better county fair than the daily display of fruits and vegetables in the San Francisco market? The regular season for any and all of them is twice as long as on the Atlantic coast at corresponding latitudes.

I traversed the much-eulogized "Alameda," an avenue of willows and poplars, of three miles, set out, in 1799, by Spanish friars. These founded a mission among the Indians at Santa Clara, to which town the avenue extends. There remains at Santa Clara the chapel of the mission, with its adobe walls, five feet thick, and flat wooden ceiling, rudely painted. It is now a part of a flourishing collegiate institution. Across the way is a clump of ruinous old adobe cottages of the same date; but we are adjured to pay no great heed to these, since we are going presently to Monterey, which has, as it were, a grand specialty of all that kind of thing.

The Alameda poplars and willows make but a moderate showing for their age, and can hardly be rated equal to New Haven elms, for instance. Behind them, along both sides of the road, are houses of a *bourgeois* comfort, as in the town. There are said to be residents of wealth and leisure who have been attracted here to pass the remainder of their days in peace. The Coast Mountains, they say, cut off the fogs and winds of the ocean, and a higher range on the other side bars out the heats of the country eastward. We endeavor to divine, in some superior refinement of taste and sentiment, the abodes of these particular ones. It is a pleasant conception, that of coming here to live for the pure physical delight in living, and highly interesting. Perhaps their daughters will stand by the gates with a certain repining mingled with their air of superior distinction, as if they, for their part, had not quite so willingly consented to abandon a world of larger opportunities. But we do not succeed. Some of these residents are simply rude mining men who have broken their constitutions in Nevada and Utah; and, after all, the desire to live a life of physical contentment does not imply taste in architecture and landscape gardening.

III.

One had expected a good deal of novelty and picturesqueness from these towns, of romantic "San" and "Santa," and "Los" and "Del," and feels rather aggrieved not to get so much of it. Its absence is explained in part by the fact that there were rarely original settlements corresponding to the present names. These are taken rather from ranches, springs, or mines in the neighborhood. On the arrival of the Americans in California there were but thirteen thousand Spanish, or Mexicans, all told, while the territory was as large as New York, Pennsylvania, and the six New England States put together.

Let us believe that the pleasing designations will act as a stimulus, and these communities will live up to their names in time, as they never could have done were they simply Smithville and Jonesville.

The impressions at San José, and in the country at large, resulting from a second visit a month later, were more agreeable. Something like the proper point of view had then been attained. The face of nature was to be parched, and the towns rather commonplace; but the continued cloudlessness of the sky, and quality of the air, were more, and the peculiar form of pleasure was settled where it belonged.

The district of villa residences of the millionnaires, when penetrated, gained much in attractiveness. There are white-oaks and chestnut-oaks, as well as scrub-oaks, in groups of a park-like appearance, and live-oaks, with long, gray Spanish moss depending from them. If there are no wild flowers, there are plenty of the cultivated sort, with lawns kept green by fountains and hose. Where there is water, the winter, or brown season, need never extend.

As a rule, long stretches of white picket-fence surround the places, and the houses themselves are white.

The bonanza kings have been invested with a greater air of magnificence than really belongs to them. Their places cost them immense sums, it is true, but a reduction should be made to Eastern standards. The outpouring of untold millions put up the prices of land, labor, and every commodity entering into the result, so that less was obtained for the money than an equal expenditure would have procured here. The Menlo Park district is inferior to Llewellyn Park, Englewood, Irvington, and others, in the neighborhood of New York.

The builders have struck out a kind of style of their own, perhaps in too great haste to wait for imported ideas. The houses are chiefly of wood. Flood, of Flood & O'Brien, and "Consolidated Virginia" when the great bonanza was struck, had just completed one of great size, on an estate of five hundred acres, at Menlo Park. There was a terrace, with a fine bronze fountain. The main steps were of polished marble with bronze sphinxes, and bronze dragons studded the ornate stables—the whole glaring, white, and over-gorgeous, like listening to the noise of a brass band.

There are some gentler, more home-like places, and recalling the tone of rural life at the East. Such a one is that of ex-Governor Leland Stanford, at Palo Alto. Here is a breeding farm for horses, one of the most complete of the kind in the world. Of seventeen hundred acres one hundred are occupied by stables, barns, and small paddocks, which, at the foot of a gentle rise of ground, make a small city by themselves. It is inhabited by a population of nearly five hundred animals, who return hither from business, as it were, in the pastures and race-tracks, and have two hundred persons employed in their domestic service. The spacious stables are uniformly floored and ceiled up with redwood, strewn with the freshest straw, and kept as neat as the most unexceptionable drawing-room.

Scions of the stock, representing the best thoroughbred

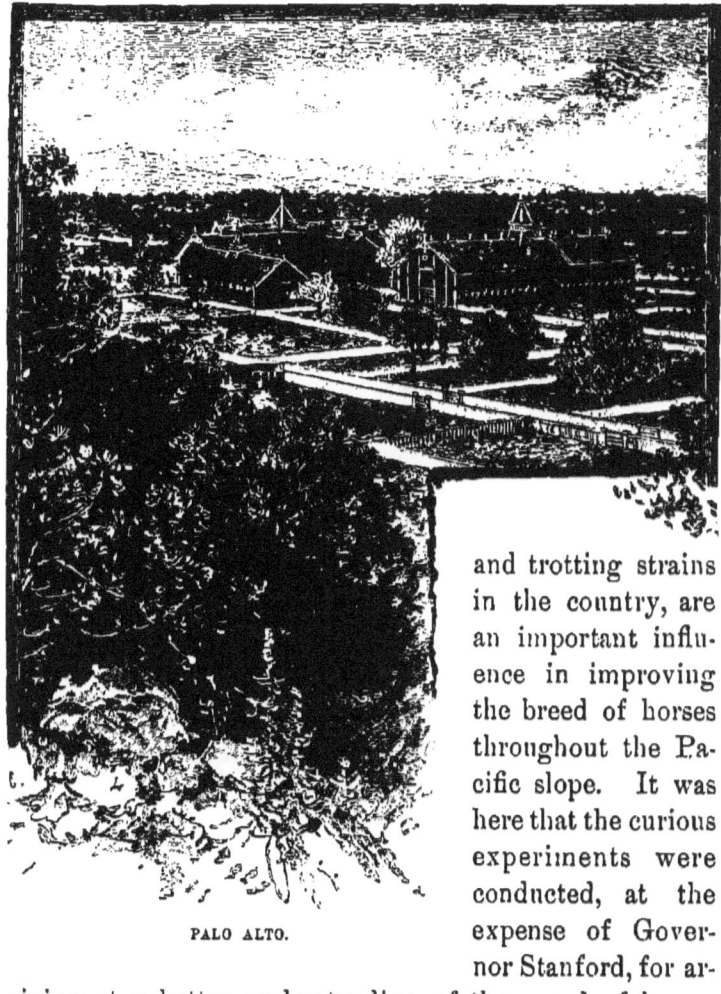

PALO ALTO.

and trotting strains in the country, are an important influence in improving the breed of horses throughout the Pacific slope. It was here that the curious experiments were conducted, at the expense of Governor Stanford, for arriving at a better understanding of the speed of horses by photographing them in motion. The photographer, Muybridge, of San Francisco, succeeded, by an ingenious arrangement of electrical wires, communicating with cameras, in securing twelve distinct views of a single stride. The attitudes are of the most unexpected sort, and some of them even comic.

From the time of foaling the colts are gently handled, and made as familiar with the touch of harness as with that of human hands. As a consequence they are tame, gentle, and even affectionate, and never need formal breaking. The effect of the system of training has been apparent in some notable records of speed. On the Bay District Association track, at San Francisco, in 1880, the two-year-old Fred Crocker lowered the record for a one-mile trot to 2′ 25¼″. Last year Bonita, a two-year-old filly, cut it down to 2′ 24½″. At the same trotting exhibition Wildflower, another two-year-old, made the mile in 2′ 21″; and Hinda Rose, a yearling filly, added to the fame of the farm by cutting down the yearling record to 2′ 36½″.

The interiors of these fine villas are, as a rule, better than the exteriors. The Mills house, at Millbrae, residence of a banking and railway magnate, now of New York, is a notable collection of *portières* and Oriental rugs, and bed-chambers done in the finest woods, with a picture-gallery of works of Gérôme, Detaille, and Bouguereau, while from all the windows are vistas of fan-palms, flower-beds, greensward, and bronzes.

Ralston's old house, at Belmont, now the property of Senator Sharon, is of those of the greatest interest, through interest in the remarkable man who built it. Starting from humble origin, he rose to be a great capitalist and the promoter of brilliant schemes of improvement, both public and private. He conducted to success a hundred projects which in other hands would have been folly, and arrived thus at such an unbounded confidence in his star that he thought he could not fail. He was entangled at last, however, in schemes beyond his control. Strong and athletic, and in the prime of life, he went down to "Harry Meigs's" wharf, in San Francisco—almost the very point from which his great prototype sailed away to Peru—and swam out half a mile into the bay. It was for refreshment in his troubles, as some say, but, as the general opinion is, with the purpose of suicide. At any rate he was never seen alive again.

The house that was his is notched into the hill-side, in a rolling country, much pleasanter than the plain at Menlo Park. A pretty gorge behind it is dammed to furnish a water-supply. There are gas-works, a bowling-alley, and an elaborate Turkish bath among the out-buildings, and a grange-like barn of solid stone, ivy-grown, which cost $80,000. The immense house is wood, white, in the usual fashion, and, with its numerous stories and windows, is not unlike a large country hotel. A peculiar arrangement and great spaciousness give it a palatial air within. The principal rooms open into one another by glass partitions, which can be rolled away, so that in large gatherings there need be no crowding through doorways. There is an arcade above, around a grand staircase, with tribunes projecting, in which young women in colors, at an evening party, for instance, would look particularly houri-like. What in another house would be the ordinary veranda is here a delightful promenade, glazed in, and provided with easy furniture and a parquetry floor. Behind a row of such main apartments as drawing-room and library comes a parallel row, of which one is a great ball-room, entirely faced with mirrors. Pianos, mantels, and stair-posts are of California laurel—a new industry encouraged by the owner among many others.

We drove from Belmont back through a succession of cup-like dells in the lower mountains, a number of them dammed to form pretty lakes, the sources of supply for the Spring Valley Water Company—a corporation of great prominence at San Francisco. The slopes at first

RALSTON'S COUNTRY HOUSE.

were tawny with grain stubble; then scattered with the thick bush known as chaparral; then bare. We passed an occasional lonely farm known as a "milk ranch," or "chicken ranch." There are no farms in California; no matter how small the tract is, it is always a ranch.

In the strong, warm sunshine chance objects on the bare slopes cast intense, purplish shadows. That of a distant tree is as dark as if a pit had been dug under it. That of a bird, flying low, is followed as distinctly as the bird itself. You are reconciled at last to the brown tone. It is like Algeria. White stands out in brilliant relief against it. One would rather like it to be a different white, however, than that of the little wooden houses. The falconers of Fromentin might career or the rival Arab chiefs of Pasini hold conferences among such hills.

XXV.

THE VINTAGE SEASON, AND MONTEREY.

I.

It was the pleasant vintage season at San José. Santa Clara County, of which San José is the capital, boasts of a number of acres of grape-vines under cultivation (over eleven thousand) second only to Sonoma County. Napa, however, to the north, and Los Angeles, to the south, greatly surpass it in gallons of wine and brandy produced.

I visited, among others, the Le Franc vineyard, which dates from 1851, and is the pioneer in making wine-growing a regular industry. Here are about a hundred and seventy-five thousand vines, set out a thousand, perhaps, to the acre. The large, cheerful farm buildings are upon a gentle rise of ground above the area of vines, which is nearly level. An Alsacian foreman showed us through the wine-cellars. A servant-maid bustling about the yard was a thorough French peasant, only lacking the wooden shoes. The long tables, set for the forty hands employed in the vintage-time, were spread with viands in the French fashion. Scarcely a word of English was spoken.

At other places the surroundings are as exclusively Italian or Portuguese. One feels very much abroad in such scenes on American soil. The foreigners from Southern Europe take naturally to wine-making and go into it, from the few hundred gallons of red wine made by the Portuguese and Italian laborers for their own families, to the manufacture of an American champagne on a large scale by the Hungarian, Arpad Haraszthy, at San Francisco. The Americans, who have not acquired the habit of looking upon wine as a necessity in the family, are not yet, as a rule, very active in its production.

A certain romantic interest attaches to this ancient industry. The great tuns in the wine-cellars and all the processes were very clean. It was re-assuring to see the pure juice of the grape poured out in such floods, and to feel that here was no need—founded on scarcity, at least —for adulteration.

Teeming loads of the purple fruit were driven up, and across a weighing scale. The contents are lifted to an upper story, put into a hopper, where the stems come off, and the grapes fall through to a crusher. They are lightly crushed at first. It is something of a discovery that the earliest product of grapes of every hue is white wine. The red wine gets its hue from the coloring matter in the skins, which are utilized in a subsequent ruder squeezing.

I shall not enter upon all the various processes—the racking off, clarifying, and the like—though, so much in the company of those who spoke with authority and were continually holding up little glasses to the light with a gusto, like figures in popular chromos, I consider myself to yield in knowledge of such abstruse matters to none. Immense upright casks, containing a warm, audibly fermenting mass, and others lying down, neatly varnished, with concave ends, are the most salient features in the dimly lighted wine-cellars.

They are not cellars, properly so called, either, since

BOTTLING CHAMPAGNE AT SAN FRANCISCO.

they are wholly above-ground. The casks rest on wooden sills upheld by short brick posts. In the cellars of General Naglee, a successful maker of brandy on a large scale, the cobwebs have been allowed to increase and hang like tattered banners. Through these the light penetrates dimly from above, or with a white glare from a latticed window, upon which the patterns of vine-leaves without are defined. The buildings are brown, gray, and vine-clad, with quaint, Dutch-pavilion-looking roofs, and dove-cotes attached. A lofty water-tank, with a wind-mill—a feature of every California rural homestead—here is more tower-like than usual.

Round about extend long avenues of eucalyptus, pine, tamarind, with its black, dry pods; the pepper-tree, with its scarlet berries; large clumps of the *nopal* cactus, and an occasional maguey, or century-plant. All is glowing now with the tints of autumn. Poplar and cottonwood are yellow. The peach and almond, the Lawton blackberry, and the vineyards themselves, touched by frost, supply the scarlet and crimson. The country seems bathed in a fixed sunshine, or in hues of its own wines.

The vines, themselves short and stout, and needing no support, yield each an incredible number of purple clusters, all growing from the top. They quaintly suggest the uncouth little men of Hendrik Hudson who stagger up the mountain, in "Rip Van Winkle," with kegs of spirits on their shoulders.

No especial attention is given to the frosts now, but those of the early spring are the object of many precautions. The most effectual is to kindle smudge-fires about the vineyard toward four o'clock in the morning, the smoke of which envelops it and keeps it in a warmer atmosphere of its own till the sun be well risen.

Three to four tons of grapes to the acre are counted

A BRANDY CELLAR, SAN JOSE.

upon; while farther south, where irrigation is used, they expect from eight to twelve. But it is claimed, in the standing controversy on the subject, that the irrigated grapes are watery, while those of lesser yield excel them in quality. The best results, we were told, are got from such vines as the Mataro, Carignane, and Grenache, imported cuttings from the French slope of the Pyrenees. There were at Le Franc's not less than sixty varieties, under probation, many of which will, no doubt, give an excellent account of themselves. They are assembled from Greece, Italy, Palestine, and the Canary Islands, so that we have all the chances of the development of something suited to our peculiar conditions.

II.

I left San José to drive along the dry, shallow bed of the Guadalupe River to the Guadalupe Quicksilver Mine, a more remote and less visited companion of well-known New Almaden. The mine is in a lovely little vale, with a settlement of Mexican and Chinese boarding-houses clustered around it. Some bold ledges of rock jut out above, and a superintendent's house surrounded by flowers hangs upon the hill-side. A weird-looking flume conveys the sulphurous acid from the calcining furnaces to a hilltop, upon which every trace of vegetation has been blasted by its poisonous exhalations.

Then I made a little tour by rail southward through the immense "Murphy" and "Miller and Lux" ranches, comprising a grain country as flat as a floor.

We turned west through the fertile little Pajaro Valley, the emporium of which for produce, and fine redwood lumber, cut in great quantities on the adjoining Santa Cruz Mountains, is the thriving town of Watsonville. We ran along a rugged coast, past wooded gorges and white sea-side cottages, at Aptos and Soquel, to the much-frequented resort of Santa Cruz. Santa Cruz has bold variations of level, the usual commonplace buildings, a noble drive along cliffs eaten into a hundred fantastic

A BIT OF OLD MONTEREY.

shapes by the waves, and shops for the sale of shells, and its summer boarders, who become, with change of seasons, winter boarders in turn. Thence finally to the long-anticipated Monterey.

Here at last was something to commend from the point of view of the picturesque without reservation. Monterey has a population which still, in considerable part, speaks Spanish only. It retains the impress of the Spanish domination, and little else. When you are told in your own country that somebody does not speak English, you naturally infer that it is brokenly, or only a little.

But at Monterey it means absolutely not a word. There are Spanish signs on the shops, and even Spanish advertisements, as, for instance, the *Wheeler & Wilson Maquinas á Coser*, on the fences.

My Mexican experience was a liberal education for Monterey, and I made the most of it. I was taken to call upon an ancient *señorita*, in whose history there was some romance.

"*Las rosas son muy secas*"—(" The roses are very dry ") she said, apologetically, as we entered her little garden, laid out in regular parallelograms, behind an adobe wall topped with red tiles. Large yellow and red roses were blowing to pieces in the wind before her long, low adobe house.

She was one of those who spoke no English. It seems as if there were some wilful perversity in it, after having been since 1846 a part of the most bustling State of the most active country in the world. It seems as if it must be some lingering hatred of the American. But the *señorita* is far too gentle for that. There is, perhaps, no reason beyond a general mental inertness by virtue of which the Mexican survivors have suffered all their other interests as well as this to go by the board.

The *señorita* is a little, thin old lady of fifty. Her romance was with an American officer, it is said, thirty years ago, and she has never since married, but has withered, like her roses, at Monterey.

As seen from a distance, scattered loosely and white on the forest-crested slope of the fine bay, the little city, which has now perhaps two thousand inhabitants, does not show its unlikeness to other places. But when entered it consists almost exclusively of whitewashed adobe houses, and the straggling, mud-colored walls of enclosures, for animals, known as "corrals." Many of them are vacant.

LOOKOUT STATION.

At frequent intervals is encountered too some abandoned old adobe barracks, or government house, or military prison of historic fame, with its whitewash gone, holes in its walls, and bits of broken grating and balcony hanging aimlessly on, waiting only the first opportunity to let go.

The travellers of my youth had a fashion of talking glibly of adobe, without explaining what adobe was. Let me not be guilty of the same error. Adobe is bricks made of about twice the usual size, and dried in the sun instead of being baked. Walls are made of great thickness, in order that, though outside and inside crumble off, there may be a good deal left. Like a number of other things, it stands very well while not assailed; and in this climate it is rarely assailed by violent extremes of temperature.

The typical adobe house of the best class is stuccoed and whitewashed. It is large on the ground, two stories in height, and has verandas. Again, it is of but one story, with an interior court-yard. It has green doors and shutters, and green, turned posts, in what we now call the "Queen Anne style," and it is comfortable and home-like to look at.

One of them contains the first piano ever introduced into California, and the owners are people who made haste to sell out their all at San Francisco and invest it here, in order to reap the greater prosperity which was thought to be waiting upon Monterey. Two old iron guns stand planted as posts at the corners of the dwelling. In front of others are some walks neatly made of the verterbræ of whales, taken by the Monterey Whaling Company. The company is a band of hardy, weather-beaten men, chiefly Portuguese, of the Azores, who have a lookout station on the hill by the ruined fort, and a barracks lower down. They pursue their avocation from the shore in boats, with plenty of adventure and no small profit.

Monterey, which is now not even a county seat, was the Spanish capital of the province from the time it was thought necessary to have a capital. The missionary father, Junipero Serra, came here from Mexico in the year 1770. It was next a Mexican capital under eleven successive governors. Then it became the American capital, the first port of entry, the scene of the first Constitutional Convention of the State, and an outfitting point for the southern mines. Money in those early days was so

CUTTING UP THE WHALE.

plenty, I have heard tell, that store-keepers hardly stopped to count it, but threw it under the counter in bushelfuls.

A secret belief in the ultimate revival of Monterey seems always to survive in certain quarters, like that in the reappearance of Barbarossa from the Kylfhäuser Berg, or the restoration of the Jews. Breakwaters have been ambitiously talked of, and it is said that the bay could be made a harbor and shipping-point and the rival of San Francisco.

The only step toward such revival as yet is a fine hotel, built by the Southern Pacific railroad, which may make it, instead of Santa Cruz, across the Bay, the leading seaside resort. Though not so grandiose a direction as some others, this is really the one in which the peculiar conditions of the old capital are most likely to tell. The summer boarder can get a tangible pleasure out of its historic remains and traditions of greatness, though they be good for nothing else. The Hotel del Monte is a beautiful edifice, not surpassed by that of any American watering-place, and unequalled in the charming groves of live-oak and pine and profusion of cultivated flowers by which it is surrounded, and the air of comfort combined with its elegant arrangements.

This is the way with our friends of the Pacific coast. If they do not always stop to follow Eastern ideas and patterns, when they really attempt something in the same line, they are as likely as not to do it a great deal better.

The climate at Monterey, according to statistical tables, is remarkably even. The mean temperature is 52° in January and 58° in July. This strikes one as rather cool for bathing, but the mode is to bathe in the tanks of a large bath-house, to which sea-water is introduced, artificially warmed, instead of in the sea itself.

THE HOTEL DEL MONTE, MONTEREY.

CLIFFS AND FOREST AT MONTEREY.

In other respects the place seems nearly as desirable at one time of the year as another. The quaint town is always there; and the wild rocks, with their gossiping gulls and pelicans; and the drives through the extensive forests. There are varieties of pine and cypress—the latter like the Italian stone-pine—peculiar to Monterey.

The more venerable trees, hoary with age and hanging moss, are contorted into all the fantastic shapes of Doré's "Inferno." They grow by preference on the most savage points of rock, and the wild breakers toss handfuls of spray up to them high in the air, in amity and greeting.

Along the beach on this far-away point of the Pacific Ocean we find a Chinese fishing settlement. Veritable Celestials, without a word of English among them, have pasted the usual crimson papers of hieroglyphics on shanty residences. They burn tapers before their gods on the quay, and fish for a living in just such junks and small boats as may be seen at Hong-Kong and Canton. They prepare avallonia meat and avallonia shells for their home market. One had rather thought of the Chinese element as confined to San Francisco alone, but it is a feature of quaint interest throughout all of Southern California.

At Monterey is found an old mission of the delightfully ruinous sort. It is in the little Carmel Valley, which is bare and brown again, after the green woods are passed, four miles from the town. The mission fathers once had here ninety thousand cattle, and other things to correspond. There are now only some vestiges, resembling earth-works, of their extensive adobe walls, and, on a rise overlooking the sea, the yellowish, low, *rococo* church of San Carlos.

The Mexican traditions in design and proportion accompanied them here, but the workmanship as they went farther from home became curiously rude, and speaks of the disadvantages under which it was done. A dome of concrete on the bell-tower is unequally bulged; a star window in the front has very irregular points. The interior does not yield, as a picture of sentimental ruin, to Muckross Abbey or any broken temple of the Roman Campagna. The roof, open now to the sky, with grasses and

CHINESE FISHING VILLAGE.

wild mustard growing from its crevices, was of stone arches, supplemented with timber-work tied with rawhides. The whole body of the church—pilasters, capitals, frieze, and all—is set on a curve springing from the floor—a peculiarity I have never seen elsewhere.

SAN CARLOS'S-DAY AT THE OLD MISSION.

There are grasses growing within, sculptured stones tumbled down, vestiges of a tile pavement, tombs, bits of fresco, and over all the autograph scribblings of a myriad of A. B. Smiths and J. B. Joneses, visitors here in their time like ourselves.

DRYING FISH AT CHINESE VILLAGE.

Once a year, on St. Charles's-day, in early November, a memorial service is held, attended by all the shabby Spanish-Indian life remaining in the country round about. The place is unique. It seems even more lonely than ruins of the same kind in the mother country, through standing amid surroundings of such a different class. Nothing is more conducive to pensiveness of a pleasant kind than, lying within this ruined enclosure, to watch the waving in the wind of the long grasses on its walls and listen to the plash of the sea on the shore, but a few steps distant.

XXVI.

A WONDROUS VALLEY, AND A DESERT THAT BLOSSOMS LIKE THE ROSE.

I.

The Yosemite, currently spoken of as the "Valley," is comprised in the belt formed by drawing lines across the State from San Francisco and Monterey respectively. It is a wild, strange nook among the Sierras, one of the few places not only not disappointing, but worthy of far more praise than has ever been bestowed upon it. It is like one of those mysterious regions on the outskirts of the fairy-land of the story-books—a standing resource of adventure to all the characters who enter it, and it is proper enough that our earthly Paradise of Southern California should have such a region of enchantment also adjoining it.

I reached it by stage-ride of sixty miles, from the Southern Pacific Railroad, at Madera, to Clark's Station, and thence by stage and horseback of twenty-five miles to the Valley. The autumn days were lovely there. The foliage, turned by a local climate quite as severe as that of New England, glowed with a vivid richness. The Merced River, a gentle stream, pursuing a devious way in the bottom, which is as level as a floor, reflected the color from many a mirror-like pool and sudden bend. Walls of rock rise on either hand to an elevation of three-quarters of a mile, varying from one-half to one-eighth of a mile in width. It is rather a chasm than a valley. At night the radiance of a full yellow moon invested all its wonders with an added enchantment. The cliffs are exactly what we think cliffs ought to be, but what they seldom are. They are of the hardest granite, pleasantly gray in color, and terminate in castle and dome like forms. The precipices are sheer and unbroken to the base, with almost none of those slopes of *débris* that detract from precipices in general. It is a little valley suitable, without a hair's-breadth alteration, to the purposes of any giant, enchanter, or yellow dwarf of them all. It is such scenery as Doré has imagined for the "Idyls of the King." One half feels himself a Sir Lancelot or Sir Gawain, riding along this lovely and majestic mountain trail; and as if he should wear chain-armor, a winged helmet, and a sword upon which he had sworn to do deeds of redoubtable valor.

It was the coast valleys and some coast towns that we took on our first journey. This time we have come down the main line of the Southern Pacific Railway through the central plain of the State. The railway is traced along the great central valley known as the San Joaquin, on a line nearly midway between the Sierra Nevadas and the Coast Range.

The road is still comparatively new, and the settlements have attained no great dimensions. It did not as a rule touch at the older towns existing, but pursued a direct course through a country where all had to be opened up. As some of the places passed by were of considerable size no little dissatisfaction ensued, and the mutterings are still heard. Frequent mention of this grievance is heard by the traveller through Southern California. Some of the neglected places even maintain that they would have been better without any railroad at all. References are thrown out to former glories of a dazzling sort which is sometimes difficult to credit, though a railroad naturally effects great innovations in trade. To the ordinary observer it would appear that the introduction of a splendidly equipped railway, even if it distribute its blessings a little unequally at first, and its tariff be high, must be a great and permanent advantage to everything remote as well as near. For the first time an adequate means has been afforded for the transport of immigrants and supplies through the whole length of the State.

The Southern Pacific Railway has completed connections which give it a transcontinental route from San Francisco, across Arizona, New Mexico, and Texas, to New Orleans. Immigrants are to be brought in by steamer from Liverpool to New Orleans, and thence by rail at a rate not to exceed that to the central West. The fares to California heretofore have been almost prohibitive, which is one of the reasons why so rich a country contains as yet less than a million of people. The languid movement hither of the valuable class of immigration which pours into the West, though ascribed by some alarmists to the presence of the Chinese, is due to the cost of travel and the lack of cheap lands for settlement. The Chinese are certainly not rivals in the matter of land, since they acquire little or none of it.

The new opportunities opened to transportation, the depression of the mining interest, and rapid increase of the Chinese, have awakened of late an exceptional interest in white immigration. A committee of some of the most prominent persons in the State has opened an inquiry into the most effectual means of promoting it. It will no doubt set forth more clearly than has ever been done before an account of such territory as is open to settlers, whether offered by the government, the railroads, or the great ranches, its advantages and the methods of reaching it.

It seems a little singular at first that lack of suitable lands can be adduced as a reason for lack of population in so vast a region, with the climate and other natural advantages of which so much has been said. It can only be understood by taking into account the unusual atmospheric dryness, and the important part played by water, which has to be brought upon the soil by costly contrivances. The locations where there is sufficient natural moisture for the maturing of crops are of small extent. They were among the first taken up. In much of the central and southern portions of the State the annual rain-fall is almost infinitesimal in quantity. At Bakersville, the capital of Kern County—whither our journey presently leads us—it is no more than from two to four inches. Light crops of grain and pasturage for stock may occasionally be got even under these conditions, but the only certain reliance is irrigation.

The springs and small streams were early appreciated at their value, and seized upon by persons who controlled with them great tracts of surrounding country, valueless except as watered from these sources. These tributary tracts are used chiefly as cattle and sheep ranges. A person owning five thousand acres will often have for his stock the free run of twenty thousand more. Cultivation is confined to the springs and water-courses, and becomes a succession of charming oases in a desert the superficial sterility of which is phenomenal.

The tenure of land by thousands of acres under a single ownership is a tradition from the Spanish and Mexican times. It has been much decried, as a great evil, and it is said that the State would be much more prosperous in a series of small farms. This is probably true, and the system as it exists may be ascribed in part to the greed of individuals, but it arises principally out of the natural features of the country. The wealth of the large holders alone enables them to undertake works of improvement, such as canal-making, drainage, and tree-planting, on an effectual scale. Perhaps the State will have to lend its assistance, and establish a public system of irrigation and drainage, before the land can be fully prepared for the small settler.

Water! water! water! How to slake the thirst of this parched, brown country, and turn it over to honest toil and thrift, is the great problem as we go southward, and the processes of irrigation are the most distinctive marks upon the landscape wherever it is improved.

II.

It is in early November that we begin to traverse the long San Joaquin Valley from Lathrop Junction, just below Stockton, southward. The side tracks of the railroad are crowded with platform-cars laden with wheat for the sea-board. The "elevator" system is not yet in use, and the grain is contained in sacks for convenient handling.

Hereabouts are some of the most famous wheat ranches. A man will plough but a single furrow a day on his farm, but this may be twenty miles long. There is sufficient rain-fall for the cereals, but not for the more exacting crops. The land gives but few bushels to the acre under the easy system of farming, but it must be remembered that there are a great many acres. The stubble of the grain-fields is whitened with wild-fowl. At a way-station a small rustic in an immense pair of boots goes over to a pool and blazes away with a shot-gun. Presently he returns, dragging by the necks an immense pair of wild-geese, almost beyond his strength to pull. The tawny color of the fields, and the great formal stacks of straw piled up in them, recall some aspects of the central table-land of Mexico. Many or spacious buildings are not necessary in the mild, dry climate of California. The prosperous ranches have, in consequence, a somewhat thin, unfurnished appearance compared with Eastern farms.

The most prominent object at each station is a long, low warehouse of the company, for the accommodation of grain. Like the station buildings generally it is painted Indian red, in "metallic" paint. The station of Merced is one of the two principal points of departure for the Yosemite Valley, Madera the other. At Merced an immense wooden hotel, for travellers bound to the Valley, overshadows the rest of the town. It rises beside the track, and the town is scattered back on the plain.

At Madera appears the end of a V-shaped wooden aqueduct, or flume, for rafting down lumber from the mountains fifty miles away to a planing-mill. Some of the hands also occasionally come down the flume in temporary boats. As the speed is prodigious these voyages abound in excitement and peril. The structure, supported on trestles, according to the formation of the ground, stretches away in interminable perspective to the mountains, which are rose-pink and purple at sunset. The scene is suggestive of the Roman Campagna, with this slight, essentially American work as a parody of the broken aqueducts and temples of the classic ancients. The lumber flume, however, is a bold and costly enterprise, though we be prone to smile at it.

By degrees we draw away from the wheat ranches, more and more on the uncultivated plain. The town of Fresno, two hundred miles below San Francisco, and about midway between two important streams, the San Joaquin and Kings Rivers, is in the midst of a particularly desolate tract, known, up to a very recent period, as the San Joaquin Desert. One should alight here. There is no better place for examining the marvellous capabilities of a soil which appears at first sight inhospitable to the last degree. Fresno is in the hands of enterprising persons, who push and advertise it very actively. We heard at San Francisco of the Fresno Colony, the Central Colony, American Colony, Scandinavian Colony, Temperance Colony, Washington Colony, and others of similar names clustered around Fresno. It is advertised as one of those genial places, alluring to the imagination of most of us, where one can sit down under his own vine and fig-tree, secure from the vicissitudes of climate, and find a profitable occupation open to him in the cultivation of the soil, and all at a moderate cost.

The aspect of things on alighting is very different from what had been expected, but all the substantial advantages claimed seemed realized, and the process of founding a home may be witnessed in all its stages.

The town has a population of two thousand, most of which it has gained in the past five years. It is set down on the east side of the railroad highway, with a thin scattering of foliage slightly veiling the formality of its lines. It consists of a few streets of two-story wooden and brick buildings. The streets cross one another at right angles, and have planked sidewalks. A slight eminence above the general level is the site of the County Court-house, which somewhat resembles an Italian villa in design, and has Italian cypresses in front. The court-houses of half a dozen counties down the line, from Modesto, the capital of Stanislaus, to Bakersfield, capital of Kern, are identical

COURT-HOUSE AT FRESNO.

in pattern, so that it is both typical of its kind and evidence of an economical spirit.

A sharp distinctness of outline is characteristic of these cities of the plain. Separated from the main part of Fresno by the railroad, as by a wide boulevard, is a row of low wooden houses and shops, as clearly cut out against the desert as bathing-houses on a beach. This is the Chinese quarter. It tells at a glance the story of the peculiar people who tenant it: the social ostracism on the one hand, and their own indomitable clannishness on the other.

There is now hardly any hamlet so insignificant, even in the wastes of Arizona, that the Chinese have not penetrated it, in search of labor and opportunities. Every settlement of the Pacific slope has its Chinese quarter, as mediæval towns had their Ghetto for the Jews. It is not always without the place, as at Fresno; but, wherever it be, it constitutes a close corporation and a separate unit. In dress, language, and habits of life it adheres to Oriental tradition with all the persistence the new conditions will admit.

The Celestials do not introduce their own architecture, and they build little but shanties. They adapt what they find to their own purposes, as has been said, distinguishing them with such devices that the character of the dwellers within cannot be mistaken.

A great incongruity is felt between the little Yankee wooden dwellings and the tasselled lanterns, gilded signs, and hieroglyphics upon red and yellow papers with which they are profusely overspread. Here Ah Coon and Sam Sing keep laundries like the Chinese laundry the world over. Yuen Wa advertises himself as a contractor for laborers. Hop Ling, Sing Chong, and a dozen others have miscellaneous stores. In their windows are junk-shaped slippers, opium pipes, bottles of *saki*, rice-brandy, dried fish, goose livers, gold and silver jewelry, and packets of face-powder and hair ornaments for the women. The pig-tailed merchants themselves sit within, on odd-looking chests and budgets, and gossip in animated cackle with customers, or figure up their profits gravely in brown-paper books, with a brush for a pen. Women —much more numerous in proportion to the men than is commonly supposed—occasionally waddle by. Their black hair is very smoothly greased, and kept in place by long silver pins. They wear wide jackets and pantaloons of a cheap black " paper cambric," which increase the natural awkwardness of their short and ungainly figures.

Up-stairs, in unpainted, cobwebby, second stories, are the joss-houses. Here hideous but decorative idols grin as serenely as if in the centre of their native Tartary, and as if there were no spires of little Baptist and Methodist meeting-houses rising indignantly across the way. Pastilles burn before the idols, and crimson banners are draped about; and there are usually a few pieces of antique bronze upon which the eye of the connoisseur rests enviously.

Other interiors are cabarets, which recall those of the French working-classes. A boisterous animation reigns within. The air is thick with tobacco-smoke of the peculiar Chinese odor. Games of dominoes are played with magpie-like chatter by excited groups around long, wooden tables. Most of those present wear the customary blue cotton blouse and queer little black soft hat, and all have queues, which either dangle behind or are coiled up like the hair of women. Some, however—teamsters, perhaps here only temporarily—are dressed in the slop clothing and cowhide boots of ordinary white laborers.

The Chinamen are servants in the camps, the ranches, and the houses of the better class, track-layers and section hands on the railroad, and laborers in the factories and fields. What Southern California, or California generally, could do without them it is difficult to see. They seem, for the most part, capable, industrious, honest, and neat. One divests himself rapidly of the prejudice against them with which he may have started. Let us hope that laborers of the better class, by whom they are to be succeeded, may at least have as many praiseworthy traits.

The town of Fresno is as yet chiefly a supply and market point for the numerous colonies by which it is environed. These colonies straggle out in various directions, beginning within a mile or two of the town. The intervening land still lies in its natural condition for settlement. It is difficult to convey an idea of its seemingly hopeless barrenness. Instead of complaining of dry grass here one would be grateful for a blade of grass of any kind. The surface is as arid as that of a gravelled school-yard. It is even worse, for it is undermined with holes of gophers, owls, jack-rabbits, and squirrels. To ride at any speed is certain to bring one to grief through the entangling of his horse's legs in these pitfalls. As the traveller passes there is a scampering on all sides. The gray squirrels speed for their holes with flying leaps, the jack-rabbits with kangaroo-like bounds. They run toward us, if they chance to have been absent from home in an opposite direction. Not one considers himself safe from our clearly malicious designs till he has dived headlong into his own proper tenement.

Here and there are tracts white with alkali. Flakes of this substance, at once bitter and salt to the taste, can be taken up in an almost pure condition. Elsewhere we pass through tracts of wild sunflower—a tall weed, charming in flower, but now thoroughly desiccated, and rattling together like dry bones.

This description applies, for the greater part of the year, not only to Fresno, but in an almost equal degree to Bakersfield, Los Angeles, and nearly the whole of Southern California. Without it the wonders which have been produced by human agency could not be understood. The face of nature in all this district was a blank sheet of paper. The cultivator had absolutely everything to do. He discovered on trial that he had a soil of remarkable capacity, and, with the aid of water and the genial climate, he could draw from it whatever he pleased.

Water is the salvation of the waste places, and makes the desert blossom like the rose. One's respect for this pleasant element is, if possible, increased upon seeing what it is here capable of. It seems that, if used with sufficient art, it might almost draw a crop from cast-iron. The vegetation of Southern California is thoroughly artificial. It consists of a series of scattered plantations created by the use of water. In these the traveller finds his flowers, palms, vineyards, and orange groves, and, burying himself among them, like the ostrich with its head in the sand, he may refuse briefly to recognize that there is anything else; but, as a matter of fact, only a small beginning has been made. What has been done, however, is an earnest of what can be done. It is found that, as irrigation is practised, the land stores up part of the water, and less is needed each year. In wells, too, the water is found nearer the surface, proving that the soil acts as a natural reservoir. As time goes on, and canals and vegetation increase, no doubt important climatic changes may be looked for. In the end Southern California may be as different from what it is at present as can be imagined.

The several Fresno colonies for the most part join one another, and form a continuous belt of cultivation. On entering their confines the change is most agreeable. Close along-side the desert, the home of the gopher and jack-rabbit, only separated from it by a narrow ditch of running water, are lovely vineyards, orchards of choice fruits, ornamental flowers and shrubs, avenues of shade-trees, fields of corn, and green pastures of the alfalfa, a tall and strong clover, which gives half a dozen crops a year. Embowered among these are the homes of happy families, larger establishments for the drying of fruits and converting the munificent crops of grapes into wine. Many of the homes are as yet but modest wooden cottages. Others, of a better class, are of adobe, treated in an ornamental way, with piazzas and Gothic gables.

The most important residence is that of a late member of the San Francisco Stock Board, who has gone into the cultivation of grapes here on a large scale. It is a handsome villa that would do credit to any town. The improvements of the Barton place were in but an incipient state at the time of our visit. A great array of young vines brightened the recently sterile soil, but timidly and as if not quite certain of approval. Young orange and lemon trees in the door-yard were muffled in straw till they should have gained a greater hardihood to withstand the frosts. Elsewhere water was being run out from irrigating ditches over fields in preparation for the first time. It is the custom to soak them, in order that they may be perfectly levelled. Knolls or any other inequalities must not be left to hinder the equal distribution of water to the crop. A wide canal stretched back from the numerous out-buildings toward the horizon. On the verge of the wide plain showed the blue Sierras, veiled by a slight chronic dustiness of the atmosphere.

In the more established portions of the colonies some charming bits of landscape are found. The Chinese farm-hand wears a blue blouse and a wide basket-hat which he calls *mow*. He pronounces this hat "heap good" if complimented upon it. He prunes the vines or collects the generous clusters of grapes; or else he digs a vegetable

PRIVATE RESIDENCE AT FRESNO.

garden by the side of a canal, in which himself, his vegetables, his cabin, a row of poplar-trees, and the blue sky overhead are all reflected together. Poplars, willows, and cottonwoods are planted along the canals to strengthen their banks. At Eisen's wine-making place, for a considerable distance, oleanders in flower are seen spaced between the trees. The water runs clear and swift. At Eisen's it turns a mill. No doubt devices for bathing in it might also be contrived if desired.

The long, symmetrical lines of trees have a foreign, or at least un-American, air. It is not difficult to recall to mind the mulberries and elms that bend over the irrigating canals of Northern Italy and drop their yellow leaves upon them in autumn like these. It might be Lombardy again, and the glimpses of distant blue the Alps instead of the Sierras. The locks and gates for the water are of an ephemeral structure as yet, made of planking instead of substantial brick and stone. The smaller ditches are often stopped with mere bits of board let down into grooves, instead of gates with handles. It is urged, however, that handles offer inducement to idlers to lift them up out of pure mischief, and waste the water.

The colonies are not quite colonies in the usual sense; that is to say, they were not founded by persons who combined together and came at one and the same time. The lands they occupy were distributed into parcels by an original owner, and, after being provided with water facilities by an irrigation company, put upon the market at the disposal of whoever would buy. No doubt a certain general consistency rules them in keeping with the names respectively set up, but it is not rigorous. Probably nothing need prevent a native American from joining the Scandinavian Colony, or a Scandinavian the American Colony, should he desire to do so.

As to the Temperance Colony, it must be sorely tried in a locality the most liberal and profitable yield of which is the wine grape. It seems hardly a propitious place to have chosen. Scoffers say that in some instances while settlers will not make wine themselves they will sell their grapes to the wine-making establishments. This I merely note as "important, if true."

The standard twenty-acre lot, as prepared for market at Fresno, has its main irrigating ditch, of perhaps four feet in width, connecting with the general irrigating system. For twelve and a half dollars a year it receives a water-right entitling it to the use of whatever water it may need. The buyer must make his own minor ditches, and prepare his ground from this point. He usually aims to establish in his fields a number of slightly differing levels, that the water may be led to one after the other. For ground in the preliminary condition described about fifty dollars per acre is demanded. Most of the earlier settlers bought for less, and the price named strikes one as high, considering the newness of the country, and the excellent farming land to be had in the older parts of the country for less. Prices are less here, however, than at Los Angeles, Riverside, or San Diego, farther south.

It is argued in answer to objectors that though land be not nominally it is really cheap, in consideration of its extraordinary productiveness. It is held that an investment here gives better returns than anywhere, and at the same time that the climate and other conditions promise a more pleasurable existence than could be enjoyed elsewhere. This Fresno land, for instance, yields four and five crops of alfalfa a year. Vineyards planted but two and a half years are shown which produce five tons of grapes to the acre. Five years is the period required for the vines to come into full bearing. It is estimated that an acre of vines in that condition will have cost one hundred and twenty-five dollars, allowing fifty dollars as the price of the ground, and it is then counted upon for an annual yield of ten tons of grapes, at twenty dollars a ton. The rate of growth in vegetation is one of the things to note. Fruit-trees are said to advance as far in three years as in seven on the Eastern sea-board.

The personal stories of the colonists are often interesting. They have generally had some previous hard experience of the world. Such a man, working sturdily in the field preparing the ground around a new cottage of his own, lost a fortune in the San Francisco Stock Board. The funds for his present enterprise were provided by his wife, who had turned to keeping boarders, and sent him her small profits monthly until he should have made ready a place for their joint occupancy. Instances were heard of where nice properties had been secured with no other original capital than a pair of brawny hands. These, however, were exceptional. The country appears to be one where it is most desirable for the new-comer to have a small capital.

In the Central Colony a comfortable estate was owned by four spinster school-teachers of San Francisco. They had combined to purchase eighty acres. One of them lived on the place and managed it. The others contributed from their earnings until it had reached a paying basis, passed only their vacations there at present, but looked forward to making it their ultimate retreat.

The idea seems both a praiseworthy new departure in the direction of female emancipation and charming in itself. I had the pleasure of making the acquaintance of the resident manager of the experiment. Her experiences, written out, would, I think, be interesting and instructive. There was an open piano in the pleasant cottage interior, and late books and magazines were scattered about. It was a bit of refined civilization dropped down in the midst of the desert.

This lady had come, she said, for rest. She took pleasure, too, in the country, and in seeing things grow. She had made mistakes in her management at first, mainly through trusting too much to others, but now had things in good control. Four farm-hands—Chinamen—were employed. The eighty acres were distributed into vineyard, orchard, and alfalfa, about one-half devoted to the vineyard. Its product was turned, not into wine, but raisins. Apricots and nectarines had been found up to this time the most profitable orchard fruits. Almonds were less so, owing to the loss of time in husking them for market. There was among other crops a field of Egyptian corn, a variety which grows tall and slender, and runs up to a bushy head instead of forming ears. The sight of it carried one back to the Biblical story of Joseph and his brethren, and the picture-writing in the Pyramids.

The grapes for raisin-making are of the sweet Muscat variety. There was a "raisin-house" piled full of the flat boxes in which raisins are traditionally packed. The process of raisin-making is very simple. The bunches of grapes are cut from the vines, and laid in trays in the open fields. They are left there, properly turned at intervals, for a matter of a fortnight. There are neither rains nor dews to dampen them and delay the curing. Then they are removed to an airy building known as a "sweat-house," where they remain possibly a month, till the last vestiges of moisture are gone. Hence they go to be packed and shipped to market.

One must walk rather gingerly at present not to discern through the young and scattering plantations the bareness beyond, but in another ten years the scene can hardly fail to be one of rich luxuriance. The site is flat and prairie-like, and I should prefer, for my part, to locate my earthly Paradise nearer the hills. Still, the taste of the time runs to earthly Paradises which are at the same time shrewd commercial ventures, and the cultivation of the plain is much easier than that of the slopes.

XXVII.

VISALIA, BAKERSFIELD, AND LIFE ON A SPACIOUS RANCH.

I.

VISALIA, capital of Tulare County, thirty-four miles south of Fresno, is one of the older towns left aside by the railroad. I put it in the most obvious way, but a patriotic Visalian, on the other hand, said to me with warmth, "Left by the railroad! Visalia left by the railroad! I guess not. It is the railroad that is left by Visalia, as it will find out."

Visalia is reached, from the junction of Goshen, by a short branch-road of its own. It is larger than Fresno, but less animated. It has perhaps twenty-five hundred people, a court-house of the pattern described, and a United States land-office.

When the epithet "old" is used of any California town not of Spanish origin it simply means an approximation to the year 1849. The building of most hoary antiquity in Visalia dates only from the year 1852. It has been government-house, jail, and store in turn, and is now decorated with the legend "Mooney's Brewery." The town was founded by one Vise, an erratic person, who came across the plains from Texas, and had followed in his life such various professions, besides that of pioneer, as preacher, trader, gambler, foot-racer, and jockey. It happened that the quarter section of land upon which he settled was at the time unsurveyed, and not legally open

FIRST BUILDING IN VISALIA.

to pre-emption. This irregularity was not discovered till years later, when the town had grown up on the site. It was brought to light by an employé of the land-office, who thereupon ingeniously undertook to pre-empt the ground for himself.

"And what came of this bold attempt upon vested interests?"

"The party was promptly fired out of town," was the reply.

Visalia is rather prolific in stories, if an "old-timer" of the right sort can be happened up to tell them. Cattle kings, whose herds once filled the San Joaquin Valley, have retired hither. You may hear how Cattle King "Pat Murray" won his wife. She was a fascinating person in her youth, the daughter of a landlady with whom Pat Murray, then struggling and impecunious, boarded, in company with numerous mates. There was great aspiration and rivalry for her hand. Pat Murray stole a march in this wise. As they were setting off in company on an expedition he said, "The trip is a rough and dangerous one, boys. I propose that we leave our money and valuables with the old lady for safe-keeping." The rest agreed, and handed over to him their property to deliver to her. The shrewd Pat Murray represented it all as his own, and obtained in this way such consideration in her eyes—as a person exceptionally well-to-do in the world—that she advised her daughter to "set her cap" at him, and all was happily accomplished before the *ruse* was discovered.

On another occasion—whether in this same courtship or not the chronicles do not say—Pat Murray disposed of rivals, who visited in the evenings a comely damsel of the general acquaintance, by soft-soaping the log serving as approach to her cabin across a small stream. Having thus arranged, he sat calmly enjoying the fair one's society, and listening with appreciative ear to the splash of the successive victims as they slid off into the water.

Stories are told of Spanish bandits and treasure of precious metals in the mountains, and of the wild administration of justice in early times, when offenders were occasionally executed first and sentenced afterward.

AN OLD-TIMER.

The first treasurer of the county is said to have carried the records of his office in his hat, and, being a person given to travel and of an absent mind, he scattered these documents far and wide behind him, even to the confines of Utah and Arizona.

At Visalia I first observed "Spanishtown," a community which begins to appear regularly alongside of "Chinatown" as we go southward. It is composed of persons of Mexican blood, poor, shiftless, and not always of the most reputable character.

Charming views of the high Sierras, now powdered with the first snows of winter, are had. The surface is more rolling than at Fresno, and strewn with fine clumps of chestnut-oaks. There are big trees back in the great mountains equalling in size those of the Yosemite. Lumbermen at work there cut down numbers which, though insignificant as compared to the very largest, are monstrous in themselves.

The water for the irrigation of this district is drawn out of Kings, Tule, and Kaweah rivers by companies, who give to their principal canals such names as the People's Ditch, the Last Chance Ditch, the Mussel Slough Ditch, and the Lower Kings River Ditch. The main ditches or canals range from twelve to forty feet in width. Wing dams confine and direct into them such portions as are desired of the wide, meandering rivers.

A California river of the south is something of a curiosity. Extravagantly wide, it is in compensation preposterously shallow. Only a few last over the dry season at all; the most evaporate and wholly disappear. Their dry beds, variegated by a few islets studded with sycamores, are more like wagon-roads than the beds of rivers. Sometimes these exhausted water-courses differ in color from the surrounding soil, and are seen stretch-

LOGGING, BACK OF VISALIA.

ing as rivers of gray or silvery sand through the general yellow of the desert.

Though irrigation be yet in its infancy its belongings have attained great dimensions. There are three hundred miles of canals of the requisite size in Tulare County, and more than three thousand miles in California all together. One main canal, that of the San Joaquin and Kings River, has a length of seventy-four miles and a width of nearly seventy feet.

II.

A branch-road westward from Goshen, a continuation of that from Visalia, conveys the traveller to the bustling, fast-growing little towns of Hanford and Lemoore, in the Mussel Slough country. This district, adjoining Tulare Lake, was recently part desert and part swamp. It has been redeemed so as to rank now among the best farming land in California. Its chief product is wheat. The inhabitants raise hardly the vegetables needed for their own use. Malaria is rather prevalent, but it is said to arise, as in many other irrigated districts, from the careless use of water rather than the fundamental situation. The water, instead of being carefully drained off, is too often allowed to lie in stagnant pools.

The Mussel Slough was the scene, in the month of May, 1880, of a bloody conflict between the settlers and railroad authorities which has become celebrated. Officers of the law, acting for new claimants, attempted to take possession of the land under a railroad title. Legally in the wrong, though perhaps morally in the right, the settlers organized to resist, put out stirring manifestoes, which read like the declarations of oppressed people struggling for their liberty, and called on gods and men to witness the justice of their cause. In the fight that ensued five settlers lost their lives, all at the hands of a single man—one Crowe, a United States marshal, who displayed a prowess and coolness under fire never surpassed in any of the narratives of sensational literature. Crowe himself was despatched. A number of the survivors were tried for their part in the affair, condemned to eight months' imprisonment, and served out their term in Santa Clara jail. They had but just been released, say a month before our arrival. Their brethren and well-wishers had received them on their return with an ovation, the noise of which hardly yet ceased to ring in the air.

III.

Bakersfield, capital of Kern County, seventy-five miles farther south, somewhat smaller than Visalia, boasted at one time the distinction of a malady peculiar to itself. The Bakersfield form of malarial fever, whatever the fine difference that distinguished it from others, had a position apart in the medical works. The sanitary condition of the place, however, has been greatly improved by the extension of drainage and irrigation works, and can, no doubt, be made all that could be desired.

Of the three lakes, Tulare, Buena Vista, and Kern, which make so large a showing on the map, the latter two, with their surrounding marshes, have been dried up, and the former is on its way to extinction also. These lakes had for me, on the map, a mysterious and important air. I seized the first opportunity to penetrate their mystery, by riding down to Tulare Lake on horseback. You cannot reach the margin, for fear of miring. Nor is the approach on foot much easier. The tules, or rushes, rise high above your head, and are infested with a dangerous breed of wild hogs, descended from vagrant deserters from the ranches. In such fragmentary glimpses as are had between and over the tules an expanse of dreary surface appears which may be either water or the alkali-whitened bed from which the water has receded. The vicinity swarms with wild fowl. Their multitudinous chatter has a kind of metallic clang in it. Now white, now dark, as they are before or against the sunlight, they flutter above the reeds and stubble-fields like autumn leaves blown by the wind.

The drying up of the lakes is occasioned by the diversion of the surplus waters of the Kern River for the redemption of desert lands. This gave rise to a controversy, lately settled by a legal decision which is a step in the crystallization into shape of a system of water jurisdiction for California. The great firm of real-estate men and ranchmen, Miller & Lux, owned the lands below; the almost equally great firm of Haggin, Carr & Tevis, those, for the improvement of which the water was taken out, above. The first-named complained of the diversion of the waters as a detriment to them, and an infringement of their riparian rights. Riparian right, it will be remembered, in the English common law, gives to the resident on a stream the right to have it flow as it was wont through his grounds without diminution or alteration.

The contest at first promised to be one of physical force. Miller & Lux endeavored to close the sluices at which the water was taken out. Just, as in Scripture, the herdsmen of Gerara strove against the herdsmen of Isaac, saying, "It is our water," the hardy *vaqueros* of Haggin, Carr & Tevis were mustered in opposition to them, with orders to lasso and throw into the canal anybody who should interfere with the sluices. This determined show of resistance prevented a conflict, and the case went to the civil courts.

The decision spoken of holds that the doctrine which prevails in California is not that of riparian right, but that of "prior appropriation for beneficial uses." That is to say, the greatest good of the greatest number is consulted. The point had been raised before in controversies about the diversion of water for mining purposes. In these cases the ruling was, that the doctrine of riparian right is "inapplicable, or applicable only in a very limited extent, to the necessity of miners, and inadequate for their protection." It was farthermore held that all of the English common law is not in force in California, but only such portions of it as are adapted to the peculiar conditions of the State. The agricultural and mining interests, therefore, are now put, in this respect, on the same footing.

Bakersfield takes its tone essentially from live stock. It has special resorts for drovers and sheep-herders. Its streets are generally full of horses, caparisoned in the Spanish style, tied to hitching-posts and awaiting their owners before the stores and taverns. The sheep-herders, a lonely race, become morose and melancholy in their long wanderings with their flocks apart from the habitations of men and human speech. They are far removed from the shepherds of Boucher and Watteau. Some are said to go insane through the monotony of their lives; and it is an occupation taken up only as a last resort, and unfitting him who pursues it for any other. Strangely enough, there is a rather English tone among them. Young prodigals of good family are found who, after trying their fortunes in Australia, India, and elsewhere, are eating the husks of repentance here in true Scriptural fashion.

The shops in Bakersfield, as throughout our travels, are kept principally by the Jews, who are great pioneers. No people are growing up more ardently with the new West; and where they are found business is pretty sure to be good.

The Chinatown is a district of compact little streets, of an extent that indicates a population almost equal to that of the rest of the place. An irrigating ditch surrounds it like a moat. The cabins along this, picturesquely reflected in it, are gray and weather-beaten, varied with patches of bright Orientalism, and shaded by a line of tall poplar-trees. The Spanishtown, close by, is a cluster of dance-houses and corrals, between which swarthy Josés and Juanitas are seen passing.

As if this were not foreignness enough already, we stumble upon a camp of strolling gypsies, their tents pitched on the borders of Spanishtown. They are English, and have come from Australia, dropping their "h's" all along the way, no doubt, as liberally as here. They are like types of Cruikshank and Dickens. An apple-faced Mrs. Jarley appears in a large velvet bonnet with plumes. A very tightly-dressed, slender individual, with a weed on his hat, might pass for Sam Weller. He is a horse-tamer and jockey. At his heels follows a belligerent bull-dog. Behind one of the tents a child of nine, Cassie by name, with fine, dark eyes, is making a toilet before a bit of cracked mirror. She pastes down her wet hair into a semblance of the "water-waves" of fashionable society. When interrupted with a compliment on the arrangement she affects displeasure, and tosses it all abroad again with a native coquetry.

The Mrs.-Jarley-looking woman is the fortune-teller. She declares that there are persons whose fortunes she would not tell for twenty—no, not for fifty dollars.

CHINATOWN, BAKERSFIELD.

Mine, however, through an especial liking she affects to have taken to me, and the dulness of trade, she promises to tell, in the most effective manner, for two dollars only.

IV.

The possessions of some of the great land-owners are prodigious. It is a favorite story that certain ones can drive a herd of cattle from the northern counties of the State to San Diego, its southern limit, and quarter them every night on their own ground. Haggin, Carr & Tevis, whose property I was privileged to examine in detail, have at Bakersfield four hundred thousand acres nearly in one body. Much of this was secured for a trifle in the condition of desert land, and has been redeemed.

One ranchman who had acquired a great estate of this kind chiefly while surveyor-general of the United States was the occasion of drawing forth one of the best *bon mots* of Lincoln.

"I congratulate you," said our martyred President. "You have become monarch of about all you have surveyed."

The owners do not often live upon their estates; they leave them in the hands of managers, and draw the revenues. The Haggin, Carr & Tevis property is divided into a number of separate ranches, each with its resident superintendent. The "Bellevue Ranch" is the centre and focus of authority. Here are the residence and office of the general manager, and a force of book-keepers, engineers, and mechanics, who keep the accounts, map, plan, supervise, construct, repair, and give to the whole the clock-work regularity of a great commercial enterprise. The numerous buildings constitute a considerable settlement. There is a "store" of general mer-

GYPSY CAMP AT BAKERSFIELD.

chandise and supplies. A dormitory and a dining-hall have been erected for the laboring hands. A tower-like water-tank, surmounted by a windmill, and accommodating a milk-room below, rises at one side. There are shops for the mechanics, capacious barns, and long sheds filled with an interminable array of agricultural implements. It is worth while to take a walk past this collection of reapers, threshers, sulky-ploughs, and rakes, and study out their uses. The immense "header and separator" rises from the rest like a leviathan. A whole department is devoted to "road-scrapers," "buck-scrapers," and ploughs of various sorts used in the construction and dredging of the irrigating ditches. The soil is, fortunately, free from stones, and the work, for the most part, easy. One enormous plough is seen which was designed to be drawn by sixty yoke of oxen, and to cut at once a furrow five feet wide by four deep. Like the famous *Great Eastern*, it has defeated itself by its own mass, and its use has been abandoned.

More than $500,000 has been expended in the item of fencing alone. An average of four hundred laborers is employed, and, in the harvest season, seven hundred. The rate of wages is from two and a half to three dollars per day for mechanics, and a dollar per day for common hands. This seems low as compared with information from other sources, and the chronic complaints of the scarcity of farm labor, in the California papers.

No great portion of this domain appears to be in the market for settlers of small means, though the intention is avowed of offering some of it in this way when thoroughly reclaimed. Tracts, however, are occupied on favorable terms by "renters," who take from 120 to 600 acres. Very many of these are Portuguese and Italians. They are usually unmarried, and work in companies of from six to fifteen persons. You see them, dark and swarthy, going about in the traditional Garibaldi shirt, with hardly a word of English among them.

The renter is provided with a house, artesian well, credit to a moderate amount at the store, and the use of some cows. He has the milk of these, but must give their increase to the estate. His lease runs three years, and he pays in rent one-third of his crop. Instances of large profits are frequent among these persons, and the same opportunities are open to others who wish to follow their example.

The superintendents and upper employés on the place are largely Southern men. California was a favorite point for Southern immigration at one time, so much that the course of the State in the war, influenced by the historic Judge Terry and Senator Gwin, was considered problematical. These that I speak of, however, are gentlemen who have come here to repair their fortunes at a later period. They have for the most part titles from the service of the extinct Confederacy, and the gentle voices and friendly courtesy characteristic of the Southern type.

A typical ranch-house, that, for instance, of our hospitable friend Major McClung, on his section of the subdivided property, is a long, two-story dwelling, painted in the Indian-red so popular throughout the country. It is raised on posts considerably above the ground, to allow of a free circulation of air underneath. There is an open hall through the centre for the same purpose. An irrigating ditch resembling a moat passes in front, crossed by a little rustic bridge.

Traces of alkali yet show white in the soil of orchard and garden, but do not prevent a plentiful growth of oleanders, roses, pear, peach, cherry, almond, and apri-

A TYPICAL RANCH-HOUSE.

cot trees. The young orange-trees were, as at Fresno, put up in mufflings of straw for the winter. The weather is very hot at noon-day, but so cool at morning and evening that wood-fires are burned. The chill in the air is of a penetrating kind, felt the more by contrast with the heat of the day, and fire is a necessity. The house-servants were clean, white-aproned Chinamen; those out-of-doors, Mexicans. One of these latter had trained a goose, "Dick," to follow him like a pet dog, and nothing was more curious than to see the pride of both master and biped in this ridiculous relation.

Cattle-raising is the leading industry; alfalfa, for carrying the stock over periods of scarcity, is the leading crop. Stacks of alfalfa of great size, one containing seven hundred tons, were seen. It is the ordinary color of hay externally, but when cut into is green.

A successful experiment has also been made in the raising of cotton. The hands were in the field going about among the white pods for the second picking.

Though out of season, a *rodeo* was organized for our benefit, to show the method of handling the roving cattle on a large scale. A number of *vaqueros* rode out in various directions till lost to sight. Presently traces of dust arose on the several horizons. The plain, on which a few cows had been peacefully feeding, was filled with stamping and lowing herds, driven toward the centre by the careering *vaqueros*. When gathered in sufficient numbers feats of lassoing the animals, by either leg or horn, separating special animals or classes, and the like, were undertaken, and carried through with marvellous dexterity. As a culmination, hats and ropes were picked up from the ground, the rider going at full speed. A silver half-dollar, placed on edge in the dust of the roadway, was seized after several attempts by a swarthy Aztec.

The herders are usually Mexicans, equipped in the Mexican style, but with the greater part of the finery left out. The bosses, who often even excel them in pure horsemanship, are generally Americans.

The ranch known as the Livermore borders Kern and Buena Vista Lakes, and is the southernmost in the tier. The herds are gathered there in the early spring, and driven to the ranch of San Emidio, in the mountains.

SAN LUIS OBISPO.

They pick up their subsistence at San Emidio till the middle of September, when they are conducted back again. Such migrations from plain to mountain pasture, and back again, recall some features of the Norwegian pastoral life of Boyesen's charming romance, "Gunnar."

At the Livermore Ranch you are at the apex of the San Joaquin Valley. Here the Sierra Nevada and the Coast Range effect a junction, and oppose a natural barrier to farther progress. The railroad has to cross this barrier by a wonderful piece of engineering, the Tehachapi (Te-*hatch*-a-pe) Pass. At one place five different lengths of track pass and repass at different levels. By the singular "Loop" the road enters a tunnel, emerges, twists spirally round the mountain, and reappears directly above itself.

At San Emidio we are on the boundary-line of San Luis Obispo County, and could make our way directly, no doubt, to its pretty, mountain-encompassed capital. This is more easily reached, however, with attractive Santa Barbara below, by steamer, or stage-road along the coast.

Returning to Bakersfield, you may ride west to the wild cañon of the Kern River, and the mining towns of Kernville and Havilah. The mining industry has never taken the same development south of the San Joaquin River as north. It is probable both that there is less ore and that the ventures have been managed with less skill. At Kernville is a quartz-mill, with a hundred stamps, which after many vicissitudes has fallen into the hands of its former workmen for debt, and is now run by them on the co-operative principle.

The rolling country by which the Kern River Cañon is approached is, if possible, even more desolate than the

418   OLD MEXICO AND HER LOST PROVINCES.

A RODEO.

plain. There is almost a necessary connection in our usual impressions between hills and trees, and when foliage is missing from hills its lack is doubly notable. An utterly parched, verdureless surface, with a texture like that of gravel, here follows all the inequalities of the

THE KERN RIVER CAÑON.

ground, up hill and down dale, to the savage and splintered granite gorge.

We fell in with an isolated sheep ranchman, "Captain Jack Barker," an enterprising man, who had created a garden spot in the waste, and showed what even this is capable of. He was engaged on a project for leading the water, by means of a flume and ditches, from the river at the cañon's mouth down upon several thousand acres of land under cultivation. In the spring-time, he told us, all this bareness is hidden by a perfect carpet of flowers, chiefly a small orange-scarlet poppy. His sheep at present seemed living on air. He had among them some Angora goats, a hardy animal, once very profitable, but now, since the decline in alpaca goods, being used by him for food.

The Kern River tumbles down a gorge four miles in length, between granite walls six hundred feet high. Its water is translucent green in deep, untroubled pools, again churned into milk-white floods, with black bowlders among them. The cañon is all but impassable. It acts like a funnel, and produces a local disturbance of its own on the atmosphere. While all around is still, a column of air will blow out of it, and, striking the tableland a quarter of a mile away, raise a chronic dust at the point of contact, like a cannon-shot.

Driving across the front of it we were nearly blown out of our wagon. We descended into it, nevertheless, and upon this experience returned to dine on ribs of Captain Jack Barker's Angora goats, and then take the railway and cross the Tehachapi Pass.

XXVIII.

LOS ANGELES.

I.

OVER the Tehachapi Pass, we are in Southern California proper. We have met already, it is true, with pretty Spanish names, old missions, leather breeches, jingling spurs, vineyards, raisin-making, and occasional orange and palm trees. But when the dividing mountain-range, four thousand feet above the sea at Tehachapi, is passed, all these are found in their greatest development. The country is older, the Spanish names are more musical; orange and lemon are not grown for ornament, but as a principal crop; and the climate is of that genial mildness which is most to the taste of seekers for health.

Famed Los Angeles, City of the Angels, is the terminus of the first day's journey which brings us into it. The watering-place of Santa Monica and the important points of San Buenaventura and Santa Barbara are not far distant to the west, while San Diego lies at a moderate remove to the southward, near the Mexican frontier. In the intervals scatter colonies of vine and orange growers, the numbers and dimensions of which are rapidly increasing.

The mountain barrier across the State is deemed by some to be of such importance that it should be a political as well as a natural division. They call for the coustruction of a distinct new State, to be called South California, its capital at Los Angeles.

TEHACHAPI PASS.

"We are different peoples," writes one of them in the *Californian*. "We are different in pursuits, in tastes, manner of thought, and manner of life; . . . our hopes and aspirations for the future are different."
The restless, uneasy population of the North, ever drifting, without local attachments, has no counterpart in Southern California; neither has the wild spirit of min-

ing speculation ever flourished here. With this peaceable life, possibly in part as a result of it, there has grown up in the people an intense love of their land.

"And it is for their own section of the State," he goes on, "that this love exists. They call themselves, not Californians, but Southern Californians. The feeling is intense. I can only liken it to the overmastering love of the old Greek for the sunny shores that lay around the Ægean.

"For myself, I feel more and more each time that I visit the upper portion of the State that I am going into a strange land. And the impression never leaves me till upon my return I look down from the crest of the Tehachapi over the warm South-land."

I have thought it worth while to quote these passages, partly because they are amusing, partly because they accentuate the topographical situation, and also because they attribute a character almost the opposite of that which exists. Everywhere is bustle, push, and enterprise. This people will sell you a corner lot or quarter-section of land with as great a gusto as any other, and at its full value. Whatever effect lapse of time may have upon them, the present inhabitants, few of whom are born here or even drafted from indolent climes, if lotus-eaters, are of a very wide-awake sort.

II.

The City of the Angels is, in general, only another San José, upon a more hilly site. Its population must be about fourteen thousand. The long thoroughfare of Main Street proceeds, from the depot, at first through a shabby Spanish quarter, locally known as "Sonora," consisting of one-story, whitewashed, adobe houses. Passing a small Spanish plaza, set with pointed cypresses, and the principal hotel, the Pico House, it becomes lined with excellent buildings of the modern pattern. Of these the handsome "Baker Block" is most notable. Continuing to the ornate "Los Angeles Bank," Spring Street diverges at a small angle, and contributes, with Main Street, to give the commercial skeleton of the town the shape of a Y with a very long stem.

On Spring Street you find a common little post-office, the municipal offices, and a brown, Dutch-looking, brick building, standing free, originally constructed for a market, and now the Court-house. If you look into the lobby of the small adobe jail you will find that some leisurely prisoner of the frescoer's trade has converted it into a resemblance to a dungeon scene at the theatre. These two streets, with a shorter one, Los Angeles Street, parallel to Main, containing fruit and produce commission houses, comprise the commercial portion of the city.

New buildings are seen going up; the shops are large and well-appointed, and placards offer, in the usual shibboleth of trade, "To Reduce Stock!" "At Wholesale Slaughter," and "For the Next Sixty Days."

A serious depression afflicted Los Angeles in 1875, at the time of the general depression throughout the State, but that has been succeeded by a new reign of activity. Trim, large residences of the more prosperous merchants are seen in the outskirts of the town. Farther out yet these become villas, in the midst of plantations of orange and lemon, ruled off into formal plots by ditches for irrigation. The class of modest means abide in the side streets, in frame cottages. The German Turn-hall serves also the purpose of theatre for such companies as come this way.

It is held that Los Angeles, with its port of Wilming-

MAIN STREET, LOS ANGELES.

ton, thirty miles away, should be now, upon the completion of the Southern Pacific railroad, the *entrepôt* and Pacific terminus of a new commercial departure. San Francisco, it is said, has too long sat at the Golden Gate "levying toll on every pound of freight that passes through," and this selfish greed is to be properly rebuked by the diversion of a part of its trade. Enthusiastic San Diego expects also to have its share. The wickedness of the proceeding would seem to depend largely upon who it is that takes the toll. Los Angeles, it is held, is to be the Lyons, and San Diego the Marseilles, of the State, San Francisco still remaining its Paris.

The pepper-tree, with its scarlet berries and fern-like leaves, forms the leading shade and ornament of Los Angeles streets. Apart from these a clump of palms grows on San Pedro Street, and, before an odd, octagon-shaped house on Main Street, a Mexican nopal of the size of an apple-tree. In the court-yard of the principal hotel droops a single ragged banana. Tropical features in the vegetation are scarce, but it is evident that this is not the fault of the climate, but of failure to encourage them. In the door-yards are the Mexican aloe and the Spanish bayonet, from the adjacent deserts of Mohave and Arizona. The castor-oil plant grows a tall weed in neglected places. The extraction of castor-oil was at one time an industry of the place, but is now abandoned.

III.

The Mexican element must be something like one-third of the entire population of the place. In the Spanish town, "Sonora," the recollection of Mexico is revived, but a very shabby, provincial Mexico. You find *mescal* and *tequila*, the two varieties of intoxicating liquor distilled from the *maguey*, or aloe. The dingy little adobe shops contain samples of dingy little stocks of goods in their shuttered loop-holes of windows. A few swarthy, lantern-jawed old-timers hang about the corners, and gossip in *patois*, and women with black shawls over their heads pass by. Much of the quarter is in a ruinous condition. There remain vestiges of the arcade system of the kind known in some form to all tropical or semi-tropical climates. The arcades of Sonora are not of massive brick and stone, but are wooden roofs, such as are put out by our corner grocers, on light wooden posts. Here and there only the battered skeletons remain, attached to ruinous houses. Most California municipalities have borrowed something of this Spanish idea. At Sacramento the thriving but flat and not attractive capital of the State, you can walk nearly all over the business part of town under cover.

There is a very respectable-looking restaurant—a vine-embowered cottage—opposite the Pico House, where the familiar *tortillas*, or pancakes, and *frijoles*, or stewed beans, may be had. Along-side is an adobe church, quaint in pattern, but modern and devoid of farther interest. From its belfry the chimes jangle loudly several times a day in familiar Mexican fashion. Out of Sonora emerges, on the 16th of September, the Juarez Guard, which escorts a triumphal car bearing the national colors of red, white, and green, and, aided by a *cortége* of dark little maidens, in white muslin and slippers, proceeds to celebrate with appropriate ardor the anniversary of Mexican independence.

This people, who have gone so much to the wall, wear no very pathetic aspect in their adversity. They are for the most part engaged in coarse labor, are improvident, and apparently contented. It is only rarely that a Spanish name—a Pacheco, a Sepulveda, or Estudillo—rises into prominence in the public affairs of the State of which they were once owners. Old Don Pio Pico, the last of the Spanish Governors, resides here, impoverished, in a little cottage, in sight of property of great value which was formerly his, and of the plaza once the centre of his authority.

Don Pio is one of the picturesque features of Los Angeles, and with his history would be esteemed interesting anywhere. Above eighty years of age, with stocky figure, square head, and bright eyes, contrasting with his bronzed skin and close-cropped white hair and beard, he has a certain resemblance to Victor Hugo. He has a rather florid taste for jewelry. He carries himself about town, in his short overcoat with velvet collar and cuffs, with a bearing still erect and stately. It is strange to tell, but true, and

DON PIO PICO.

it is evidence of the conservatism and lack of adaptability of his race, that the old gentleman, though once Governor of the State, and a continuous resident of it, as an American citizen, since he surrendered it to Fremont and Stockton in 1847, does not yet speak a word of any other language than Spanish. The talk of this historic personage gave but a rude picture of the state of society in his youth. Was there anything in the world so remote as the California of the years 1810 to 1848?

"I am but a plain and unassuming person," he said to me. "My father did not leave me a mule nor a vara of ground. I worked for the padres at the San Gabriel Mission when I was a boy, and I had little opportunity to learn book knowledge."

He disclaimed being an authority even on the events of his own fall and the encroachments of the Americans. "There are many," he said, "who have a better head for those things than I, and who will tell you better than I." .... "I was a just man, however. I treated the rich no better than the poor. Hence when they asked who was *lo mas justo y honrado*—the most just and honest man — for Governor, it was answered with one accord, 'Don Pio Pico.'"

There are differences of opinion about those ancient officials. Some of them have been charged with a wholesale issue of land-patents after the American occupation, which patents ostensibly belonged to their respective administrations. Edwin M. Stanton, sent out to look into these matters by the Attorney-general of the United States, reported at the time that "the making of false grants, with the subornation of false witnesses to prove them, has become a trade and a business."

The treaty of Guadalupe Hidalgo, in 1847, by which the war with Mexico was concluded, made valid and of full force whatever had been done before the American occupation. Spanish governors were numerous in those last days, and went in and out of office with extraordinary frequency, by reason of plots, counterplots, and the inability of the home government to enforce its own will. Alvarado, Carillo, Micheltorena, and Pio Pico reigned separately, or together, or by turns, in a revolutionary, confused, and overlapping way, which furnished excellent opportunity for fraud. One prefers, however, not to lin-

MONGOLIAN AND MEXICAN.

ger upon unpleasant suspicions, but rather to esteem these fallen dignitaries, few of whom now survive after their misfortunes and romantic histories.

Even the Chinese, singularly enough, show greater enterprise than the Spanish. Perhaps they may have a somewhat better warrant for coming in here than elsewhere, since a Chinaman is found in the list of the twelve original settlers of the town, in 1781. They have pushed into the best of the old Spanish adobe houses, once the best of their kind in the State. They occupy all those which flank the little plaza with an entire street, others debouching from it.

The populace, however, have not always been the better reconciled to the hapless Mongolians. In an outburst of deadly prejudice, in the year 1871, they were dragged out of their Spanish houses and hung to lamp-posts, wagon-tongues, and their own door-ways, to the number of eighteen, of all ages and sizes. The riot was occasioned by their resistance to some process of a deputy-sheriff. My informant described them to me as hanging like bunches of carrots.

At present they were putting up, near the site of these sanguinary scenes, an ornate open-air theatre or temple, for a triennial religious festival, to last a week or more.

IV.

One of my pleasantest days at Los Angeles was that which I spent in a drive with the Zanjero.

The Zanjero, indeed! who or what is a Zanjero?

His title is derived from the Spanish *zanja*—ditch—continued down from the times of the original settlement, and he is the official overseer of water and irrigation. He took me about with him to observe this important and entertaining part of the economy of civilization in these thirsty regions. Not that Los Angeles is so dry in comparison, for it has thirteen inches of rain against two at Bakersfield, but it is in abundant need of irrigation.

The Zanjero is elected by the City Council annually. Six deputies aid him in the summer, reduced to three in the winter, when the rains render irrigation hardly necessary. All are invested with the authority and badges of policemen.

The city, the Zanjero tells us, as we ride along, controls in its corporate capacity all the waters of the Los Angeles River. The Los Angeles River is a Southern

California stream of the typical sort. It has a wide, shallow bed, almost dry at the moment, but in spring and winter it brawls in dangerous fashion, and often carries away its bridges. We ride up to the point near a certain railroad bridge where the water is first diverted. It is taken out by two small canals, one for the city proper, one for the thriving suburb of East Los Angeles. We find that the dam by which the river is checked for this purpose is constructed of earth, with a facing of stout posts and planking. At the beginning of winter the planking is removed, and the stream allowed to sweep away the rampart of earth, which is replaced by a new one, the succeeding spring. Chain-gangs of convicts from the prison are set upon this labor.

A canal is taken out of the same river twelve miles above, which supplies water for drinking and irrigating the higher levels. There are two very different levels in the configuration of the city, one rising from the other with great abruptness, as at Santa Cruz.

Upon the height are remains of the fort built by Fremont when he entered the city. Directly at its foot is the cottage of Pio Pico; the big hotel, still bearing his name, in which he sunk a handsome share of his fortune; the little cypress-studded plaza; and the shabby white quarter of Sonora. The mass of the city lies to the right, without striking features. Beyond it, toward the river, stretch breadths of a russet bloom which we know to be vineyards, together with lines and parallelograms of orange and eucalyptus, as formal as the conventional trees in boxes of German toys. Across the river, "Brooklyn Heights" and "Boyle Heights" rise to a wide, rolling table-land (*mesa*), which extends back to the blue Sierra Madre Mountains. Toward most of the horizon stretch expanses of a garden-like vegetation of a mysterious quality — the dreamed-of orange-groves in mass.

The city has created a considerable part of its debt by its water system, in which it has spent probably $200,000. The works are of an ephemeral character, which will in time be replaced by something more substantial. The simple trenches and wooden flumes permit of wasted water, and are costly to keep in repair. One of the principal ditches, however, is carried through a hill some three-quarters of a mile in a tunnel of six feet in section. There have been formed also numbers of durable reservoirs or artificial lakes for the storage of additional water in winter to supplement the river at its lowest.

We rode out among the villas and gardens and observed the practical application of the water. The main ditches are three feet by two, the lesser about two by one. The "head" is the nominal standard of measurement of the babbling fluid. The head should be a section of one hundred square inches, delivered under a certain uniform pressure, but it is in practice loosely administered.

"The irrigators want their work *done*," says the Zanjero; "that is the main point. Some lands take more, others less, according as they are sandy or hold water. A head of fifty inches on the east side will do as much as one hundred and twenty around the city."

Fan-palms, India-rubber-trees, and tall bananas grow freely on the lawns where a little pains is taken. You stop now to exclaim at a comfortable home embowered in myrtle, orange, and vines, the dark, glossy foliage starred with golden fruit and red roses, a spot for any romance. Again, it is a long arcade or temple of arborvitæ, extending across the whole front of a garden, and framing in its arches delicious views of distant blue mountains, their tops now powdered with snow.

This land of running brooks should be a famous place for the children to sail their boats, though as a matter of fact we do not see them doing it. Perhaps there is a law against it. There are laws, at any rate, against stealing the water, wantonly raising the gates to waste it, or transferring it to irrigators outside the city limits. These latter are entitled to it only upon an extra payment and after those within the city have been supplied.

As all irrigators cannot be supplied at once, the manner of serving it out is as follows: Applications have to be made in the last week of each month. The Zanjero then apportions the supply so that it may go round among the applicants in the most convenient way. The complete circuit takes about twenty days. The applicant receives a ticket, on the payment of a fee, entitling him to receive the water on such a day at such an hour. The right for that time is exclusively his. The rates are so fixed as to reimburse the public treasury, and are not intended as a source of profit. The average charge for water is about fifty cents an hour, two dollars a day, and a dollar and twenty-five cents a night.

The subscriber has the water delivered to him by the deputy at his connecting-gate. At all other times the gate must be kept fastened with a padlock. The wooden gate, sliding smoothly in its grooves, is like a little guillotine.

Chop! goes the guillotine, when it has been raised long enough, and off goes the head, as it were, of the little stream. Thus surprised on its way among the orchards and gardens, it writhes and twists a while, rises again in its confining box, and is soon ready to begin life again on a new basis.

V.

Los Angeles is the metropolis of the orange trade, but the greater part of the culture itself is in tracts of the surrounding country, each with a thriving settlement as its nucleus. The lands are usually laid out and subdivided by capitalists, under the "colony" system, as described. Ten or even five acres in a crop of such value are a comfortable property. On Lake Guarda half an acre in lemons is sufficient for the support of a family. It is in evidence here that returns of from $500 to $1000 an acre are had from orange, lemon, and lime, after the trees have arrived at full bearing.

The piazzas of the orange-planters command attractive views; rose and heliotrope bloom round them; and specimens of all the fruits are offered for our tasting with lavish hospitality and honest pride in their perfection.

We begin with Pasadena, which is reached by a drive of ten miles from Los Angeles. Pasadena, the Indiana Colony, San Gabriel, the Lake Vineyard tract, the Alhambra, Santa Anita, and Sierra Madre tracts, and others, all of the same general character, adjoin one another. The dwellings in them are those of people of means and a certain taste. Even the least show ambition. There are pretty chapels in the Gothic style, and neat school-houses. Well-dressed children of a city air are met with on the roads. The roads are excellent. No violent storms or thawing snows in this climate tear them up, and they are kept in order with little trouble.

The door-yards are enclosed with hedges of lime, arbor-vitæ, or rose-bushes. Curious small circles from time to time attract attention, either filled with water, or dry, like the rings of a departed circus. These are reservoirs, supplementing the irrigation system. They are usually filled by artesian wells, which flow from iron pipes a few feet above the ground, the water overspreading the top in a thin film, like a globe of glass, reflecting neighboring objects. Such globe-like films, sparkling from a distance, are a frequent item in the prospect. As there has never been any forest, no unsightly stumps indicate recent clearings. The country, in consequence, does not look new. Where settled at all, it has a surprisingly old and civilized air.

The temperature, this late November day—on which there are telegrams in the papers of snow-storms at the North and East—is perfection. It is neither hot nor cold. A sybarite would not alter it. Bees hum in the profuse clusters of heliotrotpe about the porches. A single Jacqueminot rose on a tall stem, a beauty whose sway will not be gainsaid, makes its vivid crimson felt from the greensward a long way off. Among the older estates this is pointed out as the home of "Don Benito," that of "Don Tomas," so and so, the family name being usually American. Audacious in love as in other things, enterprising Americans have married into the Spanish families, both before and since the conquest, and succeeded to their acres. Very few of Spanish stock still retain any property of note.

If there be or ever existed any real earthly Paradise, I think it might bear some such complexion as that of the Sierra Madre Villa, on the first bold rise of the mountains at San Gabriel. I cannot vouch for it as a hotel, for hotel it is, but I vouch for it as a situation.

The air was heavy with the fragrance of extensive avenues of limes as I came up to it. The orange-trees were propped up, to prevent their breaking under their weight of fruit. Forty oranges on a single bough! I saw it with my own eyes. Some of the trees, by the freak of a recent

PARADISE.

gale, had been denuded of their leaves, which left only the globes of golden fruit, a lovely decorative effect, on their bare stems. A view of thirty miles is had across the garden-like San Gabriel Valley, to a strip of blue sea on the horizon. On the strip of blue sea rests a slight brown spot, the jewel of Santa Catalina Island.

Flowering vines clustered along a piazza, part enclosed in glass. In a warm nook a couple reclined in steamer-chairs, one reading aloud a novel in a gentle murmur. They were a couple of recent date, and as the place for a honey-moon it was ideal. The orange bears a close resemblance to the formal tree which the mediæval painters used to represent as the "tree of the knowledge of good and evil" of Genesis. It is appropriately placed, therefore, in our earthly Paradise.

Hist! The young woman who had been reading takes her stand archly at one side of such a tree. The man who had been listening rises also, and, with a slight yawn, places himself on the other. Oh, what is this? Is she a new Eve? She plucks a fruit, and hands it to him. Oh, this is terrible! Is there to be a fall again in Eden, and all its direful consequences? There should be some Cranach or Dürer here to take down once more the particulars of the distressing scene. What does Eve wish Adam to do? Perhaps she wishes him to buy lands—above their value —and go into orange-planting himself. Alas! he will be lost forever to the higher financial life. Perhaps Satan is the invidious real-estate man.

But really there is no pressing need of such a display of fancy because a young matron offers her husband a fresh orange before dinner.

Certain drawbacks—drawbacks attending upon an injudicious entering into this apparently fascinating kind of life—should not be overlooked. The orange-tree grows all the time, and calls for incessant care, winter as in summer. Not a few invalids who had looked to its culture as a pastime have broken down through this cause, and through having taken up more land than they could manage. The lesson of such cases is, not to attempt too much, but to keep to the five, or ten, acres, as the case may be, within one's capacity. Nor has it been politic to put everything into the single crop of oranges. The smaller fruits—peaches, plums, and especially apricots—for canning, which come into bearing quickly, are useful in tiding over the tedious period of waiting for the orange-trees to mature, and are always in profitable demand. To start existence comfortable here the new-comer should have a capital of from five to ten thousand dollars, though peculiar energy may do with less.

It requires about nine years to bring an orange-tree from the seed into full bearing. On the other hand, it is found that by deftly inserting an orange-bud into the bark of a lemon-shoot slitted in an X, and setting this in the ground, a tree can be obtained which bears marketable fruit after the second year. The controversy rages as to whether it is worth while to do this, since the product is dwarf, like the dwarf pear-tree. Though it yield early it will never yield much, and its fruit does not stand shipment as well as that of the seedling. Against this it is maintained that it lives longer than the seedling, and yields choicer varieties of fruit, and that the fruit is more uniform in size and quality, and not subject to a singular form of destruction which sometimes overtakes that of the seedling—being dashed upon its own thorns.

In the same way conflicting theories of irrigation prevail. A person who bought grapes in large quantities for the purpose of making them into wine told me that over-irrigation was rendering them watery and insipid. He proposed to meet this by establishing a standard. He would pay twenty dollars a ton for grapes containing twenty-three per cent. of sugar, and for those below standard less. Plentiful irrigation, however, is relied upon to counteract that fatal pest of the vine, the phylloxera. Some advocate the theory of irrigation in the winter or rainy season only. All the water possible is to be conducted upon the land at the time it naturally falls, leaving the soil to act as its own reservoir, and store up a portion for the dry season ahead. Others even deny the need of irrigation altogether. They write to the papers that it is only necessary to keep the surface well scratched with a cultivator, and a supply of moisture will always be found a few inches below it. It is certain that crops both of grapes and the cereals have been produced from unirrigated ground, even for a series of years. But then comes a dry year, in which everything, animals as well as plants, is scorched from off the face of the earth.

"Certainty is what is wanted," says a lively informant. "You may not need water, as you may not a revolver, all the time; but when you do, you need it awful bad."

VI.

In the plain, just under the mountains, lies the old village and mission church of San Gabriel. The mission dates from 1761. It was founded, like the other missions of California, by friars sent out from the college of San Fernando, in the city of Mexico. I recollect well the original San Fernando. It stands on the street which was the scene of Cortez's disastrous retreat from the city, and is marked with an inscription commemorating the famous Leap of Alvarado.

The Mission of San Gabriel is worthy of its picturesque origin. It has the same massiveness, color, and quaint rococo details, including the peculiar battlement, or Spanish horn of dominion. Six old green bronze bells hang in as many niches together. The fern-like shadows of a line of pepper-trees print themselves in the sunshine against the time-stained wall. No more than the church edifice now remains. Great agricultural establishments connected with all these missions were swept away, years before the American occupation, by edict of the Mexican government. Some bits of broken aqueduct, and a

A MEXICAN WEDDING AT SAN GABRIEL.

few orange-trees, above a hundred years old, in what was once the mission garden, are the only vestiges of former prosperity. The interior of the church contains a few battered old religious paintings, the worst of their kind. It is doubtful if the luxury of really good pictures was ever superadded to the excellent architecture, for which there was a natural instinct. It is a commentary on the popular estimate in which the poor old masters are held, I fear, that I was told by the neighborhood:

"You *must* see them. They are all Raphaels and Michael Angelos."

The village is piquantly foreign. Its single street is composed entirely of white adobe houses. One of them, with a tumbling, red-tiled roof, is so full of holes that it looks as if it had been shelled. All the signs are in Spanish. Here is the *zapatero*, or shoemaker, and here the *panaderia*, or bakery. The south walls are hung with a drapery of red peppers drying in the sun to prepare the favorite condiment. The population are a humble class, who gain their livelihood for the most part by day-labor on the surrounding estates. They are not too poor, however, to retain their taste for festivity still. On the occasion of some notable wedding among them they will manage to mount on horseback, and, surrounding a bridal carriage, driven postilion-fashion, return from the ceremony, at the old mission, whooping and firing pistols in the air, in the most gallant and hilarious fashion.

Near by is the large estate of Sunny Slope, known as one of the most successful instances of the putting in practice of the sanguine theories about the country. It has been acquired, and developed, from very small beginnings. It consists of some nineteen hundred acres of land, most of it in vines and oranges. There is a large wine and brandy making establishment. Eight thousand boxes of oranges and lemons, four hundred thousand gallons of wine and one hundred thousand of brandy, have been produced in a year.

The dwelling-house was approached by a stately avenue of orange-trees, in double lines, three-quarters of a mile in length. The road to the large, substantial buildings of the winery was bordered by an orchard of orange on one side and olive on the other. The vineyards stretched out in distant effect like vast reddish-tawny meadows.

THE VINTAGE, SAN GABRIEL.

At the winery, blacksmithing and cooperage were going on on a large scale, and a deft Chinaman was constructing the orange-boxes. The rich juice of the grape poured in floods, and its more concentrated form as brandy came from its still as clear as water. All distilled spirit is naturally colorless, and the hues it obtains for market are given by burned sugar, to gratify an artificial taste.

The hands are Chinamen and Mexicans. The superintendent tells us that the former do the most work and get less pay, but that there are certain things which they cannot do. They cannot plough, nor prune the vines, and they are awkward in the management of animals. Indeed, a Chinaman on horseback, or even in a wagon, seems almost as incongruous as Jack Tar.

We visited, one evening, the Chinese quarters, and it would have been hard to find a more clean, domestic-looking interior among men of any other nationality in the same circumstances of life. They seemed much more orderly in their arrangements than the Mexicans, either those from the village or those who had a settlement on a bold slope of the estate above.

There is much native Indian blood among these latter, and their dwellings were half wigwams, patched up of rubbish. Mongrel dogs, a donkey, and a foundered horse wandered at ease among them. A reddish-brown urchin, with large, liquid eyes, coming out, paused to gaze at us.

"*Cor-r-re, demonio de muchacho!*" (R-r-run, demon of a boy!) cried a slatternly mother, who appeared behind, endeavoring to urge him upon some errand of peculiar expedition.

But the demon of a boy, exemplifying the traits of his race, had no idea whatever of being in a hurry. On the contrary, having removed to a safe distance, he dawdled in the most exasperating way, and continued to stare round-eyed during all of our critical tour of inspection.

The work of the year was now the pruning of the vines. Stripped of every superfluity, the rugged little stocks, regimented veterans, were to stand bare till the exuberance of a new spring should again break forth in

IRRIGATING AN ORANGE-ORCHARD.

leaves. Faustino, Gaetano, Incarnacion, and the rest, for so they are called, appear to picturesque advantage in this work. Their swarthy faces are framed in slouch sombreros. They wear red-and-blue shirts, and bright handkerchiefs about their necks. They move forward in a line, pruning-knife in hand, and a small saw at the belt for the tougher knots. The spots of color twinkle upon the russet of the vineyard; the pruning-knives flash as they turn to the sun; the ground has a gentle, agreeable fall; and splintered granite mountains, with deep cañons among them for exploration, softened by a veil of atmosphere, back up the whole.

The orange-tree, even at a great age, is not as large as one may have expected. Even those of a hundred years in the mission garden are not above two feet in diameter. It is gratifying to be at full liberty to examine this attractive vegetation, known heretofore only in its tub in the conservatory, or on the staircase at a ball. There seems but one drawback to an orange-grove, and that is that it cannot have greensward below to lie upon. It is very exacting—requires all the nourishment the soil can give, and the soil must be kept loose and open around the roots. It is irrigated about once a month, and the surface gone over with a cultivator afterward, to prevent baking up in the sun.

The orange-grove is lovely at all times, mysterious when the long alleys are dark against the red sunset, the fruit glimmering like a feast of lanterns at twilight; and in the pleasant mornings sparkling among the glossy leaves like little suns newly risen; while we catch the perfume of blossoms heralding in a new crop, though the last still hangs upon the bough. Here and there is an example of the enormous shaddock, which resembles the orange in appearance but the lemon in character. The lemon is less hardy to rear than the orange, and is not cultivated on as large a scale. Chinamen, with ladders and baskets, gather the fruit, and chatter to one another from the trees like magpies. It is irrigation-day, and all at once the water is let on. Twisting and turning this way and that, it runs out upon the thirsty soil, as if with an eager curiosity in the embrace. Chinamen with hoes follow it, here throwing up little dams, which it tries to evade; there, when it runs sluggishly, opening little channels, and leading it where it should go. The whole orchard is soon babbling musically with running water, and in process of being thoroughly soaked.

XXIX.

TO SAN DIEGO, AND THE MEXICAN FRONTIER.

I.

These and kindred scenes are to be met with in fifty, I know not how many more, localities of a similar sort. San Fernando, Florence, Compton, Downey City, Westminster, Orange, Tustin City, Centralia, Pomona, and Artesia may be mentioned as leading examples. The "colony" government is of a simple sort, and consists of a justice of the peace, constable, water overseer, and school trustees. Anaheim, settled by Germans, was one of the first established colonies, and has become a town of importance. Santa Ana had a special bustle at present, as the terminus, for the time being, of the railroad in process of building from Los Angeles to San Diego.

Perhaps, however, the greatest general air of distinction is worn by Riverside. This colony seems to have been sought to an exceptional degree by persons in good circumstances. It is fifty-seven miles lower down than Los Angeles, and reached by a drive of seven miles southward from the Southern Pacific Railroad at Colton. Four miles north of Colton, on the other hand, takes you to San Bernardino, an important place of six thousand people, originally settled by Mormons. The regular Mormons withdrew to Utah by order of Brigham Young on the threat of the coercive war there in 1857, and only

A SYLVAN GLIMPSE AT RIVERSIDE.

a few "Josephites" now remain, whose practices do not differ greatly from those of other people.

At Riverside is found a continuous belt of settlement and cultivation twelve miles long, by two miles in average width. It will be twenty long when all complete. The population is not large, but revels in a great deal of room. The general situation is a valley of about forty miles square, at an elevation of twelve hundred feet above the sea. The access to this valley is by four several passes, one each on the north, south, east, and west, as if so many doors had been providentially left open in the encompassing mountain ranges. The settlement forms an oasis in the midst of the desert, after the general plan. Its fresh greenness, and canals of clear water, along which sylvan glimpses, almost English, are met with, derive added charm and interest from the desert. The rest of the high, quadrangular valley, capable, no doubt, of as great development, if water can be brought upon it, remains in its natural condition.

A lovely drive, called Magnolia Avenue, planted with double rows of pepper and eucalyptus trees, extends through the length of the place from north to south. It is bordered with homes, making pretensions to much more than comfort. The best of these are at the division called Arlington, four miles below the post-office of Riverside proper. The native adobe, or sun-dried brick, supplemented with ornamental wood-work, has been used as material with excellent effect. In the interiors are found rugs, *portières*, Morris's wall-papers, and all the paraphernalia of the latest Eastern civilization; and there is an archery club and a "German."

Invalidism is heard of with considerable frequency as an excuse for the migration hither. Certainly many advantages offer to the invalid. The climate permits him

ADOBE RESIDENCE AT RIVERSIDE.

to be almost constantly out-of-doors. The sky is blue, the sun unclouded, nearly every day in the year, and he can go into his orchard and concern himself about his Navel or Brazilian oranges, his paper-rind St. Michaels, and his Tahiti seedlings, with little let or hinderance. Orange culture affords him both a career and a revenue. If the unchanging blue of the sky grow sometimes monotonous, there are other distractions in the noble mountain ranges. Riverside has in this resource a touch of the charm of Switzerland. Your entertainer points out to you from his piazza the great peaks of Greylock, San Bernardino, and San Jacinto, from ten to twelve thousand feet in height, and crowned with snow for a considerable part of the year, just as the Jungfrau is pointed out from Interlaken and Mont Blanc from Geneva.

It is a description that applies to all of Southern California, that, however great the heat by day—in midsummer often a hundred and five in the shade—the nights are always cool and refreshing. Sunstroke is not known. Nor are the violent thunder-storms with which Nature, with us, endeavors to restore equilibrium after having exhausted its most oppressive warmth. The great drawback here, as there must always be some drawback, consists in occasional heavy "northers," which gather up the dust from the dry surface and produce painful dust-storms of two or three days' duration.

ADOBE RESIDENCE AT RIVERSIDE.

In autumn and winter the temperature is chilly enough to make fires a necessity morning and evening, and even all day long in apartments shut off from the influence of the sun. I was astonished to find the air so keen at these times, and a scum of ice forming upon water in the mornings even as far down as San Diego. The cold has a penetrating quality beyond its register by the thermometer. This, though usually overlooked, is important, since fuel is very scarce and correspondingly dear.

Fagots of the prunings of the cottonwoods, sycamores, and mesquit-trees along the beds of the streams are the principal resource. Such coal as can be obtained is both costly and of poor quality.

The water for the irrigation of Riverside is taken from the swift little stream of the Santa Ana River, which falls so rapidly within a short compass that it is feasible to take out two separate canals with a difference of thirty-five feet in their levels. On all sides lands are held at $200 and $300 per acre, and when the orange-trees have come into good bearing, at $1000, which but a few years ago were purchased at a dollar and a quarter an acre.

All these places have their local rivalries, though Southern California as a whole is ready to unite in vindicating its peculiar claims, against the outside world. All have their pamphlets to distribute, containing their tables of mean temperatures, altitudes, analyses of soils, and claims to regard, as based upon nearness to, or absence from, some particular natural feature. Thus the coast counties take leave to pride themselves upon a genial average of temperature, owing to their proximity to the sea. They are free, they say, from the extremes of heat and cold afflicting those which are shut in behind the mountain barriers. The inland counties, on the other hand, congratulate themselves that their lot is cast where the mountains form an efficient defence against the raw fogs and gusts which must necessarily afflict those directly exposed to the chilly ocean.

These petty rivalries are a part of the history of all new countries, and pass away with the development of population and trade. There seems no need of jealousies, since there is encouragement enough for all in their several ways. The Territories of Arizona and New Mexico have just been opened to transportation by rail from this quarter. The lands suitable for the cultivation of the "citrus fruits" are limited in extent. The market is much more likely to improve than decline, even when production shall have largely increased beyond its present rate. High railroad freights were at one time a cause of alarm. The making of an "orange wine" was proposed as a resource for using up the surplus crop of this kind. The experiment was not a success, but it is not likely to be needed. Freights have declined, and will decline more with the building of projected new roads. Shipments of oranges have been successfully made from this section as far away as Denver, Chicago, and St. Louis.

II.

Great things are predicted for Wilmington, a little port twenty-two miles to the south-west of Los Angeles. The extensive works undertaken here by the railroad and the United States government are still incomplete, and it is but a dreary little place in its present condition. However, great ports have never been selected primarily for picturesqueness, but in accordance with such commercial necessities as short lines of transit, easy grades, and convenience for shipping. Wilmington had few natural conveniences to offer. There were originally but eighteen inches of water on its bar. This has been increased to ten feet. An enormous jetty, 6700 feet long, extending out to what is called Dead Man's Island, is under construction. It is to force the tide itself to do the duty of scouring out the bottom, so that a ship channel several miles long will eventually be secured.

Santa Monica is another small port at the end of a branch railroad from Los Angeles, sixteen miles directly west, and somewhat famed as a sea-side resort. It has a hotel of considerable size, and a bold situation on a pretty horseshoe bay. The beach is of fine, hard sand; and the temperature admits of bathing, if one be inclined for it, all the year round. The hopes which were at one time entertained by capitalists, like Senator Jones, of Nevada, of making the place a great shipping point, have been for the present abandoned. It was to have been the Pacific terminus of a new through line from the East, coming by way of the Cajon Pass. A wharf 1500 feet long was built, and a breakwater proposed.

OLD MISSION AT SANTA BARBARA.

From here, or from Wilmington, you sail up the coast to San Buenaventura and Santa Barbara—favored by invalids. These places have as yet no railroad, but must before long come into the general system. Both are on that sheltered stretch of the coast which, from Point Conception, makes a sharp turn to the eastward, and has direct southern exposure and a view of the islands of

Santa Barbara Channel. Santa Barbara, on its practical side, has devoted more attention than most places to the culture of the olive—an industry still much in its infancy. Some of the cultivators have provided themselves with a machinery, which costs about a thousand dollars, for expressing the oil. As a condiment the fruit is not pickled green here, like the Spanish olive, but ripe and black. It may be that a special education is needed for liking each variety of olives, as it is for acquiring the taste in the beginning. Those here are of a small variety, descending from the old mission times, and it is hard not to find them either insipid or bitter. The leading shipment from San Buenaventura is honey. A million pounds per annum from Ventura County, of which it is the capital, is not an unusual product.

III.

I sailed from Wilmington to San Diego. I embarked in the evening in a small tug, which steamed down the tortuous windings of the channel, past black lighters that Whistler would have liked to etch, and past Dead Man's Island, and transferred us on board a coast steamer waiting without. Next morning we were at our destination, a hundred miles below. San Diego, rising on a gentle slope, makes a pretty appearance from the water. A United States barracks (yellow), with a flag-staff rising in the centre, is the most prominent object in front. You round an immensely long, narrow sand-spit of a peninsula, which contributes to form the excellent small harbor, and make fast to an immensely long mooring wharf. It is a feature of all California ports to have immensely long wharves. To the left is "Old Town," its beach where Dana once loaded hides in his famous "Two

PLAZA OF SAN DIEGO, OLD TOWN.

Years Before the Mast," now the site of a Chinese fishing village. To the right is brand-new "National City," the location of the shops and extensive depot grounds for the new railway. In the centre, at about four miles from either, lies "New Town," San Diego proper. All together have a population of about five thousand.

As we came up to the wharf a locomotive, starting from National City on the new track, made the circuit of the water-front, with one long, shrill scream, which was taken up by the hills and echoed back. Gods and men were no longer to remain ignorant that San Diego had at last caught up with its future and had its railroad.

It was cruelly disappointed when it was to be the terminus of the Texas Pacific, transcontinental, road. The panic of '73 prevented the capitalist "Tom Scott" from negotiating the foreign loan which was needed for its completion. That enterprise was abandoned, and a half-mile of graded road-bed alone remains as a sort of tumulus to the blighted hopes and bitter memories of the time. The name of the unfortunate "Tom Scott"—since defunct—remains also a byword and a reproach. Now, however, the "California Southern" is actually at work, and under contract to complete the one hundred and sixteen miles necessary to meet the Southern Pacific, at a point near San Bernardino, within a short time. It is to be a link in the new "Atlantic and Pacific," which is to follow the thirty-fifth parallel, and become a transcontinental road by means of connection with the Atchison, Topeka, and Santa Fé.

The capital and management of the California Southern are largely supplied by the same Boston company directing the Mexican Central, the line to Guaymas from the Arizona frontier, and others. A farther road is projected by them eastward from San Diego to Calabasas, passing through Port Ysabel, at the head of the Gulf of California. This can be more cheaply built below the Mexican frontier than on this side, owing to special exemptions there to be had from taxation, and the lower rates of labor. It is thought that the Southern Pacific will also be compelled by competition to build across from Yuma. Hopes are still entertained also of the derelict Texas Pacific. With all this in prospect, it will be seen that San Diego has justification for making a good deal of stir. It claims to be hundreds of miles nearer, than San Francisco, to New Orleans and New York, on the one hand, and the Orient on the other, and is correspondingly cheerful.

A hand-car on the long wharf conveyed our baggage into the town while we walked beside it. The town, being reached, is found a place of loose texture. It has a disproportionately large hotel, the Horton House, built in anticipation of the rapid arrival of its future greatness, and a loss to its original proprietor. The blue shades were down and the plate-glass windows dusty also, with an expectant look, in much of the "Horton Block," opposite. After '73 half the shutters in San Diego were put up. They have come down now, however, and probably to stay.

There is a charming view of the harbor and blue ocean from the upper slopes of the town. Part of the view is a group of bold Mexican islands, the boldest of these, Coronado, a solid mass of red sandstone, which Americans have tried to get for a quarry, without success. Yes, here is Old Mexico once more; we have come back to it. The high, flat-topped peak of Table Mountain marks it unmistakably. It is customary to drive down to "the Monument," set up on the dividing line of Baja (Lower) California, but the excursion is without special interest.

The chronic condition of shutters in San Diego "Old Town" is to be "up," that is, so far as it can be said to have any shutters yet remaining. It dates from 1769. Disadvantageously situated in regard to the bay, it began to be deserted in favor of the newer site about ten years ago. Nothing could seem more desolate than it is now. The usual old mission, with a few palms and olives about it, stands in a valley, up the pretty San Diego River, and the earthworks of Commodore Stockton, who threw them up one night before the enemy knew he was ashore, are seen on a hill. Rents should be cheap in Old Town, but, according to the gossips who still sit around the decayed old plaza, they are not. The owners hold them stiffly yet, on what theory Heaven only knows.

OLD MISSION AT SAN DIEGO.

The plaza has a toppling flag-staff, a decayed music-stand, and vestiges of a number of burned edifices, which have never been worth anybody's while to build up again. The "Merchants' Exchange" will never supply cocktails to thirsty soul again; the Cosmopolitan Hotel is without a guest; whole rows of weather-beaten adobes—whole quarters—stand vacant. It should be a great place for ghosts. But perhaps they do not care for one another's society. The children, coming from school—for there is, it seems, a school—amuse themselves with knocking at and rattling the vacant doors; then they peer in at the broken window-panes and shout, and run laughing away.

IV.

In leaving San Diego I traversed the surveyed line of the new railroad almost due northward. A thirty-mile section of the railroad was already built. The rest of the journey was made by wagon, with an occasional half-day's pedestrianism, for which the dry, smooth surface of the

DON JUAN FORSTER.

ground is well adapted. It afforded opportunity of making the acquaintance in a leisurely way of some of the ranchmen, small and great, of the old school. The principal one of these was Don Juan Forster (deceased since this visit), well known in his section. He was English by birth, but sailed with his father in a trading vessel, and became a Mexican subject and resident of California long

SEÑORA FORSTER.

before the American conquest. It was so long before that he had well-nigh forgotten his English, and had to learn it over again when the Americans arrived. The Señora, a sister of Governor Pio Pico, never learned it at all, any more than her conservative brother.

Don Juan's estate, the Santa Margarita Ranch, comprised an area of twenty-seven miles by fourteen, or one hundred and forty-five thousand acres of land. There was one fence seventeen miles in length, and another ten. The owner had made two distinct efforts to colonize a portion of his land, without great success. He had offered in London to give forty acres and the use of three cows and two horses to whoever would put upon

FORSTER'S RANCH.

the land improvements, in the shape of houses, vineyards, etc., to the amount of $1000.

The Santa Margarita ranch-house is of adobe, very thick-walled, with a terrace in front, and an interior court. The waiting at table was by a broad-faced Indian woman in calico. All the domestic service was performed by mission Indians, except the cooking, for which a Chinaman had lately been secured, with the view of having meals on time. The manner of living on these great places was found comfortable, but without the "princely" features attributed to it in some of the highly colored narratives of former travellers.

The greater part of the available land in the section was devoted to pasture. The cereals were cultivated, but not much fruit. Barley is the favorite cereal, as less liable to "rust" and spoil than wheat. Hay is made, not of grass, but of wheat and barley straw, cut green, with the milk still in it. Bee-culture is an important industry. A number of varieties of wild sage, wild buckwheat and sumac, furnish the bees exceptionally good provender. Rows of the square hives, painted in colors, were often seen districted into little streets on the hill-side, or at the mouth of some small cañon, like a miniature city.

Before reaching Don Juan Forster's the old mission of San Luis Rey is encountered, in the hamlet of the same name. It is almost Venetian in aspect. The whole exterior was at one time faced with a diagonal pattern recalling that of the Ducal Palace. The pile was ruined by a Mormon contingent of the American forces engaged in the conquest of the State. Parts of the heavy adobe walls and buttresses have fallen in, and resolved themselves back into their original element as mere earth-heaps. The images have been shot and hacked down, and a yawning cavern was excavated behind the main altar in search of fancied treasure. Upon a floor strewn with such *débris* and with fragments of red tiles the daylight falls curiously, through holes in the broken roof and dome.

SAN LUIS REY.

The railroad traverses some striking natural scenery. Most notable is the Temecula Cañon, a gorge of a wild and grand description, ten miles in length, through the Coast Range. A brawling stream runs down its centre. The gorge was filled with a busy force, as we passed, terracing up the track along its sides, sometimes on the natural rock, sometimes on a cyclopean retaining-wall of immense bowlders. Toward evening every day the firing of heavy blasts reverberated up the defile like a cannonade. The main part of the laboring force consisted of Chinamen. They had utilized the shelving ledges and random nooks by the stream for their tents and cooking-ovens with great ingenuity. The Mexicans and Indians, who formed the contingent next in importance, were in every way less provident. The surveyors were found pleasant and hospitable fellows, as surveyors at the scene of their labors are apt to be. Compactness and conveni-

20*

ence had been reduced to the lowest terms, but a pleasant existence seemed possible in their small tents. A Chinese cook was attached to each camp, and the provisions and fare were excellent.

While coming up in the construction-train over the section of already completed road we had the distinction of being waited on by a servant of rather uncommon pretensions. This was a certain "Charley," a shock-

A TICHBORNE CLAIMANT.

headed boy of fourteen, son of a later Tichborne claimant, who had strangely arisen at San Diego just then, and announced his purpose of again contesting the title.

Though serving in a menial capacity—while his father, who claimed to have good and sufficient reason for having kept quiet till now, was taking the necessary steps to secure the long-lost title and fortune—"Charley" was deaf to all banter on the subject. He was supercilious and firm in the faith that he too was a Tichborne.

"And don't you forget it," he threw out to us by way of a parting injunction.

Out of the cañon, at the van of the construction work, we were on the Temecula Plains, a part of the Upper Santa Ana Valley. The course of the road was marked henceforth only by an occasional surveyor's stake. We rode over fifty miles of absolutely treeless, verdureless desert. It was desert, however, with a certain fascination in its sterility. It had a distinct beauty of coloring. The brown, drab, and blackish waste, catching sparkles of light on its flinty surface, shimmered in the sunshine. The heat was tempered by a gentle breeze. Crags of black, water-worn rock, which had once been reefs in an inland sea, rose in bold, fantastic shapes, and noble mountain ranges stood up along the distant horizons, their rugged harshness softened into blues and purples by a delicious veiling atmosphere.

Half-way across we fell in with a single sign of human life, in the shape of an abandoned pine shanty. On going around to the rear the boards were found to have been knocked off, probably to be used for fuel. Some former travellers, halting here like ourselves, had occupied a part of their leisure with writing inscriptions in lead-pencil. One had written a direction about drinkable water in the neighborhood. Another, apparently finding this erroneous, had inscribed below it, with much more vigor than regard for adopted usages in spelling, "Lyor!!"

The sole piece of furniture remaining was a rusted cooking-stove, standing on three legs. It had a certain almost diabolic, knowing air. You suspected it of having lost its other leg in waltzing about and holding high carnival, as no doubt it did, with the coyotes, gophers, tarantulas, and lizards who dropped in to pay it visits.

XXX.

ACROSS ARIZONA.

I.

IF there be anything politically disrupting in mere topography, the section cut off by the range below the Los Angeles and Riverside country should also be made a separate State. It should clamor at any rate to be joined to Arizona, since it is Arizona that it follows in climate, and not California. South-east of the low San Gorgonio Pass the seasons are the same as those of Mexico; that is to say, the rains fall in summer, while northward they fall in the winter and spring. Thunder-storms on each side of the mountains may be plainly visible from the other, but do not pass the limit.

I myself saw, from the Arizona side, in December, in hot, clear sunshine at the time, murky clouds billowing above the range, and the lightnings playing in them, and, on returning to Los Angeles, found it drenched in its first showers of the season.

There is one excellent reason why the inhabitants of the section do not raise such a clamor, which is, that there are no inhabitants worth mentioning. For a hundred and fifty miles, from the pass, to the Arizona frontier at Yuma, the railroad hardly knows any local traffic. Its route is over the celebrated "Colorado Desert," in comparison with which previous deserts are of small importance. There are various stopping-places, with designations on the map, but these are rarely more than signal-stations where the locomotive, like the passengers, stops to slake its thirst at a series of artesian wells.

The plain is not of great extent laterally. Black and purplish mountains are always in sight, and spurs cross the track. Bowlders and pebbles are scattered thickly on the surface at first, among patches of bunch-grass. Then, near Seven Palms, the jaws of the black and purple mountains open and receive us into the genuine desert. It is strewn with bowlders still, but is itself a waste of drifting white sand, with large dunes and hills of sand. One might be riding on the shores of Coney Island or Long Branch.

A singular depression below the level of the sea for a hundred miles, and at its lowest point nearly three hundred feet, is traversed. At Dos Palmas, in the very bottom of it, a board shanty, covered with signs in amateurish lettering, indicating that it is a saloon, stands entirely alone. Surely the bar-keeper must consume his own drinks, and lead an existence unprecedented among his kind. No; a horseman in Mexican accoutrements dashes across the plain—though where he should dash from, and how he should ride anything, here in the bottom of the sea, but the skeleton, say, of a dolphin or a sea-horse, is a mystery—pulls up, and enters.

And it appears, on a better acquaintance with Dos Palmas, that a stage starts every other day for points on the Colorado River, and Prescott, the capital of Arizona Territory, and that this is but a faint survival of bustle which once reigned here before the advent of the railroad. The route of the Southern Overland Mail then came this way, and long trains of immigrant and freight wagons, carrying water in casks for two and three days' supply, were passing continually over these wastes.

Nothing, on general principles, would appear more depressing than such a country, but as a matter-of-fact it is a stimulus to the curiosity, and furnishes real entertainment. One would not wish to be abandoned there without resources, it is true, but he does not tire of looking at it from the car-window. Its blazing dryness is disinfectant and preservative. There can never exist the last extreme of sadness where the element of decay by damp and mould is not present. Chemical processes are those which are principally going on. Wonders of almost any sort may be expected, and you almost look for phantoms not of earth among the shifting mirages.

A considerable part of Arizona, as well, is of the same character, but it is estimated by competent authority that with irrigation thirty-seven per cent. of that Territory can be redeemed for agriculture, and sixty per cent. as pasturage. It will be called to mind that even the apparently hopeless Colorado Desert, which is below the level of the sea, is also below the level of the Colorado River, from which water might perhaps be spread over it with comparative ease.

The truly patriotic Arizonian in their neighborhood is not ashamed of his encompassing deserts, but rather proud of them, and with a certain reason. The desert is in reality a laboratory of useful products. Paper is made from the yucca, or Spanish-bayonet, which abounds in parts of it. There are tracts of salt, borax, gypsum, sulphur, asbestos, and kaolin, and quarries of pumice-stone, only waiting shipment. It is maintained, also, that it has deposits of the same precious metals which, mined in places where water is more accessible, have given the Territory most of its present fame.

Our train runs out upon a long wooden drawbridge, across the Colorado River, and we arrive at Yuma. The company has placed here the first of its series of hotels of uniform pattern. It is both station and hotel. Such provision on an equal scale of comfort would hardly have been judicious yet as an investment for private persons. These structures therefore become not only a typical feature of the scenery, but an indication of the extent to which the railroad has had to, and has been able to, by reason of its ample resources, take this bare new country into its own hands. They are of the usual reddish-brown, two stories in height, and surrounded by piazzas of generous width—an indispensable adjunct under the dazzling light and heat of the country.

II.

The heat of Yuma is proverbial. The thermometer ranges up to 127° in the shade. There is an old story of a soldier who died at the fort and went to the place which Bob Ingersoll says does not exist, and, finding it chilly there by comparison, sent back after his blankets.

Great heat, nevertheless, is not equally formidable everywhere. It is well attested that there is no sunstroke here, and no such suffering as from a much lower temperature in moister climates. Distinct sanitary properties are even claimed for this well-baked air. So near the sea-level, it is said to be less rarefied, and to comprise, therefore, a greater quantity of oxygen to a given bulk, than that of mountain districts, which, in purity and dryness, it resembles. It is thought to be beneficial in lung troubles. Yuma, among its arid sand-hills, has aspirations to be a sanitarium. Civilized people also may yet resort there to engage in a sensible sun-worship, basking in the genial heat, and then plunging into the river, after the fashion of the resident Indians, who make of it in this way a kind of natural Turkish bath.

THE COLORADO RIVER AT YUMA.

A transition state may have disadvantages, even when a step toward something better. Yuma has now its railroad, and is to have a shipping-port of its own, by the construction of another to Port Ysabel, on the Gulf of California. Still, it laments a greater activity it once enjoyed, as chief distributing point for the mines and upper river towns. It expects the Port Ysabel Railroad to have the effect of doubling its population in two years. It will not be a very stupendous population even then, as it is but fifteen hundred at present.

The town is a collection of inferior adobe houses, a few of the very best being altered from the natural mud-color by a coating of whitewash. The ordinary part of it resembles more the poor tropical hamlets on the trail to Acapulco than even the ordinary villages of Mexico. The houses consist of a framework of cottonwood or ocotilla wattles, plastered with mud inside and out, making a wall two or three inches thick. The roof is thatched, the floor is the bare ground. Around them are generally high palisades of ocotilla sticks, and corrals of the same adjoining.

The waiters in a Yuma hotel are of a highly miscellaneous character. You are served, in the same dining-room, by Mexicans, Chinamen, Irish, Americans, and a tame Apache Indian. One and all had a certain astounded air, ending in something like confirmed depression, on finding that we were to remain, would dine at our leisure, and did not wish to have the dishes shot at us as if out of a catapult, after the practice with the ordinary traveller pausing here his allotted half-hour. One does not expect too much of his waiter in Arizona, however. There are reported instances in which he makes you eat your steak with his hand on his pistol-pocket, and the threat of wearing it out on you if you object.

The Colorado at Yuma makes about the same impression as to width as the Sacramento at Sacramento, the Ohio at Pittsburg, or the Connecticut at Hartford. It is a turbulent yellow stream. It cuts into high sand bluffs on the Arizona side, and spreads out their contents in wide bars on the California side. It is without wharves. The light-draught, high-decked steamboats, or barges, that ply up and down its interminable reaches tie up when necessary to the banks.

Mountains of a jagged, eccentric formation follow its general course northward. Peaks impressively counterfeiting human work, Castle Dome, Chimney Peaks, Picacho, and Cargo Muchacho, loom up along the horizon, a fitting prelude to the marvels of Arizona.

It was at the close of an Indian war that this visit was made. It had been said, in rumors much exaggerated, that the whole white civilization of the Territory was in danger by the outbreak, and troops—but now on their return—had been hurried thither from all sides. The first view of Indians, therefore, at Yuma was of a double interest. They were not Apaches, it is true, but a subsequent acquaintance with the general field proved them to be even more picturesque. They are of that highly satisfactory style of savages who wear but little clothing, and none of it European. They are to be seen in numbers about the railway-station by the most casual passenger. The railroad is still new to them, and they have not satiated their curiosity. They bring friends from a distance to see it, and are observed describing to these visitors how the drawbridge swings, and how the cars are switched from one track to another.

They are met with coming across this bridge from the patch of river-bottom near the fort on the California side, where their principal settlement is. The young men run or stride at great speed, so as to throw out behind them a long red sash or band, depending from the breech-cloth, which is, in summer, the principal part of their attire. To this is added, in winter, a close-fitting gray or crimson under-shirt. They wear their thick, coal-black hair "banged" low on their foreheads, and bushy about their necks. The effect at a little distance is not unlike that of

PASQUAL, CHIEF OF THE YUMAS.

the Florentine period, when the young gallants wore jerkins and trunk hose fitting them like their skins, and just such bushy locks, which they crowned, however, instead of going bare-headed, with jaunty velvet caps.

The fort is without guns, other than a howitzer for firing salutes, and has no strength, as it no longer needs to have, except from its position on a commanding bluff. The military policy of the government now is to station its troops along a railroad or other easy line of communi-

YUMA INDIANS AT HOME.

cation, where they can be quickly massed for mutual support. All the Arizona posts, such as Camp Lowell, with its grassy parade and fine avenue of cottonwoods; Camp Grant, on its table-land; and Camp Apache, at the junction of two charming trout streams, in the White River Cañon; and the others, have only this strategic importance, and no intrinsic strength. The barracks at Yuma consist of a series of comfortable, large, adobe houses, plastered, and painted green, around an oblong plaza. They have in front a peculiar screen-work of green blinds, which shuts out the glare arising from the yellow ground, and makes both a cool promenade and comfortable sleeping apartments for the summer.

The chief of the Yumas, on whose settlement the fort looks down, chooses his sub-chiefs, but is himself appointed by the military commandant. The last investiture was made as long ago as 1852, by General, then Major, Heintzelman. He conferred it upon the now wrinkled and decrepit Pasqual, described at the time as "a tall, fine-looking man, of an agreeable disposition."

Pasqual's people cultivate little patches of vegetables and hay in the river-bottom, fertilized by the annual overflow. Their principal sustenance, however, is the sweet bean of the mesquit-tree. This they pound, in mortars, into a kind of flour. Sometimes, when on the move, the Indians float their hay across the river on rafts, which they push before them, swimming. They propel the small children in the same way, placing them in their large, Egyptian-looking *ollas*, or water-jars.

The crop of mesquit beans was so large one year as to be beyond their unaided capacity to consume, and they hospitably invited in their friends, the Pimas, to aid them. Old Pasqual describes with graphic gestures how haggard and lank were these visitors on their arrival, and what an unctuous corpulence they had attained in the end, when, after nearly eating their hosts out of house and home, they were only got rid of at last by force.

III.

Few things are more curious at this time of day than to look back at the old maps of our Western possessions previous to the annexation of Texas. Texas was not then ours; nor were a considerable part of Indian Territory, Kansas, half of Colorado, all of Utah, Nevada, California, Arizona, and New Mexico. All of this belonged to our sister republic of Mexico, which, as I have said, was within an ace as large as ourselves, and, except for its internal dissensions, could by no means be considered a puny antagonist.

An impressive vagueness attended the delineation of most things west of the Mississippi. There were great tracts hardly more known than the centre of Africa. The upper regions of Mexico were distinguished as Interna; New Mexico and Arizona were simply Apacheria —Apache Land. Our frontier ran along the line of the Sabine River to the Red, from the Red to the Arkansas, and from the Arkansas, on the 42d Parallel of latitude, straight west to the Pacific Ocean. By the peace of Guadalupe Hidalgo our frontier became the Rio Grande and Gila instead, and the line had dropped from Parallel 40° to Parallel 32°.

I have called this territory heretofore, by way of figure of speech, an Alsace-Lorraine of Mexico, though it is not probable, vacant as it was, and Americanized as it now is, that a serious grudge is still borne us for it, or that there will ever be momentous wars for its recovery. However this may be, it has been the making of us. We should be in but sorry shape indeed had we to go back to the limits of the thirteen original British Colonies, or even to these with Florida, purchased from the Spaniards, and Louisiana, purchased from the French, added. The Mexican acquisition gave us one-third of our domain—that which is now most open to the teeming millions of Europe and that which avails us our repute for essential Americanism abroad. It gave us the field of the Bret Harte school in literature, our chief marvels and wonders, our mines of the precious metals, and the command of the Pacific Ocean.

The lower belt of Arizona was not even comprised in this. An area of 460 miles by 130, below the Gila River, was not obtained till "the Gadsden Purchase," in 1853. By the payment of the sum of $10,000,000 under this treaty we obtained a number of decided advantages. We rectified our boundary line, confused through the inaccuracy of the map of one Dwinelle, on which it was based. We got rid of an embarrassing engagement, of the treaty of Guadalupe Hidalgo, to protect the Mexican frontier from Apaches—leaving them to regulate this service for themselves. We secured the right of way for a railroad across the Isthmus of Tehuantepec, which was thought desirable for speedier communication with our new possessions of California.

But above all we acquired, in the easy levels below the Gila, the natural route for a Southern Pacific transcontinental railway. The files of the Congressional *Globe* of that date are full of the necessity of binding our Pacific acquisitions securely to the rest of the country, and the most effectual of all the means proposed was considered to be a transcontinental railway.

Well, we are bowling at last along that now actually constructed Southern Pacific Railroad, once discussed in musty debates of the Congressional *Globe*. It increases our respect for predecessors to whom we may not have given any great consideration heretofore to find how sagacious they were. We reach Stanwix, with its lava beds; Painted Rock, named from huge, mysteriously-decorated bowlders; Casa Grande, from its architectural ruins of the Toltecs; and Tucson.

Adopting the policy of leaving Tucson to be examined on the return, let us push on to the extreme end of the Territory—to the eccentrically-named Tombstone. Benson, the point of departure, from the railroad, for Tombstone, is 1024 miles from San Francisco, and probably 2500 from New York.

XXXI.

TOMBSTONE.

I.

Tombstone is the very latest and liveliest of those mushroom civilizations which so often gather around a "find" of the precious metals. They live at a headlong pace; draw to them wild and lawless spirits; confer great fortunes here, the grave of the drunkard, the suicide, or the victim of violence elsewhere. A school of literature, with Bret Harte as its exponent, has arisen to celebrate their doings. At the present rate of advance of population and conventional usages westward they must shortly disappear as effectually as the dodo of tradition. While things go well with them the prices of commodities are hardly considered. Nobody haggles. The most expensive of everything is what is most wanted.

"Diamonds—two-hundred-dollar watches and chains—Lord! we couldn't hand 'em out fast enough," says an ex-jeweller, describing his experience at one of the camps in its palmy days. "Champagne wasn't good enough for me then," says a seedy customer, recalling his doings after the discovery and sale of a rich mine. He sighed for a repetition of the event, not to make provision for his old age, which sadly needed it, but that he might have "one more glorious spree" before he died.

Oftentimes this rush of life departs as quickly as it came. Some fine day the "lead" is exhausted, there is found to be no more treasure in the mines. The heterogeneous elements scatter, and the town, be it never so well built, is left as desolate as Tadmor of the Wilderness. In a certain Nevada mining town, which once numbered some thousands of inhabitants, Indians are living in rows of good brick houses, having adapted them to their peculiar conditions by taking out doors and windows and knocking holes in the roof.

A six-horse Concord coach carried us, not too speedily, over the twenty-five miles of dusty road to Tombstone. It was called the "Grand Central," after one of the prosperous silver mines of the place. A rival line was named the "Sandy Bob," from its proprietor; who preferred to be himself thus known, instead of by a conventional family appellation such as anybody might have. We should certainly have taken the "Sandy Bob Line" for its greater suggestiveness, except that it seemed to be coming down when we wanted to go up, and always coming up when we wanted to go down.

Our own proved to have plenty of suggestiveness too. A guard got up with a Winchester rifle, and posted himself by the Wells-Fargo Express box, and the driver began almost at once to relate robber stories. His stage had been stopped and "gone through" twice within the past six months. The affair had been enlivened on the one occasion by a runaway and turnover, and on the other by the shooting and killing of the driver. Of this last item his successor spoke with a natural disgust. If the line could not be drawn at drivers, he said, things had indeed come to a pretty pass. He respected a man who took to the road and robbed those who could afford it. At least, he considered it more honorable than borrowing money of a friend which you knew you could never repay, or than gobbling up the earnings of the

DISTANT VIEW OF TOMBSTONE.

poor, like a large firm lately suspended in Pima County. But as to shooting a driver, even in mistake for somebody else, he had no words to express his sense of its meanness.

He threw stones at his horses, as in Mexico, that is, at the leaders, beyond the reach of his long lash. The same stone was made to "carom" from one to the other, such was his skill, and startle them both. Long stringteams of mules or Texas steers, sixteen to a team, with ore-wagons, were met with along the road. Mexican-looking drivers trudged beside them in the deep, yellow dust, cracking their animals lustily with huge "black-snakes." Mesquit-bushes, and long grass dried to hay —not as good as it looked—covered portions of the surface; the rest was bare and stony.

We rode for a certain distance beside the branch railroad in course of construction between Benson and Tombstone. A series of lateral valleys along the tributaries of the Gila, north and south, as the Santa Cruz, Salt River, San Carlos, San Pedro, and San Simon Valleys, afford excellent stock ranges, promise of a flourishing agriculture, and easy routes for tributary railways. They have already begun to be utilized. The San Pedro has the Southern Pacific branch above mentioned, and the Santa Cruz will have the Arizona Southern, connecting the centre of the Territory at Florence, on the Atlantic and Pacific, with Mexico at Calabasas. The transcontinental road — or roads, when the Atlantic and Pacific shall have been built — will draw through these tributary valleys, as the Gila draws its waters, a trade from Northern Mexico, where mining enterprises in particular, in the hands of Americans, are making great headway.

The route began to be very much up-hill. We changed horses and lunched at Contention City. One naturally expected a certain belligerency in such a place, but none appeared on the surface during our stay. There were plenty of saloons — the "Dew-drop," the "Head-light," and others — and at the door of one of them a Spanish señorita smoked a cigarette and showed her white teeth.

Contention City is the seat of stamp-mills for crushing ore, which is brought to it from Tombstone. The latter place is without an efficient water-power. The stamps are rows of heavy beams, which drop upon the mineral, on the mortar and pestle plan, with a continuous dull roar, by night as well as day.

"That's the music I like to hear," said our driver, gathering up his reins, "poundin' out the gold and silver. There ain't no brass bands ekils it."

The route grew steeper yet. On the few wayside fences that exist were painted flaring announcements, as

"Go To Bangley and Schlagenstein's At Tombstone. They Are The Bosses, You Bet."

Then over the edge of bare hills appeared Tombstone itself, a large, circular water-tank, big enough for a fort, painted with advertisements, the most conspicuous object in the foreground.

II.

At the beginning of the year 1878 there was not so much as a tent at Tombstone. One "Ed" Schieffelin and his brother started thither prospecting. It was supposed to be an adventure full of dangers. At the Santa Rita silver mines, in the Santa Cruz Valley, for instance, nothing like so far away, three superintendents had been murdered by Indians in rapid succession.

His friends therefore said to Ed, "Better take your coffin with you; you will find your tombstone there, and nothing else."

But Ed Schieffelin — a young man yet, who has not discarded a picturesque way of dressing of which he was fond, nor greatly altered his habits otherwise—found instead the Tough Nut and Contention Mines. He made a great fortune out of them, and was so pleased at the difference between the prediction and the result that he gave the name of Tombstone to the town itself.

One of two well-printed daily papers has assumed the corresponding title of the *Epitaph*. The unreliability of epitaphs—if the remark may be safely ventured even at this distance—is proverbial. Nevertheless, they may occasionally tell the truth. From appearances it would seem that this was one of the occasions. Almost any eulogy of its subject by the *Epitaph* would seem justified. The city, but two years old at this date, had attained to a population of 2000, and a property valuation, apart from that of the mines, of $1,050,980. A desirable lot of 30 by 80 feet, on Allen Street, between Fourth and Sixth—such was the business-like nomenclature used already in this settlement of yesterday—was worth $6000.

"ED" SCHIEFFELIN.

A shanty that cost $50 to build rented for $15 a month. A nucleus of many blocks at the centre consisted of substantial, large-sized buildings, hotels, banks—Schieffelin Hall, for meetings and amusements—and stores stocked with goods of more than the average excellence in many older and larger towns.

The mining claims run under the city itself. From the roof of the Grand Hotel you look down at the shafts, hoist-works, and heaps of extracted ore of the Vizina, the Gilded Age (close to the Palace Lodging-house), the Mountain Maid, and other mines, opening strangely in the very midst of the buildings. This circumstance has given rise to disputes of ownership, so that whoever would be safe purchases all the conflicting titles, both above ground and below. On a commanding hill close by, to the southward, are the Tough Nut and Contention, and above them many others later discovered. The larger mines had extensive buildings, of wood, and in handsome draughting and assay rooms within were regularly educated scientists, ex-college professors and the like, in charge. The lesser mines put up in the beginning with commoner sheds and poorer appliances of every kind. About them all lie heaps of a blackish material, resembling inferior coal and slate, the silver ore in its native condition. A laborer above-ground earned $3.50, and below-ground $4, for a " shift " of eight hours, and the work went on night and day, Sundays and all.

I leave to others to estimate the bulk of treasure in the place. I was told that it was " the biggest thing since the Comstock," and there were forty million dollars in sight. I was offered, daily, fractional interests in mines, now by a young surveyor who was going to be married and needed money for his wedding outfit; now by new friends who were straitened for assessment funds to carry out the provisions of the law; and again by others who would kindly make any sacrifice for the pleasure of associating a traveller from a distance with the interests of the place; and yet it will be well for the novice to be wary of these seductive openings at Tombstone, as elsewhere.

This I know, however, that I descended four hundred feet or so into the Contention Mine, and found great chambers hollowed out, from which mineral had been taken, showing a generous width in the vein. The yield, from its discovery up to March, 1881, had been $2,000,000. The Tough Nut, with the Lucky Cuss, Good Enough, Owl's Nest, and Owl's Last Hoot—the racy vernacular of their names will be observed—had yielded $1,000,000.

The outskirts of Tombstone consisted still of huts and tents. A burly miner could be seen stretched upon his cot in a windowless cabin, barely large enough to contain him. There were some tents provided with wooden doors and adobe chimneys. New as it was, the business portion of the place had been once swept out of existence by a devastating fire, which originated from a characteristic incident—the explosion of a whiskey-barrel in the Oriental Saloon. Within fourteen days all was rebuilt far better than before.

I took the pains to count the number of establishments in a single short block of Allen Street at which intoxicating liquors were sold. There were the bar-rooms of two hotels, the Eagle Brewery, the Cancan Chophouse, the French Rôtisserie, the Alhambra, Maison Doré, City of Paris, Brown's Saloon, Fashion Saloon, Miners' Home, Kelly's Wine-house, the Grotto, the Tivoli, and two saloons apparently unnamed. At these places gambling also went on without let or hinderance. The absence of savings-banks or other opportunity for depositing money, in these wild communities, and the temptation arising from having it always under the eye, no doubt has something to do with the general passion for gambling. Whiskey and cold lead are named as the leading diseases at Tombstone. What with the leisure that seems to prevail, the constant drinking and gambling at the saloons, and the universal practice of carrying deadly weapons, there is but one source of astonishment, and that is that the cold-lead disease should claim so few victims. Casualties are, after all, infrequent, considering the amount of vaporish talk indulged in, and the imminent risks that are run. The small cemetery, over toward Contention Hill, so far from being glutted with the slaughtered, is still comparatively virgin ground.

III.

A farther element in addition to that of the miners is to be cited as having a good deal to do with the exceptional liveliness of Tombstone—the "Cow-boys."

The term cow-boy, once applied to all those in the cattle business indiscriminately, while still including some honest persons, has been narrowed down to be chiefly a term of reproach for a class of stealers of cattle, over the Mexican frontier, and elsewhere, who are a terror in their day and generation. Exceptional desperadoes of this class, such as "Billy the Kid," "Curly Bill," and "Russian George," have been the scourges of whole districts in Colorado, New Mexico, and Arizona, and have had their memories embalmed in yellow-covered literature.

I bought on the train, on leaving, a pamphlet purporting to be an account of the exploits of Billy the Kid. He had committed, it appeared, at least a score of horrid murders, but "so many cities have claimed the honor of giving him birth," said my pamphlet, "that it is difficult to locate with any accuracy the locality where he passed his youth." It was finally determined, however, in favor of New York. "It was on the Bowery," said the author, whose ideas of morality were peculiar even for a sensationalist, "that his mates learned to love him for his daring and prowess, and delighted to refer to him as Billy the Kid."

This promising life was cut off at the early age of twenty-two. "Curly Bill," also died young, and so did "Man-killer Johnson." I remarked upon this peculiarity, of their youth, to a philosopher of the region itself.

"Yes," he said, "they *don't* seem to live to be very old; that's so."

The recipe for a long life in this country was described as being very quick and getting "the drop" on an antagonist; that is to say, being ready to shoot first. Unless this can be done, it is the custom even to put up with some ignominious abuse at the time, and await a more favorable opportunity.

The cow-boys frequenting Tombstone were generally from the ranches in the San Pedro and San Simon valleys. There were said to be strongholds in the San Simon Valley where they concealed stolen cattle until re-branded and sent to market, and where no officer of the law ever dared to venture. They looked upon the running off of stock from Mexico, as far as that was concerned, only as a more dashing form of smuggling, though it was marked by frequent bloody tragedies on both sides.

Not to fix upon all the misdeeds of but a few, no doubt there were on the streets of Tombstone plenty of cow-boys of a legitimate sort, whose only faults were occasional boisterousness and too free lavishing of their money. There appeared to be something of a standing feud between the miners and the cow-boys, and there was besides a faction of "town cow-boys" organized against the "country cow-boys."

The leading cattle-men had a Southern cut and accent, and hailed originally from Missouri or Texas. Some appeared in full black broadcloth, accompanied by the usual wide sombrero. The landlord of our hotel described them as "perfect gentlemen," some of them good at the bar for as high as $20 or $25 a day.

The great object in life of the various factions, or of individuals who arose from time to time in search of notoriety, was to "run the town." This consisted largely in the privilege of blustering in the saloons, whooping and firing occasional pistol-shots, if thought good, in the streets, and having a moderate security from arrest, inspired by dread of their prowess.

This was necessarily a very insecure preëminence. New aspirants and rebels were continually piqued into appearing against it whenever it seemed fairly attained. Our visit happened upon the heels of a conflict making the most tragic page yet written in the annals of Tombstone. Opinions seemed divided about it—even official opinions. The sheriff extended his sympathy to one side, the city marshal, who was, in fact, its leader, to the other.

City Marshal Earp, with his two brothers, and one "Doc Holliday," a gambler, had come down the street, armed with rifles, and opened fire on two Clanton brothers and two McLowry brothers. The latter party had been practically first disarmed by the sheriff, who feared such a meeting, and meant to disarm the others as well. Three of the assailed men fell, and died. "Ike" Clanton alone escaped.

The slayers were imprisoned, but released on bail. The Grand Jury was now in session, hearing evidence in the case. It was rumored that the town party—the Earps—would command a sufficient personal influence to go free of indictment. The cow-boys were flocking into town to await the result, and on a certain quiet Sunday wore an ominous look. It was said that, should justice fail to be done them, the resolute-looking men conferring together darkly at the edges of the sidewalk would take the matter into their own hands. The jury, I have since learned, did not find an indictment, and the remaining parties to the affair, with many others, I believe, have since died with their boots on in the same cause. If anything could reconcile us to the untimely taking-off of these paladins, it would be partly their own contemptuous indifference to it.

It would seem that we ought to have at least half a dozen lives apiece, to account for such an indifference, but to be ready to toss away the only one on any and every pretext or no pretext is not at all so intelligible. It is certainly not the desperation of poverty by which it is occasioned. Many of them are in very good circumstances. The younger McLowry, a boy under twenty, had $3000 in his pocket, the proceeds of a sale of cattle, the day he fell.

The elder Clanton had played cards most of the night before with two of his deadly enemies, both parties keeping a hand on their pistols meanwhile. When "Billy" Clanton, a boy, like McLowry, lay prone on the ground in the fight, dying of his mortal wound, he still managed to get out a pistol, steadied it on a shattered arm, and fired once more at "Doc Holliday," saying,

"I'll get one of you, any way."

"You are a daisy if you do," replied Doc Holliday, continuing to advance as coolly as if at target practice, and emptying another barrel of his own into him.

And the last words of Billy Clanton, in the Nibelungen-like contest—which I am quite aware will not be quoted,

A TOMBSTONE SHERIFF AND CONSTITUENTS.

in school-readers, with those of Lawrence, Nelson, and Montcalm, since there was no sense at all in this frenzied display of pluck and tenacity — were: "For God's sake more cartridges!"

Meantime the whistles of the mining works were shrieking notes of alarm, the miners pouring forth from underground, and the reputable citizens, who might have exclaimed, "A plague o' both your houses!" arming themselves in hot haste, and coming to their doors, to prevent the spread of general anarchy.

There is a grimly humorous element in it all. It seems such an excellent joke to idly snuff out the most precious of human possessions. A cow-boy shoots a tumbler from the hand of another, just raised to his lips, saying, "When you drink with me I will teach you to take whiskey plain, and no mixtures."

A group of others sit around in a saloon where lies a fresh-made corpse. An officer of the law enters, and says, "Who claims this man?" whereupon all jump to their feet to dispute the honor.

There is a large supply of these amusing stories. To kill your man seems a way of winning your spurs, as it were, and establishing yourself on a proper footing in the community. Even the defunct, in various cases, could he be heard from, would probably find no great fault with the manner of his taking off, but only with the "luck" of it which had gone against him.

XXXII.

CAMP LOWELL, TUCSON, AND SAN XAVIER DEL BAC.

I.

The night journey returning by stage to Benson was enlivened by more shooting stories. I heard, among others, of the doings of the late Brazelton of Tucson, and at Tucson I bought his photograph, taken after death, in his mask and other paraphernalia of his craft. He robbed stages for years while apparently working quietly as a hostler in a corral. He was finally tracked to his fate through some peculiar marks of the horse he rode.

One of our passengers had just recovered from wounds received in a fight over cards with a Mexican, whom he had killed, and was now able, with the aid of morphine, to pursue his journey toward his home in New Mexico. The train men at Benson were chary of carrying their lanterns about the depot yard, a habit having arisen, it seemed, among the cow-boys of trying to snuff out these moving targets with revolvers from a distance.

There seemed a certain tameness even in the Apaches after this wild product of the higher civilization of the whites. The principal group of prisoners taken after the attempted massacre of General Carr's command was found in confinement at Camp Lowell, nine miles north of Tucson. There were forty-two of them, with Sanchez, their chief. They were of fairly regular features, and their expression, with the war-paint washed off, not unamiable.

They were handcuffed together in couples, their legs also manacled, and now wore gray army under-shirts and cotton drawers, the rags in which they had come having been taken from them. Their long black hair hung about their ears, not frowzy, like that of the Yumas, but smoothly parted in the middle, and brushed back. A number wore red bands or kerchiefs around their heads.

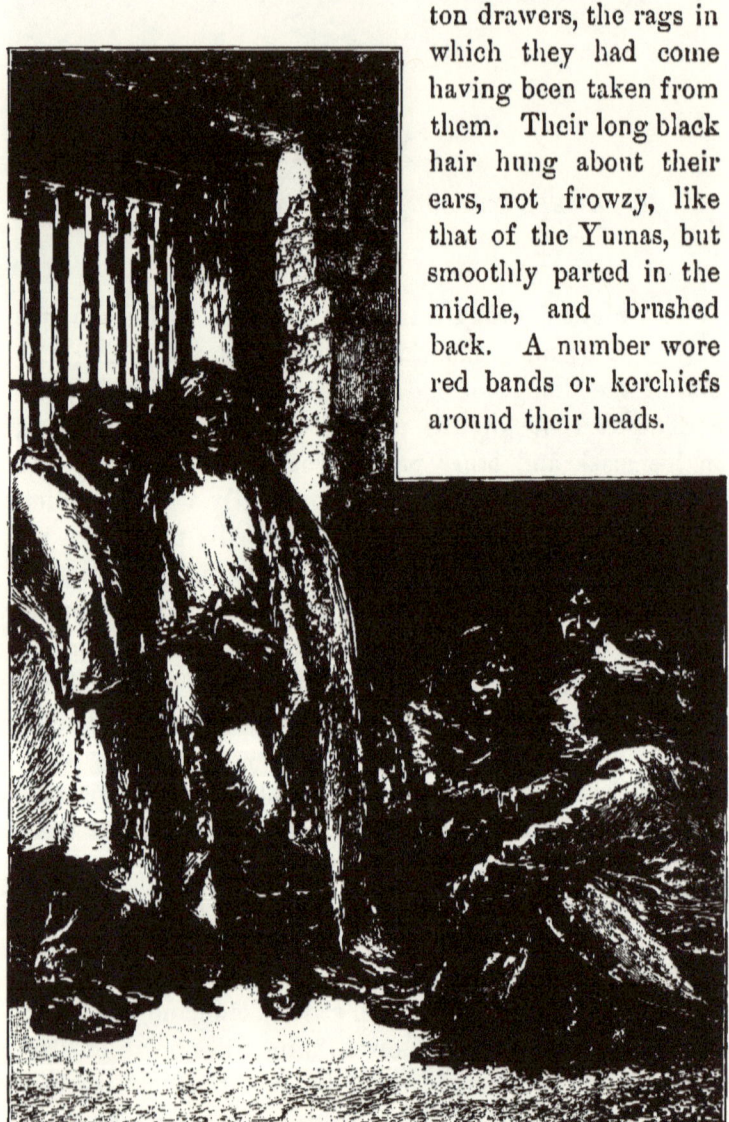

APACHE PRISONERS AT CAMP LOWELL.

Seen obscurely in the chief prison-room by side-light from à grated window, they had a certain resemblance to Greek insurgents, or the *sans culottes* of 1793, or, again, the wild Vendean peasants who fought with Rochejaquelein and Jean Chouan for religion and the king.

They were taken out for an airing in the mornings, and allowed to squat in the sun at the edge of the pleasant parade-ground, flanked by its well-shaded row of officers' dwellings. The recent rising had been the result of a fanatical delusion. A medicine-man persuaded them that he had received a revelation to drive all the whites from the land. As soon as the corn was ripe, he said, their dead brethren would arise and take arms to aid them in carrying out the decree of Heaven. He had, as many prophets have not, the courage of his convictions. Though taken in charge himself by the troops, he gave a signal agreed upon for the massacre of these to begin, calling to his people not to be concerned about his fate, as he would come to life and join them again in three days.

The bluff Arizonians are apt to indulge in a derisive way of talking of the army and its relation to the savages. They would make but short work of these latter, they say, if they took the matter into their own hands. They imply that the army does not wish to kill off, or even wholly put down, the Indians, but rather to preserve them, as a gentle stimulus to public dread, to hasten promotions, and also to furnish occasion for profitable supply-contracts. However this may be, it would seem that after the repression of this revolt, and the rapid penetration of railroads into the Territory, Indians need no longer be a deterring influence of great moment with the intending settler. This old historic source of apprehension seems as good as abolished from its last stronghold.

Eight miles to the north brings us to a ranch called

AN ARIZONA WATERING-PLACE.

Fuller's Hot Springs. This is one of the few places where a beginning of systematic cultivation has been made, and interesting besides as a typical Arizona summer resort. There was a young orchard of twenty-five acres, sheltered by a wind-break of three rows of ash-trees, doing very well in an alkali soil. The buildings consisted of a number of unpainted adobe houses, each of a single large, comfortable room, roofed with strips of cactus.

There was a "summer dining-room" made of ocotilla sticks, the intervals open; and a "winter dining-room," with tight walls, and a fireplace, in which a wood-fire was burned mornings and evenings. The hot spring, a clear, pleasant water, said to resemble English Harrogate, ran out from below a bath-house, consisting of a patched canvas tent. It became, below, a pretty brook, a pond for the cattle, and source of supply for irrigating the orchard. The mountains behind the place, the Santa Catalinas, are like the Sierra Madres behind Los Angeles. They are of the same sharp fracture, but higher and grander, jutting up here and there into as perfect castles as those of Harlech, the Trostberg, or Rheinstein. Forests of pine of large dimensions crown a part of their summits. South and south-west, across the wide plain, appear the Rincons and silver-bearing Santa Ritas.

There was a fascination in being able to examine at leisure the strange growths of the plain, and not merely to know them in glimpses from the car-windows. I made haste especially to cut down for inspection an example of the enormous saguara, the organ-cactus. Taller than that on the hill-sides of Guerrero along the Acapulco trail, it often rises to a height of sixty feet, bristles over the landscape like masts or columns, or, again, like the seven-branched candlestick of the Mosaic law. Inside it consists of a white, juicy pulp, imbedding a bundle of fibres in the form of long wands, which, when dried, serve a number of useful purposes. It has a palatable fruit, which the Indians collect from its top in August with forked sticks.

The ocotilla is simply a shrub growing as a wattle of sticks, fifteen or twenty together, only waiting to be cut down and turned into palings. The bisnaga is a thorny cactus like an immense watermelon growing on end. One need never die of thirst where it is found. The cholla is a mass of spines, which are even barbed, on the fish-hook principle. It is considered funny to hear of somebody's falling into a cholla, and nothing could better represent the traditional "bramble-bush" in which the man who was so wondrous wise met with the famous adventure of scratching out his eyes. The "deer-brush" somewhat resembles the horns of the animal. The palo verde—green stick—grows as large as an apple-tree, with the texture of a

CACTUS GROWTHS OF THE DESERT.

mammoth sea-weed. The "grease-wood" is a large bush, said to burn just as well when green as dry. Most of this vegetation is leafless, or rather the plant seems a leaf itself, since coarse bark is lacking, and the green of chlorophyll and the tenderness of structure seem equally distributed throughout.

There are homely legends and superstitions about these plants of the desert. A certain one, for instance, poisons any white spot on a horse, but not one of any other color. Another, eaten by horses, makes them lazy and imbecile. The loco, or rattle-weed, on the other hand, drives them raving crazy, and they try to run themselves to death. I do not know whether this last be wholly a superstition, for I rode in California a horse whose eccentric proceedings could hardly be accounted for on any other basis.

Tucson, from a distance, in early morning or late afternoon, is level, low, square, and brown, with a mellow light upon it and the castellated mountains behind it. In the foreground you see lazy ox-wains, a prospector, perhaps, with his pots and kettles, and a mounted Mexican towing by a lariat a bull, which ducks its head in vain resistance. From a distance it is thoroughly foreign, and of attractive promise. There is something of the Dead Sea apple in the realization of this promise. If Ruskin be right in holding that a house should be of the general color of the soil on which it stands, Tucson may lay claim to great artistic merit. It is entirely of adobe brick of the natural mud-color. Violent rainstorms occur, to the detriment of paint and kalsomine, on such a friable surface, and their use becomes a serious question of economy.

Tucson has great antiquity as a mere corporate existence. It was founded by one of the early Spanish ex-

STREET VIEW IN TUCSON.

peditions that came up the Santa Cruz Valley in quest of the reputed treasure of the Aztecs in the fabled " land of Cibola," but retains no visible trace of age. If there were ever any monuments of importance, they have effectually vanished. Even the church is new. Such foreignness as there is consists of a very provincial Mexican squalor.

The considerations of interest about it are of a purely utilitarian character, as: how it is to be paved, drained, lighted, provided with an adequate water supply, so as not to have to pay four cents a bucket for it, as at present; and how it is to get rid of its malarial fevers and shabby rookeries.

A writer in one of the papers one day paid a glowing eulogy to its peculiar situation, in the desert. He held that this was a matter not only of those material products which I have mentioned, but also of the highest moral and intellectual advantages. It was apropos of the establishment of a public library. No great idea has ever been evolved in the usual scenes of human habitation (so the argument ran), and that there is no place for study and contemplation like the desert. Christ, Mahomet, Zoroaster, and Confucius all formulated their creeds in the desert. I gathered that we are to expect from Arizona, at the proper time, some new prophet or sage, to sway again the destinies of men in the same way.

The correspondent was satisfied, at any rate, that, with a public library, Tucson could shortly become another Alexandria of the desert, "a seat of learning and fountain-head of ideas, to be sought by students from Mexico, from the Pacific Islands, from China and Japan, and the mountains and valleys of the Rio Grande," and I for one shall be very glad to see it so.

It is the commercial centre of the important Southern

EXTERIOR OF MISSION CHURCH OF SAN XAVIER DEL BAC.

mining district, and has an eligible situation for future development. It has derived in its time considerable profit from furnishing supplies to the army, and from a smuggling trade with Mexico. The goods for this latter were taken out in teams, then "packed" over the mountain passes, on donkeys, to the objective points of Altar and Magdalena, in cactus-grown, arid Sonora.

The traders at Tucson, again, are largely Jewish. A certain kind of "life" prevails freely, as at Tombstone. Roulette, faro, and other games of chance are played in a large way in the leading saloons, while the poor Mexicans gamble for small stakes at *fondas* of their own, where some wretched lithograph of Hidalgo or Zaragoza looks down on them from the walls. There is lacking, however, the choleric and dangerous air of Tombstone. People make way for you to pass if you wish, and do not seem exclusively occupied with looking about for somebody to tread on the tails of their coats.

If Tucson be without historic remains of its own, it has one of the loveliest possible in its vicinity, the old mission church of San Xavier del Bac.

San Xavier is on the reservation of the Christianized Papago Indians, in the Santa Cruz Valley, ten miles to the southward. It is a new sensation even for one from Mexico who may have flattered himself that he knew the style completely. This ancient landmark of a frontier civilization which, since its destruction, has not been even faintly approached in its kind, is not surpassed either in Mexico or out of it for the quaintness, the qualities of form and color, and the gentle sentiment of melancholy that appeal to the artistic sense. Old Father Time has trodden with heavy step on green wooden balconies in its front, broken out their floors, and left parts of them dangling free. The original sweet-toned bronze bells

INTERIOR OF CHURCH OF SAN XAVIER DEL BAC.

still hang in one of the towers. The space, terminating in a scrolled gable, between the towers is enriched with escutcheons and rampant lions, wreathed in foliage. Niches hold grotesque broken statues, and complicated pilasters flank the entrance doorway, the whole formed in stucco upon a basis of moulded bricks. Where a portion has fallen away it can be seen that the pilasters are constructed upon or held together by a centre consisting of a stick of timber.

The designer, whoever he may have been, was inspired by Venetian-Byzantine traditions. It is roofed with numerous simple domes and half-domes. The interior of these, frescoed with angels and evangelists, the chancel walls, almost covered with gilding, but stained and battered, and the painted and gilded lions on the chancel rails, recall to the least observant Saint Mark's at Venice. The style is not quite consistently carried out, however. A later rococo decoration, as exuberant as the vagaries of East Indian work, mingles with and at places overrides it. A Henri II. candlestick will give a certain idea of the pattern of the columns.

The date has disappeared from the façade, but it is believed to be about 1768, and the present edifice was built on the ruins of a former one, going back much nearer to 1654, when the mission to the Papagos was first begun. Large angels, with bannerets, their draperies formed of *papier-maché* or gummed muslin, are attached to the main chancel piers; and a painted and gilded Virgin, with a long face, and hair brushed up from a high forehead, as in the sculptures of Jean Goujon, looks down from a high altar niche.

All within is of a mediæval richness and obscurity. All without is broad sunshine falling upon the peaceful Papago village. A few old men trudge about, concerning themselves with their bake-ovens and some water-jars and strings of dried squashes, and women pass by with tall loads of hay and other produce carried in the *kijo*, a singular hamper of sticks and netting, on their backs. Nobody concerns himself about visitors, except a foolishly smiling boy, one Domingo, who has brought us the key.

To have come from that spasm of aggressive modernism, Tombstone, and to be at ancient San Xavier del Bac —it seemed to me that contrast could little farther go.

THE END.

VALUABLE AND INTERESTING WORKS

FOR

PUBLIC & PRIVATE LIBRARIES,

PUBLISHED BY HARPER & BROTHERS, NEW YORK.

☞ *For a full List of Books suitable for Libraries published by* HARPER & BROTHERS, *see* HARPER'S CATALOGUE, *which may be had gratuitously on application to the publishers personally, or by letter enclosing Nine Cents in postage stamps.*

☞ HARPER & BROTHERS *will send their publications by mail, postage prepaid, on receipt of the price.*

MACAULAY'S ENGLAND. The History of England from the Accession of James II. By THOMAS BABINGTON MACAULAY. New Edition, from New Electrotype Plates. 8vo, Cloth, with Paper Labels, Uncut Edges and Gilt Tops, 5 vols., in a Box, $10 00 per set. Sold only in Sets. Cheap Edition, 5 vols., in a Box, 12mo, Cloth, $2 50; Sheep, $3 75.

MACAULAY'S MISCELLANEOUS WORKS. The Miscellaneous Works of Lord Macaulay. From New Electrotype Plates. In Five Volumes. 8vo, Cloth, with Paper Labels, Uncut Edges and Gilt Tops, in a Box, $10 00. Sold only in Sets.

HUME'S ENGLAND. History of England, from the Invasion of Julius Cæsar to the Abdication of James II., 1688. By DAVID HUME. New and Elegant Library Edition, from New Electrotype Plates. 6 vols., in a Box, 8vo, Cloth, with Paper Labels, Uncut Edges and Gilt Tops, $12 00. Sold only in Sets. Popular Edition, 6 vols., in a Box, 12mo, Cloth, $3 00; Sheep, $4 50.

GIBBON'S ROME. The History of the Decline and Fall of the Roman Empire. By EDWARD GIBBON. With Notes by Dean MILMAN, M. GUIZOT, and Dr. WILLIAM SMITH. New Edition, from New Electrotype Plates. 6 vols., 8vo, Cloth, with Paper Labels, Uncut Edges and Gilt Tops, $12 00. Sold only in Sets. Popular Edition, 6 vols., in a Box, 12mo, Cloth, $3 00; Sheep, $4 50.

HILDRETH'S UNITED STATES. History of the United States. FIRST SERIES: From the Discovery of the Continent to the Organization of the Government under the Federal Constitution. SECOND SERIES: From the Adoption of the Federal Constitution to the End of the Sixteenth Congress. By RICHARD HILDRETH. Popular Edition, 6 vols., in a Box, 8vo, Cloth, with Paper Labels, Uncut Edges and Gilt Tops, $12 00. Sold only in Sets.

MOTLEY'S DUTCH REPUBLIC. The Rise of the Dutch Republic. A History. By JOHN LOTHROP MOTLEY, LL.D., D.C.L. With a Portrait of William of Orange. Cheap Edition, 3 vols., in a Box, 8vo, Cloth, with Paper Labels, Uncut Edges and Gilt Tops, $6 00. Sold only in Sets. Original Library Edition, 3 vols., 8vo, Cloth, $10 50; Sheep, $12 00; Half Calf, $17 25.

MOTLEY'S UNITED NETHERLANDS. History of the United Netherlands: From the Death of William the Silent to the Twelve Years' Truce—1584–1609. With a full View of the English-Dutch Struggle against Spain, and of the Origin and Destruction of the Spanish Armada. By JOHN LOTHROP MOTLEY, LL.D., D.C.L. Portraits. Cheap Edition, 4 vols., in a Box, 8vo, Cloth, with Paper Labels, Uncut Edges and Gilt Tops, $8 00. Sold only in Sets. Original Library Edition, 4 volumes, 8vo, Cloth, $14 00; Sheep, $16 00; Half Calf, $23 00.

MOTLEY'S JOHN OF BARNEVELD. The Life and Death of John of Barneveld, Advocate of Holland. With a View of the Primary Causes and Movements of the "Thirty Years' War." By JOHN LOTHROP MOTLEY, LL.D., D.C.L. Illustrated. Cheap Edition, 2 vols., in a Box, 8vo, Cloth, with Paper Labels, Uncut Edges and Gilt Tops, $4 00. Sold only in Sets. Original Library Edition, 2 vols., 8vo, Cloth, $7 00; Sheep, $8 00; Half Calf, $11 50.

GOLDSMITH'S WORKS. The Works of Oliver Goldsmith. Edited by PETER CUNNINGHAM, F.S.A. From New Electrotype Plates. 4 vols., 8vo, Cloth, Paper Labels, Uncut Edges and Gilt Tops, $8 00. Uniform with the New Library Editions of Macaulay, Hume, Gibbon, Motley, and Hildreth.

GEDDES'S JOHN DE WITT. History of the Administration of John De Witt, Grand Pensionary of Holland. By JAMES GEDDES. Vol. I.—1623–1654. With a Portrait. 8vo, Cloth, $2 50.

HUDSON'S HISTORY OF JOURNALISM. Journalism in the United States, from 1690 to 1872. By FREDERIC HUDSON. 8vo, Cloth, $5 00; Half Calf, $7 25.

SYMONDS'S SKETCHES AND STUDIES IN SOUTHERN EUROPE. By JOHN ADDINGTON SYMONDS. In Two Volumes. Post 8vo, Cloth, $4 00.

SYMONDS'S GREEK POETS. Studies of the Greek Poets. By JOHN ADDINGTON SYMONDS. 2 vols., Square 16mo, Cloth, $3 50.

TREVELYAN'S LIFE OF MACAULAY. The Life and Letters of Lord Macaulay. By his Nephew, G. OTTO TREVELYAN, M.P. With Portrait on Steel. Complete in 2 vols., 8vo, Cloth, Uncut Edges and Gilt Tops, $5 00; Sheep, $6 00; Half Calf, $9 50. Popular Edition, 2 vols. in one, 12mo, Cloth, $1 75.

TREVELYAN'S LIFE OF FOX. The Early History of Charles James Fox. By GEORGE OTTO TREVELYAN. 8vo, Cloth, Uncut Edges and Gilt Tops, $2 50; 4to, Paper, 20 cents.

MÜLLER'S POLITICAL HISTORY OF RECENT TIMES. Political History of Recent Times (1816-1875). With Special Reference to Germany. By WILLIAM MÜLLER. Revised and Enlarged by the Author. Translated, with an Appendix covering the Period from 1876 to 1881, by the Rev. JOHN P. PETERS, Ph.D. 12mo, Cloth, $3 00.

LOSSING'S CYCLOPÆDIA OF UNITED STATES HISTORY. Popular Cyclopædia of United States History. From the Aboriginal Period to 1876. By B. J. LOSSING, LL.D. Illustrated by 2 Steel Portraits and over 1000 Engravings. 2 vols., Royal 8vo, Cloth, $12 00. (*Sold by Subscription only.*)

LOSSING'S FIELD-BOOK OF THE REVOLUTION. Pictorial Field-Book of the Revolution; or, Illustrations by Pen and Pencil of the History, Biography, Scenery, Relics, and Traditions of the War for Independence. By BENSON J. LOSSING. 2 vols., 8vo, Cloth, $14 00; Sheep or Roan, $15 00; Half Calf, $18 00.

LOSSING'S FIELD-BOOK OF THE WAR OF 1812. Pictorial Field-Book of the War of 1812; or, Illustrations by Pen and Pencil of the History, Biography, Scenery, Relics, and Traditions of the last War for American Independence. By BENSON J. LOSSING. With several hundred Engravings on Wood by Lossing and Barritt, chiefly from Original Sketches by the Author. 1088 pages, 8vo, Cloth, $7 00; Sheep, $8 50; Roan, $9 00; Half Calf, $10 00.

PARTON'S CARICATURE. Caricature and Other Comic Art, in All Times and Many Lands. By JAMES PARTON. 203 Illustrations. 8vo, Cloth, Uncut Edges and Gilt Tops, $5 00; Half Calf, $7 25.

MAHAFFY'S GREEK LITERATURE. A History of Classical Greek Literature. By J. P. MAHAFFY. 2 vols., 12mo, Cloth, $4 00; Half Calf, $7 50.

DU CHAILLU'S LAND OF THE MIDNIGHT SUN. Summer and Winter Journeys in Sweden, Norway, and Lapland, and Northern Finland. By PAUL B. DU CHAILLU. Illustrated. 2 vols., 8vo, Cloth, $7 50.

DU CHAILLU'S EQUATORIAL AFRICA. Explorations and Adventures in Equatorial Africa: with Accounts of the Manners and Customs of the People, and of the Chase of the Gorilla, Crocodile, Leopard, Elephant, Hippopotamus, and other Animals. By P. B. DU CHAILLU. Illustrated. 8vo, Cloth, $5 00; Sheep, $5 50; Half Calf, $7 25.

DU CHAILLU'S ASHANGO LAND. A Journey to Ashango Land, and Further Penetration into Equatorial Africa. By P. B. DU CHAILLU. Illustrated. 8vo, Cloth, $5 00; Sheep, $5 50; Half Calf, $7 25.

DEXTER'S CONGREGATIONALISM. The Congregationalism of the Last Three Hundred Years, as Seen in its Literature: with Special Reference to certain Recondite, Neglected, or Disputed Passages. With a Bibliographical Appendix. By H. M. DEXTER. Large 8vo, Cloth, $6 00.

STANLEY'S THROUGH THE DARK CONTINENT. Through the Dark Continent; or, The Sources of the Nile, Around the Great Lakes of Equatorial Africa, and Down the Livingstone River to the Atlantic Ocean. 149 Illustrations and 10 Maps. By H. M. STANLEY. 2 vols., 8vo, Cloth, $10 00; Sheep, $12 00; Half Morocco, $15 00.

BARTLETT'S FROM EGYPT TO PALESTINE. From Egypt to Palestine: Through Sinai, the Wilderness, and the South Country. Observations of a Journey made with Special Reference to the History of the Israelites. By S. C. BARTLETT, D.D., LL.D. With Maps and Illustrations. 8vo, Cloth, $3 50.

FORSTER'S LIFE OF DEAN SWIFT. The Early Life of Jonathan Swift (1667–1711). By JOHN FORSTER. With Portrait. 8vo, Cloth, Uncut Edges and Gilt Tops, $2 50.

GREEN'S ENGLISH PEOPLE. History of the English People. By JOHN RICHARD GREEN, M.A. Four Volumes. With Maps. 8vo, Cloth, $2 50 per volume.

GREEN'S MAKING OF ENGLAND. The Making of England. By J. R. GREEN. With Maps. 8vo, Cloth, $2 50.

SHORT'S NORTH AMERICANS OF ANTIQUITY. The North Americans of Antiquity. Their Origin, Migrations, and Type of Civilization Considered. By JOHN T. SHORT. Illustrated. 8vo, Cloth, $3 00.

SQUIER'S PERU. Peru: Incidents of Travel and Exploration in the Land of the Incas. By E. GEORGE SQUIER, M.A., F.S.A., late U. S. Commissioner to Peru. With Illustrations. 8vo, Cloth, $5 00.

BENJAMIN'S CONTEMPORARY ART. Contemporary Art in Europe. By S. G. W. BENJAMIN. Illustrated. 8vo, Cloth, $3 50.

BENJAMIN'S ART IN AMERICA. Art in America. By S. G. W. BENJAMIN. Illustrated. 8vo, Cloth, $4 00.

REBER'S HISTORY OF ANCIENT ART. History of Ancient Art. By Dr. FRANZ VON REBER. Revised by the Author. Translated and Augmented by Joseph Thacher Clarke. With 310 Illustrations and a Glossary of Technical Terms. 8vo, Cloth, $3 50.

ADAMS'S MANUAL OF HISTORICAL LITERATURE. A Manual of Historical Literature. Comprising Brief Descriptions of the Most Important Histories in English, French, and German. By Professor C. K. ADAMS. 8vo, Cloth, $2 50.

KINGLAKE'S CRIMEAN WAR. The Invasion of the Crimea: its Origin, and an Account of its Progress down to the Death of Lord Raglan. By ALEXANDER WILLIAM KINGLAKE. With Maps and Plans. Four Volumes now ready. 12mo, Cloth, $2 00 per vol.

MAURY'S PHYSICAL GEOGRAPHY OF THE SEA. The Physical Geography of the Sea, and its Meteorology. By M. F. MAURY, LL.D. 8vo, Cloth, $4 00.

HALLAM'S LITERATURE. Introduction to the Literature of Europe during the Fifteenth, Sixteenth, and Seventeenth Centuries. By HENRY HALLAM. 2 vols., 8vo, Cloth, $4 00; Sheep, $5 00.

HALLAM'S MIDDLE AGES. View of the State of Europe during the Middle Ages. By H. HALLAM. 8vo, Cloth, $2 00; Sheep, $2 50.

HALLAM'S CONSTITUTIONAL HISTORY OF ENGLAND. The Constitutional History of England, from the Accession of Henry VII. to the Death of George II. By HENRY HALLAM. 8vo, Cloth, $2 00; Sheep, $2 50.

6 Valuable Works for Public and Private Libraries.

ENGLISH MEN OF LETTERS. Edited by JOHN MORLEY. The following volumes are now ready. Others will follow: JOHNSON. By L. Stephen.—GIBBON. By J. C. Morison.—SCOTT. By R. H. Hutton.—SHELLEY. By J. A. Symonds.—GOLDSMITH. By W. Black.—HUME. By Professor Huxley.—DEFOE. By W. Minto.—BURNS. By Principal Shairp.—SPENSER. By R. W. Church.—THACKERAY. By A. Trollope.—BURKE. By J. Morley.—MILTON. By M. Pattison.—SOUTHEY. By E. Dowden.—CHAUCER. By A. W. Ward.—BUNYAN. By J A. Fronde.—COWPER. By G. Smith.—POPE. By L. Stephen.—BYRON. By J. Nichols.—LOCKE. By T. Fowler.—WORDSWORTH. By F. W. H. Myers.—HAWTHORNE. By Henry James, Jr.—DRYDEN. By G. Saintsbury.—LANDOR. By S. Colvin.—DE QUINCEY. By D. Masson.—LAMB. By A. Ainger.—BENTLEY. By R. C. Jebb.—DICKENS. By A. W. Ward.—GRAY. By E. W. Gosse.—SWIFT. By L. Stephen.—STERNE. By H. D. Traill.—MACAULAY. By J. C. Morison.—FIELDING. By Austin Dobson. 12mo, Cloth, 75 cents per volume.

NEWCOMB'S ASTRONOMY. Popular Astronomy. By SIMON NEWCOMB, LL.D. With One Hundred and Twelve Engravings, and five Maps of the Stars. 8vo, Cloth, $2 50; School Edition, 12mo, Cloth, $1 30.

PRIME'S POTTERY AND PORCELAIN. Pottery and Porcelain of All Times and Nations. With Tables of Factory and Artists' Marks, for the Use of Collectors. By WILLIAM C. PRIME, LL.D. Illustrated. 8vo, Cloth, Uncut Edges and Gilt Tops, $7 00; Half Calf, $9 25. (In a Box.)

CESNOLA'S CYPRUS. Cyprus: its Ancient Cities, Tombs, and Temples. A Narrative of Researches and Excavations during Ten Years' Residence in that Island. By L. P. DI CESNOLA. With Portrait, Maps, and 400 Illustrations. 8vo, Cloth, Extra, Gilt Tops and Uncut Edges, $7 50.

TENNYSON'S COMPLETE POEMS. The Poetical Works of Alfred Tennyson. With numerous Illustrations by Eminent Artists, and Three Characteristic Portraits. 8vo, Paper, $1 00; Cloth, $1 50.

VAN-LENNEP'S BIBLE LANDS. Bible Lands: their Modern Customs and Manners Illustrative of Scripture. By HENRY J. VAN-LENNEP, D.D. 350 Engravings and 2 Colored Maps. 8vo, Cloth, $5 00; Sheep, $6 00; Half Morocco or Half Calf, $8 00.

GROTE'S HISTORY OF GREECE. 12 vols., 12mo, Cloth, $18 00; Sheep, $22 80; Half Calf, $39 00.

www.ingramcontent.com/pod-product-compliance
Lightning Source LLC
Chambersburg PA
CBHW050934300426
44108CB00011BA/721